Edward

FORTY YEARS

IN THE

TURKISH EMPIRE

OR

MEMOIRS OF

REV. WILLIAM GOODELL

Elibron Classics
www.elibron.com

Elibron Classics series.

© 2005 Adamant Media Corporation.

ISBN 1-4021-5305-8 (paperback)
ISBN 1-4021-5827-0 (hardcover)

This Elibron Classics Replica Edition is an unabridged facsimile
of the edition published in 1876 by Robert Carter and Brothers,
New York.

FORTY YEARS

IN

THE TURKISH EMPIRE.

Forty Years

IN THE

Turkish Empire;

OR,

Memoirs of

REV. WILLIAM GOODELL, D.D.,

LATE MISSIONARY OF THE A. B. C. F. M. AT CONSTANTINOPLE.

BY HIS SON-IN-LAW,

E. D. G. PRIME, D.D.

NEW YORK:

ROBERT CARTER AND BROTHERS,

530 BROADWAY.

1876.

Cambridge:
Press of John Wilson & Son.

INTRODUCTION.

In the year 1860, in a public address in the city of London, the Earl of Shaftesbury paid the following tribute to the character of the American Missionaries in Turkey : —

"I do not believe that in the whole history of missions; I do not believe, that in the history of diplomacy, or in the history of any negotiations carried on between man and man, we can find any thing to equal the wisdom, the soundness, and the pure evangelical truth of the body of men who constitute the American mission. I have said it twenty times before, and I will say it again — for the expression appropriately conveys my meaning — that 'they are a marvellous combination of common sense and piety.' Every man who comes in contact with these missionaries speaks in praise of them. Persons in authority, and persons in subjection, all speak in their favor; travellers speak well of them; and I know of no man who has ever been able to bring against that body a single valid objection. There they stand, tested by years, tried by their works, and exemplified by their fruits; and I believe it will be found, that these American missionaries have done more toward upholding the truth and spreading the Gospel of Christ in the East, than any other body of men in this or in any other age."

This volume is designed to preserve the memory and perpetuate the influence of the pioneer of this noble band of missionaries at the Turkish capital, the one most honored and beloved, according to the testimony of all his associates. A man of almost singular simplicity of character, he had a rare combination of qualities which in him were in nowise inconsistent. With the utmost firmness in adhering to his convictions of truth and of duty, which were of the most decided character, he had the gentleness of a child in his mode of expressing them. While consecrated to the great work of advancing and establishing the kingdom of his divine Master among men, and pursuing it with a singleness of aim and a seriousness of heart that proved it to be his absorbing object in life, by his cheerful disposition and his affectionate bearing toward all with whom he came in contact, he made his presence a continual benediction. He exemplified the apostolic injunction, "Let your speech be always with grace, seasoned with salt," but at the same time the spice of wit, of genuine humor, added a charm to his conversation and left a fragrance on all that came from his pen.

He kept no diary of his varying emotions. He was apparently so devoid of self-consciousness and so engrossed with his life-work that he seldom turned his thoughts in upon himself. The journal which he kept, with more or less fulness, during the greater part of his life, was simply a record of events. This, together with his correspondence, public and private, which was inimitable in style, has furnished an embarrassing amount of material for a single volume, the perplexity arising from the difficulty in deciding what to omit. His letters alone, which were unique, lively, and truly spiritual in their tone, — letters of friendship, of affection, of consolation, would fill many volumes.

His residence and labors at Constantinople covered the entire period marked by that movement known as the Protestant Reformation in Turkey. Being the first missionary on the ground; having been instrumental in establishing numerous schools for the various classes of the population; having translated the whole word of God out of the original tongues into the language of a large part of the people; and having preached the gospel daily at the capital, and up and down the Bosphorus at the various suburbs, he was one of the chosen instruments of that reformation during all its progress. On this account no inconsiderable portion of the volume is devoted to a record of this remarkable movement, which forms one of the most interesting chapters in the annals of Christian missions. This record is here necessarily confined to the work as immediately connected with the labors of Dr. Goodell.

The history of such a life, as that which is imperfectly sketched in these pages, is alone a sufficient answer to the question, " What have Christian missions accomplished?"

CONTENTS.

FORTY YEARS

IN THE TURKISH EMPIRE.

CHAPTER I.

WHEN Dr. Goodell returned to his native land in 1865, to spend the evening of his days and die among his kindred, his children united in an urgent request that he would commit to paper for their perusal and preservation such recollections of his life as he might have strength to record. With characteristic modesty he shrank for a long time from complying with their request, until by a sort of stratagem he was induced to write down some reminiscences of his earlier years. He had only begun the record when, after an illness of a few hours, he fell asleep, "and he was not, for God took him." The few sketches he had prepared are comprised in the earlier pages of this volume, and commence as follows:—

"My DEAR SON,—In complying with your request to give you some reminiscences of my early days, and of the 'Olden Time,' I cannot do better, perhaps, than to begin at the very beginning. Though I cannot testify to it from my own personal recollection, yet it has been asserted too often to be now called in question, that at Templeton, Mass., the morning of the 14th of February, 1792, was very tempestuous, and that the snow-storm was so furiously driving and drifting as almost to prevent our family physician, who lived full three miles away, arriving in season to be present at

1

my first appearance on this or any other stage. The small
room in which I first saw the light of this world was, in my
day, always called 'The Stranger's Room,' but whether it had
always been called such, or whether it was so named from
its having received the little stranger on that cold, stormy
morning, I cannot say. This room was, it may be, nine
feet by seven, and contained one window, a bed, a small
table, a Bible, a hymn-book, and two or three chairs. Adjoining this room, and to be passed through in order to reach
it, was one other room, and only one, and this was our
kitchen, our parlor, our dining-saloon, and, in fact, every
thing else which can be predicated of a New England home.
The house stood on the hill-side, and was one story high.
Under our parents' bed was the trundle-bed, which was
regularly rolled out at night, and rolled back every morning. Here three of us were nicely tucked in every night,
and here we began to repeat, with all seriousness, 'Our
Father,' and 'Now I lay me.' And here we had as pleasant
dreams and as refreshing sleep as though we were in the
king's palace.

"The vivid impressions I have of my father you already
know from the tract called 'The Missionary's Father.' And
justice to the memory of my gentle mother requires me to
say that she possessed 'like precious faith' with my father,
and that she was in every way worthy of him. She possessed, in an eminent degree, 'a meek and quiet spirit,' and
was a woman of great delicacy of feeling, an example of
taste in dress and of neatness in every thing. The comforts
she had were few, but she contrived to increase and multiply
those few as only a woman of great economy and thrift
could do. For many years an invalid, her last sickness
was long and painful, but not a word of complaint do I
recollect of ever having heard her speak. On the morning
of Dec. 2, 1809, we all assembled in that little Stranger's Room to hear her last words. And she passed away
with hallelujahs on her lips. Well do I remember with

what clearness of voice she said, 'Hallelujah! hallelujah! halle——.' Her feet seemed yet standing firm in the midst of the river. But her voice suddenly ceased; for strength and breath were both gone, and the remainder of the hallelujah was left to be finished on 'the other side of Jordan.' We all felt sure that she had gone from a world of sorrow to one of joy, from poverty to the riches of heaven.

"Eight children, four sons and four daughters, survived her, and these survived her many years. Indeed, most of them remain to this present. At the time of her death, none of her children were professors of religion; and she had to leave them all in an evil world, and very ill prepared to make their way through it. But, with confidence, she committed them all to Him in whom she herself believed. Could she have looked forward and seen their pathway through life; could she have seen all her eight children, one after another, coming forward and joining themselves to the Lord's people, and three of her four sons preaching the glorious Gospel, and one of them becoming a missionary in a foreign land: — well, I verily believe the sight would have been too much for her feeble frame, and that she would have died from excess of joy and thankfulness. O my kind mother! I often think, what would I not give to see thy gentle face once more, and, on my knees, to ask ten thousand pardons for every unkind word I ever answered thee, and for every grief or pain I unnecessarily caused thee!

"I always remember, with gratitude, that my mother, though herself ill supplied with means, was always ready to reach forth her hand to the needy. Her neighbors loved and honored her; and why should they not do so? for on her tongue was the law of kindness, and she was ever more afraid of doing than receiving an injury. 'The heart of her husband safely trusted in her,' and, as they think of all her gentle ways, 'her children rise up and call her blessed.'

"How well do I remember, even to this day, some of the

beautiful hymns she used to sing to me sixty-five or seventy years ago. How often in the days of her pilgrimage, in times of trial and pain, when spinning flax on her little wheel, did her sweet voice sound out with great clearness in the following words:—

> "'So pilgrims on a scorching sand,
>   Beneath a burning sky,
> Long for a cooling stream at hand;
>   And they must drink or die.'

Yes, and at the fountain-head of Divine consolation she did drink, and at that same fountain-head she will drink for ever. And that little spinning-wheel, the distaff, the spindle, the treadle, and all, will surely be remembered in heaven.

"There was one incident connected with my mother's last painful sickness which should not be forgotten. Her appetite was generally poor, but one morning she fancied she could eat and longed for a trout. It was early in the spring, when the ice in the rivers and brooks was just breaking up, and the meadows were all flooded with the sluggish waters. I was in those days as great a fisherman as the Apostle Peter may be supposed ever to have been, and I knew that trout were ordinarily found only in the purest and swiftest running water. But at my mother's earnest entreaty, I took my hook and line and went on horseback, riding at full speed, and singing, at the top of my voice, all the way through the woods:—

> "'Spare us, O Lord, aloud we pray,
>   Nor let our sun go down at noon;
> Thy years are one eternal day,
>   And must thy children die so soon?'

I found the meadows as I had expected, so flooded, I could not, in any conceivable way, reach the main stream, nor come anywhere near it. But I baited my hook, and threw it into the nearest waters before me; and, wonderful to relate, a much larger trout than it was common to take in that stream, even in the best season of the year, immediately seized it, and I drew it to the land, feeling that He who once directed the fish to Peter's hook directed this to mine. I at once carried it home, and made savory meat such as my mother loved, that her soul might bless me before her death. And I doubt not she prayed then, as I feel assured she had often prayed before, that I might one day become a 'fisher of men.'

"Though I never looked upon this incident as a miracle, yet I thought then, as I have always thought since, that it was by a special providence this fine trout was brought to my hook; for, in the ordinary calculations of men, there was no probability that this fish would come to my hook, or that, had I remained a fortnight longer, any other would have come. It was God who remembered us in our low estate, and especially who, in great kindness, remembered my mother in all her feebleness. And that trout, that flooded meadow, the old horse and all, will surely be remembered in heaven.

"Your affectionate father,

"W. GOODELL."

The following letter will be most appropriately inserted in connection with the preceding. It was written from Constantinople, on receiving intelligence of the death of his father, who passed away on the 4th of July, 1843. The letter has been extensively published in the religious journals, and also in the form of a tract, entitled "The Missionary's Father;" but in a mutilated form, and shorn of much of its beauty and tenderness. It was also printed in this abbreviated form in the Introduction to "The Old and the New, or the Changes of Thirty Years in the East;" a volume prepared by Dr. Goodell in 1853, as he was returning to his field of labor, after a brief visit to his native land. It is now printed just as it was originally written. Apart

from its filial character and its spiritual interest, it has often
been referred to and quoted, as one of the most graceful and
beautiful specimens of epistolary correspondence to be found
in our language.

CONSTANTINOPLE, Aug. 18, 1843.

MY DEAR BROTHER,—The intelligence contained in your
letter of the 5th ult. was not unexpected. Our father had
attained to a great age, lacking only five days of being
eighty-six years old. He was full of days, but still more
full of faith and of the Holy Ghost. How long he had
" borne the image of the earthly" before he was renewed in
the spirit of his mind, I know not; but I know he had long
borne "the image of the heavenly;" nor have I any idea
when it was, or by what means it was, that his religion assumed so decidedly a patriarchal character; but as long ago
as I can remember, he always appeared to maintain much of
that same constant intercourse with heaven, which, in his
later years, we can hardly suppose, was ever interrupted in
his waking hours for fifteen minutes at a time.

Though I can look back some forty-five years or more, yet
I cannot look back to the year when he was not living a life
of faith, and prayer, and self-denial,—of deadness to the
world, and of close walk with God. This was the more remarkable, as in the church, of which in those days he was a
member, there was never, to the best of my remembrance,
more than one individual, and not always even one, who
could fully sympathize with him in his religious views
and feelings. In Christian experience he certainly seemed
" higher than any of the people, from his shoulders and up-
wards;" and those great evangelical doctrines of the Gospel,
which his own minister never preached, and his own church
never adopted into her creed, were his meat and drink.
" *The raven, though an unclean bird, brought food to Elijah,*"
was a common expression of his on returning from church,
where he had been able to pick out of much chaff a few
crumbs of the bread of life. His privileges were few;
prayer-meetings were unknown; the sum total, or about the
sum total, of his library was the family Bible, one copy of
Watts's Psalms and Hymns, Doddridge's " Rise and Progress," Pike's " Cases of Conscience," the second volume of
Fox's " Book of Martyrs," and last, but not least, the Assembly's Catechism.

But though his means of grace were thus limited, yet, meditating day and night on God's law, his roots struck deep; and he was like a tree planted by the rivers of water, whose leaf is always green, and whose fruit is always abundant. Whoever saw him riding on horseback would, if he kept himself concealed, be almost sure to see him engaged in prayer. Whoever should work with him in seed-time or harvest would find his thoughts as actively employed above, as his hands were below. His employments were all holy, and the implements of husbandry he used were all consecrated to Christ. Whoever of the Lord's people met him, by day or by night, at home or abroad, alone or in company, would find him ready to sit right down with them in heavenly places, in order to comprehend "what is the length and breadth and depth and height" of the love of Christ. What the woman of Samaria could not understand he would have understood at once, and would have seized hold of the very first hint thrown out by our Saviour for spiritual conversation, however distant and obscure that hint might have been; for "he that is spiritual judgeth all things."

Being the youngest of the family, you can have but an indistinct recollection of the small house on the side of the hill, containing two small rooms and a garret, floored with loose and rough boards, where twelve of us were born; and of the small clump of apple-trees before the door, where your elder brothers and sisters played in the days of their thoughtless childhood. There, with no lock or bolt to any door, and no key to any trunk or drawer or cupboard; there, where, as I am told, nothing now remains but an old cellar-hole, which may even itself, long before this, have been filled up, — there our godly father prayed for us with all prayer and supplication in the Spirit; there, on every Sabbath eve, he asked us those solemn, important, and all-comprehensive questions from the blessed Catechism of the Assembly of Divines, and there, with eyes and heart raised to heaven, he used to sing to the tune of old Rochester : —

> " God, my supporter and my hope,
>   My help for ever near ;
>   Thine arm of mercy held me up,
>   When sinking in despair."

And there, too, our mother, of precious memory, — though, as she died when you were but six months old, you remember her not, —there she lived a life of poverty, patience, meekness, and faith. There she used to sit and card her wool by the light of the pine knot, and sing to us those sweet words:—

> "Hov'ring among the leaves, there stands
> The sweet celestial Dove;
> And Jesus on the branches hangs
> The banner of his love." — *Watts.*

And there, too, almost thirty-four years ago, we assembled early one morning in her little bedroom to see her die. Her peace was like a river; she was full of triumph; and she was able to address to us words of heavenly consolation till she had actually crossed over into shallow water within one minute of the opposite banks of the Jordan, — *heaven and all its glories full in view.* Precious woman! Though no man knoweth the place of thy sepulchre, and thy children have not been able to find the spot in order to erect a humble stone to thy memory, yet thy Saviour, who loved thee with an everlasting love, and in whom even in the darkest hours thou didst have such sweet confidence, will watch over thy dust, and thou shalt be recognized at the resurrection of the just. "*Were my children but pious,*" thou didst often say in thy last long sickness, "*how cheerfully could I leave them, and go away.*" But what thine eyes were not permitted to behold, have not the angels long since told thee, — that the eight children thou didst leave behind, with all, or all but one, of their partners, were partakers of that blessed Gospel "which was all thy salvation, and all thy desire;" and that three of thy sons were engaged in proclaiming it to others? Yes, God hath heard thy prayers, and "hath remembered His holy covenant," as we are all witnesses this day.

But before I close, I must say something more of the early habits and character of our venerable father. The little farm he once possessed, if it were not all *ploughed* over, was, I am confident, almost every foot of it, *prayed* over. And some dried apples from it, which a subsequent owner sent me a few years since, were to me "as the smell of a field which the Lord hath blessed." In all his intercourse with his neighbors, in the way of barter and trade, he always seemed to be more careful lest *their* interests should suffer than lest his own should, — looking on their side with his good eye, if one was better than the other, and on his own side with his evil one. And the same conscientiousness he observed in his dealings with a stranger. And judging from my early impressions, I should think that he never spoke to a stranger, or seldom saw one, without lifting up his heart in prayer for him. He was full of the millennium and of the missionary spirit long before the existence of the " Missionary Herald," or of the American Board, or of the " Panoplist " even, — and even before the Connecticut Missionary Society sent their missionaries away off to the distant regions of Ohio, praying daily for both Jews and Gentiles, saying with the Psalmist, " Let the people praise thee, O God; let the people praise thee, all of them,"— and like his uncle, Solomon Goodell, was ready and desirous to contribute something for the spread of the glorious Gospel long before he had an opportunity for so doing.

It must now be twenty-five or twenty-six years since I left my studies at Andover for a few weeks, and rode through the country to obtain evidence that he was a soldier of the Revolution. And since that time he has lived on his pension of ninety-six dollars a year. And who knows but He " who keepeth covenant and mercy " had special reference to him when he stirred up Congress to pass that pension law. He served three years in the Revolutionary war; and I was struck with the fact you communicated, of its being early on the morning of the memorable fourth of July, amidst the roaring of cannon, that he slept in peace. He is gone. And, though to his children he left no inheritance, no, not so much as one cent, yet, in his godly example and prayers, he has left them the very richest legacy which any father ever bequeathed his children. And I have often thought that should Jehovah address us, as He did His people of old, instead of calling Himself the God of Abraham and of Isaac and of Jacob, He would call Himself the *God of our father.* Oh, how little our good neighbors, who showed such kindness " to the living and to the dead" of our family knew what a rich father we had!

> " My boast is not that I deduce my birth
>   From loins enthroned and rulers of the earth;
>   But higher far my proud pretensions rise, —
>   The son of parents passed into the skies."

Yes, it is a rare privilege we have all enjoyed in being descended from such parents. They were the children of the great King. They belonged to the royal family. Their names were on the catalogue of princes, and of those that live for ever. They daily walked abroad with the conscious

1*

dignity of being heirs to a great estate, even an incorruptible inheritance. And they have now gone to sit down with Christ on His throne. "And they shall hunger no more, neither shall they thirst any more." I love to look back and see how, with no ambitious aspirings after worldly gain or pleasure or honor, they humbly walked with God; how from day to day they deliberately sought, both for themselves and for their children, first of all "the kingdom of God and His righteousness;" and how in this scoffing world they were so united to Christ as apparently to have no separate interest or existence, — it not being so much "they that lived, as Christ living in them."

It was doubtless a mercy to them that they never at any time possessed much of this world's goods, and that through much illness in the family they were at times reduced to great straits; and a mercy to us, that we had to bear the yoke in our youth, and often to make our meal of salt and potatoes; and I have often found it in my heart to bless God for all His dealings with them and with us. And oh, may neither we nor our children ever be left unchastised and uncorrected by Him! Let us choose rather to receive for our profit those chastenings, however severe, whereof all the sons of God are partakers. And why, my brother, should any of us be anxious to leave our children any other inheritance than was left to us? If we leave them this, and they avail themselves of it, then, though *we* be dead, they shall still have a Father who will provide for them, and take care of them, and bless them, and make them happy for ever.

And is our father gone, who prayed for us so much? Let us be thankful that the great Intercessor "*ever* liveth to make intercession for us;" and more than ever, let us avail ourselves of His mediation and atonement, of His grace and strength, and of His righteousness and Spirit; and more than ever, let us now pray for ourselves and for all our brothers and sisters. And is our father dead? Let us arise and give thanks to God that good men *may* die. Let us give *special* thanks that our father and mother are no longer in this world of sin and sorrow. And let us be more careful than ever to "be followers of those who, through faith and patience, are now inheriting the promises," being sinners saved by grace alone.

Thus prays your ever affectionate brother,

WILLIAM.

In his Reminiscences he gives the following account of the earlier generations of his family : —

" My father's father died young, leaving a wife and three sons. His father had four brothers, whom I used occasionally to see, and whom I always regarded as 'mighty men of valor,' viz.: —

" 1. My great-uncle, Solomon Goodell, who lived and died in Jamaica, Vt., and who, fifty or more years ago, took such a wonderful interest in foreign missions.

" Jeremiah Evarts, Esq., former Secretary of the A. B. C. F. M., wrote the following account of the gifts by Solomon Goodell to the cause of missions, and adds that his farm, which was his only source of income, did not exceed $1,000 in value.

" About the year 1800, the writer of these lines observed a donation of $100 to the Connecticut Missionary Society, published in the annual accounts, as from Mr. Goodell. Such donations were at that time very uncommon in this country, and, in regard to that society, nearly or quite unprecedented. The thought occurred that doubtless some gentleman of independent fortune had thought proper to take up his residence in the interior of Vermont, and that he considered the society just named a good channel for his pious beneficence. This conclusion was strengthened by seeing a similar donation from the same source, at the return of each successive year, for a considerable period.

" When the American Board of Foreign Missions began its operations, Mr. Goodell did not wait for an agent to visit him, but sent a message (or came himself) more than fifty miles, to a member of the board, saying that he wished to subscribe $500 for immediate use, and $1,000 for the permanent fund. He sent $50 as earnest-money, and said he would forward the remaining $450 as soon as he could raise that sum ; and would pay the interest annually upon the $1,000, till the principal should be paid. This engagement he punctually complied with, paying the interest, and just before his death transferring notes and bonds secured by mortgages, which (including the $1,000 above mentioned) amounted to $1,708.37 ; that is, a new donation was made of $708.37, to which was afterwards added another bond and mortgage of $350.

" Before this last transaction he had made repeated intermediate donations. At one time he brought to the Rev. Dr. Lyman, of Hatfield (the member of the board referred to), the sum of $465. After the money was counted, Dr. Lyman said to him, ' I presume, sir, you wish this sum indorsed upon your note of $1,000.' ' Oh no,' was his reply, ' I believe that note is good yet. This is a separate matter.' He then expressed his wish that the money might be remitted towards repairing the loss sustained by the Baptist missionaries at Serampore. He regretted that he had not been able to make the sum $500 ; consoled himself with the thought that he might do it still at some period not very distant; and said, that if any of the bank-notes proved less valuable than specie, he would make up the deficiency.

" Mr. Goodell had made what he thought suitable provision for his children, as he passed through life. After consulting his wife, he left her such a portion of his estate as was satis-factory to her, gave several small legacies, and made the board his residuary legatee. He supposed that the property left to the board by will would not be less than $1,000 ; but as some part of it was, and still is unsalable, the exact amount cannot be stated.

"It was this uncle who, having yet never seen me, sent to Mr. Preceptor Adams, of Phillips Academy, to know whether I was ' *worth raising;* ' and receiving, I suppose, a somewhat favorable answer, he soon after sent me a yoke of oxen to help draw me over the steep hills of learning. This great-uncle was excessively fond of the old poetry, and (with his long old-fashioned waistcoat, buttoned perhaps in two places, with one side reaching down much lower than the other, for he was never able to make a button and a button-hole look each other square in the face) used to sit and repeat with royal emphasis whole pages, I might perhaps say books, of his favorite Milton or Young, — his hand, when not gesticulating, resting on a table by his side, on which the old Family Bible, Baxter, Flavel, Henry's Com-mentary, Watts, &c., lay, if not in glorious confusion, yet without much order; and his gentle wife, who never wrote poetry, and was never able to tell the difference between verse which was blank and that which was not blank, would sit, as we may suppose Job's wife did, in her little corner, mending or darning, and, I doubt not, some times praying that her learned husband might be as meek as he was great.

"2. My great-uncle, the Rev. David Goodall, who was once settled over a Congregational Church in Massachusetts, and afterwards removed to Littleton, N. H., on the Connecticut River, some sixty miles North of Dartmouth College.

"3. My great-uncle, Deacon Abner Goodale, who lived in Marlborough, Mass., at the old Puritan homestead, where all these Goodells, Goodalls, and Goodales were born and learned the Assembly's Catechism.

"4. My great-uncle, Judge Job Goodell, Goodale, or Goodall (for I do not remember how he spelled the name), who died at Bernardstown, Mass., though not more orthodox or intelligent, was more polished than his three noble brothers. I have attended prayer-meetings with him in Marlborough, where he exhorted like a judge and prayed like the publican.

" These four noble brothers had three or more sisters, Miriam, and so on, each of whom possessed as marked a character as David's sister Zeruiah appeared to possess, whose big rebellious boys often drew from King David the exclamation, 'O ye sons of Zeruiah!' They were strong-minded women all of them. . . . But those four brothers stood out in bold relief among all their contemporaries. Instead of being 'behind the times,' they were always in advance, and were distinguished for their love of learning, and for their sympathy with every great and benevolent object. They and their families all had a great deal of uncommon sense, enough, perhaps, to supply the want of plain common sense, in which, though not by any means deficient, they did not so very strikingly abound. But all those men and women of pure Puritan blood have passed away, and many of their descendants, I am told, now play on the piano, eat their pudding at the close instead of at the beginning of dinner, keep Saturday night no longer, wear crinoline without stint, and imitate many other ways and practices of the Gentiles. But, as we read in the Book of Chronicles, ' These are ancient things.'

" My father's father, I said, died young. My good grand-mother afterwards married a Sawyer, and raised up a family of mighty singers in Templeton, — Uncle John, Uncle Jotham, Uncle Job, Aunt Dinah; dear me! how they used to chase one another up and down those *fugue* tunes till they got safely out of the jungle, and found themselves, unexpectedly to others if not to themselves, all safe home at last. My good grandfather and grandmother Sawyer lived to a great age, and she was blind many years before her death. Though they lived more than three miles from church, they were always there in season, however severe the cold, deep the snow, or pouring the rain; and on their return home they never failed to find the baked pork and beans, with the orthodox pudding, warm from the oven, where they had been religiously deposited twenty-four hours before.

" In looking back to the days of my boyhood, few scenes come up so vividly to my mind as those connected with our Sabbath days and our going to church. Although we lived three miles from the house of God, we were never absent on the Sabbath day. Be it wet or dry, cold or hot, we were always there, and the more tempestuous the weather, the earlier we were found in our places. The old, puritanical-looking horse seemed to know as well as the most pious of us that it was holy time, and he stood at the door saddled and bridled, with his head bowed reverently down, as if in solemn meditation upon the duties he was expected to perform. My father, with one of the children in his arms, rode before; my mother sat behind him on a pillion, and carried one of the children in her arms, and still another child rode behind, clinging as closely to her as she did to her husband. I recollect on one occasion in ascending a steep, sandy hill the girth of the saddle gave way, and there was an avalanche of the whole load, father and mother and three children, with saddle and pillion, over the horse's tail, plump into a sand-bank. The old rheumatic horse never seemed amazed at any thing that might happen, but this time he simply opened his large eyes wider than usual, and, wheeling half round, looked to see whether he could help us in any way. Had he taken it into his head on that occasion to use his heels instead of his eyes, that avalanche might have proved as fatal to us as those more terrible to the dwellers and travellers among the Alps.

"After reaching home on Sabbath afternoon, and telling where the text was found, we sat down to our dinner, of baked pork and beans, which had been put into the oven the day previous, and left there overnight. When dinner was over, we were all summoned to the Assembly's Catechism, which we were expected to repeat *verbatim et literatim*, from 'What is the chief end of man?' to the end of the primer. Our father asked the questions with book in hand, and we were expected to answer as promptly without the book as he asked with it. And, indeed, we were so familiar with the Catechism, that we could not only repeat the Ten Commandments, with all that was required, and all that was forbidden, together with the reasons annexed, but would also answer the three great questions, What is justification? adoption? and sanctification? and tell also 'the several benefits which in this life do either accompany or flow from them.' When these recitations were ended, we had family prayers, and by that time we were sufficiently fatigued to retire to our slumbers.

"In those days there were no Sabbath schools. Indeed, I never heard of such an institution till I was more than twenty years old. Professor Bradbury's beautiful songs had then no existence. With what joy should we have hailed them! Our good old minister, the Rev. Ebenezer Sparhawk, though an Arminian, used to appoint two days in the year, one in the spring and the other in the autumn, for all the children of his congregation to assemble at church, on some week-day, and repeat to him the Lord's Prayer and the Catechism. These appointments were made, it may be, quite as much for the parents as for the children, that they might have the duty of catechising their children kept constantly before their minds. This Catechism is now pretty much superseded by the Sabbath school; and although I should be slow to recommend a return from the Sabbath school to the Catechism, yet might not this Catechism be included in the Sabbath school, and be made to form a part of its interesting exercises? In the days of our fathers and grandfathers, that Catechism was certainly a wonderful institution, and the descendants of those families that were most thoroughly drilled in it are now undeniably the very bone and sinew of New England, whether considered politically, socially, or religiously.

"Mr. Sparhawk was extremely careful in the performance of all the duties appertaining to his office as a settled minister, such as catechising the children twice a year, visiting the sick and afflicted, preaching on the Sabbath, and once on the Friday preceding the communion, three times a year; but prayer-meetings and revivals being considered pure innovations, never met with favor in his eyes. Indeed, such newfangled notions were hardly known to his people. Not one of his deacons, although all of them were exemplary men, ever opened his lips in public to offer public prayer or give a word of exhortation! On the Sabbath he preached under a large sounding-board, and some of the youthful and the thoughtless members of his congregation watched with trembling anxiety, lest it might one day fall on his head and crush him. But in spite of their fears he died in his bed, in a good old age, greatly respected and universally lamented. His numerous descendants are among the most intelligent and excellent men and women of the land.

"After Mr. Sparhawk's death it seemed much easier for his people to slide down into Unitarianism than to rise up to what was considered more evangelical and orthodox. His successor, the Rev. Charles Wellington (afterward D.D.), was equally exemplary in life, but still more lax in doctrine. Though not at first an avowed Unitarian, he was at length

known to be such. Like his predecessor, he was greatly and
deservedly respected in the town, and much beloved by all
who knew him. Of him I have many very pleasant recollections; for although knowing that my father's family had
no sympathy with his creed, he always treated us with great
kindness, and did what he could to help and encourage me
in my studies. In his day the more evangelical portion of
the church seceded, built a new place of worship for themselves, and called the Rev. Lewis Sabine to be their pastor.
With him and his church I always feel at home, for they
have full sympathy with missions, with revivals, and with
all those doctrines of the Gospel denominated Evangelical.
The Rev. Dr. Wellington had, several years before his
death, a colleague, the Rev. Mr. Adams, who is now his successor, and who, like himself, is a pleasant and exemplary
man. I greatly revere the memory of both Mr. Sparhawk
and Mr. Wellington, and of their deacons, and of many others
in my native town. May their children and their children's
children be blessed of the Lord who made heaven and earth.

" Let me not here omit to mention the Baptist minister,
the Rev. Elisha Andrews, and his pleasant family. His
elder children were just about the ages with myself and
some of my sisters. They were fine scholars, and our two
families had much delightful intercourse. Their father was
an excellent townsman, a good neighbor, and an earnest,
judicious preacher. His prayer-meetings were to my father's
family like oases in the desert. As the Baptist meeting-
house was much nearer than the Congregational, we were
not unfrequently found there on the Sabbath; and had it not
been for disowning the Abrahamic covenant confirmed in
Christ, and especially had it not been for close communion,
which was strictly adhered to as an article of faith, some of
us might have joined that church, for many of its members
were earnest Christian men and women, loving the Bible,
and speaking often one to another on the great subjects
which concern our common salvation.

"Among the reminiscences of the years when I was yet a child in my father's house, there are some incidents connected with the social habits of that period which, in these days of temperance, come up with a peculiar and somewhat of a ludicrous force to my mind.   More than threescore years ago, when punch, egg-nog, and a mixture of molasses and rum, called black-strap, flowed almost as freely through the sweet vales of New England as pure cold water does now, I remember a good old man, who, like my own orthodox parents, believed in the Assembly's Catechism, together with 'the reasons annexed' to the whole ten commandments, and who usually came once or twice a year to confer with them on the prophecies in general, and the millennium in particular; and to converse also about those devoted missionaries who had recently taken their lives in their hand, and gone to the desolate regions of Ohio to preach to those benighted people.   On those occasions all servile labor was suspended, and we children sat down with eyes and ears opened wide; yea, and mouths too, for we hardly dared breathe in the usual way, lest we should lose a word.

"At the close of their long and interesting session, my good father always rose with the greatest possible seriousness in his whole demeanor and made the good man a glass of toddy, if it were summer, or a mug of flip, in winter, the sugar at the bottom being invariably reserved for the longing palates of us little ones.   Altogether, the old folks seemed to have a grand good time, and we young ones were easily persuaded to believe that there was somehow, and in some way, 'a good time coming' for us.

"It happened one day we saw the good man's horse (and we knew his horse, with the white spot in his forehead, almost as well as we knew the good man himself) turning his head towards the door of our house.   Our parents were absent, and, as they would not be at home till towards evening, I felt that it became me, as the oldest son of the family, to be treating the servant of the Lord with all due respect.

And, indeed, we all of us hastened to put every thing in readiness to give him such an honorable reception that we need have no fear that the bears would come out of the wood, a little to the east of our house, to devour us, as they once came out upon and tore in pieces the unmannerly children in good Elisha's degenerate days.

"At the proper time, therefore, I retired to make the good man a glass of toddy. On tasting it I thought it too strong, and put in more water, with sugar to match. Tasting it again, I thought it was too weak and too sweet; and, therefore, made another change, and still another. As it still did not suit my taste, and as there was no room left in that glass for further experiments, I poured the whole out into a more capacious tumbler, and then went on changing and tasting, and tasting and changing, till I quite lost the idea how it ought to taste. And, finally, beginning to pour some of it into a large bowl, I found I must have mixed almost enough for a 'raising;' at least quite enough for six men, instead of one. With all due reverence, I then carried a tumblerful and presented it to him. He took it and drank off a part of it, and, patting my head, said I had been too bountiful. He then lifted up his hands and gave us all his blessing, with plenty of good advice, and adding that I had better put the remainder aside till my father came home, he mounted his nag and rode off.

"After he had gone, I thought within myself, Now, what shall we do with all this toddy; for we should be ashamed to have our parents come home and see it, and to throw any of the 'good creature' away would be quite wicked. So, taking counsel with my brothers and sisters, all but one younger than myself, we sat down, in high earnest, to see what we could do towards reducing the fearful amount. And we drank and drank till our heads turned round. I presume the children in our Sabbath schools can, almost any of them, tell us of a more excellent way of honoring these servants of the Most High God; but those were days of darkness.

As this was the first time, so I am happy to add it was the last time, I ever made this vile compound for such a holy purpose.

"Another scene, illustrating the ignorance of those times on the subject of temperance, I well remember. A very godly minister, who lived in an adjoining town, had occasion to pass by my father's door several times a year, and as in those days of rank Arminianism my father was almost the only one on that road who fully sympathized with the good man in the doctrines he preached, and as our house was about the half-way house for him, he often stopped and passed an hour with us. My mother was for a long time an invalid. And one day when the good man called, our family physician happened in. Very soon, before the door of the house, where I was sitting, I heard him consult our physician on the following very difficult problem. (It should here be premised that both the physician and the minister were above reproach, neither the one nor the other having ever given occasion to be suspected of a too free use of the glass.) The minister said he had to be around among the people every day, visiting the sick and dying; directing inquiring minds to Christ, and comforting mourners; praying with the aged and infirm, and explaining to the simple-minded those things that were difficult to be understood, &c.; that wherever he went, liquor under some form and name, was offered him to drink, which, in order not to give offence, or be considered guilty of a breach of good manners, he felt bound to take. Moreover, that, after calling at a number of places, his head invariably became affected, and he felt himself in danger of saying or doing some foolish thing. Would the good doctor, therefore, prescribe something for him to take, or give him suitable advice as to what he should do in this emergency.

"I remember just where the good minister stood, and how he looked. I remember also just where the good doctor stood, and how he looked. He had in his hand a cane, with the end of which he kept digging in the ground; and the more earnestly he was questioned, the more earnestly and the deeper he dug. (And what more natural than that our Saviour, under similar circumstances, should 'stoop down and write on the ground.') At length he straightened himself up, and, standing before his questioner with his arms crossed, he uttered the following advice, viz., that, after he had called at several places, and had begun to feel the effects of the liquor taken, he should go straight home, while he was yet able to walk, and, entering at once into his study, should sit there in silence and solitude, till the dizziness should pass away, and then, taking some food with a cup of tea, he could go out without fear to finish his pastoral visits. The idea of total abstinence from intoxicating beverages seems not to have entered the mind of either the one or the other. That he *must* drink was taken for granted, if he would not be guilty of an unpardonable offence. The only thing was to drink without feeling the effects of it ; and on this point the good physician was sadly perplexed. In those days everybody drank, old and young, rich and poor, male and female ; and our whole country seemed rapidly descending on the steep and slippery side of the hill towards ruin. But New England at length arose in the greatness of her strength, and, in the firmness of her principles, signed the temperance pledge ; 'and the land had rest for forty years.' "

CHAPTER II.

AT what period "the great change" in the subject of these memoirs took place, no one, not even he himself, knew; for, notwithstanding the vivacity of his nature and his sparkling humor (traits which characterized him from his earliest years to the day of his death), there was ever a vein of seriousness as strongly marked, and a strict conscientiousness, which even in his boyhood seemed that of the true Christian. A revival in his native town the early part of the year 1811 was the occasion of his publicly declaring himself on the Lord's side; but even then he did not seem to become fully awake to the great ends of a Christian life. It was not until he was brought in contact with educated minds devoted to the service of the Redeemer that he began to exhibit that consecration of spirit which so signally marked his subsequent career. This will appear as we continue his Reminiscences.

"You will naturally infer from what I have written that my father's circumstances were none of the best. It was even so. But he had seen better days. I remember when he owned a hundred acres of land without any incumbrance upon it, well fenced and well stocked. He owed no man any thing, and had money at interest. But he was laid low one winter with lung fever, and for more than a year was unable to attend to his farm. Before his recovery my mother had a serious illness, and remained an invalid the rest of her days. The doctor's bills were heavy, and the loss he sustained by being unable to attend to his farm was still heavier. His affairs thus became so involved that he was never able to extricate himself from the embarrassment.

"It had been long seen and felt at home that, being feeble from my youth, I could never obtain a livelihood in any of the ordinary ways of manual labor; but it was thought possible I might at length be able to teach small children their A-B-Abs; for I could read with fluency, and my memory was so retentive that I readily learned any thing by heart. Though I was a professor of religion, yet, on looking back from this distance of time, it does not appear that a supreme desire to preach the Gospel had yet taken possession of my heart. Of my father's heart, however, it had taken full possession, and, with that view, he encouraged my attempting to get an education. But he could not furnish me with any means, and there were at that time no education societies.

"At length we heard of Phillips Academy, where pious and promising students sometimes received pecuniary assistance in prosecuting their studies, and hope now sprung up in my mind that I might one day become a preacher of the Gospel. I, therefore, made a journey to Andover, walking and riding by turns, and presented myself before the great preceptor, John Adams, Esq., afterwards honored by Yale College with the title of LL.D. I learned from him that there was a charity fund, but that more than twice as many as could be received had been long waiting to enjoy its privileges. Mr. Adams advised me to come to Andover at the commencement of the next quarter, encouraging me to expect that my tuition would be provided for; but I must be prepared to bear the whole expense of my education up to the time when there should be a vacancy in the charity fund. I turned my steps homeward, footing it the whole distance, sixty miles, with a heavy heart, reaching my father's house, foot-sore and weary, on the third day after leaving Andover.

"From the time of my return from Andover all our thoughts were bent on the great question of raising funds to meet the necessary expenses for one quarter. On the

one hand, poverty so stared us in the face as to look us out
of countenance wherever we turned our eyes; and, on the
other hand, the desire and the necessity of my trying to get
an education rose up before me like the image in Nebuchad-
nezzar's dream, with all its mighty proportions. And so
we thought and thought; but the more we thought the more
we knew not what to think. And we finally began to
think less and pray more; and thus we continued till it
was found I must return to Andover, in order to be found
there at the commencement of the quarter. So, without
money and without credit, and without any plan; and with
no thoughts but the most confused; and with no prayers
except ejaculations, — your father strapped on his trunk, as
though he intended this to be his final departure, and turned
his face towards the 'Land of Promise,' — small promise,
indeed, though even this was little better than 'hoping
against hope.' In this trunk were all his books and clothes,
— indeed, all his worldly effects. Its lower edge pressed
hard against the small of his back, to his great annoyance
at the time, and to the permanent injury of this feeblest
part of his very feeble frame in subsequent years. In many
of the towns through which he passed boys would hoot after
him in the street, and, with an air of proud superiority,
ask if he had in his trunk a monkey or an anaconda to
exhibit. But, as he had no strength or courage to spare
for discussion, his replies were always faint and few; and,
in order not to take any extra steps, he seldom passed from
one side of the street to the other, but kept straight on,
in the middle of the road, till his feet at length stood on
that sacred hill whither all his thoughts and expectations
had been for a long time turning with anxiety, but with
fond desire.*

* This trunk was destroyed in the great fire at Constantinople in
1831. In one of his letters written at the time of the fire he says:
"The celebrated trunk, concerning which you made inquiry, and
which I intended to leave as a rich legacy to my children, was thrown

" Here a new trial awaited me. For the protection of the students, the trustees had adopted a rule that the students should board only in such families as they had licensed for this purpose. Mr. Adams gave me the names of some half dozen or more, and, leaving my trunk in his entry, I went forth to make application for board and lodging; but not one of them would receive me, the security I had to offer appearing to them very much like that which the Turks offer when they simply say ' *Allah Kareem,*' *i.e.*, ' God is merciful.' I got another list of names, and then another, until I had visited every house in town that was licensed, and no one would take me in. I returned to Mr. Adams's house, and could not refrain from weeping. At length I determined to take matters into my own hands, and, slipping out unperceived, I knocked at the first house that I saw, and asked if a poor student who wished to enter the Academy could find board and lodging with them. The woman of the house answered in the affirmative, and her husband confirmed it, and a bargain was soon struck.

" Mr. Hawley, the husband, was a poor shoemaker, and so very poor he could not possibly lose any thing, for the very plain reason he had nothing to lose, and possibly he might turn a penny. He was a profane and intemperate man, and some of his apprentices were of very ungodly manners. Mrs. Hawley was an earnest Christian woman. She had an impediment in her speech, and could not utter a single sentence intelligibly on ordinary subjects; but on the love of God she could speak with scarce any stammering, and it was said that in praying she never stuttered at all. Certainly, in singing her sweet hymns, no impediment could ever be noticed. She did what she could to make my stay comfortable, and doubtless hoped I should bring the family

from the window of the upper story, and broken to pieces. I have seen nothing of it since; but many of the precious things contained in it I saw scattered around the garden of the English palace, and the fire licking them up as it would stubble."

2

into some state of decency and order. He, I doubt not, was pleased to have what he would call the aristocratic and absolutely arbitrary rules of the trustees trampled under foot. And Mr. Adams was evidently disposed to wink at my being found in such an unsuitable place, and to give me a chance of finding a better one for myself. On my return from Dartmouth College, four years afterward, to Andover Seminary, I found Mr. Hawley low with consumption. I often visited him and prayed with him, and there was reason to hope that before his death he had become a new man.

"Having, as you perceived, secured a boarding-place, next morning I stood before the desk of the great Preceptor, and had my seat assigned me, in which it was expected I should always be found in study hours. My first lesson in Latin grammar, which I was to commit to memory, Mr. Adams also marked out for me.

"After some hours he called me up to recite, when it was found not only that I had learned all that was printed in large type, which students were expected to learn, but that I had committed to memory all that was in Italics, though only designed to be read over, and not recited; and, moreover, that I had gone over in this perfect manner more pages than he had marked out for me. Mr. Adams now opened his eyes wide, and looked at me from another stand-point, to see of what stuff I was really made.* And I began to

---

* In a letter which John Adams, LL.D. wrote many years afterward to his son, Rev. William Adams, D.D., he makes mention of this first recitation in the Latin grammar : —

"Before the close of the morning session I called him (William Goodell) to recite. He repeated all the first page, *verbatim*, notes and all, then the second and the third, in the same exact manner. I said, 'You must have studied this before.' He replied, 'I never saw a Latin grammar before you gave me this.' He advanced in his studies with great rapidity and accuracy. He proved himself an excellent scholar, a pious youth, and so obtained all the aid he needed. He had no more tears to shed but those of good humor and gratitude."

open my own eyes wider, and to look at him with more fearlessness than I had dared to feel before; for he smiled and wept by turns, and it was plain that a favorable impression had been made upon his great mind and still greater heart. I now felt sure there was no danger of my being sent away from that unlicensed house, unless another and a better one were provided for me.

"Mr. Adams, at the time I entered Phillips Academy, was in the full strength of manhood and vigor, at the very zenith of his long and brilliant career as a teacher of youth. His influence over me was greater than that of any other teacher. I came under his instruction at the most plastic and critical period of my life, and I gave up my whole being to be moulded by him as clay by the hands of the potter. Every thing he said and did, his example, his casual remarks, his prayers, all were to me exceedingly impressive. Andover was at that time blessed with such mighty men, men of God, as Professor Stuart, Professor Woods, and Professor Porter, and I often heard them preach; but neither at that time nor in subsequent years did their words fall on my ear and heart with such weight as those of Mr. Adams, during all the time I was his pupil. Many of his remarks I wrote down, parts of his prayers I remember to this day. Almost every sentence he uttered seemed an aphorism containing a world of meaning. I seemed to myself to have just waked up to a new life, and to be living in a new world. And even now, at this distance of time, I often lift up my heart in thankfulness to God that I was blessed, at such a time, with such a teacher.

"With Mr. Adams's family, though knowing them all by sight, I did not then become so well acquainted as several years afterward, when, having finished my collegiate course, I returned to Andover to pursue my theological studies. The acquaintance I then formed with them all was intimate, and to me very pleasant and precious. Never shall I cease to remember it with gratitude."

To one of the children of his old preceptor he wrote, on hearing of the death of Mrs. Adams, in 1830 : —

" When I heard of the death of your dear mother, I felt that she was indeed the mother of us all, and that there were those in the four quarters of the globe who would mingle their tears with yours, and who would pray that the Lord would sanctify to you this bereavement, and pour consolation into your bleeding hearts. The brief Memoir by Professor Stuart, which some friend was kind enough to send me, I read with deep interest, and lent it to others; and I said, if her name had not been once mentioned in the Memoir, I should have known to whom the character belonged. I doubt not you love to dwell upon her virtues, and talk over the instances of her humility, kindness, and benevolence.

" How much I would give to sit down one evening in your quiet family, and talk over with you all the good things the Lord hath done for Israel and for you and us since we last met! I am sure, after we had talked a while, we should say, ' He hath not dealt with us after our sins, nor rewarded us according to our iniquities.' I would take every one of your children up in my arms and bless them ; and, after I had listened to the story of the Lord's dealings with you and with your little ones, I think I should pray with a great increase of fervor that you might be ' the seed of the blessed of the Lord, and your offspring with you.' "

The Reminiscences continue : —

" While I was yet a member of the Academy, Mr. Adams's youngest son, William (now the Rev. Dr. Adams, the eloquent preacher and beloved pastor of the Madison Square Presbyterian Church, New York City), entered the Academy. I remember, with great vividness, how daintily and gracefully he stepped in with young Blanchard (Rev. Dr. Blanchard, of Lowell, Mass.), and presented his little self, then six years old, before the desk of the venerable Principal. In those days of his childhood, I often carried the lively little fellow on my back to school and to other places ; and I am thankful to acknowledge that, as one good turn deserves another, I am now, in my second childhood, often helped by him and his worthy friends over some of the steep and rugged places always incident to the decline of life.

"Just about the time I entered the Academy, two others also entered, both of whom proved to be remarkably fine scholars. One of them has since been known to the Christian world as the Rev. Asa Cummings, D.D., for many years editor of the 'Christian Mirror,' in Portland, Me., and the biographer of Dr. Payson; and the other was the Rev. Alva Woods, D.D., at one time President of Transylvania University in Lexington, Ky., and afterwards Professor in Brown University. Brother Cummings had rolled logs in the densest forests of Maine, till his legs had literally become quite crooked; but his mind was a diamond of the first water. I thought I had never known a person of so clear and candid an intellect as he appeared to have. My classmate, Woods, was the son of a Baptist minister in the Green Mountains of Vermont, and was nephew of the Rev. Dr. Woods, one of the distinguished professors in the Theological Seminary at Andover. These two, together with myself, Mr. Adams put into a class by ourselves, and he always seemed much gratified with our conduct and our progress; for no mark of tardiness, of absence, or of an imperfect lesson was, it is believed, ever placed against either of our names. With all promptness we could answer any question which would naturally arise from our lessons; and with all ease we would decline any noun in any declension, naming it in every case, from the nominative singular to the ablative plural, and going through the whole at one breath. And then we could go backward through the whole at another breath, naming the word in every case, from the ablative plural to the nominative singular. To us this was real fun, and to Mr. Adams it seemed real fun to hear us.

"But the quarter was at length drawing to a close, and so many were standing between us and that charity foundation to which we three were looking forward, that there appeared scarcely any hope of our ever receiving any benefit from it. And it was evidently becoming a subject of deep thought and earnest discussion with Mr. Adams and some of the trustees what provision should be made for us, without diverting any of this charity fund from its prescribed channels. A few days before the end of the quarter, Mr. Adams called us up, and, after informing us how many had been waiting much longer than we to receive the aid, told us that Lieutenant-Governor Phillips, of Boston, who was one of the trustees, and I think one always present at the examinations, had come forward, and, on account of the present great disproportion between those funds and the numerous applications for them, had voluntarily offered to bear our expenses through one year. This was to us a great and sudden relief. It was like the year of jubilee, and we gave special thanks to Him ' who remembered us in our low estate, for His mercy endureth for ever.'

"Early in the year, Mr. Adams informed me that a relative of mine in Vermont, on hearing that I was at the Academy, had sent word to ask whether I was worth raising. What answer Mr. Adams made I never inquired, nor did he ever tell me. But the year was not far advanced when a drover, with some scores of cattle for the Boston market, knocked at the door of the Academy, and, to the amusement and wonder of the pupils, asked to see me. Mr. Adams beckoned me to go and see what was wanted. Amidst the lowing of oxen, I went with some trepidation, when, lo and behold, he turned over to me a fine yoke of oxen, which he said my father's uncle in Jamaica, Vt., Solomon Goodell, had sent, to draw me up some of the steep and rugged hills of science. With the oxen came the following characteristic note addressed to Mr. Adams. It was a mere scrap of paper, carelessly folded in the form of a letter, and containing the following words:—

" ' Sir, I send you a pair of fat oxen for William Goodell, in your school.'

" I immediately stepped back and asked permission to be absent the remainder of the day, telling Mr. Adams I had suddenly become possessed of some live stock, and ' must needs go and prove them.' I drove them at once to my lodgings and put them into the pasture, but was so much afraid somebody would steal them I hardly dared take my eyes from them, and the very next day I sold them to a butcher. And thus in this my last year at the Academy I paid my own bills.

" This year would close my preparatory studies; but to what college should I go? and how should I be supported? My classmate Cummings, having friends in Boston and that vicinity, was going to Cambridge. My classmate Woods, — who was my chum for one whole year, — being a Baptist, would naturally go to Brown University. We had in the mean time become acquainted with Daniel Temple, who entered the Academy soon after us. Although his boarding-place was some distance from ours, yet, as he had just been converted in a powerful revival of religion and was full of faith and the Holy Ghost, his influence was felt far and near. Mr. Adams proposed to him and to me to go to Dartmouth College, saying that the Kimball Union Academy had been recently established at Meriden, N. H., and that this Academy had funds to aid in their studies those having the ministry in view, and, as there were not students enough to exhaust all the funds, the College came in for a share. Some of the professors had written Mr. Adams on the subject, promising to take two, whom he should recommend, and allow them each one hundred dollars a year for the four years. Mr. Temple and myself thankfully accepted the proposition, and at once made arrangements to room together. The aid proffered would not indeed be sufficient to meet our expenses, but the long winter vacations would enable us to earn something by keeping school. I entered Dartmouth College Sept. 24, 1813.

" The one hundred dollars per annum allowed me from the funds of the Kimball Union Academy, together with what I earned by teaching, enabled me to pass through college with comfort to myself and without being a burden to others. Every winter found me occupied in teaching school; and I was so fond of the employment, and moreover the opportunity of doing good appeared to me so great, that I would have been willing to teach even without compensation. The places where I taught were Wardsborough, Woodstock, and St. Johnsbury in the State of Vermont, and Keene and Hanover in New Hampshire. I also taught a small school in a corner of New Marlborough, N. H., before I went to the Academy. In many of these schools, I had reason to believe, my efforts were blessed not only to the minds, but to the souls, of my pupils. How I should love to see them all, and converse and pray with them all once more! Several of them are in the ministry, and may they be able ministers of the New Testament!

"In my school in Keene the religious interest awakened was long-continued and very deep. Oh, what precious meetings we had! and what blessed recitations of the Assembly's Catechism! My soul with great joy and thankfulness hath them still in remembrance. And what would I not give for the privilege of again sitting with those dear youth 'in heavenly places in Christ Jesus'! Well, we hope in those heavenly places to sit together for ever. The commencement of the revival was under the following circumstances. One of the boys had been guilty of using profane language. After conversing with him some time on his sin, and telling him that without repentance and forgiveness he could never enter heaven, I tied a string round his neck, and charged him to remember, whenever he felt that string, that he could not go to heaven without being pardoned, and that he could not expect pardon without asking for it. When he came to school the next morning the string was gone, it having been taken off by his father. As parental authority was superior to mine, I could not take him to task; but I again addressed him and the whole school on the sin of profanity, reminding them of what God had said of him that taketh His name in vain. I then asked him if he wished me to pray that God would forgive this sin and all the sins he had ever committed, and save him from eternal punishment. On his assenting to this I took him by the hand and rose for prayer. The whole school rose as by a sudden impulse. The boy wept, and the whole school were deeply moved. When I ceased praying, all the pupils seemed so much affected that I continued to speak to them for some minutes on sin, repentance, and salvation; and from that time for many weeks onward it was as easy to speak to them on those infinitely important subjects as it was to breathe. Christ was there, and every word spoken in His name seemed to tell. They all appeared to feel that in that prayer they had come directly into the presence of God, — much nigher to Him than they ever came before, — and that they were transacting business with Him for eternity; and I doubt not 'the Lord will count, when He writeth up the people, that this and that one were born there.'

"Among the first letters of welcome I received, when visiting my native land in 1851, was one from a daughter of Judge Newcomb, who in that memorable winter began to breathe the breath of spiritual life, — a life which shall never end. And among the first letters of welcome I received upon my final return home with my family, in 1865, was one from this same beloved daughter, who still has life, and has it more abundantly.' Though wanting in some measure the sense of hearing, she could and did, and I doubt not does still, hear the whispers of the Spirit, and the sweet and precious words of Jesus. And should any of the beloved youth of this school, or of any other school I have taught, read these lines, may I not hope they will offer up this one petition for their old teacher, that, after having pointed out to them and to many others the way to heaven, he may not himself be ' a castaway ' ? I have reason to be very grateful that one so unworthy should have been employed to such a degree in these blessed services, while at the same time I ought to be no less humble and penitent that in those blessed

2*   c

services I did not feel more of the 'constrainings of the love of Christ' urging me on to action.

"In the winter of 1314 I taught school by day, and a singing class also in the evening, at St. Johnsbury, Vt. Here I found myself among some of the very best of people. The church was emphatically a *working* church; and perhaps, with even more propriety than many of the apostolic churches, might be called *a model church*. Every member appeared to be a living branch of the true vine, and to be always standing in his or her lot, ready for any and every service which was to be performed for Christ. The church had no pastor, and, I think, had always been without one; for pastors were then few in that part of the country. But the public services of the sanctuary, together with the prayer meetings maintained by the church on the Sabbath and at other times, were of the most interesting character; special pains being taken to procure the very best sermons that could be found in the whole country; and the reader being always expected to look over very carefully beforehand the sermon he was to read in public, in order that the emphasis might in every case be laid right, and the meaning brought out with clearness and power. They also took special pains to sing well, often meeting together for the sake of practising, and employing a teacher to perfect both themselves and their children in the science as well as in the art of music. Their prayers were devout and edifying, for they were offered by those accustomed to 'lift up holy hands without wrath or doubting.' Those parents, both men and women, took strong hold of the Abrahamic covenant; and as much expected their children to be heirs according to the promise as the good patriarch himself expected his son Isaac would be. In fact, whenever I see or hear the word *St. Johnsbury*, I always think of the place of which God said, 'This is my rest for ever; here will I dwell, for I have desired it.'

"That church was composed of such members as the very godly parents of Professor Lawrence, late of East Windsor

Theological Institute; the Hon. Luther Jewett, M.D., himself a host; Governor Fairbanks, that wonderful man, whose very name in all that region was a synonyme of every thing that was upright, honorable, benevolent, and good; together with his earnest and excellent brother, he, I mean, the inventor of the celebrated Fairbanks scales. The last mentioned Fairbanks was, on account of his wonderful mechanical genius, a man after Dr. Hamlin's own heart (the Rev. Dr. Hamlin, I mean, President of the Robert College in Constantinople), he being, as is well known, a great mechanic; and when I told him that this Fairbanks had once been a pupil of mine, shutting up one eye and squinting at me with the other, he very naively, as if with the most unaffected simplicity, remarked, 'You must have taught away to him all your own knowledge, reserving nothing for yourself; for you yourself have been utterly deficient in that line from the first day I knew you.' A bit of pleasantry to be sure not much to the credit of the one addressed; but I have at least the satisfaction of feeling that I taught it all away to one who knew how to employ it to some good purpose.

"On Sophomore Quarter-day, in 1815, the Faculty, to my surprise, gave me the first appointment, which was the Latin Salutatory. But when we graduated, in 1817, I had the Greek Oration, then considered the third appointment; Marsh, afterwards President of Burlington College, had the first, which was the Valedictory; and Chase, now Bishop of New Hampshire, received the second, which was, I think, the Philosophical. During the greater part of my senior year I was engaged in teaching, and was able to attend but few recitations. Had it been otherwise, had I spent the whole year in hard study. it is not likely that I should have deserved a higher appointment than the one given me; for the class was a large one, and there were many very good scholars in it. One thing is certain, and I think of it even now with satisfaction, that for the sake of a collegiate honor I never studied fifteen minutes the more, no, not ten,

nor even five, during my whole course; and that my eyes
and health were as good at the end as at the beginning.
My health was indeed always feeble; and three hours a
day were just about my average time of study. But then,
when I did study, it was in good earnest, concentrating my
whole mind directly on the subject. It was much the same
during all my term at the Theological Seminary, and during
much of my missionary life I have been able to devote but
a few hours a day to close study. But though feeble from
childhood, I have hardly ever been sick a day. In fact, I
have been growing stronger ever since I was born; and
should 'the days of the years of my life' run parallel with
those of Methuselah, might it not be reasonably expected
that I should be more hale and vigorous in the nine hundred and sixty-ninth year of my life, than any of the
hypochondriacs of any generation of students, past, present,
or future?

"During the revival at college, the pious students were
in the habit of going out, if not daily, weekly, into the
neighboring villages and towns to conduct meetings, sometimes in a school-house and sometimes in the church itself;
and as they carried the revival spirit with them, and as
much expected a revival in every place as they expected
to reach that place themselves, the flame was kindled everywhere, the Spirit was poured out from on high, and very
many, it is believed, were created anew in Christ Jesus
unto good works. Before the commencement of this revival a Moral Society had been formed in college, which
embraced a large number of the students, and which promised to be very useful. A regular meeting of this society,
occurring in the very height of the revival, very few of the
members, especially of those who had been recently converted, or who had been most active in those revival scenes,
were present, and this gave occasion for the complaint that
we had become too religious to be any longer moral, and
that we were devoting so much time to religion, that we had

none left for morality. We were then young and inexperienced, and very zealous, and were doubtless much less discreet than we ought to have been in regard to many things. The revival was indeed one of remarkable power; and yet college duties were not in general suspended, but the studies and recitations for the most part went on as usual. On one occasion, however, when one of the professors was hearing a class in the recitation-room, in the room immediately above 'many were gathered together praying.' And the singing of sweet hymns in that same room, where boisterous mirth had been previously often heard, so deeply affected the Professor and his whole class, that their recitation that morning was turned into a meeting for thanksgiving and praise. And that was the only instance I recollect of any interruption to the regular duties of the college.

"One day a student, observing his heart more filled with wicked thoughts than he had previously supposed possible, and alarmed to find his own powers altogether too feeble to control them, undertook to escape from himself. Throwing off his outer garments, he ran as if for dear life; and those who saw him in this earnest race knew as little what his object was, as those who hastened to get out of John Gilpin's way knew of his. He ran and ran till well nigh exhausted; but, finding all his bad thoughts still clinging as closely as ever, he became discouraged, and, slowly returning to his room in college, cried, 'Lord, save, or I perish.' That runaway has now been for many years a steadfast preacher of the glorious Gospel, directing the attention of men to the Lamb of God, who alone taketh away the sin of the world.

"The most of our fellow-students at Dartmouth had, like ourselves, to struggle hard to get an education; and we did not any of us make so much use as we might of the unlimited credit we had on the Bank of Faith, viz., 'Trust in the Lord and do good, so shalt thou dwell in the land, and verily thou shalt be fed.' And in those days we heard the story of

another bank, as it might be called, with which we were
sometimes tempted to do business. It had, indeed, in its
vault no specie, — I mean, no Scripture promises; yet it
strangely secured the confidence of many desponding minds.
The story ran thus: A poor student, very inattentive to his
studies, and extremely careless as to both his manners and
his morals, was repeatedly, though to little purpose, admonished by his tutors and professors. At length the President
sent for him, and, after giving him plenty of good advice and
solemn warning of his danger in the course he was pursuing, asked him, ' How do you ever expect to get through the
world in this way?' The fellow at once and very archly
replied, ' Did you ever hear of any one sticking by the way?'
' Yes, surely: all get through by hook or by crook, *and nobody ever sticks by the way.*' These few words, '*nobody ever
sticks by the way,*' spoken to the ear of one sunk low in despondency, often had a talismanic potency to drive away his
anxious forebodings. I have seen the face of our good
brother Temple lighted up with smiles and joyful hopes, by
simply repeating those talismanic words, ' *nobody ever sticks by
the way.*'

    " Of some of my college classmates the following are well
known: President Marsh, of Burlington College, the vale-
dictorian of our class; President Cushing, of Hampden
Sidney; Professor Fisk, of Amherst; Emory Washburn,
LL.D., Governor of Massachusetts, and Professor of Law
at Cambridge University; Benjamin Dorr, D.D., Rector of
Christ Church in Philadelphia; Carlton Chase, D.D., Bishop
of the Diocese of New Hampshire; and Lyndon A. Smith,
M.D., of Newark, N. J. I should love to mention by name
many others of my class, whose countenances I can in some
cases still recall, but whose names, during a long absence
from the country, have faded from my memory. I hope to
see them in that world where their faces will shine as the
brightness of the firmament, and they will all of them be
found to have ' received a new name, which the mouth of the

Lord shall name,' and which shall not be forgotten for ever. In the class before me were such men as Professor Haddock, Professor Torrey, President Wheeler, of Burlington College, Rev. Dr. Absalom Peters. Another member of the class, who afterward became a member of Congress, and who secured from his Alma Mater the honorary degree of LL.D., like many of us sprung from poverty, but earned a pittance by ringing the college bell. Receiving very deservedly a high appointment at Sophomore quarter-day, as it was then called, he was much encouraged by this honor, and his friends were not a little elated with his success. Indeed, he became so inspired with self-reliance that he was accustomed afterwards to stand out on the steps in front of the college, and by the hour together discuss the great questions of the day with the greatest wranglers in the three upper classes in college. And his step was now so firm, and his carriage so erect, that the words of the poet were often applied to him : —

> ' At every step his advanced head
> Knocked out a star in heaven.'

" Thus potent is a little encouragement received at the proper time by a poor, timid student. The Rev. Levi Spaulding, D.D., the distinguished missionary in Ceylon, was my junior in college, but I knew him well both before and after. So also Professor Upham and Professor Bush, together with Rufus Choate, LL.D., who were in the classes after me, were well known to me, for that wonderful revival which took place in Sophomore year threw all the classes into one indiscriminate mass, and all class distinctions were for the time being entirely obliterated.

" During our Freshman year at college, the number of pious students in the upper classes was very small. In the senior class there was, I think, but one professor of religion, and he, in point of scholarship, stood among the lowest in the class. There was no prayer-meeting conducted by the students, and, of course, although Professors Shurtliff, Moore, and Muzzy were not only able, but very earnest Christian men, yet there was no spiritual life in college. Thus passed one whole year of death-like stupidity. In our Sophomore year we began to have more courage. About this time it was that the members of the Theological Society, that met every Saturday evening in secret session, with doors locked and windows barred, that we might not be interrupted by the thoughtless ones in college, unanimously adopted that famous resolution that we would, each one of us, converse with at least three of his fellow-students on the subject of personal religion during the coming week, giving them also a special interest in our prayers. We had hardly commenced our work when the Spirit was poured out upon us from on high in a most remarkable manner, and instead of conversing with three of our fellow-students, we (certainly some of us) conversed with more than thirty times three. My room-mate, Temple, being everywhere known as a man of God, and of deep Christian experience, our room was thronged from morning till night with those who 'would see Jesus.' I have seen many precious revivals, but I have never since witnessed a work so mighty as was that at Dartmouth College in 1815, embracing some of the finest scholars in every class in college, together with most of the distinguished families that lived in its vicinity, and extending its saving influence even to subsequent classes in following years.

"I recall the names of some of the subjects of this work of grace who in after life became distinguished men: Professors Torrey, Fisk, Bush, and Upham; President Wheeler, President Marsh, President Cushing, Bishop Chase, and last, but not least, that beloved missionary of the cross in Ceylon, Levi Spaulding. All these were men of note, and, besides, there were many who, though less known, became earnest and useful ministers of the New Testament. A large number of students, with members of the principal families in the neighborhood, joined the college church in one day. And then it was we felt, and some of us said, as we stood on a knoll in front of the college buildings, 'The winter is past, and the rain is over and gone, and the flowers appear on the earth, and the time of the singing of birds is come.' I well remember the first public prayer which Haddock made. He had always been strictly moral, and such was the gentleness of his manner, and such his native politeness, that he was often pointed out to us as an example of what we might all of us become, even though we should never attend a dancing-school; but it was not generally known that he was indulging hope in Christ, nor even that his mind had of late been unusually impressed with the great things of eternity. When, therefore, at the close of a meeting in the old school-house, I asked him to offer prayer, and he arose at once with all the grace and dignity so natural to him, and poured out his heart in a prayer of great fervency and peculiarly appropriate, the effect was overpowering, and the glory of God seemed to fill the place. Every heart trembled for joy or with fear, and we hardly dared speak to one another as we walked silently away from the place.

"At one of those little, but never-to-be-forgotten prayer-meetings, there was present a member of the senior class. He was a distinguished scholar, and excelled particularly in mathematical studies. As we did not in those days wait for much ceremony, and as we scarcely thought of what was due from a Sophomore to a Senior, we pounced upon him at once with such tremendous questions that he soon found his mathematics at fault, for he could not solve the principal problem, 'What shall it profit a man, if he gain the whole world and lose his own soul?' He took his hat and retired, and some forty years afterwards, describing the scene in a letter to some friends, he said: 'I went out under a pine-tree, and gave myself up to God, and that pine-tree (said he) will be remembered in heaven.' Yes, indeed, Brother Spaulding, and many pine-trees will be remembered in heaven. And many such rocks and trees, and old school-houses, will be remembered there. From under that pine-tree where he groaned, and wept, and prayed, and gave himself to God, Spaulding went to that school-house, 'where many were gathered together praying.' He came in, look-ing as though he had never seen such a sight before. But he arose almost immediately, and, throwing his spectacles back on his head, while rivers of water ran down his eyes, he brought out all the mathematics he ever knew, demon-strating every truth with more than mathematical precision, even with the power of the Spirit, so that every thought-less heart in that crowded house quailed. Those were, indeed, the years of the right hand of the Most High. And I do not know that we were ever more honored of God as His instruments in doing good than during those blessed years.

"How much would I give to revisit all these scenes of college life, and especially all those interesting spots made sacred by the presence and blessing of the Holy Spirit! I would go to our good Deacon Kellogg's. I would go into the old school-house, feeling that the Lord will assuredly count, when He writeth up the people, that this and that one were born there. I would go over 'Mink Brook,' and think of all the precious memories of those who lived and were born again on its banks. I would go into the ceme-tery, and feel what a blessed thing it is to work and suffer for Christ in this world. I would go and see all the young professors, and the new president, and say to them: 'Instead of the fathers shall be the children,' and, in com-parison with those who have preceded you, may you be like 'princes in all the earth.' Last summer I saw at Brock-port, N. Y., a lady who lived on the plains of Dartmouth, amidst those scenes of glory. She said I assisted her in inaugurating the first Sabbath school ever known in this country. This, I assured her, could not have been, — though it may possibly have been the first Sabbath school estab-lished in the State of New Hampshire, or at least in that part of the State.

"Many years have elapsed since those wonderful days, and it is not to be supposed that in describing them I have stated every thing with perfect accuracy or in due order. But, in every remembrance, I always exclaim, 'Not unto us, O Lord, not unto us!'"

At what period Mr. Goodell first became interested in the subject of foreign missions as a question of personal duty does not appear from any records which he has left. When he went out from his father's house to obtain an education, his purposes for life were altogether indefinite. He did not even have the ministry of the Gospel distinctly in view. But the instructions of his beloved preceptor at Phillips Academy seem to have awakened new and higher views of Christian obligation, and to have inspired him with nobler aims. Almost at the beginning of his studies the stern purpose which led him to seek preparation for a wider sphere of usefulness ripened into a humble and complete consecration to the work of his Master, and a willingness to do His will, whatever the work might be.

While he was at Phillips Academy, the first missionaries of the American Board to India, Messrs. Newell, Judson, Hall, Nott, and Rice, were ordained at Salem, Mass., about twenty miles from Andover. This service young Goodell attended, and he thus describes the scene in his Reminiscences: —

"The ordination took place at the Tabernacle Church, Feb. 6, 1812. The students in the Academy had repeatedly seen the most or all of them, and had heard Judson and some others of them preach. Mr. Adams kindly gave permission for any of the older students to go who wished; and, with my classmate Cummings, I at once embraced the opportunity. The day was one of the coldest known that winter. It was exceedingly slippery, and we had to strain every nerve and exert every muscle to keep on our feet, while, at the same time, we had to press forward with all the eagerness possible in order to arrive in time. The sea, a ship, a wharf, a city, a seaport town, were all new and strange things to me, my eyes never having looked upon such things before ; and, after arriving and taking some refreshment with the relatives of Mr. Cummings, I spent the time before the ordination services in running every where, and seeing every thing. My fatigue was already so great that a bed would have been a much more fitting place than a church. But only the latter was open, and I entered with the crowd.

" The church was filled to its utmost capacity. The news of the approaching ordination had spread far and wide, and the excitement was of no ordinary kind, — to see five young men, of great promise, possessing talents and attainments of a high order, and voluntarily devoting themselves, at the call of Christ, to all the poverty, the hardships, and the perils of a mission for life. Ann H. Judson and Harriet Newell were there, both to be afterwards embalmed in the memory of the Church, and to have an imperishable record in its history. And there were also present those men of God, the Rev. Drs. Worcester, Griffin, Woods, Morse, Spring, and many other great and good men, several of whom took part in those very solemn ordination services. The interest manifested was universally very deep. God was there, and in that great assembly there was, at times, a stillness 'like the stillness of God, when He ariseth in silence to bless the world.' At times the whole great assembly seemed moved as the trees of the wood are moved by a mighty wind. As may well be supposed, the feelings of the audience, and especially our own, were wrought up to the highest pitch.

" Immediately at the close of the services we had to start, without rest or refreshment, to walk back to Andover. Long before we reached home I had ceased to have any control over the muscles of locomotion, but staggered like a paralytic. Some theological students, who had also been to Salem, overtaking us, assisted in supporting me along. Being placed between two of them, and bearing my whole weight upon them, they, by taking turns, succeeded in carrying their load. Through a kind Providence we reached the house where I first boarded at Andover. The family immediately spread a bed for me on the floor, before the fire, and tried to make me comfortable; but I shook and shook, till it seemed as if my nerves and muscles would never again become quiet. It was certainly a wonder I did not become permanently paralyzed by this exposure, excitement, and excessive fatigue. But God preserved my life; and the next day I was able to walk to my lodgings, and soon to attend to my lessons. I felt amply repaid by being so thoroughly inoculated with the missionary spirit, that a re-inoculation has never been found necessary."

This ordination seems to have made a deep impression upon his mind; but we find no record in his diary giving any indication of his having seriously proposed the question of duty to his own heart until near the close of his Freshman year in college, when he wrote, under date of May 20th, 1814 : —

"This day Brother Nealy called upon me. He expects soon, with Brother Russel, to go to the missionary establishment in Gosport, Eng., to prepare himself to be a missionary. Lord, hast thou called them by thy grace to preach the unsearchable riches of Christ to millions who are perishing for lack of vision? Wilt thou prepare them for it? But what shall I do? Lord, what wilt thou have me to do? Here am I; send me. I desire to labor where thou wilt have me. I am ready to follow thee wheresoever thou leadest."

The bright example of self-devotion and the early death of Harriet Newell seem to have deeply affected his heart. Mr. Newell was married on the 9th of the same month on which he was ordained at Salem. He sailed with his young wife on the 19th for Calcutta. On the 19th of November, in the same year, Mrs. Newell died at the Isle of France, at the early age of nineteen. Her years were few, but her life was long in the work which it accomplished. The brief memoir which was published the following year was the means of kindling the missionary spirit in many hearts, and we know not how much influence it may have had upon William Goodell in leading him to consecrate himself to the same service. That he was deeply impressed by its perusal appears from the following entry in his diary, made only four days after the last-quoted extract from his journal : —

" *May* 24. A few days since I received the Memoirs of Mrs. Harriet Newell. I had long wished to become more acquainted with her life and writings. My curiosity was so excited, and my desire to read the book was so great, that I could not sit down and read it through by course, as usual, until I had turned over nearly every leaf, reading a few lines in one place and a few in another. I could not restrain my tears while looking on her likeness. It brought to my mind her piety, devotedness to God, and ardent love for the millions in Asia. When I consider her activity, self-denial, and readiness to forsake all for Christ, I feel as if I had no religion. Oh that a flame of that divine love which warmed her breast might be kindled in this heart of mine ! "

While he was at Dartmouth, he enjoyed again the privilege of attending the ordination of a band of missionaries, of which he wrote in his journal : —

" *July* 4, 1815. This day I returned again to college. My health is much improved by my journey. I was present at the ordination of six missionaries (Mills, Richards, Meigs, Warren, Bardwell, and Poor) at Newburyport, June 21st, and at the grand convention of ministers at Royalston. They were such occasions as I seldom enjoy. The sacramental season at Newburyport was peculiarly interesting. To sit at the Lord's table with so many of the redeemed servants of Christ, assembled from various places, seemed next to being in heaven."

CHAPTER III.

IN the autumn of 1817, having completed his college course, he returned to Andover, and entered the Theological Seminary. The day on which he became a member of this institution he made the following record : —

"*Wednesday evening, November* 5, 1817. Was this evening admitted a member of the sacred institution at Andover. On this holy ground, consecrated by the prayers and tears and offerings of many who are now sleeping in the tomb, I purpose to spend three years, and 'give myself to reading, meditation, and prayer,' hoping in due season to be in some measure prepared to preach the unsearchable riches of Christ to a dying world, and not be as those who are 'ever learning and never able to come to the knowledge of the truth.'"

From the time of his entering the Theological Seminary his associations tended to increase his interest in the cause of foreign missions, and to fasten more deeply upon his heart the conviction that the call from the perishing in distant lands, which had been ringing in his ears, was addressed to him personally. The controversy in his mind, and the decision to which he came in connection with his classmate and most intimate friend, Daniel Temple, he describes in his Reminiscences : —

"At Andover we at once joined that little sacred band, whose constitution and by-laws, correspondence and records, together with all the signatures of the members, were written with an alphabet which had been invented expressly for the purpose by Gordon Hall and his noble compeers, and which none but the members could understand. This secret society

was like 'a wheel within a wheel,' which, though unseen, was
not unfelt, for it moved and controlled all missionary societies
and missionary operations in a way which, to the churches
and even to the secretaries themselves, seemed perfectly
unaccountable.   Here we came under the influence of such
men as Pliny Fisk, that excellent missionary pioneer of
Palestine, who afterwards died at my house in Beyrout; and
of Levi Spaulding, the veteran missionary in Ceylon, whom
we had known at Dartmouth College, and who now questioned us as closely as we had once, during that great revival
in college, questioned him.   We were professing to follow,
and to be entirely willing to follow, the leadings of Providence, wherever we might be directed.   And we were ready
to declare further, what in fact we had been doing for several
years, that should the state of the world, at the close of our
studies, be such as it then was, it would undoubtedly be our
duty to engage personally in the work of carrying the Gospel
to the heathen.   What need was there of our coming to a
determination more positive and decided?

" These brethren, together with Levi Parsons and several
other strong men of that generation, were not satisfied with
this, and solemnly assured us that unless we were prepared
to take a step much in advance, it was morally certain we
could never be missionaries.   This at first seemed to us little
better than atheism, and we began to urge some objections
from our stand-point.   We had been following the leadings
of Providence in regard to every thing all our days, and we
had each of us been in a remarkable degree the child of
Providence, and ought we now to renounce Providence, and
take things into our own hands, especially this great matter
of personally engaging in the missionary work?   But our
strongest objections and arguments did not seem to have the
weight of a feather with these men of God.   On that evening they had evidently brought together all their strongest
men in order to knock away the platform on which our feet
were planted.   Naming over all the missionaries who had

ever gone from Andover, they showed most clearly that every one of them had been obliged to close his eyes against all the doors which Providence seemed most invitingly to open for him in his own country, and to stop his ears against all the apparently reiterated calls of Providence to remain at home. They declared that if a man were fit to go on a mission, most unexpected doors would be opened on every hand, and calls would come from every quarter, some of them louder than when seven thunders utter their voices, all of them earnestly urging him to remain here. And that all the churches, and all the venerable pastors, and even all the professors of the theological seminaries, would endeavor to persuade him that Providence evidently designed that he should stay at home; that, in fact, he was the only man who could fill this or that important place, and that for him to close his eyes against these open doors, and to shut his ears against these loud calls, would be to rebel against the light, and to make himself wiser than God and all God's people. Much of this we ourselves knew, for we had already seen it in the case of our own associates who preceded us in the missionary work. And we soon felt the necessity of coming under laws like those of the Medes and Persians. These strict rules were necessary, not only for our safety, but for our comfort, saving us from distractions and difficulties without end. It was soon understood that every thing had already been considered and settled, and that it was altogether in vain to think of turning us from our purpose, our minds having been made up in full view of all these circumstances which they thought new and providential."

In February, 1818, he wrote from the Theological Seminary to his father an extended letter, communicating to him for the first time his views and feelings on the question as to where he should spend his life in the service of Christ, expressing his conviction that the claims of the Eastern world far outweighed those of the country in which he was

3   D

living, and concluding with the following reasons for considering the call to engage in the work of missions as addressed
personally to himself:—

"1. I was consecrated to God in infancy by my parents, to
be His child and servant for ever.

"2. I have, I trust, dedicated myself to Him who formed me
for His glory, and I no longer consider myself as my own, but
as bound by every possible obligation to be as active in His service as are those ministering spirits of His that excel in strength
and do His pleasure, to go wherever He shall send me, and most
cheerfully execute all His commands. I have often said to Him,
' Help me to serve thee with all my powers, and I refer it wholly
to thee in what place, under what circumstances, or even in what
world this shall be.'

"3. My business is not merely to pass through the world with
comfort, reputation, and perhaps with a degree of usefulness,
but to attempt the greatest possible good, to practise any kind
of self-denial, to exert every faculty, and be willing to follow
Him who was a man of sorrows, and had not where to lay His
head, to promote the benevolent object for which He became
incarnate.

"4. For several years I have, I hope, desired the conversion
of the heathen; and when I have looked upon the extensive
fields already white unto the harvest, and considered how few
the laborers, I have at least professed to pray the Lord of the
harvest to raise up many who should enter these fields; who
should go to the east and west, to the north and south, and
preach glad tidings of good things to all people. And since
God has raised me up, and that, too, almost by a miracle (and
for some purpose, else I had never existed), if I now without
sufficient reason refuse to go (and I can offer none which appears to me to have much validity), how can I ever again make
this an object of prayer?

"5. The grand scheme of divine Providence which has been
unfolding to the admiring view of those who are looking for
redemption, and God's providential dealings with myself, have
all conspired in directing my attention to the East. Add to all
this, if you please, —

"6. The facility with which I can acquire a new language,
and the adaptation of the work of a missionary in many respects to my constitution, and its harmony with all my feelings,
and I think you will be equally convinced with myself that it is
my duty to think seriously whether I ought not to leave my
dearest connections, and give up all that is interesting in Christian society and friendship, in order to extend the knowledge of
salvation to the ruined, dying millions in pagan lands.

"On this subject I have asked no man's advice, because I

thought no one capable of determining for another. But a father's advice and blessing I account no small thing. And for this reason I have stated my views and feelings that you may communicate yours in return to one who, I hope, will ever thankfully receive reproof and counsel from an affectionate parent."

In his letter to his father he alluded to one obstacle, without naming it, which seemed to stand in the way of his devoting himself to the work of missions. It was the dependent condition of his father; but this he immediately set about removing. Leaving the Seminary, he visited several places in New England, to obtain the evidence of his father's service in the Revolutionary army, in order to secure for him a pension. In this he was successful, and nothing now remained but for him to receive his father's approbation and blessing. These were freely given, and he made the following record of his final decision : —

" *February* 12, 1818. This evening had an important interview with missionary brethren. And now 'tis done! I am thine, O thou who didst die for the world! Send me where thou wilt; arm me with Christian courage, and most cheerfully I go to the ends of the earth to publish thy salvation ! "

From this time onward until he breathed his last breath, he never faltered in his absorbing devotion to the great work of Christian missions, — that of making known the Gospel of Christ to the whole world.

On the 4th of November, 1818, he attended the ordination of Pliny Fisk, Levi Spaulding, Miron Winslow, and Henry Woodward, as missionaries, which took place at Salem, Mass. Of this interesting occasion he made the following record in his journal : —

" This has been to me a most interesting day. Several of my missionary brethren were set apart and publicly consecrated to the work of the Lord among the heathen. The audience was numerous and attentive, — the exercises solemn and calculated to make a favorable impression. May the Spirit of the Lord God rest upon these my dear brethren, —the spirit of counsel and might, the spirit of knowledge and of the fear of

Jehovah.   And when they walk in the midst of trouble wilt thou revive them!

" Spent the evening with those who were ordained, and with those who intend, unless detained by Providence, to go to the heathen.   There were eleven of us together, — a number equal to that of the apostles when they returned unto Jerusalem from the mount called Olivet, and went into an upper room and continued with one accord in prayer and supplication with the women.   We had no expectation of spending another evening together on earth; and on parting sang, ' When shall we all meet again,' and pronounced Moses' benediction: ' The Lord bless thee and keep thee; the Lord make His face to shine upon thee, and be gracious unto thee; the Lord lift up His countenance upon thee and give thee peace.'   Amen and Amen."

We prefer to state in his own words, penned only the week before his death, how God provided for him a loving companion and faithful helper for his missionary life; one who delighted to share in his toils and trials, and who, surviving him, after awaiting with joyful expectation the hour when their blessed intercourse, so long enjoyed on earth, should be made still more blessed in heaven, went up, on the 11th of July, 1871, to be for ever with him and with the Lord.   He says in his Reminiscences : —

" And here I might as well introduce another, even a new and important personage, whose influence on all my subsequent life has been as good as it has been great.   Mr. Temple had been my chum during the whole four years at college, and was still my room-mate at the Theological Seminary.   But I heard incidentally that he had been looking out for a more permanent room-mate, and had already obtained the promise of one.   It must be confessed that I was at first a little vexed that he should have taken so important a step without giving me even a hint of such an arrangement, and I at once determined not to be left in the lurch.   It is true that there was a large circle of very estimable young ladies whose acquaintance I had made in vacations and in the schools I had taught; but oh, how often I wished that some maternal association, or that the whole church, Moravian fashion, would select for me a suitable companion.   But as such wishes were vain, I had to keep on praying, having already prayed more in reference to this subject than in reference to any other temporal subject whatever. I now began to watch as well as pray.

"In passing, one vacation, through various towns in New England to hold meetings of a religious or educational nature, I came to the town of Holden, Mass., and was there most providentially introduced to a lady of singularly sweet disposition, modest appearance, and dignified demeanor, bearing the name of Abigail P. Davis. But though our acquaintance continued and increased for more than four years, yet I was unable to hear from her lips that short monosyllable, that long-desired word, *Yes*, till Nov. 19, 1822, when, in the presence of her good minister and of numerous other friends, it rang out with such clearness as quite startled me, for I had nearly begun to fear that there might be some defect in her organs of speech in reference to this little word. And to this very day I have always been so thankful that the business was not left to any maternal association or to any church, be it Moravian or any other organization under heaven. It was all as if manifestly arranged in the divine decrees before the foundation of the world, and there has never been any disposition on her part or mine to alter these decrees.

"Several months after letters had begun to come to me from Holden, Mr. Temple, to whom I had never spoken a word on the subject of his so unceremoniously changing his room-mate, said to me one day, with a serious air, ' Let us see, who is that young lady at Holden whom you hope to secure for a more permanent room-mate than your present one?' On telling him, with all honesty and frankness, and perceiving he began to smile, I inquired, 'Who told you any thing about it?' He immediately replied, ' You yourself have just told me, and I thank you.' And so, after mutual congratulations, we both of us went on our way rejoicing.

"This excellent lady I led away from her native land in 1822. And now I have brought her back, almost, if not quite, as good as new! 'Goodness and mercy have indeed followed us all the days of our life, and we hope to dwell in the house of the Lord for ever.' And there may our nine children and our children's children, with all our Eastern friends also, dwell for ever with us! Had the Prophet Samuel been present with his horn of oil on our first introduction to each other, he would, doubtless, have heard the words (with the pronouns altered) which he heard upon first seeing the youthful and ruddy David, 'Arise, anoint her, for this is she.'"

Although he was apparently disposed to refer a matter of so much importance to himself as the choice of a companion for life wholly to the divine decrees, he did not seem quite so scrupulous in regard to the marriage of another. The letter which follows, the last he ever wrote, shows that he was not unwilling to be an instrument in the hands of Providence in promoting the happiness and usefulness of a fellow-missionary, and so of helping to execute the divine decrees.

"Among those associated with Mr. Temple and myself in that sacred secret society at Andover were Bingham and Thurston. They belonged to the class before us in the Seminary, and were already designated to be the pioneers of the mission to the Sandwich Islands. Early in September, 1819, the Prudential Committee, hearing of a good opportunity in the brig 'Thaddeus,' directed these brethren to complete all their arrangements and repair to Goshen in Connecticut for ordination, and hold themselves in readiness to embark on the very shortest notice. But those brethren were still in the Theological Seminary; nor would their studies terminate before the middle of the month, and of course they had very many arrangements to

make, the most important of which they had considered
already settled. But, alas! at this the last moment the
mothers of both the young ladies who had engaged to accompany our brethren to the Sandwich Islands interfered and
refused to let their daughters go. It was an unexpected and
very severe trial to them, and a time of great sorrow
and deep sympathy to us all. Something must be done,
and that speedily; but there seemed to be no time to accomplish so important a matter. That they should go unpro-
vided with suitable companions, was not to be thought of
for a moment; for they were not expected ever to return,
nor would an opportunity of sending to them be likely to
occur (as they supposed) oftener than once in twenty-five
or thirty years, while the voyage itself was one of six months'
duration, around the terribly tempestuous Cape Horn. We
had many consultations and some very earnest prayer-meetings on the subject. The result was, that the society
clubbed together and procured for me a fine horse that
would carry me full ten miles an hour, and sent me on, if
not a Quixotic, yet a most delicate mission.

"Receiving from Mr. Thurston what was perhaps equivalent to a *carte-blanche* in regard to one of two young ladies
whom I had described to him, I started early one morning
and 'streamed' through the country after a wife for a poor
destitute brother, being borne on by the best wishes and
fervent prayers of the whole Theological Seminary. Remembering that 'the King's business requires haste,' I
'saluted no man by the way,' but galloped on to the accomplishment of my work. After a forty miles' ride I slackened
my pace, and put up my horse in a stable in one of the
principal towns of Massachusetts. And though unsuccessful
there, yet fully believing in the perseverance of the saints,
and being thoroughly persuaded that what hath been fore-
ordained will surely come to pass, early next day I turned
my horse's head and partly retraced my steps, though not
by the same road, to a school-house, where I knew a distant

relative of mine was teaching, some twelve miles from her father's house.

" Dismounting and hitching my horse, I bolted into the school-room, and, not having much time for any long conference, I opened my business at once. Well, after a brief introduction of my errand, I told her I knew she had often thought of the subject of missions, and had decided long ago whether she herself would go on a mission, if she had a good opportunity. The only question, therefore, for her to decide upon in this case would be, ' Wilt thou go with this man ? ' Having described to her his character and appearance as well as I could (the days of photographs had not yet come), I added : ' After all, there are ten thousand little things, and thousands of little matters of taste, which no one can decide for you. You must decide them for yourself. And you shall have the opportunity. Next week is the anniversary at Andover, and the next day Mr. Thurston will start to go to the ordination in Connecticut. Your father's house is on the way. I will accompany him, and spend the night under your roof; and you will have an opportunity of becoming acquainted with him. No person ever need know the object of our stopping there overnight, nor need you feel under any obligation to encourage his suit in consequence of any thing I have said, or in consequence of your meeting him.'

" Had she, Priscilla like, asked, ' Why don't you speak for yourself, John ? ' the natural answer would have been, John is already provided for. On her agreeing to this, and after I had, Eleazer like, lifted up my heart, I rode to see her father. He replied ' that he had given her to God once, and had no right to take her back now.' The next morning I returned to Andover, and, 'having gathered the disciples together, I related what things God had wrought by my ministry.' And there was great joy among the brethren.

" On the day appointed, I took Mr. Thurston, and walked with him to the town of Marlborough. The sun was already sinking in the western woods when we arrived, and all the front windows were reflecting his rays most gloriously, which I took for a good omen. We knocked at the door, and were soon admitted, when lo and behold! the house was full of people, all of them kinsfolk and acquaintances; for they had done what Cornelius did when he was expecting Peter, not knowing but this one, called Peter, might prove to be the very Messiah himself. Somewhat startled, we bowed rather nervously, as would naturally be expected under the circumstances. Before we had time to be seated, I saw the black-eyed damsel entering from a door at the other end of the room; and, making my way through the crowd, I took her hand, and said, ' How do you do, cousin?' I then stepped back, and drawing Mr. Thurston, *nolens volens*, through the throng, I put his hand in hers, as much as to say, ' Behold the handmaid of the Lord. Behold the one whom God hath chosen to be the companion of thy life.'

" The company then made room for us to sit down ; but I must confess it required all the tact I possessed to relieve the embarrassment of our position, and introduce pleasant topics of conversation. To whatever point I turned, keen eyes were fastened on my poor brother, as though they would read his very thoughts. I tried to get him to converse on a great variety of subjects; but the words strangely stuck in his throat, although they scarcely amounted to more than a single Yes or No! I tried to get him to sing with me; but, although one of Israel's sweetest singers, his voice seemed to come, like Jonah's, out of the whale's belly, rather than from his own blessed throat. It was a most awkward position for him and for me and for her and for all present. On looking back to all the circumstances, I think, however, it was admirably managed.

" At an early hour the company began to disperse, and we were soon left alone with the young lady. We now almost began to wish some of our friends would return; for we were at first more confused than ever to know what to say and do next, and really began to tremble at the sound of our own

3*

voices. This was, however, but momentary. There were too many important points to be settled that night for any time to be lost; and, finding my efforts to remove the embarrassment of the two parties crowned with success, I retired hopefully to my slumbers.

"The next morning I was directed to go to the town-clerk, and get him to publish far and near 'that *marriage was intended* between the Rev. Asa Thurston and Miss Lucy Goodale.' As there would not be three Sabbaths before the time of their embarkation in which to publish the banns (which the laws of Massachusetts required), I requested him to make use of three town meetings, which occurring the next week would fulfil all the requirements of the law. I then hastened to Boston to get her outfit; and this included not only what was necessary for a six months' voyage, but a complete stock of clothing for a whole lifetime, as it was not supposed possible ever to send back for any thing. Miss Frances Irving, of Boston, an active and intelligent Christian lady, did all this business for me. I accompanied her solely to pay the bills and carry the parcels. I then returned to Marlborough with all this abundance of material, calling on every praying widow in the neighborhood, and employing every woman, old and young, to drop their own work, however urgent, and make up these garments I had brought, in order to have them in readiness by a certain day the next week, when I promised to call for them.

"Having thus put all these things in train, and appointed the wedding day, I resigned my commission and laid down my office, being fully determined, in my own mind, never again to engage in so fearfully responsible a business. That in this case I acted right is beyond doubt, for it was one of necessity and mercy. It was under extraordinary circumstances, and not to be judged of by common rules. The union proved a comfort and a blessing to the parties concerned. In various letters from both of them they are not slow to acknowledge the good hand of God upon them, and to acknowledge also their indebtedness to me for my zeal and agency in the case. Although this fashion may do among the crowned heads of Europe, yet it is hardly to be recommended to missionaries. What if the union had not proved a happy one? Alas! alas! it almost makes me shudder now to think of it.

"Every thing being thus happily arranged, I went on with Mr. Thurston to the ordination. We found Mr. Bingham already there; but *he* was still unblest. People from far and near came to attend the ordination, and the hospitality of the Goshenites was taxed, though not beyond the power of endurance. Among others who came directly to the parsonage, to be shown where they would find accommodations, was Miss Sibyl Mosely, who had been teaching a very important select school in Canandaigua. She, with a younger sister, drove up in a buggy; and the kind minister not being successful in pointing out the road to a good deacon's with whom they were to be housed, Mr. Bingham, who stood on the door-steps, at once offered to drive them over, as he had been there the day before. This was his first interview with Miss Sibyl Mosely; but it is to be inferred that it was by no means the last, for within a brief week this excellent lady became Mrs. Bingham! As they were not under the laws of Massachusetts, which required intention of marriage to be published three weeks, they hastened down to Dr. Hawes's lecture-room, in Hartford, Conn., and were married at once, and then hurried on to Boston to embark. Mr. Thurston and myself returned to Marlborough in time for the wedding, and immediately after the ceremony we accompanied them to Boston. Henry Homes, Esq., had already given notice that he would entertain us; so we drove directly to the court where his house stood. This was my first introduction to his very pleasant family. Our stay here was longer than had been expected; for, although the captain had been very anxious lest we should not be in time, we had to wait several days for *him* to get ready. In the mean while we attended

many interesting meetings, and sung many precious hymns;
for Mr. Thurston's voice had again become, as in former
days, most sweet and captivating. At length, on Saturday,
Oct. 23, 1819, we were all summoned to assemble on the
Long Wharf, to unite in religious services preparatory to the
last farewell. In the reports of the Board, which were published, we have the following:—

"'The assembly united in singing "*Blest be the tie that
binds*." A fervent and affectionate prayer was offered by the
Rev. Dr. Worcester; a closing address was made by Hopoo,
a young convert from the Sandwich Islands; and Messrs.
Bingham and Thurston, assisted by an intimate Christian
friend, sung with perfect composure, "*When shall we all meet
again?*" A fourteen-oared barge, politely offered by the
commanding officer of the Independence 74, was in waiting;
the members of the mission took leave of their weeping
friends, and were speedily conveyed on board the brig
"Thaddeus." They were accompanied by the committee and
other particular friends. In a short time the vessel weighed
anchor, and dropped into the lower harbor, and the next day,
the wind and tide favoring, put to sea. To the favor and
protection of that God "*who maketh the clouds His chariot, and
walketh upon the wings of the wind*," this little band is commended by many prayers.'"

Under date of Sept. 6, 1818, he makes mention of his
first attempt to conduct the worship of the sanctuary:—

"To-day, for the first time, I entered the sacred desk at Dra-
cut. In the morning I read a sermon from these words, 'The
Spirit of the Lord God is upon me, because the Lord hath
anointed me to proclaim the acceptable year of the Lord, and
the day of vengeance of our God;' and in the afternoon from
these words, 'This is my Beloved, and this is my friend, O
daughters of Jerusalem;' both Cooper's sermons. Five persons were propounded for admission into the church, whom I
assisted in examining the day previous. I was enabled to go
through the exercises with some degree of satisfaction to myself,
and, if I mistake not, to general acceptance. Whenever I
attempt to preach the everlasting Gospel, may the Spirit of the
Lord God rest upon me, 'the Spirit of counsel and might, the
Spirit of knowledge and of the fear of the Lord;' and may my
labors be ever attended with a divine blessing; and may I have
the unspeakable joy of introducing many into the fold of Christ."

Another extract from his journal, showing his fidelity and wisdom in leading souls to Christ, is interesting also as an illustration of the phases of spiritual experience through which the sinner passes in coming out of darkness into the light of the Gospel: first, thinking of his own safety; then, of being delivered from sin, and being made holy; then, desiring to know more of God and of His excellency; and, at last, losing all thoughts of self in an earnest desire for the salvation of others; which last is one of the clearest evidences of having passed from death unto life. The person alluded to was the daughter of his beloved preceptor at Phillips Academy. She afterward became the wife of Rev. George Cowles, who was several years pastor of the First Church in Danvers, Mass. They both perished in the wreck of the steam-packet "Home," near Ocracoke, N. C., Oct. 9, 1837.*

"*April* 29, 1819. As I have had occasion to converse and pray frequently with Elizabeth Adams, I have remarked several distinct and important eras in the course of her trials of mind. She requested me to pray, —

"1. That God would forgive and save her. This request continued three or four days. Then, —

"2. That she might have a broken heart and contrite spirit, and might submit to God unconditionally. This continued about the same length of time.

"3. That she might know more of God, of the Saviour, and of herself. This for several days has been her request. But to-day —

"4. As she was of little consequence, and as she did not know as it would do any good to pray for her, she desired me to pray for her brothers and sisters.

"May she soon forget herself, and embrace the world in her prayers."

* An account of this calamity, by which ninety out of one hundred and thirty persons on board were lost, published at the time, says: "When last seen, Mr. and Mrs. Cowles were reclining side by side on the luggage, and a kind Providence permitted a survivor to report, as the last words which fell from the lips of Mr. Cowles, 'He that trusts in Jesus is safe, even in the perils of the sea.'"

CHAPTER IV.

DURING the vacations of the Theological Seminary Mr.
Goodell gave himself to evangelistic labors, going out
into destitute places and performing the work of a home
missionary, visiting from house to house, distributing books
and tracts, holding religious meetings, and exhorting the
people on the subject of their souls' concerns. One of his
vacations he spent on the island of Newcastle, at the mouth
of Portsmouth Harbor, N. H., of which he gave an account
in a letter to a friend at the time : —

" *Theological Seminary, June* 23, 1819. I did not spend
the vacation at the Isle of Shoals, but at Newcastle, which
is situated at the entrance of Portsmouth Harbor, three miles
from Portsmouth, the largest of those islands which lie at
the mouth of the Piscataqua. It is a mile long, and a mile
broad; was incorporated in 1693; and contains a meeting-
house, a school-house, about seventy dwelling-houses, one
hundred and twenty families, and seven hundred inhabitants,
exclusive of those connected with Fort Constitution. The
fort and light-house are at the north-east extremity. The
first minister was ordained here previous to 1689, and has
been succeeded by eight or nine others. Since the death of
the last, about twenty years ago, nothing has been proposed
by any person which would have the least tendency to reform
the morals of the people and make society better. Almost
every law of the State of New Hampshire is trampled under
foot. Indeed, the place has had all the corruptions, without
any of the moral advantages, of seaport towns."

He had hardly entered upon his work at this place before
he found a coadjutor in an unexpected quarter. Colonel
Wallack, a Roman Catholic, who was in command of the

fort on the island, warmly seconded his efforts for the religious improvement of the people, attended with his family the public services which Mr. Goodell had inaugurated, and required all the soldiers composing the garrison to attend. When Mr. Goodell first went upon the island, he was insulted by the boys in the street; but he soon organized a Sunday school, gathering these boys into it; and before he left they treated him with the greatest respect, taking off their hats and saluting him with two or three bows apiece when they met him. His labors here were attended with a spiritual blessing, a number receiving religious impressions that resulted in their hopeful conversion.

Mr. Goodell was licensed to preach the Gospel by the Kennebec and Somerset Association, at Pittston, Me., May 10, 1820, a short time before completing his studies at Andover. He thus records the preparation of his first written sermon: —

" This day completed and commended to the Saviour my first sermon. Whenever I exhibit it in public, may I be enabled by divine assistance to do it in a tender and impressive manner. It is my highest satisfaction to lay all my attainments at the feet of my Redeemer, and to say, ' Here am I, and here are my preparations; make such use of them as thou pleasest. All I am and all I have are at thy disposal. Thou needest not my services. I beg the privilege of serving thee.' "

On the 28th of July, 1820, while he was yet at the Theological Seminary, he wrote to the Rev. Pliny Fisk, then at Smyrna: —

" What will become of Temple, Bird, and myself still remains in uncertainty. We have had no communication with the Prudential Committee, but contemplate it within a week. We feel ready to put ourselves under their direction; but what are their views of the expediency of sending out missionaries to Smyrna immediately we do not know. Dr. Woods told me none would probably be sent within a year, owing principally to the embarrassed state of the funds. It is presumed we shall be employed much of the next year as agents, — business in which we are truly reluctant to engage, and in which nothing would induce us to engage but the importance of that cause which it is designed to promote. . . . In the Middle Class we cannot calculate upon more than two good missionaries; in the Junior Class three are 'brethren,' and two or three more will probably soon join the association. We are now about preparing some missionary tracts, to be published as soon as funds sufficient for the purpose can be raised, and to be distributed in connection with tracts of the New England Tract Society, with this difference only, — that they will be distributed gratuitously. We have it in contemplation also to have a missionary almanac, to be distributed gratuitously or sold at a very reduced price.   O Brother Fisk! I would never go among the Turks were they not embraced in those blessed promises which relate to the universal extension of the Gospel.   I should not dare to take one step forward, had not the Saviour said, ' Lo, I am with you alway, even unto the end of the world.'   And still I feel that if I had as many bodies as there are missionary establishments, one body should be worn out at each station. Pray that God may give me grace to employ my one poor self wholly and faithfully in His service.   Our views are directed to that quarter of the globe where you are gone; and our daily prayer is that our Redeemer would permit us to go and serve Him to the end of our days among the heathen."

After his mind had been fully made up to devote himself to the missionary service, he wrote: —

" I used to think of great trials, — such as leaving friends and country, being burned at the stake, having one's head chopped off, &c.   I now think less of these, and more of the ten thousand little ones that will occur every day probably till I die.   God's grace will be sufficient for all."

The first number of "The Missionary," dated May 21, 1819, has an elaborate paper from his pen on " The History and Present State of Armenia as a Missionary Field," embodying a vast amount of information in regard to the state of the country, and the religious condition of the people.   The paper would fill a small volume, and was evidently the result of much research.

On the 12th of August, 1820, he had an interview with Dr. Worcester and Mr. Evarts, which resulted in his making an engagement to spend a year, after his graduation at the Seminary, in visiting the churches as an agent of the Board, to awaken an interest in the cause of foreign missions, and to raise funds for the prosecution of its work. On the 28th of September he recorded in affecting words the parting with his classmates at Andover, and their dispersion into different parts of the great vineyard.

From Andover he returned to Dartmouth College, to spend the remainder of the year attending medical lectures, to prepare himself more fully for his future labors. With the commencement of the new year (1821) he entered upon his agency for the Board. Leaving his home in New England, he visited a number of towns along the Hudson River. Arriving at Catskill about the first of March, he met with an accident which came well-nigh terminating his earthly labors, but which, by his long detention at this place, was overruled to the awakening of a deep interest in behalf of the cause which he came to plead. As he was driving down a steep hill, his horse became unmanageable, ran, and threw him from the carriage. His ankle was badly sprained, and he was otherwise severely injured. The horse then ran over a poor woman, breaking her arm, and afterwards dashed the wagon to pieces. In a letter to a friend, a few days after the accident, he gave the following account of it and of his condition : —

"There was indeed but a step between me and death; but God preserved me. On the very spot where I fell there happened to be a little snow; had I fallen anywhere else I know not what could have preserved me.

> 'That life which thou hast made thy care,
>   Lord, I devote to thee.'

"I have every possible attention, — am surrounded by fathers and mothers, brothers and sisters, who delight to

E

serve me. After my fall I was immediately carried into the house of Judge Cooke, who and his wife are excellent Christians. Two of his children have recently become pious, and others of them are inquiring with much concern about religion. Both my physicians are devoted Christians; the servants in the family are godly; and the whole church are praying for my speedy and perfect restoration. Some of the best people in the world are here. I would rather break my bones in this place than almost anywhere else I know of.

" As I could not bear the thought of idleness, I yesterday took charge of the Female Academy, the instructor being sick. I have between twenty and thirty young ladies; half of them are pious, and several of the others not far from the kingdom of heaven. As I can get round a little by the aid of crutches, I assure you I scatter missionary seed with an unsparing hand. It is a good time now; the Spirit of God is poured out, and the fallow ground is broken up. Since I wrote last the good work, both here and at Hudson, has rapidly increased; but the opposition in the latter place exceeds all I ever before heard of. Tracts and pamphlets, dialogues and essays, are constantly issuing from the press filled with blasphemy. The whole city is in an uproar. The convicted and converted are assailed from every quarter with ridicule and threats, and sometimes with blows."

The Rev. David Porter, D.D., of precious memory, the friend of revivals and of missions, was pastor of the church at Catskill. Among his parishioners was the Hon. Thomas B. Cooke, into whose house Mr. Goodell was providentially thrown, and who became deeply interested in the cause to which his guest had devoted his life. He entered into a contract to contribute to the funds of the American Board fifty dollars a year, on condition that Mr. Goodell should send him an annual letter, whatever part of the world might be his home. This contract was faithfully fulfilled by both parties, until the death of Judge Cooke, which occurred more than thirty years after. We have before us a large number of the letters, which, with a single exception, were written on the 1st of January in each year.

One of these, dated at Constantinople, January 1, 1834 (thirteen years after), is here inserted, and others will follow under their respective dates : —

"MY DEAR SIR, — Amidst the bustle and the ten thousand compliments, not to say *white lies*, with which the new year in these countries is always ushered in, I never fail to remember you and my dear friends and benefactors at Catskill. 'I was hungry, and ye fed me; thirsty, and ye gave me drink ; a stranger, and ye took me in; sick, and ye visited me,' watched with me, gave me medicine, and with the blessing of God cured me. And this, I doubt not, ye did (at least in some measure) 'in the name of a disciple.' You received me as a 'messenger of the churches.' You thought I belonged to Christ, and you received me as His servant, and as though you expected I should make a report to Him of your hospitality, of your habitual feelings toward Him, and conduct toward His ministers. I always wonder that those who know and love Christ should ever take me as having any part or portion in Him; and my soul is humbled within me when I think of the thousand kindnesses I have received from you and other friends of Christ in America. But He, He is worthy of all the attentions which you and others have ever shown me for His dear sake. He is worthy of all the money, books, clothes, time, influence, every precious thing you have ever given Him, and every precious thing you have not yet given Him. In the estimation of the 'ten thousand times ten thousand round about the throne,' who know immeasurably better than we do, He is worthy, infinitely worthy, to receive it all. Let all, then, be consecrated to Him, — 'power, riches, wisdom, strength, honor,' — whatever can in any way be employed in His service. When we get to heaven, we shall for ever wish Him to have the whole, our hearts and all. And, my dear sir, if you and yours, and we and ours, ever go there, we shall be there sooner by one year than when I last wrote you. Let us, then, be 'girding up the loins of our mind,' and be 'looking for that blessed hope, and the glorious appearing of the great God and our Saviour Jesus Christ.'"

In a letter to Judge Cooke, written from Constantinople, January 1, 1836, he made the following mention of the one who was injured at the same time with himself : —

" The poor unfortunate woman who was passing, and was knocked down and run over, and in the most imminent danger of being killed, I do not forget. I was sorry to have been even the innocent cause of pain and trouble to her; but it was all ordered by Him who cannot err in judgment, or be resisted in the execution of His will. If she be living, will you remember me to her very kindly; and will you say to her that I hope *neither* of us will be crushed, but *both* of us escape, when the world, instead of my poor horse and wagon, shall ' flee away, and be no more found.' "

When sufficiently recovered from his injuries to leave Catskill, he travelled westward in the State of New York, a large portion of which was then comparatively unsettled. From Whitesborough, near Utica, he wrote: —

"*May* 25, 1821. In the last four Sabbaths I have preached three times each day, and sometimes once or twice a day during the week. The missionary pulse beats high in this region. In one town five acres of land have been consecrated for five years to be cultivated for missionary purposes. In another, one man has resolved to cultivate one acre for the Lord as long as he lives. In another, a man told me he would give some land to be cultivated in this way as long as the sun shines and the water runs."

Rochester, N. Y., at that time was a small village, having one Presbyterian Church of less than a hundred members. In this church he preached the first missionary sermon ever heard in the place. An aged resident sends the following reminiscence of the occasion: —

" Notice was given that a missionary sermon would be preached by Rev. William Goodell. A prominent man in the congregation was much opposed to foreign missions, and declared he would not give a cent to any of these beggars, and got up quite an excitement on the subject. After the sermon a collection was taken up; and at the close of the services, while the officers of the church were counting the money, this opposer came up to the table, and exclaimed, ' I thought I put all I had into the bag, but here is some more. After such a sermon, who could help giving?' "

Travelling westward into the States of Ohio and Indiana,

he found in many places an unexpected interest in the cause of missions to the dark portions of the world, the result of a gracious outpouring of the Spirit upon the churches of that comparatively new region of country; but in other places there was literally a famine for the bread of life, and the Gospel message which he carried to them was heard with gladness. He wrote at the time (Feb. 18, 1822): "There are but two settled ministers, of the Presbyterian or Congregational order, in the whole State of Indiana. I preached in one place where some of the people said they had heard but three sermons from Presbyterians there before."

While in the West, he received a letter from Mr. Evarts, Secretary of the Board, stating that it was the wish of the Prudential Committee that he should extend his journey to the Indian missions in the South-west. Leaving the Ohio River, he travelled on horseback through Kentucky, Tennessee, and Alabama, much of the way through the wilderness. At Columbus, Miss., he was detained a number of days by a flood. Here he gathered the scattered families from day to day, breaking to them the bread of life, while the waters prevented his progress, and then made his way through the flood, sometimes wading, sometimes on horseback, and sometimes in a log-canoe, until at length he reached Mayhew, a station among the Choctaw Indians, where he received a hearty welcome, and where he greatly enjoyed the physical, but still more the spiritual, rest among the people of God, some of whom a short time before were savages. From Mayhew he went to Elliot, another station, one hundred miles west, where he was hailed with the same delight by the missionaries, one of whom wrote to the Board of the "rare and precious privilege" they had enjoyed "of welcoming one who has just come from visiting a great number of the churches, and who is expecting one day to preach the Gospel at Jerusalem." After the death of Dr. Goodell, the Rev. Cyrus Byington, who was at Elliot at the time of his visit there, and who had previously been with him at Andover

Theological Seminary, wrote a touching reminiscence of the visit, recalling, together with other incidents, the text of the sermon that Mr. Goodell preached, and the hymn with which the services were opened on the Sabbath, —

> " We are a garden walled around,
>   Chosen and made peculiar ground."

Mr. Evarts, Corresponding Secretary of the Board, was at Brainard when Mr. Goodell visited that station, and they left together on the morning of May 21, 1822, on their journey to the North.

CHAPTER V.

IN September, 1822, the annual meeting of the American Board of Commissioners for Foreign Missions was held at New Haven, Conn. The Board convened early on the morning of the 12th, and then adjourned to take part in the ordination services, which, by previous arrangement, were to be held at ten o'clock. William Goodell, destined to the mission in Palestine, William Richards and Artemas Bishop, who were to join the mission at the Sandwich Islands, were then set apart to the work of the Gospel ministry. The sermon on the occasion was preached by the Rev. Samuel Miller, D.D., of Princeton Theological Seminary, from Isaiah lxi. 4: "And they shall build the old wastes; they shall raise up the former desolations; and they shall repair the waste cities, the desolations of many generations." The prayer of ordination was offered by the Rev. Joseph Lyman, of Hatfield, Mass.; the Charge to the missionaries was by the Rev. Abel Flint, of Hartford; and the Rev. Joel Hawes, of Hartford, expressed to them the fellowship of the churches. The Ordination took place under the authority of a council of neighboring churches. After a recess of half an hour the sacrament of the Lord's Supper was administered, a large congregation of communicants joining in the celebration.

On the 19th of November, 1822, Rev. William Goodell was married at Holden, Mass., to Miss Abigail Perkins Davis, daughter of the Hon. Lemuel Davis, of Holden.*

---

* Her grandfather, Rev. Joseph Davis, was ordained Dec. 22, 1742, as the first pastor of the church at Holden, on the day of its organization, and continued his ministry in the same place more than thirty years. Since the organization of the American Board this church has sent out nine foreign missionaries.

The beloved wife of his youth was the cherished companion of his whole subsequent life, the faithful and efficient helper in all his labors, and such an earthly consolation and joy as is rarely given to man in this vale of tears. In his Reminiscences, with which this volume opens, he penned, only the week before his translation to a better world, a beautiful tribute to her exalted worth; and it will not be inappropriate to insert in this place an extract from a letter which he wrote on the tenth anniversary of their marriage.

" *Constantinople, November* 19, 1832.   Ten years ago to-day the tenderest of all unions known in this world was formed, or rather was then publicly recognized; and, through the kind providence of God, this union, which we know must sooner or later be dissolved, has been preserved to this hour. On the sea and on the land, in fire and tempest, in pestilence and war, our Heavenly Father has suffered no evil to befall us, but in tender mercy He has continued us a comfort and a blessing to each other, and has permitted us to bring thus far on their way through the wilderness the children whom He has graciously given us.   What shall we render to Him for all His benefits?

"Mr. Dwight, with whose family we are now living, tried his best to get a turkey for the anniversary, but, not succeeding, he sent for a quarter of beef; and, failing in this, the cook, by chance or design, prepared us a dinner of *sheep's liver*, which coming, as you know, from the region of the heart, answered the purpose admirably.   I doubt whether even Elijah made a better meal from what the angels cooked in heaven.   Surely we can say, ' Goodness and mercy have thus far followed us all the days of our life,' and we hope we shall hereafter go and ' dwell in the house of the Lord for ever.' "

A few days after their marriage Mr. and Mrs. Goodell were summoned to New York to embark in the vessel in which passage had been engaged for them and for Rev. Isaac Bird and wife, designated to the same mission.   Mr. Goodell preached in the Murray Street Church on Sabbath afternoon, December 1, from Matt. xvi. 2, 3, on "The Signs of the Times," Rev. Dr. Romeyn and Rev. Mr. Whelpley taking part in the services. Mr. Bird preached in the evening, in the same church, from John x. 16: "Other sheep I have which are not of this fold." On Monday evening, several congregations united in the monthly concert of prayer at the Middle Dutch Church. Mr. Evarts, Secretary of the Board, Rev. Dr. MacAuley, Rev. S. H. Cox, and Rev. Messrs. Goodell and Bird took part in the exercises, which were reported in full at the time. Mr. Goodell, in the course of the same week, preached in the churches of Rev. Dr. MacAuley, Rev. Mr. Matthews, Rev. Mr. Whelpley, and Rev. Mr. Patton. On Thursday, the day appointed for annual Thanksgiving in the State, a meeting was held at Rev. Dr. Romeyn's church, in Cedar Street, at which the missionaries received their final instructions from the Corresponding Secretary of the Board. They were appointed to join the mission in Palestine. A sermon was preached on this occasion by Rev. Mr. Bird.

Late on the following Sunday evening, after having attended public services, they were summoned to go on board the brig " Shepherdess." The departure of a band of missionaries for a far-distant land awakened at that time far deeper interest than at the present day. Thirty or forty friends, who had heard at the close of the evening service of the summons which they had received, assembled at ten o'clock at the house of Mr. Moses Allen, where they had been hospitably entertained during their sojourn in the city, and after engaging in religious services, conducted by the Corresponding Secretary, accompanied them to the ship. Nor did they say farewell until they had again commended the missionary band in prayer to the grace of God. Early on the morning of the 9th the vessel sailed.

When these missionaries left the shores of their native land, they had "set their faces to go to Jerusalem." The Syria mission had been established by Rev. Pliny Fisk and Rev. Levi Parsons, who left this country in 1819. On the death of Mr. Parsons, which occurred at Alexandria, Feb. 10,

4

1822, Rev. Jonas King, who was then studying Oriental languages at Paris, offered his services to the Board for three years, to supply the place of the lamented Parsons, and reached Palestine in April, 1823. Messrs. Goodell and Bird with their wives expected not only to enter the Holy Land, but to take up their residence in the Holy City, doing the work of their divine Master on the spot that had been consecrated by the labors of his life, and by his death.

On the 21st of January, 1823, the " Shepherdess," after a pleasant and prosperous voyage, arrived at the island of Malta; and they were soon at home with the Rev. Daniel Temple, who had preceded them. As they were to spend several months at this place, in the study of the languages of the East and in the work of translation and printing, they found it necessary to take a larger house, of which Mr. Goodell made mention in his usual style : —

" *February* 25, 1823. We all removed this day to Strada Reale, No. 187. This house is much larger and much more convenient for our printing-press, our chapel, and our own apartments than the other. To the Saviour would we consecrate all these rooms, with all their furniture; especially the chapel, with its desk, its seats, its candlesticks, and snuffers. May the Saviour have free access to every room, and here take up His abode!"

Malta was then a sort of school-house, where the missionaries bound for the Orient prepared for their future labors, and from which they made some aggressive movements upon the kingdom of darkness. February 13, Mr. Goodell wrote from Valetta : —

" Malta is altogether unlike any thing we ever before saw or thought of. There is nothing here that reminds one of America. Every thing looks more like romance than reality. The city is full of people, — Jews, Greeks, Italians, English, Maltese, &c. The Maltese are most numerous, and are invariably Roman Catholics. The Catholic priests pretend to forgive all sin except the unpardonable sin of reading the Scriptures. Whoever is guilty of perusing the Sacred Volume must never expect forgiveness, unless he gives the priest a great deal of money or performs some extraordinary penance. Some of the people, however, have become so bold as to read the Bible in defiance of priest and pope; and a few, it is hoped, have become truly pious."

At a later date, July 24, he wrote: —

" This is an excellent place for American missionaries to commence the study of the languages, and to learn something of the customs and habits of the Eastern world; but we must not say of it, ' This is my rest for ever, here will I dwell.' We have many opportunities of doing good to the English who reside here, but very rarely opportunities of benefiting the Maltese. The English government does not permit us to distribute any of *our tracts* here; does not permit the circulation of the Maltese Gospel of St. John; and (I would say it softly) is far more afraid of the influence, not of us simply, but of all missionaries, than of all the Roman Catholics in the world.

" I have no idea of being shut up in this island more than two or three months longer. We must break forth upon the right hand and upon the left. We have concluded to ' take up our carriages' and go towards Jerusalem. We go not knowing the things that shall befall us there, in that land where the blood of Jesus was shed, and which has been long under the curse of God. We expect many privations and difficulties to which we have been strangers heretofore. But we desire to feel that through Christ we can do all things, and, without him, nothing. 'O Emmanuel, if thy presence go not with us, carry us not up hence!' The land to which we go is still the land of promise, and is yet to become the joy of the whole earth. The curse will be removed; the tears will be wiped away from the eyes of the daughter of Zion. Jerusalem shall be built; and the sweet influences of heaven, like the rain and the dew, shall descend copiously upon the mountains of Israel. The Lord hasten it in His time!"

He describes the circumstances of their departure from Malta, and the incidents of their voyage to Beyrout: —

" *October* 22, 1823. We have engaged passage on 'La Divina Providenza,' a Maltese brig, bound to Cyprus and Beyrout. As we shall probably sail before the Sabbath, we this evening commemorated the death of our Lord and Saviour. The ordinance was administered by Mr. Temple, and by Rev. Mr. Wilson, of the London Missionary Society. Between forty and fifty persons, most of whom have been our constant hearers, united with us in this feast of love. Of these persons one was of the Roman communion, one of the Greek, and the rest of the Episcopal, Presbyterian, Independent, Baptist, and Methodist connections. About fifteen persons sat down to the Lord's table on this occasion for the first time in their lives, having, as they trust, been translated from the kingdom of darkness into the kingdom of God's dear Son within the last eighteen months. Many of the spectators, as well as the communicants, were melted to tears. With the former we trust there were 'great searchings of heart;' and while with the latter we never expect again in this world to drink of the fruit of the vine, we hope to drink it new with them in our Father's kingdom, and to sit with them in heavenly places for ever.

" *October* 24. Our dear brother and sister Temple, and other Christian friends, 'accompanied us to the ship.' We united in singing, 'Blest be the tie that binds,' &c., and the Rev. Mr. Wilson commended us in prayer unto Him whose blood was shed at Jerusalem. Our Christian friends at Malta on this occasion have shown us the most marked attention and kindness, preparing many things for our voyage, and for our comfort at Jerusalem. Indeed, we can say with the Apostle, that during our whole stay 'they showed us no little kindness, and when we departed they laded us with such things as were necessary.'

" *Lord's Day, October* 26. A strong, contrary wind, anciently 'called Euroclydon;' a high sea; all of us much distressed with sea-sickness. This is the first Sabbath since we left our native country on which we have been unable to worship God in a public manner. To-day, instead of being permitted to go up with glad hearts 'unto the altar of God with a multitude that keep holy day,' we find ourselves 'exceedingly tossed with a tempest,' and are compelled to lie down amidst dirt and vermin, hardly able to speak, or to take the least care of ourselves. 'Think upon us, O our God, for good.'

" *November* 1. In sight of Candia, the ancient Crete. Here Paul preached to those who were, to a proverb, addicted to lying, the glorious Gospel of the blessed God. Here he planted a church, of which he appointed Titus the overseer, that he ' might set in order the things that were wanting, and

ordain elders in every city.' Here he touched and advised
to winter in that memorable voyage to Italy, in which he was
shipwrecked at Malta. Oh that we may have more of the
spirit of that great apostle, and be ready to follow him in the
path of duty and suffering.

"*Friday, November* 7. Instead of being in port, as we had
hoped, we are still 'sailing under Cyprus, because the winds
are contrary.' An admirer of the Greek classics might easily
fancy that his eyes now behold the very mountains which the
poets have rendered immortal by making them the birth-
place of Venus, and the abode of the Graces. In the Scriptures of the Old Testament this island was called 'Chittim.'
In the Acts of the Apostles much mention is made of it under
its present name. It was to Cyprus some of those came
'who were scattered abroad upon the persecution that arose
about Stephen, preaching the word to none but unto the Jews
only.' It was here Barnabas was born, who, 'having land,
sold it, and brought the money, and laid it at the apostles'
feet.' It was here 'one Mnason' lived, 'an old disciple with
whom,' said Paul (when on his way to Jerusalem for the
last time), 'we should lodge.' It was to Cyprus Paul and
Barnabas sailed, after they had 'been sent forth by the Holy
Ghost' to preach to the Gentiles. It was at Paphos, in this
island, 'the deputy of the country desired to hear the word
of God, and Elymas the sorcerer sought to turn him away
from the faith,' for which he was smitten with blindness.
And it was here Barnabas sailed, after he and Paul had con-
tended, and 'departed asunder the one from the other.' The
Lord in mercy grant 'that there may be no divisions among
ourselves, but that we may be perfectly joined together in
the same mind and in the same judgment'!

"*Friday, November* 14. Left Cyprus at seven o'clock this
evening. As fellow-passengers, we now have one Turk, two
Greeks, an English gentleman, and two Armenians, a bishop
and a priest, going with their servants to Jerusalem. The
bishop has resided there thirty years. Amongst us all, we
are now able to speak and read no less than fifteen different
languages. Oh that we may all learn the language of the
citizens of Zion!

"*Saturday, November* 15. Find ourselves this morning in
sight of 'that goodly mountain, even Lebanon,' which Moses
prayed so earnestly to behold. Its summits are covered with
snow. 'Will a man leave the snow of Lebanon, which

cometh from the rock of the field? Yet,' saith the Lord,
' my people have forgotten me.'

" *Sabbath, November* 16.   Were hailed at four this morning
by a Greek privateer.   All on board were in the greatest
consternation lest it might prove to be not an authorized
vessel, but a pirate.   The bags of money flew wherever they
could find a place, some to the berths and some to the hold;
some of the most important papers and most precious articles
were intrusted to the keeping of the ladies, Mrs. Bird and Mrs.
Goodell.   The poor Turk, quaking with fear, threw off his
turban, supplying its place with an English cap, and concealed himself in the hold.   To the general cry, ' What shall
we do?' one answered, ' Let each one think and act for
himself;' another, ' We can die but once;' and another,
' We are at the mercy of God.'   We let our trunks, garments, &c., remain as they were, committing our property,
our liberty, our life, and our cause unto Him who preserved
Paul, not only ' in perils in the city, in perils in the wilderness, and in perils in the sea,' but also ' in perils of robbers;'
and who has said, ' I, even I, am He that comforteth thee;
who art thou, that thou shouldst be afraid of a man, that shall
die, and of the son of man, that shall be made as the grass;
and forgettest the Lord thy Maker?'   The Armenian bishop
kept crying, ' Il diavolo! il diavolo!' (the devil! the devil!)
this being about all the Italian he knew.

" Our captain was ordered to set his sails, and wait till the
morning light.   When he made some objection, the reply,
' If you do not obey, we will sink you to the bottom,' was an
argument of sufficient weight in our circumstances.   As soon
as there was light sufficient to distinguish countenances, a
boat came with twelve or fifteen men; and the commander,
with four or five others, came on deck.   They looked more
like savage than civilized men, were miserably clad, and
appeared half famished; but they conducted themselves in a
very honorable manner, made inquiries about our voyage,
and what Turkish vessels we had seen, and wished to purchase tobacco and provisions.   When we offered them some
of our Greek tracts, they seized them with great avidity;
and we only regretted that we had not a greater variety at
command.   Among those we gave them were ' The African
Servant' and ' The Life of William Kelley;' and our prayer
is that a divine blessing may attend the reading of them.

" At eleven o'clock we came to anchor, four miles distant

from the city. It was a morning without clouds; and we discovered, on the sides of Lebanon and in the environs of Beyrout, many trees, and more that appeared verdant and lovely than we have seen since we left the hills and dales and fruits and flowers of our own happy country. May the countenance of our Redeemer ever be to us 'as Lebanon, excellent as the cedars.'"

A few days after his arrival at Beyrout, he sent to a friend in America the following account of their entrance into the Land of Promise: —

" Monday, the 17th, we went on shore. The British consul, Mr. Abbott, received us politely. Indeed, he had already sent his nephew on board, kindly offering us every assistance which it was possible for him to render, and inviting us to make his house our home, saying there was not a single house where it would be proper to take our wives. We immediately, thankfully accepting his kind offer, returned to the vessel for our families and baggage. There is no wharf at Beyrout, and when the boat struck, the half-naked, barbarous Arabs leaped out, and carried us, one at a time, through the billows to the dry land, amidst the multitude who ran to witness so novel a scene. We were in the English costume, and the ladies were without veils. The Turkish governor sat with his pipe, and looked on very composedly. Mr. Bird remained with the boat and baggage, and I walked with the ladies to the house of the consul, a Turk carrying the infant child of Mrs. Bird, and leading the way. Many Arabs followed in the train to see what the end would be; and the boys and girls frequently ran across the street before us, in order to see the color of our eyes and the cut of our garments to better advantage. The consul lives in the country, about a mile from the landing-place. His family is the only English family at Beyrout. Himself and daughter, aged twelve years, speak the English language; his wife is from Italy, and speaks French and Italian. They all received us with the greatest cordiality, and made us welcome to all the comforts which their house afforded. Yesterday we were engaged in bringing our goods on shore. Late in the evening Mr. King arrived from Der el Kamar to meet us. He was in the Oriental dress, and wore a venerable beard. Mr. Fisk had gone to Jerusalem."

Owing to the unsettled state of things at Jerusalem, it was deemed advisable to remain for the present at Beyrout, and accordingly they engaged a house, and established themselves for the winter, fully intending to go up to the Holy City the

ensuing spring. In his truly devout spirit, and in the Scriptural language which seemed to be his native dialect, Mr.
Goodell records their entering upon housekeeping: —

" *Tuesday, Novemb r 25*, 1823. Engaged in removing our baggage to ' our own hired house.' In the evening took up our abode
there. We read the 132d Psalm : ' Lord, remember David and
all his afflictions; how he sware unto the Lord, and vowed unto
the mighty God of Jacob: surely I will not come into the
tabernacle of my house, nor go up into my bed; I will not give
sleep to mine eyes, nor slumber to mine eyelids, until I find out
a place for the Lord, an habitation for the mighty God of
Jacob.' We consecrated our house and ourselves to the
Redeemer. We prayed that He would take up His abode with
us, and that He might never witness any thing in any of our
rooms which should grieve Him to depart from us. ' O Thou
the Hope of Israel, why shouldst thou be as a stranger in the
land, as a way-faring man that turneth aside to tarry for the
night? ' Say, we beseech thee, of this place, ' This is my rest
for ever, here will I dwell, for I have desired it.''

He subsequently described their home: —

" The house which we occupy belongs to a wealthy Turk.
It stands on a delightful eminence, about a mile from the landing-place, and nearly half a mile from the English consul's;
entirely overlooks the city, and most of the adjacent country,
and is surrounded by mulberry-trees. Like all the houses of
this country, it did not contain a single pane of glass,* and in
storms and tempests we had nothing to do but close every aper-
ture designed for the admission of air or light, wrap ourselves
in our cloaks, and *let it rain.* Now, through the kindness of the
consul, we have a few panes of glass in each room, and have
light sufficient to read or write, in rain as well as in sunshine.
The principal room was entirely open towards the north; but
we have suspended a large sail-cloth, which serves to defend us
in some degree from the cold winds and rains of this wintry
season. In this room we have a table filled with Bibles and
tracts in various languages. Here we receive our company and
take our meals. Here we give the Arab his coffee and his pipe,
read with him in the Arabic Scriptures, and tell him of the
glorious Gospel of the blessed God. And here, too, we ' bow
the knee unto the Father of our Lord Jesus Christ, that we
may be enriched in all utterance and in all knowledge,' and
that ' the Spirit may be poured out from on high ' upon the
people among whom we dwell, and for whose salvation we desire

* The English consul's was the only house in Beyrout at that time
that had a glazed window.

to spend and be spent. We are, indeed, in the midst of Arabs and armed Turks, and we sometimes cannot but feel how easy it would be for them to destroy us in a moment. But 'the Lord is our light and our salvation.' We sit down quietly to the study of Arabic, eat our morsel with contented and thankful hearts, and at night lie down in peace and safety under the shadow of the Almighty. 'Blessed be the Lord who loadeth us with His benefits, even the God of our salvation.' "

The winter was spent in the study of the Turkish, the Arabic, and the Armenian languages; but the missionaries entered at once upon their work of preaching Christ in the house and by the way, wherever they found an opportunity or could make one. They distributed the Word of God in various languages, the books being furnished by the British and Foreign Bible Society. Their house was a Bible depot, and the people of all tongues came to read it or hear it read, thus enabling them to scatter the good seed extensively, and with strong hope of its speedily bearing fruit. As yet no prejudice against their work had been excited, and curiosity induced great numbers of all religions to come and see the strangers and hear what they had to say. The missionaries who had preceded them, Messrs. Fisk, Parsons, and King, being unmarried, appeared more like passing travellers; but when these men came with their wives, in strange costumes, and settled down among them, it was natural that their advent should be the theme of universal remark, and that it should awaken a general desire to know more about them and about the object of their coming. Scarcely a day passed without the house of the missionaries being visited, and sometimes it was thronged, with Arabs and Turks, Jews and Greeks, Maronites and Franks, &c. Some extracts from Mr. Goodell's journal will show how speedily and how fully their work opened up before them:—

"To-day our house was crowded with Arab women who came to look at us. We also received visits from an English captain, a Jew, and a friar, with all of whom we had some religious conversation." Again: "Some women called, to

4* F

whom we read the Scriptures. One of them appeared anxious to learn to read, but doubted whether it was possible. Everybody said a woman could not learn; the experiment was once made in a convent, and only two out of a large number were found to have any understanding." Another day: "Three men called to read the Scriptures; two of them borrowed the Bible to carry home with them. In walking out afterwards I stopped at a house and found one of the men reading the Scriptures to his family. Two Greeks called, to whom I gave Greek tracts, and I informed them that many were printing for them at Malta. Three Catholic priests called. I gave a French Testament to one, who requested it, and Greek tracts to them all." Again: "Three Turkish ladies, the wives of a wealthy Turk in the city, called upon us. Like other ladies of this country, they had their golden 'chains and bracelets and head-bands and ear-rings, and ornaments of the legs and tinkling ornaments of silver about their feet.' Mrs. Goodell read to them from the Arabic Scriptures."

"*December* 4. In the city met with a Maronite priest, who said he lived very nigh us, and asked the privilege of visiting us. In the evening he called, and brought to the ladies two beautiful doves, as white as the snow of Lebanon. In return we offered him an Arabic Bible; but he refused to accept of it as a gift, saying, 'It is a good book, and worth paying for; you are worthy men for bringing such books into the country.' He then took out a Spanish dollar and gave it for the Bible; the first Bible, probably, he ever possessed, though, judging from his venerable white beard, he is not less than fifty years old. We told him we should like to see him every evening; and if he would teach us to speak Arabic we would teach him to speak Italian. He accepted the proposal with great pleasure, and said he would teach us to speak Arabic like a nightingale.

"*December* 5. The Maronite priest called and brought again the doves, which in the course of the day had made their escape. We thanked him for his kindness, and he replied: 'When the infant Jesus was first brought to the temple, and the aged Simeon took him in his arms and blessed him, the parents of the child, being poor, had nothing to bring but two doves; and when I heard of the arrival of these good women, I thought, What have I to bring? but, being poor, I could think of nothing but the two doves to bring to them as a present.'

"*December* 6. Mr. King's instructor taking notice of the attentions we bestowed upon the ladies, it gave us an opportunity of speaking to him on the importance of female education; of telling him many of the customs of America, especially of the intelligence and influence of the female part of the community in our country, and of the good which they did by instructing youth, by their epistolary correspondence, and by their benevolent efforts. He frequently laughed heartily when we served the ladies at table before we served him or ourselves, and when we assisted them in doing any little thing. He said, if any person should come into his house and speak to his wife first he should be offended. We told him we had so much love and respect for our wives that we were better pleased when they were honored than when we were ourselves. He said, ' English ladies have understanding; but not so the Arabian women.' The women here are treated as slaves. Whenever they go abroad they wrap themselves up in a large, white sheet. They never walk out with their husbands; they never eat with them. And to ask a man after his wife, that is, about her health, is almost an unpardonable offence."

As much of the time of the missionaries was necessarily spent in the acquisition of the several languages spoken in Syria, it was a matter of prime importance to obtain native assistants who were qualified to give them instruction and at the same time to aid them in their work. In this they were remarkably successful. Within the first year of their entrance into the country, a kind providence sent to their house an Armenian bishop, a man of extensive learning, who had spent the most of his life in the Armenian convent at Jerusalem. He had become disgusted with the superstitions of his church, and, coming to Beyrout, he met with Mr. Goodell, who took him into his service as interpreter and assistant in translating. He was known in his own church by the name of *Dionysius*, but was called in the mission *Carabet*. When he first came to Mr. Goodell he was far from being a serious-minded person, — he was even profane in his language; but he soon became impressed with the truth as he learned it for the first time from the teachings of evangelical ministers. He subsequently gave evidence of being truly converted, and was of great assistance to the mission. He remained in the service of Mr. Goodell until after his removal to Malta, in 1828; during which time he renounced all connection with the Armenian church, and, in token of his renunciation of its orders, he took to himself a wife.

Another excellent assistant was an Armenian ecclesiastic named Jacob, known also as Wortabet. He was a young man of good parts and education, but at first without any settled principles. After he had been in the service of the mission about a year, as literary assistant, he became deeply serious; the truth had taken hold of his heart and conscience. He too renounced the church with which he had been connected, as having apostatized from the faith and become utterly corrupt.

A single passage from Mr. Goodell's journal will show how many languages it was necessary the missionaries should be more or less familiar with, in order to prosecute the various branches of their work : —

"We almost daily read the Scriptures in Ancient Greek, Modern Greek, Ancient Armenian, Modern Armenian, Turkish Armenian (or Armeno-Turkish), Arabic, Italian, and English, and frequently hear them read in Syriac, Hebrew, and French. Seldom do we sit down to our meals without hearing conversation at the table in Armenian, Greek, Arabic, Turkish, Italian, and English, and prayer daily ascends from this house — I hope to heaven — in all these languages, excepting the Italian. In translating the Scriptures, we have open before us the Bible in Ancient and Modern Greek, Ancient and Modern Armenian, Turkish, Armeno-Turkish, English, two translations in Arabic and three in Italian, and occasionally Hebrew and Syriac."

CHAPTER VI.

ALTHOUGH Mr. Goodell had entered Syria with the full expectation of going to Jerusalem to make it the scene of his labors, it soon became evident that the point where, in the providence of God, they first landed and were detained was one of great importance in connection with the mission work. Jerusalem was then in a disturbed state, and events soon after transpired which made it doubtful whether they could go there at all with their families. Beyrout, on the other hand, enjoyed British protection; and Mr. Abbott, the consul, took a warm interest in the missionaries personally, and in the cause in which they were engaged. The trade, too, with other parts of the Mediterranean was rapidly increasing, and the free communication with the interior afforded an opportunity for exerting a wide-spread influence. They determined, therefore, to go on with the work which had opened so auspiciously, and here they continued to labor with encouraging success. Mr. Bird, who had gone to Jerusalem in January, 1824, and who was there arrested on an accusation of distributing "books which were neither Mussulman, Jewish, nor Christian," returned in May; and Messrs. Goodell and Bird prepared to begin anew in Syria the proclamation of the Gospel which had been heard in that land eighteen hundred years before, the echoes of which had long since died away.

Beyrout thus became the head-quarters of missionary operations in Syria; and as it was the only spot where missionary homes were established, it was frequently visited by the different missionary brethren who had come to the country. Mr. King spent much of his time at a monastery in Mount Lebanon, engaged in the study of Arabic; but he often joined the families on the coast. Pliny Fisk, who was engaged in exploring the country with a view to future operations, was also several times welcomed to the homes and the hearts of those who had known him as a brother beloved in their native land. And when his short work was done, just two years after Messrs. Goodell and Bird landed, this devoted servant of Christ, whose name in connection with that of Levi Parsons, the first missionaries to Palestine, will ever be kept in sweet remembrance, came here to die. Returning from one of his tours, he reached the house of Mr. Goodell in his usual health, but was soon attacked with a fever which he had contracted while watching with an English gentleman. For several days there were no alarming symptoms; but, although every thing that love and tender care could do for him was done, and with apparent success, his disease suddenly took an unfavorable turn, and, rapidly sinking under its power, early on the morning of the Lord's day, Oct. 23, 1825, he entered into rest. Of this event Mr. Goodell wrote at the time: —

"It seems a great mercy that he died with us, and not abroad among strangers. This he often mentioned with thankfulness in the course of his illness. It appeared a comfort to him to have us about him to converse with him, pray for him, and strengthen his faith in God. Some of the Arabs were deeply affected, as they stood around his dying bed; they were amazed at his peace of mind, and could not conceive it possible that any one could be so willing to die. They wept. We explained to them the cause of his tranquillity and joy, related to them much of his religious views and experience, and told them of Christ and heaven. Indeed, we sometimes felt that Christ and heaven were present. It seemed but a step 'to Him that sitteth upon the throne and to the Lamb,' where God himself wipes away all tears."

The following suggestion, occurring in a letter to a friend in America, written at this time, will be appreciated by all missionaries, and may help those who correspond with them to write letters that will be no less acceptable and no less useful because containing items of earthly intelligence : —

" Tell us every thing, good, bad, and indifferent. Do not say, ' I suppose this one and that one have written so and so,' but write every thing; for but few tell us any thing. Some write us very *good* letters, but tell us no news, supposing that because we are missionaries we have no flesh and blood, and no concern with mortal things. Tell us every thing!' "

For a time every thing connected with the missionary work in Beyrout went on prosperously, and without restraint from either civil or ecclesiastical authorities, and without the manifestation of hostility on the part of the people. Mr. Goodell and Mr. Bird mingled with Turks and Arabs and Maronites and Jews and Greeks, distributing the Bible and reading it to them, without molestation or hindrance.

But this state of things was not to continue. The words of the Master to His disciples, " If they have persecuted me, they will also persecute you," were again to be verified in the land where He suffered. Within the first year an order from the Maronite Patriarch was read in the church at Beyrout, forbidding the people to receive the Holy Scriptures circulated by the missionaries, specifying the editions published in England, and requiring all to return or burn those they had received. The Pope's vicar-general subsequently called on Mr. Goodell and Mr. Bird, and assured them that this order was issued without his knowledge and without any authority from Rome ; but the outbreak proved to be only the first breath of a coming storm.

The first severe trial through which Mr. and Mrs. Goodell were called to pass was incidental, and did not spring from their character and work as missionaries. The attempt to throw off the Turkish yoke, made by Greece in 1820, was still carried on when they landed at Beyrout in 1823, and for several years longer. It was in consequence of this war that the scenes occurred which are described in the following extracts from Mr. Goodell's journal; scenes in which not only was he stripped of his property, but the lives of himself and his family were often in imminent peril:—

" *Sabbath, March* 19, 1826. Yesterday two Greek vessels came in and anchored at the river, about two miles east of Beyrout. As they frequently come in to visit European vessels and to seize whatever Turkish property they may find on board, we suspected nothing uncommon. At daylight this morning we were awakened by a brisk fire of musketry. Ten other Greek vessels had come in during the evening, observed in the city but not observed by ourselves, and had landed about five hundred men, who were now before the walls of the city, attempting to scale them. The city was in an exceedingly defenceless state; but the Turks, knowing it must be victory or death, acted with great spirit and energy, and succeeded in driving the Greeks from the wall, in doing which they killed four or five and lost of their number near twenty.

" The twelve Greek vessels, which, to the shame of their commanders, had till now been at anchor, immediately sailed forth with a fine breeze and in fine order, directly before the town, and commenced a heavy cannonading. The Turks were able to return only about one ball for twenty received. We expected nothing but that the city would have a change of masters in a few moments, and looked to see the Greek flag hoisted in Beyrout. But the Greeks, though to human view they could have landed with the greatest ease, made no attempt of the kind, and apparently came out in mere wantonness to take revenge for the unsuccessful effort made at daylight to take the city. After an hour and a half, during which time they gained nothing, and lost the finest prospect of success, they returned to their place of anchorage. One of their balls carried away both the legs of a poor Greek lad in the city; three balls entered the house of the French consul, and two that of the Austrian. The house of the English consul was much exposed to the firing both by land and by sea, but was not touched. The Greeks that were killed lay in plain view from his house and within a stone's throw of his door.

" The Greeks who had landed in the night immediately, on being driven from the walls of the city, took possession of all that part of the country where I live; entering every house, eating, drinking, smoking, and, in some instances, pillaging Many parties of them came to my door; but, on my telling them I was English, they departed. (As we have English protection, we are known in no other character in this country than as English.) The people out of the city fled in all directions, taking with them all that was possible of their property. All that could do so escaped to the mountain. My house was immediately filled with men, women, and children, who came trembling and screaming from all quarters, bringing with them their most precious articles as their little all. About two o'clock, P.M., the Greeks all retired to a fort about a mile distant, half-way between the city and the anchorage at the river, some of them carrying away what they did not bring with them, viz., *Greek tracts.*

" *Wednesday*, 22d. Since the Greeks left us on the Sabbath, we have been under no government but that of God. My house has been filled with the poor Christians who were preparing to escape to the mountain. Twenty-seven slept in one room of my house one night, and the other rooms were equally well filled. To these I daily read the Scriptures, and exhorted them to trust in God. Most of the houses are now forsaken, all the most valuable articles removed, the highways are unoccupied, and far and near scarcely a human being is to be seen except the poor of the land who have nothing to lose. The gates of the city have been shut since the Sabbath, and we should have been entirely destitute of bread, meat, rice, oil, and charcoal, had we not been able to purchase a little from the fleeing inhabitants. To the west of us are the Turks, fortifying their city and castles, and beginning to rage like so many bears, whom it is better to avoid than to meet. On the east are the Greeks, who must pass by us, whether they attack the city by land or by sea. The Emir Beshir, head of the mountain tribes, has come down from the mountain with his troops, and encamped about half an hour's distance to the south of us; and whether he will assist the Greeks or the Turks, or attempt to become master of the city himself, in opposition to both, is a perfect secret. To the north of us is the Bay of Beyrout. We are therefore hedged in on all sides; and the English consul being within the walls of the city, we have no protection but that of the Almighty. We wait with anxiety for the result, as it respects the fate of the city and the interests of this mission.

" *Thursday*, 23d. The Greek vessels spread their sails this morning before sunrise, and, with a very light breeze, moved out of the river. All eyes were fastened upon them. The Turks were at their posts, and the most solemn silence prevailed. The Greeks passed the city at a respectful distance, without throwing a single ball. Just at this time a large number of troops arrived from the Pasha of Acre, consisting principally of Albanians and Bedouins. These, finding the Greeks out of reach, immediately poured forth into all that part of the country which had been, on the preceding Sabbath, in possession of the Greeks, and commenced plundering every house. A French merchant, whose house was near mine, they seized by the throat, took a gold watch from his pocket, his money from his belt, and articles from his house, to the value of five thousand Spanish dollars. My own house, being about the centre of their depredations, was much exposed. Many parties came at different times and demanded entrance; but on my telling them the house was English, and they must not presume to enter, they departed.

" After being annoyed by them in this way more than three hours, with a full and painful view before my eyes of their nefarious operations, a party of six or seven, most or all of whom were Bedouins, who appeared only ' fit for treasons, stratagems, and spoils,' came and very insolently and peremptorily bid me open the door. I reasoned with them a long time from the second-story window, but to no purpose. One of them cocked his gun and levelled it at my head. I told them I should not open the door; and, if they opened it, they did it in violation of the treaty between England and the Ottoman Porte; and they did it, too, with full evidence before their eyes, from the windows in my house, from my dress, language, &c., that I was a European. At this moment four or five respectable Turks of the city passed along, and exerted their influence in my favor, protesting to the Bedouins that I was an English consul, and that, if they broke into my house, it would be at their peril. They listened a moment, and then renewed their attempts, saying they knew neither consul nor sultan.

" Not being able to break open the door, they cut it down with their hatchets, and rushed upstairs like so many tigers eager for their prey. The Turks from the city hastened after them, and took their station at the door of Mrs. Goodell's room, not allowing a single Bedouin to enter. The Bedouins seized whatever came in their way, and we snatched from them all that we could and threw into that room. They became very angry, and one of them drew his sword. Seeing it was vain to reason with them, I assumed a tone of authority, and ordered them to leave the house immediately, telling them that I had already sent a message to the city, and that the pasha would surely take off their heads if the case was represented to him. This had the desired effect. They became calm, and listened to a long and severe reproof from me. They asked me why I remained there; why I did not go to the mountain. I told them I could not go, and gave as a reason Mrs. Goodell's peculiar situation. The villains prayed that God would bless my wife abundantly, and make her exceedingly fruitful, to which I added my hearty Amen. They then left. (Some of the rogues came a few days afterward to inquire after her health and happiness. One of them also came to claim some tobacco which he said I stole from him while he was plundering my house.)

" The gates of the city being now open, and the English consul, hearing of our situation, had sent three times to the Kehya Bey, commander of the pasha's troops, to protect me, and the Kehya Bey had sent horsemen to assist me; but not one ever came nigh me. After leaving the city they galloped away to commit depredations themselves. Being thus unprotected, and the Turks from the city refusing to remain with me through the night, as the Greeks might return, I accepted an invitation from the English consul to take refuge in his house. ' We took joyfully the spoiling of our goods,' and passed safely through the crowds of armed robbers to the city, where we were received by Mr. Abbott and his family with all that attention and kindness which they have shown us on former occasions.

" *Thursday. April 6.* Mr. Bird's house now contains all the missionaries that are to be found in Syria. It is a garrison, and as such affords protection to a few houses in the neighborhood. But most of the houses without the city are desolated and greatly injured; those lovely gardens, the glory of Beyrout, lie uncultivated; the leaves of the mulberry-trees have put forth, and the silk season, which is the most busy and profitable season of the whole year, is just at hand; but the possessors of these houses and lands have not yet dared to come forth from their hiding-places, and their ruin seems inevitable, whether they come forth or continue concealed. If they come forth, it is to suffer imprisonment and stripes, and almost unprecedented extortions; and, if they do not come forth, their possessions are all sequestered by the Kehya Bey. Yesterday I had an interview with the Kehya Bey, the cadi, and the governor, on the subject of the robbery committed upon me. I afterwards sat two hours with the sheikh of the Bedouins among his troops, with the hope of recognizing some of the robbers; but the villains, knowing the object of my visit, thought it prudent to keep out of the way.

" *May* 15. It is impossible to describe the system of falsehood, injustice, oppression, and robbery which has been in operation here for the last two months. Human beings, whose guilt is no greater than that of their proud oppressors, are condemned without a trial, their flesh trembling for fear, their religion blasphemed, their Saviour insulted, their comforts despoiled, their lives threatened, and their bodies filled with pain, and deeply marked with the blows inflicted by Turkish barbarity. Some of them were so badly beaten that they could not walk, but were carried by soldiers, as they went from house to house to obtain a trifle here and a trifle there towards paying the enormous exactions made upon them. One poor creature was brought to my door half dead. I spent several hours in endeavoring to restore him; applied cupping-glasses to his back, bound up his feet, gave him cordials, and finally kept him two days till he could walk. I have never known before what it was to see 'all faces gather darkness, men's hearts failing them,' every bosom tortured with the most gloomy forebodings and the deepest distress.

"*May* 19. This is the first week for two months that I have opened a book for study. The force of the storm appears to have spent itself, and we are now quietly pursuing our work. We have our hopes and our fears, our encouragements and our discouragements. All our schools upon the mountain continue to prosper, and we have sold more copies of the Holy Scriptures within three months than all our number sold during the twenty months preceding. Our schools in Beyrout are of course suspended for the present; but the protection we have afforded to many persons of all the different Christian sects appears to have made a favorable impression. Within a few days we have also had evidence that the truth is prevailing, that some of the good seed sown is springing up, and that the little leaven which has been cast into this mighty mass is spreading. We bless God that we were brought here, even though we should now be destroyed. We believe the good work will go on, though we should be cut off."

Through the English consul, Mr. Abbott, Mr. Goodell made application for indemnification for his losses to the Pasha of St. John d'Acre, who had sent the troops to Beyrout. His application was accompanied with an extraordinary kind of evidence, which had an equally remarkable influence in determining the case in his favor. He employed a Greek artist with whom he was well acquainted, and who was familiar with all the circumstances, to paint a rough but accurate picture of his house, with the Bedouins in the uniform of the Turkish troops forcing their way in. With the letter demanding indemnification, this painting was presented to the pasha, who at once received it as proof positive that his troops had committed the depredation, and exclaimed, "Mashallah! Truly these are my men." He immediately issued an order that the full sum demanded should be paid, amounting to 2,875 piastres (about $230).* The Kehya Bey of Beyrout, who had made many promises of payment without the least intention of their fulfilment, was greatly enraged when the order came; but there was no resisting the command of the pasha, and he was obliged to pay it.

* The compiler of these memoirs has this painting now hanging in his study, a greatly valued memorial of the scenes described.

The calamities which had been visited upon the people, and in which the missionaries shared, were afterward acknowledged as having been the means of averting a disastrous interference with their work, — an interference which subsequently drove them from the field. In regard to this matter Mr. Goodell wrote : —

" Had not God sent terrible judgments upon the people, it is impossible to say to what extremities they would have proceeded against us. A deep plot was laid to drive us all from Beyrout. The Maronite bishop had arrived, and had prepared an excommunication for every Maronite who should permit his house to be hired by us ; and he was endeavoring by bribery and intrigue to bring the Greek bishop and the Mohammedan rulers to act in concert with him, and thus force us to retire from the field or to stand out in the rain with our wives and little ones. But God in His holy providence sent the Greeks here at that very moment ; the bishop had to flee in the night, and has not since dared to return ; and the very best houses of the Maronites fell into our hands by the earnest request of the owners. Moreover, just as the Armenian patriarch at Constantinople was ready to sally forth with a firman from the grand seignior against Jacob Aga, and also, as it seems probable, against the men that were in my service, God let the janissaries loose upon their capital, and permitted the fires which they kindled to rage with greater fury in the Armenian than in any other quarter of the city, and to burn to ashes, among many thousand buildings, the palace and the most splendid church of the Armenian patriarch ; and thus to furnish him sufficient employment for the present, without his meddling with the reformation in these parts."

When the commotions described in the preceding pages had passed over, the missionaries resumed their various labors. Before the close of the year thirteen schools had been established, containing about seven hundred scholars, of whom more than one hundred were girls, — a remarkable evidence of a change of sentiment in regard to the education of women ; their intercourse with the people was resumed ; and more Bibles than ever before were circulated. Mr.

Goodell wrote: "The number of those who come to read with us every evening is increasing; the largest room in my house is sometimes well filled, and, as a few of them find it inconvenient to return home the same evening, I have provided beds for them. They usually sit up more than half the night, conversing on what they have seen and heard."

But what was most cheering was the evidence that the Spirit of God was moving upon the minds of many who had been under instruction, leading them out of the darkness and superstition in which they had been groping, into the light of the knowledge of the glory of God, — a light to which few eyes in that land had been opened for many centuries. Some extracts from Mr. Goodell's journal will show in what circumstances another year opened: —

"*January* 1, 1827.   Blessed be God for the mercies of the last year!   It has been a year of much opposition and of some encouragement; a year in which sinners, as we believe, have been converted.   We met to-day at twelve o'clock, and sung, ' We are a garden walled around.'   I read the fifth chapter of Isaiah and the second chapter of Ephesians, and offered a prayer appropriate for the monthly concert.   We then received into our communion Dionysius Carabet, formerly Archbishop of Jerusalem, and Gregory Wortabet, also Mrs. Maria Abbott, wife of the English consul, an Italian lady, and formerly a papist.   The two former assented to the Articles of Faith and to the Covenant in Arabic, and Mrs. Abbott in English.   Mr. Bird then offered the consecrating prayer in Arabic, for those who had publicly given themselves to God.   We afterwards addressed them on the importance of living godly lives and of adorning their profession.   I broke and distributed the bread, having offered the prayer in English.   Mr. Bird then prayed in Arabic, and distributed the wine, and we sang, —

> ' Why was I made to hear thy voice,
>   And enter while there's room ? '

" After the benediction was pronounced, all, as if unwilling to leave the place, took their seats; and we again, in Arabic, addressed those who had recently professed to renounce the world.   I made some remarks to the spectators who were present.   The whole was a scene of deep solemnity and interest. It was the day (always dear to us) of the *monthly concert;* it was the first day of the year; it was a renewed consecration of ourselves to Christ, and a presentation to Him of the first-fruits of this mission ; it was the 'reviving of the stones out of the heaps of the rubbish,' amidst the desolations of many generations; the rearing up of a church 'upon the foundation of the apostles and prophets, Jesus Christ Himself being the chief corner-stone,' which church, we have confidence to believe, will live and flourish long after we have gone to render up our account.

" We prayed for our beloved Asaad Shidiak, who would doubtless have been with us were he not in bonds for the testimony of Jesus. We thought of our beloved Fisk and Parsons, whose benevolent hearts would have been filled with unspeakable joy at such a sight before they went to heaven. We looked around upon several weeping individuals present, of different communions, some of whom are desirous of uniting themselves to us, and whom we shall probably admit to Christian fellowship on the next sacramental occasion, at the monthly concert in February. Oh that this mission might henceforth be like 'the tree of life, bearing twelve manner of fruits, and yielding her fruit every month!'

"*January* 14. Some time since the people of the mountain were forbidden to speak the word *Bird*. But *bird*, in Arabic, signifies *cold;* they therefore were under the necessity of using a different word. Afterwards came an order that nothing should be said in reference to us; no questions should be asked about us; no hints given respecting us and our labors; that we should not be in remembrance. To-day an order was read in the church in Beyrout, which had been previously read on the mountain, that no one should speak to us, enter our houses, serve us in any capacity, buy or sell, receive any of our books, receive our charity, &c. It was read with loud vociferations and threatening aspect. We were called 'heretics,' 'accursed,' &c. Something of the same nature was proclaimed in the Latin church, and also in the Greek church. ' No person shall buy or sell, except those who have the mark of the beast in their foreheads'! O Lord, we are oppressed; undertake for us.

"*January* 23, *Sabbath.* To-day there was another blast in the Greek church, similar to that in the Maronite. Great were the threatenings against all who should presume to have any connection with us. They are to be carried to the *moot selim* * to be bastinaded. The *wakeel* † is very furious. But to-day we had more than usual to read with us. One saved himself from a bastinading by twice fleeing to me. Next Sabbath all are to be excommunicated who do not leave us.

"*January* 29. The Greek priests are active to-day in prohibiting and threatening from house to house; but the work goes on. If we had a church, and the people were left at liberty, we should have the largest congregation in the city."

* Governor.   † Lieutenant.

The monthly concert and communion season in March was another occasion of very deep and tender interest. There were present, besides Messrs. Bird and Goodell, Rev. Eli Smith, who had just arrived in the country; Mr. Nicolayson, of the London Jews' Society, who had been some time in Syria; Messrs. Gobat (now the venerable Bishop of Jerusa lem) and Kugler, destined for Abyssinia, and Mr. Mueller, missionary to Egypt, all of the Church Missionary Society; and an Abyssinian, who had been sent to Egypt by the King of Abyssinia to procure a bishop for the church in that country, and of whom Mr. Goodell said: "The Abyssinian, 'though black,' is 'comely as the tents of Kedar, as the cur-tains of Solomon,' possessing, as we have reason to hope, the graces of the Holy Spirit." The missionaries above named all took part in the services of the day, which was observed as a day of fasting and prayer.

"Among those who surrounded the table of the Lord," says Mr. Goodell, "were individuals who belonged, or had belonged, to the Episcopal, Congregational, Lutheran, Lutheran Reformed, Moravian, Latin, Armenian, Greek Catho-lic, and Abyssinian churches. Indeed, we were from Europe, Asia, Africa, and America; spoke about as many languages as were spoken on the day of Pentecost; and represented almost all the principal denominations of Christians in the world. But, though we were literally from the four quarters of the globe, and represented so many churches and spoke so many languages, we were in all but sixteen souls."

Fiercer and still more fierce raged the persecution against the missionaries and against all who were under their instruc-tions. The former could not be molested legally; but all sects and classes were aroused against them, and whatever power the various ecclesiastical authorities possessed over their own people was used to the uttermost to break up their intercourse with the mission families. To give the ordinary salutation to one of the missionaries, or to render them any service whatsoever, was made a penal offence. For such offences some were thrown into prison, others were beaten, others had soldiers quartered on them, and one was persecuted unto death. Nor was it only the nominal *Christian* sects that rose up against the missionaries. All the *Turkish* authorities in the pashalik were bribed or stirred up to throw obstacles in the way of their prosecuting their work. For months the missionaries did not dare to be seen upon their house-tops or in the street, from fear of personal violence; and when they lay down at night they knew not what assault might be made upon them before the morning. Mr. Goodell subsequently wrote in regard to this period and its perils:—

" During the last two years of our stay at Beyrout, I seldom closed my eyes in sleep without first thinking over ways and means of escape, if our slumbers should be disturbed by enemies. I seldom walked abroad without looking for rocks and bushes and caves and pits into which the persecuted might flee in the hour of danger. Often have I thought of Obadiah's two caves, in which he hid a hundred prophets of the Lord, and fed them with bread and water; and often have I said to myself, What would I not give for one such cave, to which we and our friends might repair in case of need! For several months before we left Beyrout I had many of my things packed up, that I might be ready to go anywhere at the shortest notice, and my money so separated and disposed of that I might not even be hurried off to prison penniless."

Cases of extreme persecution occurred. The name of Asaad Shidiak, already mentioned, is one which will always be associated with the history of modern missions in Syria, as is that of the martyr Stephen with the annals of the early Christian church. He was a Maronite youth, highly educated, who had been in the service of Mr. King as literary assistant, although not at that time fully enlightened in regard to the errors and superstitions of his own church. When Mr. King's farewell letter on his leaving Syria was published,—a document which produced a powerful impression throughout a large portion of the Turkish empire,—Asaad attempted a reply to it. His studies and meditations while preparing this reply were in a measure instrumental in opening his eyes; and when he afterward entered the family of

5 G

Mr. Bird as his teacher in Arabic, he came also to learn the truth of the Gospel, and to be renewed by the Holy Spirit.

After his conversion, he made rapid progress in the divine life; but his defection excited the wrath of his former ecclesiastical superiors, who forbade him to have any further connection with the " Bible-men." The patriarch, he was informed, " had received instructions from Rome to persecute these men by all means in his power so long as one of them should remain in the country." With great mildness of manner, but with firmness, he adhered to the truth as he had learned it in the school of Christ, never fearing to meet his adversaries, and to reason with them out of the Holy Scriptures. More than once, at the invitation of the patriarch, he went into the interior, where he held long controversies with his former teachers, and where they used every effort, even resorting to imprisonment and violence, to induce him to renounce his new opinions and submit to their control. Twice he made his escape from confinement, and returned, once in disguise, to rejoin his friends, the missionaries, at Beyrout. At length, after repeated attempts to persuade him to put himself in the power of his enemies, he was treacherously thrown into the hands of the Maronite patriarch, from which he never escaped. He endured almost unheard-of tortures. He was kept in prison with a heavy chain around his neck; and, although he survived for years, he never regained his liberty. The manner of his death, and even the time, are not known to this day, except to his persecutors, who never relaxed their hold or ceased to torment him until he joined the noble army of martyrs before the throne.*

In the midst of these troubles, in May, 1827, the plague broke out at Beyrout. All classes were seized with a panic, which immediately suspended the persecution; but the people being allowed to come to the houses of the missionaries,

* The Memoirs of Asaad Shidiak, containing all that was known of the circumstances of his death, were published a few years since in a volume, written by his beloved teacher in Christ, Rev. Isaac Bird.

where they heard the word of life unmolested, the visitation was overruled for the furtherance of the Gospel. The fears of an invasion by Mohammed Ali had the same beneficial effect.

In the fall of 1827 fresh troubles arose. The Greek revolution was still in progress; and when it became known that the European powers had determined to interfere in behalf of Greece and against Turkey, all who enjoyed English protection (including the American missionaries) were in great embarrassment. Many of the Franks left the city, and the native Christians fled in alarm to the mountains. The Turks were more and more exasperated with every fresh rumor in regard to the war, and the situation of the missionaries became exceedingly perilous. By the advice of the English consul, Mr. Goodell sent his family to Der Kalaat, formerly a Roman castle, but now a Maronite convent, on the mountain, about three hours distant. He remained at Beyrout, prosecuting the work of the mission among the Greeks and Arabs. It was only by stealth that he was able to visit his household, being closely watched by the enemies of the mission in the city, and watched for by those on the mountain. Of the circumstances in which he saw his beloved ones, he wrote : —

"I visited my family several times in their retreat, going up in the evening after dark, climbing in at a back window, staying as a sort of prisoner in Mrs. Goodell's room during the day, and climbing back out of the window again in the night, or, rather, very early in the morning, and coming down to Beyrout. Thus I repeatedly went and came without turning the mountain upside down. The monks generally, if not always, found out that I was there; but my stay was too short to excite much alarm. They had previously threatened to burn down their convent and leave the place, if I presumed to go up; but whether, being made entirely of stone, except the doors, it was found to be fire-proof, or whether from some other cause, it still remains a monument of their long suffering.

"In one of my visits, I was unintentionally detained a day longer than usual, staying two days instead of one, which gave much uneasiness to the more orthodox monks, especially as they saw that some of their number were swerving from the rules and duties inculcated, and were fond of stealing away from the convent to the Druze Chapel to converse with our Armenians. A complaint was finally made against me to the English consul; and when, a short time after, a monk, whom they had bound, to prevent his going any more to the Druze Chapel, mocked them by an unexpected escape from their hands, they made still louder complaints against me. They thought it very unreasonable that I should be permitted to walk abroad like other men upon the face of all the earth; for, besides all the injury I might do to their convent, I might perhaps, on the way in going or returning, salute some person; and, if he should return the salutation, he would be, *ipso facto*, under the patriarch's great excommunication! Or some individual might have the ill-luck to give me a glass of water, and thereby fall into the same condemnation. The consul, in the course of different conversations with them, told them we had as much right to go to any part of the country as they had; for we had a firman from the grand seignior, giving us the privilege; and he assured them that, while they were pouring out curses upon *us*, we were praying that God would bless *them*, and while *they* were attempting all manner of evil against us, *we* were attempting all manner of good for their souls and bodies."

While environed with such perils, he wrote to a friend in the United States, under date of Aug. 20, 1827 : —

"An executioner in this country, who had become famous for taking off heads gracefully, is said to have boasted one day to his friend that he could take off a man's head without his feeling it. His word being disputed, he challenged his friend to stand forth and submit to an experiment. His friend immediately laid his neck bare and stood forth. The executioner made a flourish with his sword; the latter stood firm and said, 'You did not touch me.' The former replied, 'Nod and see.' He nodded — and his head dropped to the ground. I assure you, we almost nod now and then to see whether our heads are really on our shoulders or not in these critical, perilous times."

In November he wrote from Mansooreea, another retreat, to which he was compelled to fly with his family : —

"MANSOOREEA, Nov. 27, 1827.

" MY DEAR SIR, — I prepared letters to send you on the 7th inst. by a French corvette, which came in early in the morning to convoy vessels, it was said or supposed, to Alexandria. As one had been daily expected for this purpose more than a week, and as favorable accounts of the progress of the negotiations at Constantinople had been received, nothing of an adverse nature was apprehended. I sent twice into the city, however, in the course of the day to know if there was any thing new, and was assured there was nothing. Just at dark the unexpected intelligence reached us that a terrible battle had been fought somewhere on the 20th ult. between the combined European fleets and the Turkish fleet,* in which the latter were entirely destroyed; and that all the Franks in Beyrout had already fled in great precipitation from the city, some to the mountains, and others on board the corvette.

" It was one of those dark nights of thunder, storm, and tempest, when every man in this country, who has a cloak and a hut, feels happy in wrapping himself up, and lying secure in a dry corner. The corvette, it was said, would be off before morning, to go we could not learn whither. Mrs. Goodell was very ill in bed, and unable even to sit up. It had become no longer advisable for me to go to Der Kalaat, much less to reside there, even if I should succeed in getting my family there in safety. The flight of the Franks at such an hour, in such a storm, and on the arrival, too, of the corvette, very justly excited much alarm in the city; and it could not be conjectured what the Mussulmans would do in their rage and fury, when they should first hear the report of the battle. There was no time for delay. There was no one to advise. And we must, if possible, be in some place of security by morning light. We promised a handsome reward to an Arab, if he would grope his way through the darkness and storm with a few lines to the English consul at Der Kalaat, and return with an answer before three o'clock in the morning. After having consulted very seriously with one of us whether he should take his pipe on so perilous an expedition, he finally

* The battle of Navarino.

concluded to go without it. In the mean time, we put into trunks, boxes, and pillow-cases our books, papers, and whatever was most valuable and most important to be preserved, and endeavored to procure camels, mules, and asses, to convey away ourselves and effects we knew not yet whither. But, as all the animals had been previously engaged by others, we were able to find only two asses. Precisely at half-past two o'clock, the messenger returned, and had as much to say of his hairbreadth escapes, amidst darkness and thunder and headlong steeps, as though he had barely survived some bloody political revolution. The consul wrote that, only a few hours before, he had very providentially taken of the Emeer Shedeed a large and, for this country, commodious house at Mansooreea; and he advised that we betake ourselves thither, where he and his family would join us at their leisure, and consult what steps were to be taken for our further security.

"At daylight we were all ready to start, except Mrs. Goodell, who appeared really too ill even to leave the bed. Fortunately, at this moment several Arabs came and reported to us that the governor sent ten soldiers after the French consul the evening before, who followed him till the darkness and storm forced them to give up the chase. This so counteracted the debilitating effects of pain and disease that before sunrise we were all, in company with Mr. Smith and an English gentleman, on the way, most of us of course on foot. As it was very muddy, and as we had to stop occasionally to rest, we did not reach our place of destination till near noon; but we all escaped safe, — Mr. Smith and his companion to Der Kalaat, and the remainder to Mansooreea. The storm had providentially spent itself in the night; but we experienced the effects of it to such a degree in the badness of the road that we could not but remember the exhortation of our Saviour, 'Pray ye that your flight be not in the winter.' We immediately despatched a messenger to inform Mr. Bird of what had happened; and about sunset obtained some refreshment for ourselves and little ones, having tasted scarcely any thing for twenty-four hours. The fright and flight, together with the change of air and of circumstances, has entirely restored Mrs. Goodell to health; and our children were never more lively and healthy than they are at present.

"With affectionate salutations, yours, &c.,

"W. GOODELL."

CHAPTER VII.

MR. GOODELL and his family returned from their mountain retreat to Beyrout, December 27, and were rejoined by Mr. and Mrs. Bird, from whom they had been separated about five months. They hoped now to be able to resume their labors ; but the political disturbances continued, and with the opening of another year, 1828, they had the prospect of losing all consular protection. On the 28th of January a French man-of-war arrived at Beyrout from Alexandria, and one from Smyrna, to lower the French flag and take on board the French consul and subjects. The English consul also received instructions to strike his flag, but it was some time before he was able to leave the country. Early in the year also the plague reappeared at Beyrout. It was at length decided that duty required the mission families to leave the country until quiet should be restored. Even to leave was a matter of great difficulty, the authorities for a long time withholding permission ; but, having chartered a vessel to take them and their effects to Malta, Mr. and Mrs. Goodell and Mr. and Mrs. Bird, with their families, including their Armenian helpers and their families, Mr. Smith and Mr. Nicolayson and family, set sail on the 2d of May.

Notwithstanding the violent opposition which their labors had excited, and the disastrous circumstances in which they were called to leave their interesting field, the mission had thus far been remarkably successful. The actual state of things when they came into Syria, and indeed up to the time of their leaving, so far as the nominally Christian churches and people are concerned, was thus described by Mr. Goodell:—

"I came to Syria with the hope that I should find at least some individual, however obscure, who sighed for the abominations committed, and who worshipped God in spirit and in truth; and I do not now say that no such individual is to be found, but I can say in truth that no such person has been found in Syria by ourselves (those of course excepted who appear to have been benefited by our instructions), and that all our researches have not brought to light *one* who appeared even ashamed or afraid to lie, and profane the name and Sabbaths of the Most High. On the contrary, the more we have seen and heard, the more we have conversed with the people, and the more diligent our inquiries have been to ascertain their real state, the more painful has been the conviction and more overwhelming the evidence that in all these churches, Jewish and Christian, ' there is none that seeketh after God.' "

But although they had found the land and the people in such a state when they entered the country, seldom has missionary work been crowned so speedily with such encouraging results. The Gospel had not only been proclaimed extensively among the people, but from among the Armenians, Greeks, and Maronites, men had been raised up who were preaching the truth faithfully and fearlessly from house to house; schools had been established, in which hundreds of children and adults of both sexes were taught; a decided impression had been made upon the Oriental prejudice against the education of women; tracts had been widely distributed, which were eagerly read and discussed by a people peculiarly given to controversy; a spirit of inquiry, although in the main accompanied by a spirit of opposition, had been extensively excited; all classes of people, of all nationalities, had been aroused, — Armenians, Greek and Roman Catholics, including Maronites and Mohammedans, — moved as much, perhaps, by the zealous opposition of their religious teachers as by the truth itself, but thoroughly aroused to the consciousness that a new element of power had been introduced among them. All these were exceedingly hopeful indications;

and sad was the disappointment when those who had begun to see the fruit of their labors were called to abandon the field and leave the harvest to perish. They left, however, in the full expectation of returning as soon as the political storm which was passing over the land should subside.

The voyage from Beyrout to Malta was far from pleasant. There were in all twenty-one persons, besides the ship's company, crowded together in a little Austrian trabaccolo of a hundred tons. Only about half the number could get into the cabin at once. They were obliged to live and take their meals chiefly on deck in all kinds of weather, without table or chairs; and when, after being thirty days at sea, the vessel reached port, they were obliged to go into quarantine for thirty days more.

From the lazaretto at Malta Mr. Goodell wrote to a friend in America: —

"It grieves me to say that all our missionary operations in Syria are at present suspended, and 'all our pleasant things laid waste.' The step we have taken in securing a temporary asylum in this island will not probably be altogether unexpected, if you have had an eye to the political tempest that has been for several months gathering in the East, though you may not have seen and heard so distinctly as we have the lightnings and thunderings which gave a more fearful aspect to the impending storm. It is with emotions peculiarly tender that we look back from our present retreat to the former scene of our labors; to the schools that once flourished; the individuals that wept for their sins and listened with deep earnestness to the story of redeeming love; to the church gathered there; small, indeed, and despised, but literally taken from 'many nations and kindreds and tongues,' and ' *builded together* for a habitation of God through the Spirit;' to our various labors, public and private, for the spiritual benefit of the people, together with the shame, reproaches, and sufferings to which we were exposed for the sake of the glorious Gospel of our blessed Lord; and to the travels and researches and sacrifices and toils and sorrows and life and death of him (Mr. Fisk) who sleeps sweetly in our own garden, undisturbed by the rage and blasphemy of God's enemies."

5*

The missionaries of the American Board to the countries lying on the Mediterranean were now nearly all gathered at Malta, on account of commotions which were agitating the Turkish empire. Malta, being under English control, was a place in which they were sure of protection in all circumstances, and on this account it had been selected as a printing-house for the Orient. The mission was supplied with fonts of type for printing in Italian, Modern Greek, Armenian, and Arabic. After his arrival at the island, Mr. Goodell took the superintendence of the press, devoting himself at the same time to the work of translation and to preparing books and tracts for publication. Some idea of the extent to which the press was used may be gained from the statement that from July 1, 1822, to Dec. 31, 1828, there were issued at Malta, of books and tracts, 7,852,200 pages, and more than 5,000,000 pages were put in circulation. Mr. Temple left for a visit to the United States, a few days after the arrival of the brethren from Syria, and Mr. Bird made a missionary tour on the coast of Barbary in the spring and summer, preaching in Arabic, and disseminating the printed word.

There was little of incident in the life of a missionary at Malta during the sojourn of Mr. Goodell, while he was waiting for the troubles in the East to subside. This quiet life gave him an opportunity to cultivate the acquaintance of his family, such as he had not enjoyed before. He wrote, Oct. 19, 1828: —

" This is the first time that I have lived alone with my family since my marriage. On our arrival at Malta, in 1823, we lived in the same house with the families of Messrs. Bird and Temple. When we first arrived at Beyrout we lived for nearly a year with Mr. Bird, and when we took another house, we had immediately Carabet, and soon after his wife, with us constantly, besides many Arabs continually about us. We have now for a whole month been alone, and we bless God for this retirement and relief from care and anxiety. Though I spend most of my days at the press, yet I see and enjoy more of my family than I ever have before. The society of my wife and children is indeed a comfort, which my circumstances have never before permitted me to enjoy."

In January, 1829, he wrote: " On the 8th Mr. Anderson took tea with us, and we had a fire in the evening, the first we have had since leaving America," which was more than six years before.

To a friend at Andover, Mass., he wrote from Malta, under date of March 24, 1829 : —

" We thank you and all our good friends at Andover for so affectionately and prayerfully ' remembering us in our low estate.' Though we feel unworthy of such remembrance, yet we are, I trust, of ' the goodly company ' of those who constitute ' the body of Christ ; ' and if so, we are ' members in particular, and members one of another.' We ' believe in the holy catholic church, the communion of saints.' We love to feel united in spirit, labors, sufferings, privileges, and blessings, with all ' the household of faith,' with all ' the elect,' who ' have obtained like precious faith,' whose ' names are written in heaven,' and who ' are come unto Mount Zion, the city of the living God, the heavenly Jerusalem ; ' with all who ' are builded together for an habitation of God through the Spirit,' and who ' in every place call upon the name of Jesus Christ our Lord, both theirs and ours.' Whether, like Asaad Shidiak, they are in prison for the testimony of Jesus ; like Dr. Carey, translating the Scriptures ; like the pious poor, exhibiting ' an example of suffering, affliction, and of patience ; ' or like the students of Andover, making their particular study those mysteries of redemption, to look into which the angels again and again turn away their minds from other glories and wonders in heaven ; wherever they may be found, and in whatever circumstances, we pray that ' grace may be to them, and peace from God our Father, and from the Lord Jesus Christ.'

" My mind has, I believe, been the more led into this train of thought from our having been recently called to part with our beloved friends, Mr. and Mrs. Nicolayson, with little prospect of our ever being permitted to live and labor with them again here below. Though *he* was German and *she* was Irish and *we* were American, and though we were all strongly marked with our national peculiarities, they sometimes smiling at our singularities and weaknesses, and we in our turn at theirs, yet we all loved one another as 'fellow-heirs and of the same body.' We have been together in many scenes of affliction and of consolation ; have often united in prayer and praise in social and public worship ; have many times surrounded the table of the Lord together, to eat of the same bread and drink of the same cup, and I trust that we have all been made to drink into the same Spirit ; and, though separated in body, we shall never be separated from the love of God, which is in Christ Jesus our Lord.

"It is pleasant to think of the hours of religious intercourse and enjoyment we have had from time to time with many of the dear servants of God, who are either already now in heaven or on their way thither. And it is pleasant to think of that day when the last pilgrim from this vale of tears shall arrive at his long-sought home, and shall stand on Mount Zion with all that have been 'redeemed from the earth,' with 'an innumerable company of angels,' and with ' the general assembly and church of the first-born,' and with ' Jesus the Mediator of the New Covenant.' May we be there ! And may none of those near and dear to us be missing.

" Brother Temple writes to us that America is '*Emmanuel's land*,' and he gives us such glowing descriptions of the increase of the fruits of righteousness there, that we should really like once more to go over into that garden to see 'the fruits of the valley,' and how ' the vine flourishes and the pomegranates bud.' But whether we are ever indulged with this privilege or not, our prayer for you all shall ever be, ' Awake, O North Wind ; and come thou South ; blow upon this garden, that the spices thereof may flow out,' more and more, ' to the glory and praise of God ' !

"*Malta, May* 26, 1829. Two Greek pirates are to be executed to-morrow morning at Florian. They appear to be deeply criminal and awfully hardened. A circumstance brought forward in the course of the trial, day before yesterday, strikingly illustrates the distinction made in the papal and Oriental churches between the religious and moral character. It appeared that the beef and anchovies on board one of the English vessels which they pirated were left untouched, and the circumstances under which they were left appeared to the court so peculiar that the culprits were asked the cause. They promptly answered that it was at the time of the great fast, when their church allows neither meat nor fish to be eaten. They appeared to be hardened and abandoned wretches, enemies alike to their own and every other nation, and yet rigidly maintaining their religious character, and, while robbing, plundering, murdering, and stealing the women and children of their countrymen and selling them to the Turks, and committing other atrocious deeds, they would have us understand that they were not so wicked as to taste of meat or fish when prohibited by the canons of their church. The religion of these countries has nothing to do with moral character. The priests do not and dare not interfere with this, their business being only with religion. The priest here, in confessing these men, remarks that they are very religious, and quite resigned to their fate.

"*February* 14, 1830. My birth-day. I am now thirty-eight years old. I have been affected this morning in thinking how good God has been to me ever since I was born, and how great are my obligations to Him. What a mercy that He has permitted me to enter His vineyard and take part in the work of spreading the Gospel! In reflecting on His kindness towards me through the whole period of my life, the following things affect my mind, as particularly calling for gratitude and praise to the Giver of every good and perfect gift, viz.: religious education by pious parents; divine influence at an early period of my life; opportunity to acquire a liberal education; advantages of the Theological Seminary at Andover; the privilege of being a minister and missionary of the cross; an affectionate, wise, and discreet partner in life; and children to bring up for God. These are the great points which are the first to strike my mind on every retrospect of my life; and in fixing on each of them separately, how many blessings to be thankful for under each one, or connected with each one! May my heart be always fixed on God, that I may always sing and give praise to Him!

"*May* 1, 1830. Mr. and Mrs. Bird and their little ones, with Mr. and Mrs. Whiting, left us, amidst our prayers and tears and benedictions, and sailed for Beyrout. We believe that they went forth in obedience to the divine command, and that the pillar of cloud will go before them by day and the pillar of fire by night, and that God Himself will be with them, and will bless and comfort them. To those of us who had been so long associated in missionary labor, who had passed together and helped each other through so many scenes of trouble and of joy, who had so often met and been refreshed together at the table of the Lord, and who had brought the little ones whom God hath graciously given us to the same baptismal font to be dedicated to the Lord, the separation was a heavy cross, but it was one which we felt we must take up and bear cheerfully for the sake of Jesus and His cause."

The following, written on the occasion of the visit of the American Episcopal missionaries, Rev. Messrs. Robertson and Hill, at Malta, on their way to Greece, in November, 1830, exhibits the truly catholic spirit which he breathed from the day that he entered upon his missionary work until he rested from his labors : —

" I cannot express how happy we were to have these beloved missionaries with us during their short stay in this island, and ' to help them on their way, after a godly sort.' To all missionaries, of whatever denomination, who come with such a spirit and with such enlarged views as these manifested, we will most gladly extend the right hand of fellowship, and bless them in the name of the Lord. Indeed, I believe we felt that we belonged to but one church, and that the church universal."

While in Syria Mr. Goodell, with the aid of his Armenian helpers, Carabet and Wortabet, had commenced the translation of the Holy Scriptures into the Armeno-Turkish. He continued the work after reaching Malta, and his connection with the press at the latter place afforded a favorable opportunity for printing it under his own supervision. Accordingly, the New Testament having been completed and carefully revised, the printing of it was commenced on the 8th of January, 1830, and finished within a little more than a year. When the last proof-sheets had been corrected, he wrote : —

" My obligations to God are exceedingly great that He has allowed me the privilege of serving Him in so sacred and important a work, and that He has prolonged my life, and given me health and strength to bring it to a close. I have great occasion to implore forgiveness that from day to day I have with so little fervency sought the aid and have been so little under the influence of that same good Spirit by which holy men of God were moved when they spake and wrote these everlasting truths. May the sins of all those who have been in any way employed about the ark of the Lord be forgiven through the merits of Christ! And may all who shall read the words of this book 'obtain the forgiveness of their sins and an inheritance among them who are sanctified'!

"Nothing now remains but that it should be commended to the blessing of God, to be used for His own glory, for the increase of holiness on earth, and for the salvation of many souls. May it go forth accompanied by that Spirit without which the mere 'letter killeth'! May it be 'received with all joy,' and prove a 'savor of life unto life'! May those who read it not attempt to teach *it*, but be willing it should teach them! May they yield their minds to all the information it contains, their hearts entirely to its government, their conduct to its direction, and their opinions to its decisions! May the priests and bishops read it, and learn what that faith is for which they are to contend earnestly! May the people read it, and learn to 'prove all things, and hold fast that which is good'! May the proud read it, and learn to be humble; the worldly, and learn to 'lay up treasure in heaven;' the self-righteous, and learn to 'count all things but loss for the excellency of the knowledge of Christ;' the ignorant, and become 'wise unto salvation'! May parents and children, rulers and subjects, masters and servants, read it, and learn the duties of their respective stations! May the afflicted read it, and learn where true comfort can be found; the miserable, and learn how to be happy, both here and hereafter! May the anxious and inquiring read it, and find it to be a light unto their feet and a lamp unto their path! May sinners of all descriptions read it, and by faith 'behold the Lamb of God, that taketh away the sin of the world;' may they read it, and 'have right to the tree of life, and enter in through the gates into the city'!"

CHAPTER VIII.

THE following year Mr. Goodell received instructions from the Prudential Committee of the Board to repair to Constantinople, and commence a new mission at that place. The letter of instructions reached him on the 26th of April, 1831. The next day he began to make preparations for removal, and on the 21st of May he left Malta with his family in the ship "Banian," Captain Smith, for the Turkish capital. The special object of his mission was to reach the Armenian population of the city,— an intelligent, enterprising, and wealthy part of the people, who might be expected to exert a powerful influence for good throughout the Turkish empire, when once they should embrace the truth as it is in Jesus. For this service Mr. Goodell was specially qualified by his previous study, labors, and experience.

He reached Constantinople on the 9th of June. His description of Stamboul and its suburbs, as seen on his approach, is not excelled in graphic force and beauty by any of the numerous pictures that have been drawn of the grandeur of this magnificent Oriental scene : —

"*June* 9. We all rose at an early hour to see Constantinople. The storm had passed away, the stars were fading out of their places, the winds breathed soft, and the morning had all the freshness and coolness of one at this season of the year in New England after a refreshing shower. The view of Constantinople was at first indistinct, and presented nothing striking. We began to call in question the correctness of the opinions expressed by writers, of the unrivalled beauty of its situation and of the scenery around. But as we approached the city the prospect became enchanting.

On our left were fields rich in cultivation and fruitfulness. On our right were the little isles of the sea, and beyond the high lands of Broosa, with Olympus rearing its head above the clouds and covered with eternal snow. In the city, mosques, domes, and hundreds of lofty minarets were starting up amidst the more humble abodes of men, all embosomed in groves of dark cypress, which, in some instances, seemed almost like dense forests; while before, behind, and around us were, besides many boats of the country, more than twenty square-rigged vessels, bearing the flags of different nations, under full sail, with a light but favorable breeze, all converging to one point, and that point Constantinople.

" When we first caught a glimpse of Top-Hana, Galata, and Pera, stretching from the water's edge to the summit of the hills, and as we began to sweep around Seraglio Point, the view became most beautiful and sublime. It greatly surpassed all that I had ever conceived of it. We had been sailing along what I should call the south side of the city for four or five miles, and were now entering the Bosphorus, with the city on our left and Scutari on our right. The mosques of St. Sophia and Sultan Achmet, with the palaces and gardens of the present Sultan Mahmoud, were before us in all their majesty and loveliness. The latticed windows of the women's apartments, the gilt doors, with the titles of the grand seignior inscribed over the massive gates in letters of gold, were coming into sight like enchantment. Numberless boats were shooting rapidly by in all directions, giving to the scene the appearance of life, activity, pleasure, and business. The vessels before us had been retarded and those behind had been speeded, and we were sweeping around the Golden Horn in almost as rapid succession as was possible, every captain apparently using all his skill to prevent collision with his neighbor, or being carried away by the current; and every passenger, like ourselves, apparently gazing with admiration on the numerous objects of wonder on every hand. Around us in the harbor, among the boats and vessels, were porpoises tumbling, and sea-fowls, exceedingly tame, flying, hovering, swimming, and catching whatever eatable might be thrown overboard. The Turks never molest them, and they have in a great measure laid aside their natural fear of man."

Mr. Goodell was soon at home in his own hired house at

Pera, one of the suburbs of Constantinople. It will seem strange at this day, when so many Americans annually visit the Turkish capital, and when not a few are residents, that after his arrival he wrote to a friend in this country: " My family is said to be the first that has ever visited this place; and Mrs. Goodell, Mrs. Smith, wife of our captain, and Miss Reynolds, who came with us from Smyrna, the first American ladies ever seen here."

Mr. Goodell, on reaching Constantinople, took a house at Pera, directly across the Golden Horn, the suburb chiefly occupied by the Franks. He had just begun to look about him and to lay his plans for commencing systematic labor, when his work was suddenly arrested by one of those terrible conflagrations to which the city of the sultans has been peculiarly liable. Of this disastrous fire, by which he lost nearly every thing of an earthly nature that he or his family possessed, we find in his journal the following graphic account: —

" BUYUK-DÈRÈ, Aug. 12, 1831.

" About nine o'clock in the morning of the 2d inst., when the alarm of fire was first given, I saw the smoke ascending, and immediately repaired to the spot. It was about a mile from my house, and nearly in the direction of the Frank burying-ground. As I approached, the scene became more terrific, — men and boys running; children crying; women screaming, or beating their bosoms, and nearly fainting; some carrying their babes or infirm relatives; others dragging a part of their clothes and furniture; some making a feeble effort to check the progress of the fire; and a multitude of others, who felt themselves secure, looking on as mere idle spectators. I was not at all aware of the danger which those around me seemed to apprehend, and did what I could to calm their fears and inspire confidence. For near two hours I labored in a large garden, assisting some Armenian women to extinguish the fire, with which their beds and clothes were still smoking. In the mean time, the wind very considerably freshened, and the fire, which it appeared to me might easily have been suppressed at first, began to spread rapidly, and to defy all attempts to arrest its progress. Fire-engines had arrived, and were arriving, but the element, like a wild beast that had escaped from the hand of its keeper, was raging too violently, and had acquired too much power, to be subdued.

"I must, I think, have made a mistake as to the real situation of my house, or as to the real direction the fire was taking, for I had not the least idea that my own neighborhood would be disturbed. The owner of my house, also, whom I met in the vicinity of the fire, had the same views in regard to the part of the town likely to be affected. I concluded, however, to go home and rest, and after a while return again to afford any assistance in my power. On the way I met Mr. Lazarides, who has the charge of the Depôt of Scriptures at Galata, and who had also the superintendence of a school at Pera on the Lancasterian system, which he had been encouraged to establish by Messrs. Brewer, Barker, and others at Smyrna. He, with many others, was wringing his hands and weeping, and anxiously asked what he should do. I assured him that I fully believed he was in no danger; but, if he thought otherwise, he had better send the slates, books, &c., of the school, and whatever else he pleased, to my house, where they would *certainly* be safe. I went with him to the school, and with several porters we took every thing except the seats, also much of his own private property, and *all* his brothers', and started for my house. It was now almost impossible to pass, on account of the crowd of men, women, and children; some carrying off their little ones or their goods to a place of safety, others returning for a fresh load; while a company of firemen, hastening with their engines towards the fire, would now and then break their way through, to the no small danger of the limbs and lives of those with whom they came in contact. Some appeared to be in danger of suffocation, and some, with loads on their backs, were thrown down, and literally passed over.

"On reaching home, I found the house nearly filled with the goods of some of our neighbors, and my family somewhat alarmed, and already engaged in closing the iron shutters. The fire now for the first time appeared to me to be spreading towards the part of the town in which I lived. Mr. Cunningham, who lived in a stone house near by, came in, and assured me that such houses as his and mine were always known to resist the effects of fire, and advised me to let every thing remain in the house, as he should in his. I had all the shutters well fastened, the windows removed, water carried up to all the rooms and upon the roof, and every thing done which I was able to do. The owner of the house, a rich Armenian, also came in, and flew about, and seemed to exercise authority, like the 'angel who had power over fire,' and I felt that we were safe. Mrs. Goodell was in the mean time engaged in arranging our things, and putting up as many of them as possible in trunks and baskets.

"Every house was like touch-wood, and the wind and flames increased, and rolled on towards us like waves of liquid fire. The iron shutters of my house soon became red hot; the rooms were like a heated oven ; but we made plentiful use of water, and were able for a considerable time to extinguish the fire, wherever it caught.

"About this time Mr. Churchhill came in, and insisted that Mrs. Goodell and the children should immediately go to his house, quite in the lower part of Pera, towards Galata, and there remain till we should come, as he was sure my house could not stand long. They left in company with Messrs. Offley and Roboli, clerks in Mr. Churchhill's counting-house. Soon after, Mr. Cunningham came to tell me that his house, with every thing in it, was gone, and that mine could not resist much longer. Every house back of mine was in ashes, or nearly so ; every house on the left hand was all on fire, and the house next to mine on the right had just caught. In front, and separated from me by a narrow street, was the large garden of the English palace, surrounded by a very high wall. Assisted by Mr. Churchhill and Panayotes, a friendly Greek, who came over from Constantinople and stayed by me during all that day, and several of the succeeding ones, we threw from the projections or balconies of our chambers into this garden whatever came to hand, till my strength was exhausted, and Mr. Churchhill declared that we could not remain in the house another minute in safety. The fire had passed through the adjoining house to the very front, and was sweeping the front part of mine, which was not defended by iron shutters. He started, and bade me follow. I called to my servant Giovanni, and then passed through a shower of tiles, windows, and firebrands, that were falling into the street from the adjoining house. My hat caught fire, but, praised be God, I passed unhurt. The servant, who was not a quarter of a minute behind, was not able to follow, and had to return into the house, and was somehow saved by the firemen through the ashes and fire at the back part of the house.

"We hastened to the garden, and towards the spot where we had thrown so many things, and where I expected to find them all secure. We found it impossible to make a near approach; the fire had passed the garden wall; not a single article of all we had thrown from the windows could be seen; and the whole front part of my house was wrapt in one entire sheet of blaze. We afterwards found in another part of the garden a very few of our things, some of them broken, and others partly burnt, which had been rescued from the fire by the exertions of Messrs. Offley and Roboli and other friends; but almost all of them were consumed before they could be taken from the spot where they were thrown. With 'the spoiling of our goods' we removed from place to place in the garden, till the palace itself took fire, and no place of safety could any longer be found there. We then proceeded to Mr. Churchhill's, a large and very strong stone house. The fire followed us, and in about an hour the fire was at the next door. We hastened to Top-Hana, and, hungry, thirsty, and fatigued, we came the same night in a boat to this place, a distance of about eighteen miles. Mr. Churchhill had a house here, which his family were already occupying. We were 'strangers, and they took us in,' and very hospitably entertained us, till we could look round and find a dwelling, and purchase a few things necessary for commencing housekeeping. We found ourselves at once destitute of almost every comfort, and had, as it were, to begin the world anew. Not a single cup nor a single utensil remained. Two single beds, partly burnt, three sheets and two coverlets, partly burnt, and one pillow, constituted the whole of our conveniences for the night.

"Panayotes, the Greek above mentioned, threw many of my books from the window, a part of which were preserved; but all my Grammars and Dictionaries in the English, French, Italian, Arabic, Hebrew, Greek, Armenian, and Turkish languages; all my Geographies, Gazetteers, Histories (excepting two odd volumes of Mosheim), Commentaries on the Bible, manuscripts, translations, &c., with many of my private papers, are gone, — all 'into smoke have they consumed away.' I had visited most of the places here which are objects of curiosity to a stranger, and had taken copious notes of what I had seen and heard; but not a trace of them is now to be found. We had provided at Malta a good supply of clothing for ourselves and children, but of many articles we are entirely deprived, and of others to a great degree. I have not a single shirt to put on. We had a pretty large stock of medicines, but not one article was saved. We had many little comforts which are considered indispensable in case of sickness, but *not a single one is left;* nor can many of them be obtained here now at any price. Keys we have in full complement, but scarcely any thing to unlock.

" The little girls thought it very hard that the fire paid no respect to their toys or their books. Their 'Little Philosopher' books and all the rest are gone. The second day after our arrival at this place there was an alarm of fire where we are staying, and they began to cry, and said they would go back to Malta. The trunk that I carried so far on my back when I left home to enter Phillips Academy, and which I intended to bequeath to my children for their inheritance, is also gone.

" But, though cast down, we are not destroyed. We have been afflicted, but not given over unto death. And one reason why I have dwelt thus particularly on our own circumstances is that you may form some idea of the losses and circumstances (and in some instances great distresses) of from seventy to eighty thousand of our fellow-sufferers. Of all that part properly, I understand, called Pera, only eight private houses are said to remain. One of these is Mr. Churchhill's. Of all the palaces, only the Austrian and Swedish were saved. Of all the churches, only one Greek and one Latin (with the new English chapel then in building) escaped the general conflagration. The people in crowds made the best of their way to the burying-grounds with whatever they could take with them; and for several days and nights from ten to twenty thousand persons might be seen there, many of them with scarcely any other covering than the canopy of heaven, or any other bed than the graves they slept upon. Multitudes of men, women, and children might be seen lying against a grave-stone, to defend their head from wind and cold during repose.

"In such times of calamity it is not in these countries as it is in America, where the sufferers meet everywhere with sympathy and assistance. Many persons here will, indeed, '*take you in*,' but it is generally in the wrong sense. Almost every one with whom you have to do hopes and endeavors to profit by your losses. Are you very anxious to have any particular article saved? Perhaps not a porter will lift his finger to save it without an extravagant compensation, demanding in some instances nearly or quite as much as the article originally cost. And if for a moment you lose sight of him, he will perhaps take the road to his own house, or will turn aside into some lane, and carry off your treasure. One of my trunks I found, a week after the fire, at Ters-Hana, more than a mile from my house; another I found more than a mile in another direction. The former was broken open, and all, except two, of the silver spoons which our dear friends in America had given us were gone.

"But my heart sickens and my eyes fill as I think of the wickedness, the sufferings, and the horrors of that day! More than one hundred persons are reported to have perished by fire and falling walls. Nine men were buried in the ruins nearly opposite Mr. Churchhill's house, and an entire week elapsed before they could all be dug out. Others were cut off from doors and streets by surrounding flames, and, with millions of cats and other quadrupeds, were burnt alive. The space of ground burnt over is about two miles long, and in some instances a mile broad, making, as the Rev. Dr. Walsh thinks, rather more than a mile square. The destruction of property was greater and the fire more irresistible than has ever been known here before, and reminded one of the fires of the last day. It seemed, indeed, like 'the great and terrible day of the Lord,' when 'the heavens, being on fire, shall be dissolved, and the elements shall melt with fervent heat, the earth also, and the works that are therein, shall be burnt up.' The Lord grant that we may all 'find mercy of the Lord in that day,' and may our treasure be laid up where the last fire cannot reach."

The losses which he sustained in this great fire were in a measure made up by the generous aid of friends in the East and in the United States. When the news of the disaster reached Smyrna, several American merchants, shipmasters, and residents sent nearly three thousand piastres (about two hundred and forty dollars) to Mr. Goodell, together with a box of clothing, which it was impossible to obtain at Constantinople, excepting at extravagant prices. Among the many pleasing expressions of remembrance and sympathy which he received from his native land, and one doubly valuable at a time when nearly every memento of home was "consumed away into smoke," was a box from a society of ladies in his native town, with the familiar names of the respective donors written on the several articles.

Driven from Pera by the conflagration, he was obliged to seek quarters in one of the more distant suburbs of Constantinople. He found a temporary home at Buyuk-Dèrè on the Bosphorus, about fifteen miles from the city, and four or five from the Black Sea.

"*August* 6. We are now occupying a part of a house belonging to two Greek princesses, whose father was beheaded at the commencement of the Greek revolution. Besides ourselves and these princesses there are several other families and individuals in the house. Indeed, we form a community by ourselves, of 'many nations, kindreds, and tongues,' being from ten different nations, belonging to eight different religious communions, and understanding sixteen different languages. May we all dwell together in that 'house not made with hands, eternal, in the heavens'! In every place where we have sojourned; in every island or country we have visited; in every road we have travelled, or ship in which we have sailed; in every house we have rented, and every room we have occupied, — how many things have the eyes of infinite Purity seen amiss in us! How many mercies have we, in all places and at all times, received! and how few and how poor returns have we, in any place or at any time, made! And the fire which burns up all things else does not consume our sins, nor destroy the remembrance of them. May they all be washed away in the blood of the Lamb, that precious blood which cleanseth from all sin!"

Among the occupants of this house were three American gentlemen, — Dr. James E. De Kay, of New York, who had been sent from the United States as a medical commissioner, to study the new and mysterious disease, the Asiatic cholera, that was then sweeping over the continent of Europe, and which made its appearance on the American shores the following summer; Mr. Hènry Eckford, also of New York who was employed by the Turkish government to superintend the construction of its navy; and Mr. Charles Rhind, — all of whom became for a season members of the family of the missionary. This association was the source of mutual pleasure, the guests sharing in the privileges of an American Christian home, and by their society and kind attentions contributing to the enjoyments of the household. The arrival of another American, with whom Mr. Goodell had for many years the most agreeable intercourse, and from whom he received substantial aid and encouragement, is mentioned in the accompanying extract from his journal: —

"*August* 21. Preached at Commodore Porter's. He has just arrived as *Chargé d'affaires*, and has kindly opened his doors for public worship on the Sabbath. All the American travellers and visitors who happened to be in the village attended, among whom were a Jew, a Quaker, an Episcopalian, Socinians, and Congregationalists. The subject of the discourse was Searching the Scriptures. Whatever offices we or our countrymen may fill; where or for whatever purpose we may travel by land or by sea, in all places and among all people; of whatever languages, religions, or customs, — may we feel and say, 'Thy word is a lamp unto my feet and a light unto my path,' and may our conduct ever be in accordance with such a sentiment."

Of one of these services an American traveller who was present wrote at the time: —

" Our worthy friend, Mr. Goodell, celebrated divine worship at home, and such of the inmates of the palace as felt disposed attended the service. As many did not understand English, Mr. Goodell delivered an impressive discourse in Italian. It is certainly not among the least of the novelties of our situation to hear a Yankee clergyman preaching in Italian on the banks of the Bosphorus to an audience composed of half a dozen different nations, assembled from

6

various quarters of the globe." — *Sketches of Turkey, by Dr. De Kay.*

Mr. Goodell's journal continues: —

"*Saturday, August* 27. The plague increases in the village. This morning an Italian physician died of it a few doors from us. There is much consternation. We established quarantine regulations, as most others around us had done previously.

" *Tuesday, August* 30. In the midst of cholera, plague, and conflagration the Lord has hitherto been our preserver. Other families around us have been 'minished and brought low,' but ours has in great mercy been built up, and has this day been increased by a son, — an event, however, in no way deserving special notice, except that he is the first American child born in Constantinople or its suburbs. May he be born again, and seek 'a better country, even an heavenly.'"

On the same day Mr. Goodell received from Commodore Porter the following note: —

AMERICAN HOUSE,
Tuesday afternoon, Aug. 30, 1831.

MY DEAR SIR, — I congratulate you and Mrs. Goodell on the accession to your family, and hope the boy may long live to be a blessing to you.

I had been endeavoring to get a room fitted up for his accommodation, in expectation of the event, but did not succeed in time. It shall be ready, however, by the time Mrs. Goodell will be able to move, and then, as I shall be alone, I beg you to come and take up your residence with me as long as it may suit your convenience.

With the best wishes to you, Mrs. Goodell, and all the little ones.   Yours truly,

DAVID PORTER.

The spirit in which this graceful hospitality was accepted is expressed in the following extract from the journal of Mr. Goodell: —

" *October* 19, 1831. Accepted of the kind and pressing invitation of the American *Chargé d'affaires*, Commodore Porter, to spend the winter with him, and removed to his

house. He has assigned us four rooms, two of which he has
entirely fitted up for us at his own expense. All the return
we have it in our power to make him for this kindness is to
pray that we may be to him what the Ark was to Obed-
edom, — a blessing to his house. May He who made Joseph
useful in Egypt, Nehemiah in the court of Persia, and Daniel
in Shushan the Palace, make us useful in our present residence; and 'in simplicity and godly sincerity, not with
fleshly wisdom, but by the grace of God, may we have our
conversation in the world.'"

This was the commencement of an intimacy that continued
with little interruption until the death of Commodore Porter,
in 1843, while he was yet representing the government of
the United States at the Sublime Porte. The American
ambassador for many years took the liveliest interest in the
work of the missionary, giving him his protection and the
warmest personal friendship; accompanying him on his missionary tours, and affording him material aid in carrying out
his plans for the welfare of the people to whom he was sent.
Still more valuable was the return which the ambassador
for Christ made by his Christian counsel and kindness and
fidelity and prayers, which never ceased to encircle the
Commodore, until he breathed his last while Mr. Goodell
was kneeling at his bedside in prayer.

Sabbath, September 25, Mr. Goodell preached as usual at
the house of the American *Chargé*, of which he made special
record, as being the occasion of the baptism of his own child,
Constantine Washington. This name was given at the suggestion of several American friends then at the Turkish
capital, on account of his being the first American child born
at Constantinople. Several German, Greek, and Papal-
Armenian friends were present at the service.

In the early part of October, Constantinople and the
vicinity were visited with one of the most remarkable hail-
storms of which we have any authentic record, the hail
falling in masses of ice. Mr. Goodell describes it in his
journal: —

" *October* 5, 1831. At seven o'clock this morning occurred the most dreadful hail-storm that I ever witnessed. The roaring of the storm was heard for fifteen or twenty minutes before it reached us, and was at the time supposed to be the rumbling of distant thunder. As it approached, our attention was arrested by the very singular appearance of the Bosphorus. It seemed as if some person was, at intervals, throwing brickbats or paving-stones into it from the roofs of the houses. Observing, however, the same appearance at a distance from the shore, I concluded for a moment it must be large fish jumping out of the water. But immediately the storm rushed on with awful fury; the stones fell, indeed, thick as hail; almost every pane of glass that was exposed was broken; the tilings of the houses were cut to pieces, and the water came down in streams into our chambers; while the whole surface of the Bosphorus was splashed up into the air in a manner it is impossible to describe. Our rooms were covered with glass, hailstones, and water. Several persons received severe contusions on their limbs, geese were killed, and the poor dogs ran in every direction in the streets yelping, and wondering who could be pelting them so unmercifully with stones. Some of the hailstones weighed 130 drachms, and some are reported to have weighed 150 drachms. We ourselves measured two of the hailstones, that were five and six inches in circumference; and one of our neighbors, an apothecary, measured one, of which Dr. Walsh took a drawing, that was fourteen inches in circumference.*

---

* This statement of the size of the hailstones, with their weight, a pound and a half, may appear incredible, but much larger masses of ice are recorded as having fallen. "On the 4th June, 1814, hail from thirteen to fifteen inches diameter fell in Ohio. In Orkney Islands, on the 24th July, 1818, during thunder, a very remarkable shower of hail took place. The stones were as large as a goose's egg, and mixed with large masses of ice. In June, 1835, hail fully three inches in circumference fell near Edinburgh, from a dense cloud during a thunder-storm. On the 8th May, 1832, an immense mass of aggregated hailstones fell in Hungary, measuring about a yard in length, and nearly two feet in depth. A hailstone, described by Captain Delcrosse as having fallen at Baconniere in July, 1819, was fifteen inches in circumference, and had a beautifully radiated structure, showing it to be a single hailstone." — *Buchan's Meteorology, Edinburgh*, 1867.

The storm lasted near half an hour, though not the whole time with such fury; and the oldest residents and the greatest travellers amongst us say they never saw the like before.

" *October* 8. Yesterday and to-day have been cold, stormy, uncomfortable days, and the rain still continues. The tiling of our house was so much injured by the hail-storm, and the windows so broken, that our rooms are scarcely in a habitable state. The water comes down or through in almost all parts of them, and we have to huddle together like sheep from corner to corner to get a dry place, and we can hardly find a spot to lay our heads at night. The judgments of God have certainly been various and very terrible in this country. 'He gave them hail for rain, and flaming fire in their land.' "

CHAPTER IX.

THE city of Constantinople, at the time of Mr. Goodell's arrival, contained, including the suburbs, a population of about 1,000,000, of various nationalities and religions. The Turks and other Mohammedans comprised more than half; the Greeks and Armenians each numbered about 150,000, the former being the more numerous; there were about 50,000 Jews; the remainder was made up of Franks and people from almost·every part of the world. These several classes formed distinct communities, which for the most part occupied different quarters of the city, or different suburbs, — the Turks having almost exclusive possession of the city proper; the Greeks, Armenians, Jews, &c., occupying Galata, Pera, Hasskeuy, and other adjacent villages. They were all living, as now, under an anomalous form of government, the Sublime Porte, as the Sultan's government is called, being supreme, while each separate nation had its own head, with a regularly organized system of government, subject only to the Sultan. Of this peculiar political constitution of things we shall have occasion to speak more at large in a subsequent chapter.

When Mr. Goodell went to Constantinople, his mission was to the Armenians, who were descendants of the ancient inhabitants of Armenia. The nation embraced Christianity about the commencement of the fourth century; but, like all the Oriental churches, the Armenian had become exceedingly corrupt. It was almost wholly given up to superstition and to idolatrous worship of saints, including the Virgin Mary, pictures, &c. The Armenians hold to transubstantiation, and worship the host; and, indeed, have adopted most of the errors of popery. Nearly half the days of the year are fast-days. Their feast-days are regarded as more sacred than the Lord's day. As with all rigid formalists, the weightier matters of the law and of the gospel are considered of small account compared with the punctilious performance of religious rites and ceremonies. They have numerous grades of the clergy, at the head of which is the Catholicos. The Patriarch at Constantinople is only a bishop, and is the civil head of the Armenians in that part of Turkey. The priests are required to be married men, but no priest can be married a second time. If his wife dies, he may become a *vartabed*, — a sort of preaching monk, — of whom many are attached to different churches, but he cannot become a bishop. This restriction to one wife for a lifetime is said to make the priests exceedingly careful of their wives, and far more ready than lay husbands to relieve them of the cares and burdens of life. A traveller speaks of seeing a priest in the interior engaged in hanging out the clothes he had washed, who gave as the reason that his wife was delicate, and he wished to preserve her as long as he could, for if he lost her he could not have another. The bishops, contrary to Paul's special injunction, are not allowed to marry at all.

The Armenians were an enterprising people, and the great wealth of the bankers, who were nearly all Armenians, made them very influential throughout the empire, even with the Turkish officials, who were largely dependent upon them for pecuniary advances and assistance. The various connections of this people with different parts of the country, and the influence which they were in a position to exert, in promoting the spread of the Gospel in Turkey, made it exceedingly desirable that they should embrace the truth; and as priests and people were alike in the grossest spiritual darkness, and "had need that one should teach them which be the first principles of the oracles of God," the first mission to Constantinople was for their special benefit. But the way was providentially hedged up for a time. The circumstances which turned the attention of Mr. Goodell temporarily to the Greek and Turkish population are detailed in the following communication to the Board: —

"*November* 21, 1831. You may, perhaps, wonder that I have done so much for the Greeks and so little for the Armenians. The reasons are: 1, That in the various plagues with which the country has been afflicted I have, in the providence of God, been brought much more into contact with the Greeks than with the Armenians; and, 2, that as regards Lancasterian schools, I had absolutely nothing to begin with among the Armenians, — no lessons, no suitable books, no master; nor could I well give them an idea of the system without a living model, such a model as these Greek schools do actually present. In an interview which I had with the Armenian Patriarch, soon after my arrival at Constantinople, he spoke favorably of such schools, and wished us to take some Armenian priests or schoolmasters, and instruct them in the system. Those terrible dispensations of Heaven which soon followed interrupted the plans we were maturing for their good, and for a season cut off, in a great measure, all intercourse with them; indeed, since the burning of Pera, and the consequent dispersion of its inhabitants, I have not seen one of the Armenians with whom I had previously formed an acquaintance, and it was not till very recently that I found among them a teacher in whom I felt sufficient confidence to employ him and appoint over this business."

In the course of a few weeks he established four Greek Lancasterian schools at the capital and in the suburbs, and these after a few months were largely increased in number; one of them, almost as soon as it was opened, had more than a hundred boys. The Russian ambassador became warmly interested in the enterprise, and assumed the expense of the tuition of a number of boys, after providing them with suitable clothing at his own cost. Commodore Porter also stood ready on all occasions to second these efforts of the missionary. Great wisdom was needed in the management of the schools and in the instruction of the pupils, owing to the strong prejudices of the people. The Greeks were very jealous of evangelical principles, and preferred that their children should be taught the doctrines and trained in the ceremonies of the church, rather than that their minds should be developed and enlightened. The Armenians were still more bigoted. The papal priests, on learning that the New Testament was used in the Greek schools, endeavored to excite opposition; but as the schools were not intended for their people, and as they enjoyed the approbation of the Russian ambassador, and of others connected with the Greek Church, they were unsuccessful in their opposition.

It was the policy of Mr. Goodell to induce the people to establish schools for themselves, while he furnished the plans, and, as far as possible, selected suitable teachers, making the people responsible for their maintenance and management. They were thus saved from the charge of being under foreign control. Before the end of a year he gave the following hopeful account of his educational work: —

"Of the importance of Lancasterian schools in this country, we think that we and our patrons at home can have but one opinion. To afford them encouragement and patronage, and to aid in extending the system as much as possible, we are confident, should occupy a large portion of our attention. More than twenty such schools have been established among the Greeks in this neighborhood within the last year, one of which is in our own house, and contains between twenty and thirty girls; and, did the room admit of it, it would doubtless contain twice the present number. In these schools there cannot be much less than two thousand children, one hundred of whom may be girls. And though with all of them we have not so much connection as we could wish, yet it is matter of devout thankfulness that this work has to such a degree fallen into our hands, and that we have been permitted directly ourselves, or indirectly through our agent, to exercise so much influence over them. I love to think of these schools, particularly as the business of instruction is thus taken away from bigoted and vulgar minds, and put into the hands of those who are more liberal and enlightened, and who teach something besides the liturgy and mummery

6*   I

of the church; and we hope and pray that many of the rising generation may be a generation to praise God."

In the mean while, he was prosecuting the general work of the mission, embracing every opportunity for bringing before the minds of the people the truths of the Gospel. Some extracts from his journal and correspondence will give an idea of his work, and of the character of the people among whom he was called to exercise his ministry. The first of these extracts contains a simple but complete answer to the sacramentarian view of the Lord's Supper, prevalent even now among more enlightened communities: —

"*October* 24, 1831. Read and conversed with the two papal Armenian youth, as indeed I do with one or both of them almost every evening. The portion of Scripture, which came in course, was part of the twenty-sixth chapter of Matthew, which gave me an opportunity of explaining the nature both of the passover and of the Lord's Supper. The design of both, I remarked, was similar, and it was very remarkable that the language used in respect to both was similar. Thus, in the one case, it is said, ' Prepare the passover,' 'kill the passover,' ' eat the passover,' &c. But the passover was the *passing over* of the houses of the children of Israel, when the first-born of Egypt were destroyed, and was not, therefore, a thing which could be either killed or eaten, or on which any such sort of thing could be predicated. The disciples did not and could not eat this *passing over of houses;* they only prepared, killed, and ate the lamb which commemorated this event. In the other case it is said, 'Take, eat; this is my body.' But the disciples neither took His body nor ate it; they only took and ate the bread which represented it. The language in neither case is literal, but in both is figurative, and in both is easily understood, and in both is to be understood in the same way.

" *November* 28. Every thing in regard to schools seems to be going on better and better, and my influence seems to be widening and strengthening every day. The schools are also, as might naturally be expected, exciting a desire and creating a market for the Holy Scriptures and for religious tracts. These angels have troubled the waters of the pool. I hope all the first ones who step in will be healed; and I am glad I am here to help some of the poor, impotent folk in, who would otherwise, I fear, lie a long time in their diseased state. Indeed, as Mrs. Goodell has already observed to some of her correspondents, ' We evidently came to Constantinople at the very right time, and, notwithstanding our losses and privations, we rejoice that we came when we did.' "

The memory of the one to whom the following letter was addressed, as well as of the writer, will give to it special interest : —

"CONSTANTINOPLE, Dec. 5, 1831.
"TO MRS. JOANNA BETHUNE:

" DEAR MADAM, — As Dr. De Kay, of your city, is proceeding directly from this to New York, I avail myself of the opportunity of replying to your esteemed favor of July 6. It was received early in October, though the books for Infant School No. 1, which you sent at the same time, were not received until very recently. I received also with these several other books, of which your letter made no mention, and I therefore conclude that I am indebted to other friends in New York, as well as yourself. All the books, both yours and theirs, were very acceptable, and the more so as we had recently suffered such a loss by the conflagration at Pera, of which you have doubtless heard. Indeed, by that terrible visitation we were, in almost every respect, excepting that our persons were untouched and the lives of our children graciously preserved, reduced in one short hour to the condition of the patriarch Job. But our friends in this quarter, instead of sitting down, like his at the first, upon the ground with us, and not speaking a word of comfort, at once manifested great sympathy and kindness toward us, which they expressed in deeds as well as in words. And if those at a distance do the same, we and they shall be like Job and his friends at the last, when they all came to comfort him ; and he prayed for them, and every man also gave him a piece of money, and every one an ear-ring of gold ; and the Lord blessed the latter end of Job more than his beginning.

" As to our circumstances, our schools, and our prospects, I beg leave to refer you to Dr. De Kay. He has resided here about four months, and near half the time in our own family ; and to his professional advice and services on several occasions, as well as to his friendship, and that of Messrs.

Eckford and Rhind, who are also from New York, we acknowledge with pleasure our obligations.

"We commend ourselves and our labors, and those whose temporal and everlasting good we are seeking, to your prayers.   We love to think of the good people of your city ; of the intercourse we enjoyed with some of them in former years ; of our many obligations to them for their repeated kindnesses ; and of the visitations of the Holy Spirit, and the great increase which has in consequence been made to your churches.   The Lord add to their number a thousand-fold, and increase you more and more, you and your children.

"Mrs. Goodell unites in Christian salutations.   Remember us also to all our friends in New York who may inquire after us.   May you and their families, all of them, be like the interesting family at Bethany, where the Saviour often visited, and where every one loved Him and was loved by Him ! May the children of your infant and Sabbath schools also cry in the temple, ' Hosanna to the Son of David ! '   And may every one of them be taken up by Him in His arms and blessed.

"Excuse haste, and believe me, my dear madam,
"Yours truly,
"W. GOODELL."

"*January* 14, 1832.   Went to Galata, and thence nearly to the Seven Towers, to visit the Armenian patriarch in his palace.   He appeared to be about fifty years old, his beard long, black, and thick, befitting his exalted station, and his deportment in all respects marked with dignity.   Both he and his vicar received me very graciously, and conversed with much apparent interest about America, schools, &c. The patriarch was very inquisitive respecting our religion, and wished to know whether we followed Calvin or Luther, the vicar having previously laid it down as an incontrovertible proposition that all Protestants were followers either of one or of the other.   I replied that in America there was the most perfect freedom in regard to religious sentiments and worship, and that there were various denominations of Christians ; and that, though some of these, it is true, were called Calvinists and some Lutherans, and others by still different names, yet I knew the fact to be that they did not generally inquire what Luther, Calvin, or any other man believed in order to know what to believe themselves, but were remarkably free from all shackles of this kind, and inquired simply what God had said in His holy word. To this they at once bowed assent. The patriarch then inquired about missionary operations in China, which led me to speak of the missions recently established there; of those also in India and Burmah; and of the wonderful change that had been produced in the moral condition of the inhabitants at the Sandwich Islands. He was very anxious to know what kind of Christians our missionaries made them, what sect they were made to follow, what name they took, &c. I told him that they were not baptized in the name of Calvin, Luther, the pope, or any one else, but simply 'in the name of the Father, and of the Son, and of the Holy Ghost;' that they embraced Christianity in its primitive purity, without any thing foreign being mixed with it; and that they were formed into churches that ' knew no man after the flesh,' but received the pure unadulterated word of God as the sufficient and only rule of faith and practice. To this he, with his vicar, again gave the fullest assent, but seemed at the same time to be filled with wonder at so extraordinary and yet so reasonable a course. He expressed for me and for America much of the Oriental kind of love, of which every man here seems to keep always a large stock on hand, and said if he had not seen me he must have gone there, but in being favored with a sight of me, he had seen America, and was glad.

"*January* 18. The Epiphania of the Greeks. Went to the Greek church a quarter before six, while it was yet dark, and found a great crowd assembled in the yard or inclosure of the church, and the priests chanting their service over a barrel or large firkin of water, with the cross planted by the side of it. As soon as they had finished blessing and consecrating it, and were retiring to the church, there was a universal rush of the people for some of the holy water to drink, and to carry away in bottles; and such pushing, pulling, scrambling, bawling ensued as I have seldom seen even at football.

" On entering the church, I was conducted to the seat belonging to the principal priest, and where I, of course, had a good view of all that passed. In the midst of the chants and prayers, this priest went at different times through the crowd with a basin or cruse of the holy water in one hand

and a small brush, made of a few twigs tied together, in the other ; and, while the people bowed down to kiss his hand, he sprinkled them with the brush dipped in the holy water, and crossed them on the forehead with it.

" Near the close the same priest carried round the broken bread; and again there was a general scramble of men, women, and children to get a bit, and, on bowing the head to receive it, they always kissed the hand that gave it.

" A large procession was now formed, and the principal priest carried the cross with great formality and ceremony to baptize it, as they term it ; that is, to throw it into the Bosphorus, and see who will plunge in and get it first.   They proceeded, chanting as they went, to a fine quay opposite the Russian palace.   I stood on the lowest step, with the priest on the same step next to me on one side, and six naked fellows, shivering with the cold, on the other, while an immense crowd of people were behind, stretching along the shore to the right and left, or were in boats directly in front.   In order to deceive the poor fellows, and put them off their guard, the priest several times raised his hand and *made as if;* they laughed at the artifice practised upon them, and the people laughed, and the priest looked at me, and laughed as heartily as any of them.   At length he flung it two or three rods from the shore, and instantly there was a headlong plunge after it, and a momentary but vehement struggle who should first get possession of it.   The successful candidate first immersed it the whole length of his arm beneath the waves, then kissed it, and presented it successively to the lips of his comrades for a salute from each of them.   The ladies in the boats now vociferated to him, all unclothed as he was, to come to them, that they might next enjoy the privilege of kissing it.   This, as it appeared, he felt constrained to do, though the priests and elders on shore were in the mean time bawling after him to hasten back to them, that they might give it the same token of love, and march it back in triumph to the church.

" The aga of the village was present to keep order on the occasion ! a Mussulman, with a whip in his hand, to keep Christians from devouring one another, or committing any excesses during their religious solemnities !   The whole appeared like a farce.

" *February* 14, 1832. My birth-day ! A severe snow-storm. I recollect to have heard from my mother that there was a

tremendous snow-storm the day I was born, forty years ago
to-day, both as to the day of the week, Tuesday, and day of
the month, 14th. My life has been a stormy one, but the
Lord has ever afforded a shelter from the blast. How many
of my beloved friends and acquaintances have gone to heaven,
while I am still a pilgrim and a stranger, not yet arrived at
the heavenly rest! One, the Rev. R. Cushman, with whom
I have spent hours and hours in singing the songs of Zion, is
now tuning his harp before the throne, while I must sing the
Lord's song in a strange land.

> " ' When shall I bow amongst them there,
>   And view thy face and sing thy love ? '

> " ' I would not live alway; I ask not to stay
>   Where storm after storm rises dark o'er the way.'

"I am now as old as Caleb was when he was sent by
Moses to spy out the country. I have lived as long as the
children of Israel were wandering in the wilderness, and of
me, as of them, can it now be said, ' Forty years long was
I grieved with this generation.'

" *February* 15. The snow fell yesterday about mid-leg deep,
the storm continuing from morning till evening. It seemed
an old acquaintance, and I went out both yesterday and this
morning in the midst of it and bid it welcome, and took it in
my hands and made a snowball. I also took with me our
three eldest children, to introduce them to it. They were delighted with its appearance, saying it looked like soap-suds.
I set W. down in the midst of the snow, and when he began
to sink in it he cried out, not knowing how deep he was
going. Many fine icicles were hanging from the houses,
some of which I succeeded in getting, and presented to my
children as old friends. Some of the snow and icicles they
brought into the house to see what they were, and what would
become of them when placed near the fire. It snowed only
once at Beyrout all the time we were there, and that was
the second winter. At Malta it never snows.

" *March* 24. This morning took our final departure from
the Commodore's. We have lived with him since the 19th
of October, a little more than five months, and have every
day shared his hospitality and kind attentions; and no
unpleasant word has ever passed between us. May he at
last have ' a building of God, an house not made with hands,
eternal in the heavens.' The house I have taken here be-

longs to Ismail Effendi, who has once been ambassador to England, who was, several years since, sent into exile by the present Sultan for his infidel sentiments, but was afterward permitted to return to the capital. This house is the one in which we found shelter the first and second nights after the great fire. In all our removings may we, like Abraham, erect an altar unto the Lord, and call upon the name of Jehovah. May every room in this house be consecrated, and here may the Lord come unto us and bless us.

" *April* 2.   Baptized a child, infant daughter of the Dutch consul, by the name of Sophie Hortense. The father is a Frenchman and a Protestant; the mother, a Polish lady and a Catholic. The whole house of Scanavi were present, also all of my own family, together with Panayotes, whom I met in the street. I read portions from the Modern Greek Testament, baptized the child in Italian, prayed in English, and conversed in Turkish, which Panayotes translated. Mr. Borelli and Madame Scanavi were very anxious I should baptize the child, and the mother was fearful lest it should die, as it was not well. May it be baptized with the Holy Ghost.

" *April* 27.   As our excellent friends, Dr. and Mrs. W., are about returning to England, I accepted an invitation to join them in a short excursion. We first went to Beshik Tash to see the Sultan go to the mosque. He was attended with much less pomp and ceremony than when I have seen him on former occasions; but I observed what I never did before, that, on his leaving the mosque, and appearing on horseback in the presence of the multitude, two persons burnt incense before him as though he were a deity. Perhaps, however, no idea of that kind was intended to be conveyed, as the custom of burning incense prevails in all the Oriental churches.

" We afterwards went to what is called the Ballukly, or Fish Church. This is a Greek church, or rather the ruins of a church, for it was torn down by the Janizaries at the commencement of the Greek revolution. It is outside the Silivria Gate, near Top-Kapusi, where the Turks made an entrance when they took Constantinople. The story on which the great celebrity of the church was founded is this: The day on which the city was captured was a fast, and the priests belonging to the church were preparing a fast-day dinner of fried fish. While they were thus engaged, some one brought them word that the city was taken by the Turks.

An incredulous priest said, that sooner than believe this he would believe that the fish that were then frying in the pan would jump out into the fish-pond, and swim about alive; which was no sooner said than done, and, according to the story, if not the faith, of these people, the fish are to be seen swimming about, fried on one side, unto this day. To-day is the anniversary of that event, and wonderful miracles are said to be wrought there on these occasions. We found multitudes of people assembled, — men, women, and children, — not only Greeks, but Turks, Armenians, and Franks. The place is in the midst of a very extensive Turkish burying-ground, and everywhere in the midst of this mighty congregation of the dead was heard the sound, if not of the *viol*, yet of the *bagpipe*, — the players sitting upon the sepulchral monuments, and the Greeks dancing merrily among the thick graves. To go to the graveyard to make *kaif*, *i.e.*, to have a jollification, — to dance, drink coffee, tell love-stories, and show their gayest dresses and liveliest manners and most beauteous forms, is very common in Constantinople, and with others besides Greeks.

"The fish-pond is below, under the ruins of the church. The entrance to it was guarded by Turks, who exacted tribute of all that went in. ' But the fish, — where are the fish ? ' said I, rather impatiently, to some priests, who were selling candles to assist our vision in the broad light of mid-day. They replied, with great calmness and becoming gravity, that the multitudes of people had frightened them away, so that not one was to be seen. But though we saw no fish, we saw *fishing* enough ; for there was an abundance of priests, holding plates at every corner to receive offerings. The maimed, the deaf, the lame, the halt, and the blind were there ; but I saw them return as they came, — *without benefit*. I gave some of these miserable objects a few paras ; but I did not see one 'walking and leaping and praising God' for the gift of healing.

"As it was too late to return to Buyuk-Dèrè, I went with Mr. F., who has rooms in a khan in Constantinople, and we finally dined and spent the night with his Turkish teacher, Halim Effendi, who is at the head of a large Mussulman school in the city. He reads and speaks Greek as well as Turkish ; and he had in his library copies of the New Testament, both in Turkish and in Greek, also Mr. Temple's spelling-book, and other useful works. He is a great friend to these schools of mutual instruction, one of which he has visited; wishes much that the system may be adopted by the Turks, and says that if the capudan pasha or the seraskier pasha would patronize such a school, the experiment would not fail to succeed. I told him I thought I would make use of my friend, Mr. Eckford, in bringing the subject under their consideration.

" Halim Effendi is distantly related to Ismail Effendi, and, like his distinguished relative, he drinks wine, curses the prophet, speaks highly of the life of Christ, and contemptibly of that of Mohammed. In the course of the evening he closed the door, and asked me, 'Who is Christ? Whom do you consider Him to be?' I replied that I knew Him to possess human nature; in other words, to be a man, because He sustained the relations, performed the actions, and suffered the infirmities of man; He was a son, a brother, a neighbor, a master, a friend; He walked and talked, and ate and slept, and learnt and worked at His trade; was hungry, thirsty, fatigued, sorrowful, glad, &c.; that I knew Him also to possess a divine nature, or to be God, because He did the works of God, claimed an equality with God, and fully substantiated His claims by miracles. Upon this he immediately seized my hand, and kissed it, and declared that he had never heard such an answer before from the mouth of any one, Armenian, Greek, or Frank; that it expressed his belief exactly; and that Christ must be a most exalted personage, — *God*, if we pleased to call Him such. On his remarking something about the Christians of these countries, I told him he must not call them Christians; he might call them any thing else he chose, but the name *Christian* was most inappropriate; he must not judge of Christianity by their works or their ceremonies; they had forsaken the Gospel, and adopted other things instead thereof, which were any thing but Christianity. Here he again seized my hand, and declared that my words were true, as he could testify.

"*May* 2. Called at the palace of the Armenian patriarch; visited the schools there, which contain five hundred boys of different ages, and in several apartments. I afterward called upon the patriarch's vicar, first sending up word to know whether a visit would be acceptable. I was no sooner seated on the sofa than he began to examine me very closely on my religious faith, and to sift my answers in the presence of the priests and others in the room. As the object of my

visit was *schools*, I was sorry to have any thing of a contro-
versial nature introduced, and was disposed at first to waive
the subject; but I did not long think it best to decline giving
him a frank disclosure of my sentiments. He first brought
forward the subject of the eucharist; and, after asking how
often we received it, he wished to know what we considered
it to be. In order to avoid an answer, which I foresaw must
end in a dispute, I replied, in general terms, that we celebrated the ordinance in remembrance of Christ, of His love,
His sufferings, and His death. Not being satisfied with this,
he put the question in a still more direct manner. I told
him that we always used the Scripture language on this subject, — 'This is my body,' and 'This is my blood.'

"*Q.* Is it not, then, real flesh and blood that you partake of?

"*A.* No; everybody among us knows better than that
from the *taste*.

" *Q.* But do they not consider it to be changed?

"*A. How* changed? Changed into *what?*

" *Q.* Do they not, at least, suppose the power of God to
be in it, in an especial manner?

"*A.* When Christ says, 'I am the door,' and 'I am the
vine,' is the power of God in the door or in the vine in a
more especial manner than it is in the *window* or in the *fig-
tree?*

" Here all present burst into a hearty laugh, in which the
vicar himself joined. He then asked whether I did not
believe that there was something in it *essentially spiritual.* I
replied that every bit and particle of it went into the stomach
and was there digested, and was then 'cast out into the
draught;' that the way to a man's heart was not through his
mouth; that nothing entering in at the mouth goes to the
heart, but to the stomach, and can neither purify nor ' defile
the man' in any other sense except a *physical* one. Is it
not so, Effendi?

" Yes, true; but is it, then, of no benefit to our *souls?*
said he.

"*A.* Certainly; it was given us for no other purpose.

" *Q.* But if it be not *changed*, not made in some way
essentially holy, how can it be of any *spiritual* benefit
to us?

"*A.* Are the letters of the alphabet *spiritual* substances,
or *material,* — *things made with men's hands?*

" The latter, certainly.

" But when we make use of these material things in reading the Scriptures, are not our souls benefited?

" To this he, in the midst of another general laugh from those present, assented, and pressed me no more on the subject. I then told him, what he seemed little prepared to expect, that we in America consider the ordinance so sacred that we never profaned it by giving it to the whole congregation indiscriminately, but to those only who in the judgment of charity were true Christians.

" After this he asked about our funerals, our way of making priests, confession, &c. And I gave him a very particular account of our customs in these respects, with which he and the others seemed rather pleased than otherwise. He then appointed one of the teachers present, an interesting and intelligent youth, who has visited our school at Galata, and who is much pleased with the system, to come and spend several days in the school, in order to make himself master of the system, and to introduce it among the Armenians."

In May, 1832, Mr. Goodell, accompanied by Commodore Porter, made a journey to Broosa, which is about eighty miles south-east of Constantinople. As the object of the journey was to examine the religious condition of the country, he took the route by land, around the head of the Gulf of Bithynia, thereby doubling the distance, but enabling him to visit some of the more important cities and villages by the way. He stopped at Nicomedia, the former capital of Bithynia, the residence of the Emperor Constantine and of several of his successors. Here, too, Dioclesian had his winter palace, and from this place he issued his edicts against Christianity, and began the terrible persecution by which he hoped to erase the Christian name from the earth. The route lay also by the almost deserted city of Nice (or Isnik, as it was then called), where two of the ancient councils were held, the one called by Constantine A.D. 325, at which the Arian heresy was condemned; the other in 787, under the Empress Irene, and her son, Constantine VI., at which image-worship was established. The desolate condition of this once famous city he describes as follows : —

"The city cannot be much less than six miles in circumference, and it is surrounded by double walls, the inner one of which is twenty-five feet high, and at the base fourteen feet thick. These walls are forty-eight feet apart, with a fosse between, and at the distance of every forty paces they have upon them a double line of marble and brick towers, square-built. The gates are triple, one within another, evidently rebuilt at an ancient period, from materials still more ancient. Indeed, almost every thing seems to have been rebuilt again and again. Even the very mud cottages of the present generation are composed of fragments of the fine arts; and in them, as well as in those parts of the walls of the city that have been repaired, are inserted here and there mutilated bas-reliefs and Greek inscriptions, often turned upside down. But most of the habitations of this once crowded population are totally obliterated. The ploughshare now passes over a great part of the ancient city; the sepulchres of the dead are ploughed up, and fields of wheat and mulberry now occupy the sites of ancient palaces and temples and mausoleums. The ivy runs over the wall; the wild bird screams upon the mouldering towers; the tall grass waves in the midst of deserted halls; and briers and weeds luxuriate where nought but taste and elegance and beauty and fashion and gayety and pleasure once existed.

"Here we saw the stork build her nest, and the gray squirrel revel without fear amidst marble figures defaced and fractured, but still disclosing the charms of symmetry and proportion, and the design of the ancient Greek chisel. Here we saw mosques and baths that were built from the ruins of pagan and Christian temples, themselves crumbled to ruins; and shafts and capitals of marble columns strewed upon the ground, and literally turning to dust by natural decay. Indeed, the tooth of time has left here more signal marks of his ravages than I have ever seen in any place before. It is very common in this country to find an extensive burying-ground connected with a comparatively small village, showing the population to have once been much greater than at present, or the congregation of the dead to be far greater than that of the living. But here even the burying-grounds are themselves buried; the sepulchres are literally sepulchred. Pagan priests and Christian bishops, councils of prelates and armies of crusaders, potentates and powers, countless myriads of this once populous and luxurious city, have passed away, and not even the repository of their ashes can be found any more at all.   Thou, Lord, in the beginning hast laid the foundation of the earth ; and the heavens are the work of thy hands ; they shall perish, but thou remainest ; and they all shall wax old as doth a garment ; and as a vesture shalt thou fold them up, and they shall be changed ; but thou art the same, and thy years shall not fail.' "

He spent four or five days at Broosa, visiting the Armenians, Greeks, and Jews in their homes, calling upon the ecclesiastics, and gathering information in regard to the spiritual condition and wants of the people.   The impressions made upon his mind he communicated to the Board in an earnest recommendation of Broosa as a desirable point to be occupied for missionary labor.   On his return to Constantinople, he wrote : —

" This whole tour has been made in the ancient Bithynia, the three principal towns of which are Nicomedia, Nice, and Broosa, all of which, with many others, we visited.   Paul and his companions once 'assayed to go into Bithynia, but the Spirit suffered them not.'   The Gospel, however, was introduced there soon after, and flourished ; and it was 'to the strangers scattered throughout' not only 'Pontus, Galatia, Cappadocia, and Asia,' but also 'Bithynia,' that Peter addressed his first epistle.   We experienced much kindness from the people in almost every place we visited in this interesting country ; but such 'strangers,' 'strangers and pilgrims on the earth,' whose treasures and hearts are in heaven ; who 'desire a better country, that is, an heavenly ;' and who feel and act as though they are travelling through the wilderness to their eternal inheritance, — I fear are not now to be found in the whole country.   They need some one to 'expound unto them the way of God more perfectly ;' to 'teach them again which be the first principles of the oracles' of God ;' to show them 'what manner of love the Father hath bestowed upon us ;' to 'turn away their ears from fables ;' and to call their attention to 'Him that speaketh from heaven.' "

The place was occupied as a mission station in 1834, by the Rev. Benjamin Schneider, who not long after was joined by other laborers; and it has enjoyed the signal manifesta-tions of God's presence in a blessing upon their labors ever since.

A large number of schools for Greek boys being in success-ful operation at Constantinople, Mr. Goodell, in May, 1832, opened the first school for girls, which in the course of a few days had twenty-five scholars. This last movement, being such a decided innovation upon the customs and opinions of the people, roused the ecclesiastics. On the 5th of August the Greek synod issued an excommunication against all who gave it any encouragement. The document ran thus: "Since the man" (Mr. Goodell) "who has a school in his house is different from us in his form, habit, and ethics, therefore, whoever send their children to the school, let them be excommunicated."

The action of the synod awakened a counter-excitement. The people, and especially the women, began to see a new light dawning upon them and upon their daughters. If they did not in turn excommunicate the bishop, through whom the edict was promulgated, they did not fail to bestow upon him some of their choicest anathemas. The bishop, when remon-strated with for his course in attempting to break up the girls' school, replied with great emphasis, " Why should girls learn to read and write ? They will be writing love-letters next!" which, in such a country, would of course be a heinous crime, and was not to be thought of for a moment.

Amidst the excitement and controversy among the Greeks and the Armenians, almost unexpectedly there sprang up a desire on the part of the Turks to have schools established for the benefit of their own children, a few enlightened men taking the lead, and taking also the responsibility, which was not light. " At an examination of the school at Arnaut-Keuy," wrote Mr. Goodell, " several Mussulmans were present, among whom was a *bin-bashy* and an *on-bin-bashy* (Turkish officers). They are determined to have a school among the Mussul-mans, and had a long talk with Mr. L. on the subject.

They have already selected a house at Beshik-Tash, and prepared seats, with the knowledge of the Sultan, but intend to keep it a secret from the seraskier pasha, and in the course of a month will invite the Sultan, and surprise him with their progress."

This project was fully carried out. One school for Turkish children was established at Beshik-Tash and another at Scutari, suburbs of Constantinople, which were visited by the Turkish officials, who manifested the warmest interest in the wonderful progress made by the children under the new system of instruction, so different from the old and useless routine. Azim Bey, the son of a former ambassador to England, a highly educated man, was foremost in promoting the enterprise, and on one occasion he addressed the scholars as follows : —

" His most sublime Majesty, Sultan Mahmoud, desires your good. These schools are no benefit to him, but he designs them for your benefit. You have come from different parts of the empire; you are in the morning of life, and it is now in your power to become learned and wise. In the old Mussulman schools nothing of any value was learned ; men were asses ; but here asses may become men. This badge of rank which you see on my breast was given me by my sovereign, as a token of his regard. To-morrow he can take it away, and then I shall be as undistinguished as any other man. But what knowledge I acquire he cannot take away from me. The terrible conflagrations which, you see, consume almost every thing else, cannot burn it; nor can the floods overwhelm it, or tempest sweep it away. Knowledge, therefore, young men, knowledge is the best property you can possess."

Varieties occur in missionary life, as shown by the following extracts from his journal : —

" *July* 24. Was visited by the father of a young lady in Yeni-Keuy. He was my most humble servant, and one of his daughters was still more so, as she wished me to give her a shift, a pair of stockings, or something to help her to marry. He had heard my fame from afar.

"Another man called, a shoemaker living in Pera, who, pulling off his hat and bowing, introduced himself in the following singular manner: 'I have the honor to find you at home, sir. I am an Englishman, sir. I've heard you preach on board the cravat (corvette), sir. I've come on a curious business; you'll not believe me, but it's true, sir. I must take an oath 'fore you, sir, that I'll not drink a drop of ardent spirit for a whole year. I'm not in liquor now, that's true, sir,' — at the same time thrusting his fingers instead of a comb into his hair, and looking altogether like one who was, as the sailors would say, *half seas over.*

"I told him that I was no magistrate, and had no authority to administer an oath, and that, moreover, it was my duty as a minister of Jesus Christ to endeavor to persuade men to leave off *swearing* as well as *drinking.*

"'I *must* swear to it,' said he; 'I must down on my knees 'fore you, sir; and you must read a chapter over me from the Bible; and I must swear on the Holy Gospel not to drink spirit, sir; nothing else will save me. I once took such an oath, and it answered the purpose for a year, and I must now renew it, or I'm a ruined man, sir. And unless I stop drinking I cannot be married to a young lady shortly.'

"I replied, you must regard the authority of Jehovah. If His high commands do not bind you, how can I suppose you will feel bound by an oath.

"'I know all that,' said he; 'I've been t'New York, and t'Philadelphia, and all along the coast of the Carolinas; I can repeat half of Mark, sir;' and, beginning at the second chapter of Matthew, he began to repeat it verbatim.

"At length I suggested that he might enter into a solemn *obligation,* similar to that which the members of the temperance societies take upon themselves in America. The poor man, who, notwithstanding his odd way of introducing the business, yet seemed really in earnest about it, was very doubtful whether such a pledge, without the formal administration of an oath, would be strong enough; but he finally concluded to make a trial. He wished the obligation to be for *one year only.* We told him that *for ever* would be still better. He thought *for ever* would be too long, but consented it should be for *five years;* and solemnly promised to drink nothing stronger than coffee for five years from July 24, 1832."

The following incident occurred about the same time : —

"After service on the Sabbath, I tied an Englishman to a papal Armenian lady. *Him* I tied in *English*, and *her* in *Turkish*. To *him* I read portions of the New Testament in *English*, and to *her* in *Greek*. She understood both Turkish and Greek, but some of her friends present understood only the *latter*. They had never seen Protestant worship before ; and, when we kneeled in prayer, they looked round, and, seeing no images, really thought at first, I believe, that we were worshipping our chairs. However they afterwards appeared gratified, and wondered to find us so religious a people, Protestants and atheists being synonymous terms with them. Not long ago we had to marry a couple in French. As we are constantly liable to be called upon to perform the ceremony in various languages, we concluded it best to prepare a *form* in these languages, that we might be ready for any emergency."

To a stranger visiting Mohammedan countries few incidents are more impressive than the cry from the minaret, calling the people to prayer at regular periods by day and during the night. The musical voice of the trained muezzin, the liquid intonations of the Arabic tongue, together with the sentiments expressed in the call, all make it to a reflecting mind seem like a voice from heaven, especially when heard in the stillness of night : —

> "Allah ekber ! Allah ekber !
> Esheden en la Allah, illa Allah," &c.

> " God is great ! God is great !
> I testify that there is no god but God.
> Come to peace ! come to happiness !
> Come to the garden of delights !
> God is great !" &c.

Or, as it is sometimes varied at night : —

> " God is great ! God is great !
> Prayer is better than sleep," &c.

The writer of these memoirs will never forget the impression made by this call, as he was wakened by it in the dead of night, on the plains of Sharon, in the land of Palestine. And once again these words seemed still more strikingly appropriate and suggestive. He had joined a company of missionary families on the shores of the Bosphorus, at the evening twilight, in their weekly meeting for social prayer. In the few moments of silence that immediately preceded the opening exercises, a musical voice from the minaret of a mosque near by was heard: "God is great! God is great! Come to peace! Come to happiness! Come to the garden of delights!" Could any summons be more appropriate to an assemblage of Christians met to draw near to the throne of the heavenly grace? It was near this same spot that Mr. Goodell wrote, Nov. 15, 1832: —

"Our house was next to the Turkish mosque, and five times a day did the white-turbaned muezzin ascend the minaret and proclaim the hour of prayer. The infidel Greek, whenever he could put his head out of sight, never failed to burst forth into contemptuous merriment; but it seemed to be a call to me to come boldly to the throne of grace by a new and living way, of which the Moslem knows nothing, and thus to lift up my heart with my voice unto God."

In the year 1832, Mr. Goodell was permitted to welcome to his field two fellow-laborers, who became literally fellow-apostles in the great reformation which by the Gospel and the grace of God was wrought among the nominal Christians of Turkey. The Rev. H. G. O. Dwight (who had previously made an extended tour of exploration in Armenia in company with Rev. Eli Smith) arrived at Constantinople, with Mrs. Dwight, on the 5th of June. His mission was to the Armenians. The Rev. William G. Schauffler arrived on the 31st of July, to labor among the Jews. These three families for a long time occupied the same house, and never was one family more perfectly united in feeling and service. This intimacy of fellowship was broken off only by the translation of Dr. Dwight, who was killed on a railway train in 1862, while on a visit to this country. Dr. Schauffler still survives, an active and efficient worker in the great cause in which they were so long and so happily engaged together.

CHAPTER X.

THE summer of 1832 was one of trouble and anxiety at the Turkish capital. First came the plague, of which we shall have occasion to speak more particularly hereafter. It prevailed in its most fatal form in the immediate neighborhood in which Mr. Goodell was then residing. He wrote at the time: "The vials of the wrath of God seem to be poured out upon this country; and though the people gnaw their tongues for pain, yet they repent not of their evil deeds. My little daughter asks whether there is any plague in heaven, for it says in the Revelation, 'Seven angels had the seven last plagues.'" After the plague, the cholera again made its appearance, and prevailed most fatally at Orta Keuy, the village to which Mr. Goodell had removed in August. Many of his neighbors were swept away by it, and he himself had a slight attack.

After these visitations of pestilence came rumors of war. The ambitious Viceroy of Egypt, Mohammed Ali, having exterminated the Mamelukes and extended his conquests in Arabia, sent an army into Syria under command of his adopted son, Ibrahim Pasha, took Acre by storm, and on the 20th of December, 1832, gained a complete victory over the Turkish forces, routing the entire army and taking the grand vizier prisoner. When the news of these events reached Constantinople, Mr. Goodell wrote to a friend: —

"*January* 1, 1833. You have doubtless heard from time to time of the successes of Ibrahim Pasha. The grand vizier is now his prisoner, and the whole Turkish army is cut to pieces, or entirely routed; and no sort of obstacle now remains to prevent Ibrahim Pasha from marching directly to Constantinople. On receiving the news of this disaster, the Sultan in his great rage, it is said, broke one of the splendid mirrors of his palace; but this is certainly better than to break men's heads, according to the ancient custom of this most ungracious government. Halil, who was Capudan Pasha in the last expedition, has been despatched as envoy extraordinary, or rather plenipotentiary, to the court of Mohammed Ali in Egypt, to conclude a peace on as good terms as possible. He sailed on the 7th inst., in the corvette which Mr. Eckford sold to the Sultan last year. A Russian brig-of-war has also sailed for the same port, having on board, it is said, three commissioners, from the three great powers, England, France, and Russia, who go to Egypt for the benevolent purpose of giving to Halil Pasha their countenance and support, and to Mohammed Ali their counsel and advice, unasked."

On the 21st of February he wrote again: "You will doubtless hear that this place is likely to be the seat of war. Ibrahim Pasha is close by. The Russians are already on the march for Constantinople, or rather, I should say, twelve men-of-war, including several line-of-battle ships, have already arrived at Buyuk Dèrè; and England and France will not be idle spectators. You will be able to form some idea of the feelings of the *divan* (council of government), when I tell you that they have strictly forbidden any person in the street to speak with his neighbor or friend of the *weather*, of the course or change of the *wind*, of the time of day, of his own health, or of that of anybody else: all which, strange as it may seem, is actually carried into effect; and we are told that an individual in this village, for a slight and unintentional violation of the order, was immediately hurried off to the bagnio. Now the meaning, or hint given, is simply this, that no person is to lisp a word about the affairs of government; for if he is not permitted to utter a syllable even on his own most common affairs, how shall he presume to *whisper*, or even to *think*, about the great concerns of the vast empire of mighty Sultan Mahmoud."

Still later he wrote: "Every thing continues to have a warlike appearance. Notwithstanding all the talk of peace which we occasionally hear, the real fact is, *there is no peace*, nor does there appear to be any probability of peace at present, unless it be a good large *piece* for the Russians; they are pouring down upon us every day from the North, like the Goths and Vandals upon Rome."

The apprehensions of an attack upon the capital were removed in the spring of 1833 by the conclusion of a treaty, in which the Sultan ceded Syria to the Viceroy.

About this time Constantinople was visited by a band of missionaries of a peculiar type, the St. Simonians of France, who came to propagate their socialistic views. They met with no success or encouragement. No record is made of their arrival, but the journal of Mr. Goodell contains this amusing account of their departure: —

"*April* 24, 1833. The mission of the St. Simonians was short, and as unsuccessful as short. Yesterday I saw them put, by order of the Sultan, on board a small, dirty, open vessel of the country (such as is used to carry charcoal or wood), and sent to the Dardanelles, the pasha of that place being directed to send them forward, and put them on shore somewhere beyond the limits of the empire. Their coming has produced a prodigious sensation among all classes. Not Ibrahim and all his conquests, nor the presence of the Russian fleet, with all the uncertainty hanging over the subject of their departure, have produced any thing like it. The Perotes, in particular, will now have subject-matter of conversation for a whole month to come; while all good papists among them will feel bound to place additional candles before the Virgin, in token of their gratitude for her timely interference in saving them from antichrist. And were it not for ourselves, they might now hope that 'the land would have rest for forty years.'

"These men, it is said, went one day last week and stood in a conspicuous place to see the Sultan, and, when he passed along, they remained like statues, not showing the least sign of respect; but, whenever they saw a female, of whatever age or of whatever nation, they would run to her, even in sight of the Sultan himself, throw off their caps, bow down before her, gaze upon her face, and compare her features with the model of female beauty they had in their hand, in order to ascertain whether the individual they had accosted were the female messiah. Now, you know, even the *com-*

mon Turks do not consider it very genteel, to say the least, for strangers to take such liberties with their wives and daughters. And the high Sultan was so indignant to see them give to the harem of his subjects that honor which he considers due to him alone, and give it, too, in a manner which would shock common decency even in civilized countries, where woman is accustomed to receive attention, that he ordered them to be arrested and thrown into prison.

" A multitude of people of all nations were assembled to see them off. The Turkish guard offered them no abuse, nor did they allow any others to insult them. The Turks carried their baggage on board with as much gravity as they would charcoal, and the prisoners, thirteen in all, walked out two and two and embarked. They were all dressed in livery, having red pantaloons fitting as tight to the legs as their skin ; neat boots, reaching half-way up to the knee ; a sort of Albanian petticoat, though much less full and much shorter, not reaching half-way down to the knee ; a girdle round the waist ; black cloaks thrown over their shoulders and tied before ; red, three-cornered caps on their heads ; their beards long ; and their hair, like that of Nazarites, hanging over their shoulders. They were all young men, with interesting countenances, and they appeared perfectly at their ease.

" After they were gone, I asked the captain of the port, from whose office they had just been conveyed on board, ' Who were these singular-looking men you have been sending away ? ' He replied, ' They are Frenchmen, whose father is imprisoned in Paris, and who came here to look round in our harems for their mother.' They certainly displayed great ignorance of the customs of the country, and a great want of common sense, to say no more ; but when men ' turn away their ears from the truth, and are turned into fables,' what can be expected but that, like ' wicked men and seducers, they should wax worse and worse, deceiving and being deceived.' They are called *missionaries* by the people here, which is, of course, not much to our honor. Yesterday I was in a store at Pera, and heard several persons conversing about the imprisonment of these thirteen. I told them I had understood that there were twenty-four of them in all. ' No,' replied a flippant clerk, whom I took to be a papal Armenian, ' there are only *thirteen of these ;* the Americans at Orta Keuy are bashkah,' *i.e., not the same ;*

different. Some of those present must, I think, have known that I belonged to the *bashkah;* but they said nothing."

At that period, and for many years later, the most absurd forms of respect for the Sultan were exacted from foreigners, as well as from the subjects of the Sublime Porte. No one was allowed to ride in passing the palace of the Sultan; all must dismount and walk, and this, too, whether the palace was occupied or not. Even in passing the palace on the Bosphorus in a boat, parties were rigidly required to lower their umbrellas, no matter how furiously the sun or the rain might be beating upon them. Nothing could justify such a breach of etiquette as keeping an umbrella or parasol spread. The Turks generally were extremely fanatical in their notions. Green was claimed as sacred to the descendants of Mohammed; and a Frank lady would at any time be liable to be stoned if she were seen in the street wearing a green veil, or any other article of dress of this color. Mr. Goodell makes mention of these absurd requisitions : —

"The Sultan is spending the winter in the village next below us on the Bosphorus; and when we pass by his palace, if on horseback, we have to dismount and walk by; if with an umbrella over our heads, we have to close it. Yesterday in passing we dismounted without waiting for orders to do so. To-day one of us on foot in the rain was ordered to close his umbrella. But if the Sultan is not ashamed to *give* such orders, why need we be ashamed to comply with them? Whenever it is not too inconvenient, however, we, as well as all other Franks, take another road, wishing his highness no greater humiliation than bowing the knee to Jesus, and confessing Him to be Lord, to the glory of God the Father."

The letter which follows, although written more than forty years ago, has not been superseded in interest, especially in the analysis which it gives of Turkish character and life, by the notes of any of the numerous travellers who have visited that part of the world in later years. It was addressed to Sidney E. Morse, Esq., then senior editor of the " New York Observer," who had been his fellow-student at Andover : —

7*

ORTA KEUY (Constantinople), Oct. 17, 1832.

MY DEAR BROTHER : — I have to acknowledge the receipt of the " New York Observer," which you have had the kindness to forward regularly to me for some time past.   We read every number with lively interest, rejoicing at the unexampled prosperity which God has given to our country, and especially at the numberless spiritual blessings which He has graciously bestowed upon it, — blessings which have scarcely a parallel in the whole history of the church.

There is but little in this part of the Old World that looks like the industry, virtue, thrift, enterprise, rising greatness, and moral dignity of your part of the New.   A striking trait in the character of the Turks, as you probably know, is indolence.   They seem, in general, to have almost a mortal antipathy to labor and to the exertion of muscular strength, and even to masculine exercises, except such as they take on horseback and in the use of arms.   Hence they neglect agriculture ; and large tracts of most fertile and beautiful country are left comparatively a desert.   Their manufactures, too, are generally in a languishing state ; and all the instruments, utensils, and machines they ever use in doing any thing are for the most part as few, as simple, and as rude as can well be imagined.

But the Turkish character is not altogether a compound of ignorance, grossness, barbarism, and ferocity, as it has been sometimes represented, for they have certainly some redeeming qualities.   As a nation, they are temperate and very frugal.   They make much less use of animal food than is common with ourselves ; and it is only within a few years that they have begun in some places to transgress the laws of their prophet by indulging in wine.   They are hospitable, but ceremonious ; very easy and dignified in their manners, but, if report be true, vicious and beastly in their habits ; extremely kind to their domestics, and especially to their slaves ; exercising unbounded benevolence towards the whole canine race, and not unfrequently a moderate degree towards some of their fellow-men ; but furious in anger, and in executing vengeance on their enemies, terrible.   They are much inclined to superstition, and, in general, attend strictly to the externals of their religion.   Their natural gravity and taciturnity give them, in the view of strangers, the appearance of being haughty and disdainful ; and, indeed, they have a lofty national pride, which is in some instances so prominent as to be extremely offensive.

But, after all, there is something in the Turkish character which I always admire; and I have frequently made the remark that, should they be brought under the influence of the Gospel, they would, to my taste, be the most interesting of all the Orientals. Their gardens are retired and romantic, their dwellings are distinguished for simplicity and quietness, and the stork loves to come and build his nest on their chimneys. Their children have fine healthy countenances, and are in general neatly dressed and well-behaved, — the girls being modest and retiring, and the boys manly, but not rude. It is very rare to see them boxing or hooting in the streets; indeed, I do not recollect to have ever seen an instance of the kind. A stranger to our athletic and boisterous sports, to our more effeminate exercise of dancing, or to the bustle and conviviality of our social circles, the Turk reclines on his soft cushions with all composure; partakes of his *pilaff* and his, in general, vegetable fare, with few words and little ceremony; smokes in silence the mild tobacco of Syria, or the still milder tömbecky of Persia; regales himself at short intervals by sipping the superior coffee of Moka; troubles himself little with politics, and, if possible, still less about the weather; is easily reconciled by the doctrine of fate to all the calamities that may befall his neighbors or his country; knows nothing of hypochondria; and, if he wishes any excitement, the Jews and Greeks will do any thing for money to amuse him, or he has only to take a few grains of opium, and he is at once in an ecstasy.

Our families recently had an invitation, with Commodore Porter, to attend the circumcision of Ali Bey's eldest son, — a ceremony which a Frank or a Christian has very seldom an opportunity of witnessing. Ali Bey resides at Kady Köy, the ancient Chalcedon; and he is a near and a good neighbor of our *Chargé d'affaires*, who, besides ourselves, was the only Frank present on the occasion. He is of the higher class of Turks; and, holding an important office under government for many years, he has acquired both wealth and renown. The poor among the dogs lie down at his gate, and look up to him for protection and support; and the birds of the air build their nests in his *salamluk*, or room for receiving company, where they lay their eggs and rear their young without molestation.

His son was an interesting youth, of a fine form and countenance, pleasing manners, richly dressed, and adorned with various ornaments of diamond and pearl. He was thirteen years of age, which is a later period than usual for the performance of the rite; for up to this time they are considered as belonging to the *harem*, — the hair of their head is suffered to grow, and is plaited by the women with much neatness; but after this time their head is shaved, according to Turkish usage, and they are taken from the women's apartments, and admitted only to the society of men. Two other boys from families in the neighborhood were to have been introduced into man's estate at the same time, but the courage of one of them failed him, and, when the moment came, the rogue took to his heels and ran away, and did not show his face again till he was assured he could do it with safety.

Ali Bey invited all his friends and acquaintance, and made a great feast. The guests were numerous ; and, as we arrived at half-past ten o'clock, A.M., and did not leave till five o'clock, P.M., we had an opportunity of seeing much of Turkish manners. Ali Bey conducted himself with great dignity and propriety, manifesting no levity, nor giving utterance to an idle or unnecessary word, showing much affection and tenderness for his children, and appearing to consult the comfort and happiness of his friends. Many of his guests were equally courteous and dignified; and, indeed, almost every one maintained a decorum, both of speech and behavior, which it would be well for some who boast of their superior civilization to imitate. I was amused and gratified to see the spirit of *equality* that seemed to animate them all : the poor and the rich met together ; the slave sat down in the presence of his master; and every one that entered received a *salaam* from one and another all round the room, which he returned with the same easy and graceful manner with which it was given, and with the same apparent consciousness of being a man among men.

But, though they did not condescend to be foolish themselves, yet, I am sorry to say, Ali Bey hired others to play the fool for them. I say nothing now of their music, except that it is always rude, nor of the sentiments of their songs, except that in most cases it is well that so few of the words can be even understood, from the barbarous manner of singing; but three paltry Jews, occasionally relieving the musicians, endeavored to amuse the company by a variety of artful tricks and ridiculous pranks, now practising legerdemain, and now exhibiting the most antic gestures and postures, accompanied with low jests. Indeed, they were jugglers and buffoons, and one of them personated folly to perfection. As the company were introduced from one apartment of the house to another, they had in every room the musicians to entertain them with song, or the Jews with sleight of hand and vulgarity. The Turks did not seem transported by either the one or the other, but looked on with all the gravity becoming sages ; and, when they had smoked out one *chibook*, the slaves brought them another.

The principal room in the *harem* was the one appropriated to the ceremony which was to be performed, and it was elegantly furnished for the occasion. Cashmere shawls and other drapery of great beauty and value were hung tastefully round the walls, and a superb couch for the son, with a suitable one for the other two boys, was fitted up at one end, with hangings enriched with various devices in diamonds and brilliants, and a *garlick* withal, suspended from the centre, to *keep off the evil eye*. Whenever we entered this *sanctum sanctorum* of Ali Bey's tabernacle, his wives, of which he has several, retired with their female friends and attendants to an adjoining apartment, where through the lattice, or, as it might very properly be called, the *jealousy windows*, they could see us and every thing that transpired, without exposing their own charms to the profane gaze of any but their husband. We could just perceive their moving forms with great indistinctness. But a little daughter, perhaps six years old, dressed in the long, rich, and splendid robes of the Orientals, and certainly a child of singular sweetness and modesty, was present most of the time, as also a little girl of about the same age from another family.

We dined at four o'clock, P.M. ; and, for at least an hour before this, portions were sent to the needy, — not the fragments, or the refuse, as is the custom with us, but whole plates of *pilaff* and other savory dishes, of which none of the guests, hungry as we all were, had yet been permitted to taste. One table was prepared *à la Frank* for the Commodore and his friends, and Ali Bey and a brother of the last Reis Effendi sat down with us ; when, according to our custom, we implored the blessing of our Father in heaven upon our food and upon all our brethren of the human family, in the name of our Lord and Saviour Jesus Christ. The food was excellent and abundant ; soup and *pilaff ;* flesh, fish, and fowl, cooked in various ways ; different kinds of jelly ; and almost every kind of fruit. The table was also furnished with wine, of which Ali Bey and his brother Turk drank as freely as any other person at the table; and, indeed, the latter of the two manifested a fondness for it which I was not gratified in seeing, as he seemed to me to be in danger of exchanging one of the best virtues known in Turkey, viz., temperance, for one of the worst vices prevalent in Christendom, viz., intemperance. He begged the Commodore to send six bottles of wine to his brother, the late Reis Effendi, who now resides at Kandeli, in the house where the exchange of ratifications of our treaty with the Sublime Porte took place a year ago. This man was treated by all with marked attention and respect. He appeared to possess a good share of intelligence, and I had a pleasant conversation with him about America and its customs. He at first expressed the opinion that we were to be pitied in being confined to one wife; but, on my telling him that ours could read and write, and enlarging on the ten thousand other good qualities they are allowed to possess, he at length acknowledged that one good wife was worth a dozen poor ones, and that, in this respect as well as many others, the people of Turkey were, to use his own expression, *barbarians* and *brutes*. His daughter is espoused to Ali Bey's eldest son, — perhaps the same little girl we saw in company with Ali Bey's daughter.

Though urged by our host and his friends to spend the evening, and even the night, to witness some theatrical exhibitions, we left immediately after dinner. On returning home, I could not but reflect that those people, in common with ourselves, belong to the race that has rebelled against their Maker; and that like ourselves they need " the grace of God, which bringeth salvation, teaching them that, denying ungodliness and worldly lusts, they should live soberly, righteously, and godly in this present world." And assuredly the time will come when these followers of the false prophet shall be enlightened by the True Prophet, and, forsaking their delusions, shall be " looking for that blessed hope, and the glorious appearing of the great God and our Saviour Jesus Christ." Let us pray and labor that the day may be soon ushered in.

With Christian and affectionate salutations,

Yours truly,

W. GOODELL.

Having been invited to be present at the ordination of fifteen priests at the Armenian patriarchal church at Constantinople, Mr. Goodell gives the following account of their induction into office : —

"*September* 7, 1833. It is a rule or custom with the Armenians that the newly made priests must remain in the church forty days and forty nights, without once going out, and without once putting off any of their priestly garments, and must during all this time practise the most severe abstinence, and keep reading over and over the Psalter and the ritual of the church ; and also that their wives must be muffled up, or rather literally sewed up, in cloaks and other heavy prescribed garments, and must remain during all these forty days and nights at home, in a darkened room, not being allowed to taste any pleasant food, nor indeed much of any kind, and not having it in their power to divest themselves of a single article of their clothing, nor even to loosen a stitch for the sake of brushing away the vermin, however much they may be teased by the accumulation of a variety of the little tormentors. Hohannes suggested to Peshtimaljian that there was much discomfort, not to say discredit, in all this, while there was no use whatever ; and the latter, who is decidedly the most learned man we have seen in the country, and who is very liberal in his views, and a great friend to us, went immediately to the Synod, and induced them to dispense entirely with every thing that related to the poor wives, leaving them at liberty to go out and come in, attend to their families and enjoy the comforts of life, as at other times. Their husbands, too, have been permitted to change their linen ; and instead of saying the church service over and over, a thousand times repeated, they are permitted, or rather required, to spend part of the time in studying the Gospel. May they therein learn how to become able ministers of the New Testament ! And may they thereby be taught that 'the letter killeth, but the Spirit giveth life !' We were taken to see some of them in the church when their forty days were about half expired and their beards had begun to grow. They approached and kissed our hands, and I implored for them the gift of the Holy Spirit."

One of these priests, Der Kevork, who was evidently much affected at the time by the supplication offered by the missionary on his behalf, afterward became an earnest preacher of the truth as it is in Jesus. Although he never formally left the Armenian church, he exerted a powerful influence in promoting the wonderful revival and work of true religion among his people, which took place a very few years later. Other native laborers also gathered gradually around the standard of the cross.

When Mr. Goodell reached Constantinople, in 1831, a young Greek, Panayotes Constantinides, called to see him, and gave him an unexpected welcome. He was a book-binder, employed by the Turks in the Mussulman quarter of the city; but from intercourse with an English clergyman, who had spent a few weeks at Constantinople, he had become interested in the truth, and gave evidence of being a sincere Christian. It was not long before he ceased attending the services of the Greek Church, and cast in his lot with the missionaries. He was a good Turkish as well as Greek scholar, and was familiar with Turkish literature. This man seemed to have been raised up by Providence for an important work in connection with the American mission. He became at once a valuable assistant to Mr. Goodell in the schools and in the work of translation. He was subsequently licensed to preach; and continued to be a faithful helper to the day of his death, which occurred in 1861. Of his valuable labors mention will be made, in connection with his death, in a subsequent chapter. As he had occasion to go out at one time in missionary service, Mr. Goodell gave him the following unique passport or letter of introduction:—

" KYRIOS PANAYOTES,

" My translator, dragoman, counsellor, and helper, aged thirty-seven years, having a wife and three children, and weighing about two hundred and eighty pounds (Turkish), is a fine Turkish and Greek scholar, having some acquaintance also with the English, Armenian, and Hebrew, together with all their cognates; but, above all, is a great lover of the truth, and of all good men, being ' an Israelite indeed, in whom is no guile ; ' and he will, I doubt not, hereafter ' eat of the tree of life, which is in the midst of the paradise of God.' Amen. "As witness my hand,

"W. GOODELL."

Not long after, Mr. Goodell was visited by two young Armenians, Hohannes Sehakyan and Senakerim, who came with an evident and earnest desire to have "the way of God expounded unto them more perfectly." They had been for several years under the instruction of Peshtimaljian, an enlightened Armenian, and one who, before the advent of the missionary, had given much evidence of being taught by the Holy Spirit. These young men, like Nicodemus, came by night, and often, week after week, to converse upon the word of God, and to read it in a language with which they were familiar. Both subsequently came to the United States, and spent several years in study, to qualify themselves for usefulness among their countrymen in Turkey. In July, 1833, they formally gave themselves up to the guidance of the missionaries, affording at the same time pleasing evidence that they had already submitted themselves to the teachings and devoted themselves to the service of the great Master. Senakerim was employed by the mission, and was immediately useful in the work of translation. Hohannes was placed at the head of a school of a higher grade, established for Armenian youth.

Their conversion produced great excitement among the priests, and awakened no little alarm among the people. The Armenian bankers and merchants were more influential, even in ecclesiastical affairs, than the ecclesiastics themselves, and had a controlling influence in matters which in some other parts would be decided entirely by the priests. When the defection of these two promising young men became known, a wealthy Armenian jeweller, of great respectability and influence, instigated, as was afterward learned, by a Romish priest, attempted to stir up an excitement. The school of Hohannes was closed by clerical interference. The

K

jeweller also endeavored to obtain ecclesiastical action that
should deter others from following the example of these
youth.   He went to their former teacher, and preferred
charges against them, as having been bribed by foreigners to
take a stand against their own people, and for having adopted
pestilent heresies.

The accused were summoned before Peshtimaljian, and
the accuser, with no little violence of manner and great bit-
terness of spirit, proceeded to support his charges.   The
young men were about to vindicate themselves, when Peshtimaljian prevented them by spreading before the astonished
jeweller such a mass of evidence from the Holy Scriptures
and from history in favor of the evangelical doctrines they
had embraced, and in opposition to the heartless mummeries
and the idolatrous practices of his own church, that the man
was utterly confounded.   Hohannes and Senakerim also
helped to pour light upon his mind ; and the result was that
the jeweller was convinced of his own errors, and became an
open and powerful advocate of the pure doctrines of the
Gospel.   Another Armenian, Sarkis Varjabed, also renounced his errors, and became a useful assistant to the
missionaries in the work of translation.   Thus God raised
up helpers to carry on His work.

The year 1834 was ushered in with manifest tokens of the
divine presence, of which Mr. Goodell wrote, under date of
February 1 : —

" Our weekly service in Turkish, which is attended statedly
by half a dozen Armenians and a few Greeks, had all along
been increasing in solemnity and interest.   Kyrios Panayotes,
of the latter nation, appeared to be growing in grace ; and Senakerim and Hohannes, of the former, to be getting more and
more under the influence of truth and of the Holy Spirit.
We felt prepared to go a step farther ; and the first monthly
concert season in the year 1834 we observed in *Turkish*, as
well as in *English*.   This is probably the first time the
monthly concert for prayer was ever observed in that language.   Kyrios Panayotes made one of the prayers, and

from one of our Greek tracts, printed at Malta, he gave in Turkish an interesting account of Obookiah, and of the commencement of the mission at the Sandwich Islands. Every ear seemed to be open, every eye to be moistened, and every voice that uttered a syllable was in a tender and subdued tone. One of the Armenians then gave an extract from a sermon which was preached by their patriarch in Constantinople, a day or two previous, and which had given them much satisfaction. The following is the substance of the extract: Those Christians who love the Gospel have caused it to be translated and printed in every language; and all, even the heathen nations, are now beginning to read it. Let us, therefore, see to it that we conform ourselves to its precepts, lest those who have but just received it should point at us and reproach us with neglecting the duties it enjoins, and we should thus give occasion to them to blaspheme. This was truly monthly concert intelligence, and was as cheering as it was unexpected.

" After the Turkish, we had our usual English service for the occasion. Our little company represented six nations and six churches. One was a Baptist brother, the master of an English vessel now in this port, and a man of intelligence and serious piety. The day previous he had united with us in celebrating the Lord's Supper, feeling that in doing it, though he had acted contrary to the rules of his church, he had acted in strict conformity to the rules of the Gospel: ' Receive ye one another, as Christ also received us.'

" Senakerim's heart was now full, and he could no longer restrain his feelings, but with most animated countenance and an earnest manner, and with tears now and then gushing from his eyes, he gave an interesting account of his and Hohannes' experience, and of the way in which Providence had led them and brought them to a knowledge of the truth. During the remainder of the month we had frequent precious intercourse with these young brethren. Sometimes their hearts were filled with darkness and sorrow, and their heads bowed down like a bulrush, and they came to us, and with the docility of little children inquired concerning pardon and salvation through atoning blood. At one of our meetings, it devolved upon Senakerim while in this state of mind to read the following verse: ' And she said, Truth, Lord; yet the dogs eat of the crumbs which fall from their master's table.' It seemed to express the very feelings of his own heart, and it was with difficulty he could finish the sentence, owing to the tender emotions which were awakened by it in his bosom, and which were struggling for utterance.   Both he and his companion appear now to be filled with light and love and comfort and zeal.   They lay hold of the divine promises, and plead them in a manner quite unusual ; and, like Peter, they seem ready to go to prison and to death, though, like him and like most young converts, they doubtless have much less genuine faith than they think they have. A few storms, such as we have in these countries, will give it a trial."

In company with Commodore Porter and Commodore Patterson, of the frigate " United States," Mr. Goodell was invited to visit the new summer palace of the Sultan at Beylerbey, near Scutari, where they were received and treated with the utmost attention.   Mr. Goodell writes : —

"*March* 3, 1834.   It was gratifying to us as Americans to see the respect in which our country is held by the Ottoman government.   The high officers of the empire seemed to vie with each other in doing honor to it.   And, indeed, how could it be otherwise when the grand seignior himself set the example ?   Namik Pasha, who has command at Scutari, had been appointed by the Sultan to conduct the party through the palace and the gardens, and this he did with the politeness which characterizes many of the present race of Turks at Constantinople.   As we retired, he asked me to visit the Turkish Lancasterian schools as often as I thought proper, and to make such suggestions as might seem to me necessary. Both Commodore Patterson and Commodore Porter visited the schools at Dolma Baktchè and Scutari, and expressed themselves highly pleased.   The Turkish officers were also delighted, and declared at the time, as they have frequently told me since, that they had seen English, French, Russians, &c., but that they had never seen *friends*, *real friends*, till they saw the *Americans*.   Such complimentary expressions, however, weigh not so much here as they would in the United States.

" I am happy to say that two more Lancasterian schools are just going into operation at Constantinople, under the direction of the Seraskier Pasha himself.   The Seraskier, or generalissimo, ranks, I believe, about the third in the kingdom. He is now more than eighty years old, but is as full of fire as ever, and his power and influence seem scarcely less than that of the Sultan himself. For these two schools we furnish a copy of the same lessons which we prepared for the school of Azim Bey, the Alai-emini, or commissary-general, at Scutari.

"On a recent visit to the barracks at Dolma Baktchè, we were agreeably surprised to find that a third Lancasterian school had been established there. This makes now seven in all, besides the rooms appropriated for learning the French language, and for drawing maps, charts, &c., connected with all these schools. Not less than two thousand Mussulman youth are now enjoying the advantages of education in these schools. Four hundred and fifty are in the three schools at Dolma Baktchè; and quite a number, who six months ago did not know a single letter of the alphabet, now read any book with ease. Rifaat Bey, Kaimakam at this place, with whom I had had previous intercourse both here and at my own house, said he hoped that all the rooms in the whole establishment would one day be converted into schools; and to this expression of his feelings we added our most hearty amen. It is truly matter of most fervent gratitude that so many doors of usefulness are now opening before us, and that we are permitted to exert, directly and indirectly, so important an influence in the changes that are taking place, and that seem destined to give an entirely new impression to the character of the different people dwelling in these countries.

"Since I commenced writing, our agent has been to see the Greek patriarch. He says the priests break his head; that he must have rest; and he intimated strongly to our agent that he should resign his office. The patriarch is learned and candid, and is not at all the man to delight in a storm; but the incessant cries, 'The people have all become Lutherans!' 'They have all become Protestants!' 'They have all become infidels!' 'We are all polluted!' &c., 'while you, O patriarch, sit still, and see it all,'—have greatly discomposed his spirits.

"*May* 8. There is at present a prodigious excitement among the Greeks in regard to the Lancasterian schools; the priests have taken some 'lewd fellows of the baser sort,' have stirred up the patriarch, threaten him with the loss of office, and demand the utter destruction of every school. It is impossible to see what will be the result; but the waves have been running higher and higher for more than a month, and certainly appear now ready to swallow up every thing. The patriarch weeps, and says that if this state of things goes on for three years more, as it has for three years past, there will not be another Christian left in all Constantinople ; *i.e.*, I suppose, there will not be another Greek to kick up his heels at the sound of the bagpipe on Sundays. And this spake he not of himself, but, being high-priest, he prophesies that it is better for the schools to perish than the orthodox Greek religion. However, I had no idea that our influence here had been so great ; and I am sure the patriarch must have exaggerated. But He that sitteth in the heavens is higher than they ; and all the weapon we shall think it best to use against them is ' *all-prayer.*' We shall not even enter into an argument with them on the subject, but let them fight it out alone among themselves, for the less noise the better."

On becoming acquainted with the origin of the opposition that from time to time sprang up against the missionaries, the circulation of slanderous reports, the stirring up of public excitement, the breaking up of schools, and other measures of hostility, it was often found that the Romish priests were at the bottom of it all. They had no immediate power, as in Roman Catholic countries, but they could and did secretly instigate the Greeks and the Armenians to hinder the good work that was going on among them. Utterly false statements in regard to the books that were used in the schools, the teachings of the missionaries, and their designs in coming to the country, were circulated by the Jesuits. But only once did they make an attempt to convert the Protestant missionary to the Roman Catholic faith. The record of this effort is so interesting and peculiar, it is here transcribed in full from Mr. Goodell's journal. With all the apparent seriousness of the interview, there is a vein of irony running through the interrogatories and replies of the missionary that seems to have escaped the notice of the Jesuit emissary.

" *April* 6, 1834. Was visited to-day by a Jesuit, who, as it would appear, came on purpose to convert me to the papal faith. He was full of Peter, and his zeal knew no bounds. As this was the first instance that had ever occurred in my intercourse with the people of these countries of any individual who even so much as pretended to feel any interest in my spiritual concerns, or to have any care whether I am saved or lost, I was much struck with it.

" He began by lamenting the divisions in the Christian Church, and by showing how sincere was his desire and how great the importance of union ; and in all this I was not backward to express the most cordial sympathy, quoting from the prayer of our blessed Lord, and commenting particularly upon the words, ' That they all may be one,' &c.

" He then lost no time in introducing the Church of Rome, and at once urged me to become a member of it. I told him that I needed no urging at all, for that I was as ready as he could wish me to be to do whatever he could convince me was right, and that the only thing I required of him was *sufficient reasons;* let him produce these, and the work was done. I then proposed this question, What excuse shall I offer at the day of judgment for taking such a step as you are now pressing me to take? As he appeared to be confused, or hurt, by the interrogation, and as I felt that, if he was really seeking my good, I ought not to confound him at the outset, but rather to encourage him, and give him every advantage, I retracted the question, and requested him to take his own way. His reasons were then produced, and I attempted to answer them, till from his whole manner it was to me as clear as the sun that he was not thinking of the honor of Christ, or of my conformity to His image and advancement in holiness, but only of the strength of his own party and the glory of the Church of Rome, — an object which appeared to me so infinitely mean and unworthy, that I could endure it no longer. I then, in my turn, pressed him with some close questions, and forced him to say, not by inference, but in so many words, —

" 1. That the Scriptures are not a sufficient rule of faith and practice, and that no person can be saved by simply following their directions. And,

" 2. That the blood of Christ will not, cannot, and never did, cleanse any one from all sin, however great might be his faith in the efficacy of it, and however frequent and undoubted his personal application of it to his own soul. The whole, in fact, must be seasoned and spiced with the mummery of

Rome, or it is like 'salt that has lost its savor, and is good for nothing but to be cast out, and trodden under foot of men.'

"Among other reasons that he presented to induce me to profess Romanism, he said that in their church they had Christ brought very near to them, — that in the consecrated wafer, for instance, he held the very Christ of God in his hand. I replied, that the Lord Jesus was already much nearer to me than my hand, for that He was in my heart, and that I had become a temple for the indwelling of His Spirit. He said that whenever he ate the consecrated bread *he* also had Christ in his heart. I told him that not a particle of the wafer ever went to his heart, but that every bit of it which passed down his throat went straight to his stomach, and was 'cast out into the draught;' for that (except in the case of very small children, or very childish people, and in quite a different sense) the way to the heart was never through the stomach.

"Of his assertion, so often and so positively made, that Peter was the head of the church, I asked for proof. He quoted, 'Thou art Peter, and upon this rock,' &c. I asked him whether he supposed that Peter and the other disciples understood the passage. 'Yes, certainly,' was his reply. 'But,' said I, 'they never understood it the way you do; such a meaning as you affix to it, and such inferences as you deduce from it, they never dreamed of. For several times afterwards they came to our Lord, and put the question to Him directly, Who of them was to be the greatest? But in no instance did He refer them to this discourse, and say, Do you not see that that matter is already settled? Have not I already declared that Peter is to be your head and chief? No; so far from this, He made use of the strongest language and most expressive symbols to assure them that, though such things were usual in the kingdoms of this world, yet whoever entertained such thoughts and views in relation to His kingdom was to be for ever excluded from it."

"To his oft-repeated declaration that there is no salvation out of the pale of the Romish Church, I replied, 'I am without the pale of the Romish Church; and if Christ has no pleasure in me, if I do not belong to Him and do not keep His commandments, why does He manifest himself unto *me*, as He does not unto the *world?* Why does He visit me and dwell with me, softening and purifying my heart by His Spirit, and drawing my affections away from earth to heaven? Does He ever do this for any whom He is not saving from sin and hell, and whom He is not leading to heaven? He certainly does not.'

"In conclusion, I told him that so long as I believed in Christ, received His laws, and felt assured of a judgment to come, I could not, I dared not, as I valued the life of my soul, turn from the holy commandments delivered unto us, and give myself to the guidance of the Roman Catholic Church. And if this is to be a heretic, he certainly left me a more confirmed one than he found me."

8

CHAPTER XI.

ONE of Mr. Goodell's most striking characteristics as a man, and one of his most eminent qualifications as a missionary, was his practical wisdom. As in social life, so in dealing with the great diversity of characters that he met with in the discharge of his official duties, and especially in the multiplied emergencies that were constantly occurring in such a city as Constantinople, he seemed to have an intuitive apprehension of what was best to be done, and to be able to do it without exciting the opposition which some men would be sure to call forth. He made no compromise of truth or duty to please any one. Where principle was involved he was unyielding. But his gentle, conciliatory temper gave him an advantage in dealing with all classes of people. He had his full share of "the contradiction of sinners," as he went on with his work, and, in common with his brethren, he escaped the woe pronounced on those of whom "all men speak well;" but few have ever accomplished so much in similar circumstances, and at the same time awakened so little personal hostility. It seemed perfectly natural to him to exemplify the words of the Saviour, when commissioning the first Christian missionaries: "Behold, I send you forth as sheep in the midst of wolves; be ye therefore wise as serpents and harmless as doves."

He was evidently just the man for the peculiar and multiplied types of human character to be found among the Orientals. His plan was to exert an influence over those with whom he came in contact, without having the appearance of influencing them at all, and so to avoid exciting opposition. He aimed at securing a moral and religious reformation among the people, not by outside demonstrations so much as by leading the people to adopt by themselves those principles and measures that would secure the end. In employing the important agency of schools, which accomplished so much in enlightening the people in the early years of the mission, he preferred to infuse a new element into the schools already existing, or to give the entire control of the schools that he organized to the different religious communities, while he quietly suggested the course of instruction, the books that should be used, and, indeed, the whole system of management and education. This he was the better able to do, because the Greeks and Armenians had no schools that were worthy of the name, and they were, at first, quite willing to receive suggestions for their improvement.

And so, when some of the Turkish officials came to him and expressed an earnest desire for the establishment of Lancasterian schools for the Turkish youth, instead of taking the work into his own hands, or exercising any sort of control over them, he wisely left the Turks to do the work themselves, while by his advice he secured their proper management. By pursuing this course he secured the establishment and continuance of ten, where there could have been but one, had he kept it under his own control, and in this way he avoided all collision of authority.

So, also, in the work of evangelization. He had not come to do a work of proselyting. He did not feel called upon to make an open assault upon the Greek and Armenian churches. This would utterly defeat the object for which he came to Turkey, which was to make known the Gospel in its simplicity, and lead the people to embrace the truth. To pursue such a course would at once excite opposition, and close the door against the reception of the truth. His aim was to cast the leaven into the existing church organizations, leaving it to work by the power of the Divine Spirit. His desire was to see the work of reformation going on within the Greek and Armenian churches, knowing that when those who were truly enlightened could endure the mummeries and idolatry of these churches no longer, the movement for a purer church would come from themselves. And this was precisely the result that came about in the course of a few years.

He was so much impressed with the importance of pursuing this quiet course, that he often, personally and in his correspondence with other stations, delicately urged his views upon his brethren, some of whom differed from him. Having more than once, in his correspondence with the Board, expressed these views, he was requested by the Secretary at Boston to draw them out in full. This he did in 1834, in an extended series of papers, entitled, " Hints and Cautions to a Missionary," which have been preserved, and which would make a volume of moderate size. No portion of these " Hints " can be given here, but some extracts will be made from his more familiar correspondence on the same subject.

In one of his letters to the Corresponding Secretary he wrote : —

"We must follow Christ. That is a general proposition. When we are in circumstances which call for the exercise of patience, or of a forgiving spirit, we must follow Christ in that particular. When we are in circumstances which call for bold and fearless declarations of divine truth, as is the case with our brethren in America, we must follow Christ in that respect. And when great caution and consummate prudence are required, may we not also follow him in this ? Christ always adapted His instructions to the circumstances of the people. You aim to do the same in America ; and may we not do the same here ? And if you in America can, under certain circumstances, follow Christ in one particular, why may we not here, under other circumstances, follow Him in another particular ? Why should we judge you as not being universal in your conformity to Christ, or why should you judge us? Suppose we should change places, and, of course, circumstances; you would then have to become much more cautious, and we much less so, or else neither of us would follow Christ."

To one of the missionaries in Syria he wrote : —

" The great principle upon which we act you will find in the example of our blessed Lord : 'I have many things to say unto you, but ye cannot bear them now. And with many such parables spake He the word unto them, as they were able to hear it.' Now this is not a mere theory with us, but it is literally reduced to practice ; and we endeavor, in this respect as well as in others, to 'walk in His steps.' Nor in applying this principle here have we any, even the most remote, reference to what Christians can do or say in America, or to what men can bear there, or to what the government will admit there. No : we are to look at the ignorance, prejudice, and bigotry that prevail here ; at the state of society, &c., — and then apply the principle in all its length and breadth. And I feel no hesitation at all in doing it. It appears to me that if a missionary should do nothing for the first three years but simply mix with the people, and learn how weak and ignorant and foolish and prejudiced they really are, it would be an acquisition worth a million times more to him than that of all the languages spoken in the Ottoman empire.

" In every, or almost every, place individuals are found who are so far enlightened as to see and feel that their churches are abominably corrupt, and who do sincerely desire a reform ; and it is a most desirable thing to secure their influence and co-operation. But, by taking too high ground, do we not effectually preclude this ? They are not prepared to go to such lengths ; and they are forced, even against the convictions of their own conscience, to take sides against us. Do you say they should be prepared to venture all consequences ? I reply, if they were so prepared, our services would not be necessary ; the work would be done without us.

" We ourselves, at this place, have nothing to do with the church, its dogmas, ceremonies, and superstitions ; nor do we ever think of meddling with the convents, the priests, the celibacy of the clergy, &c. In fact, we stand nearly as far aloof from what may be called ecclesiastical matters, as we do from political matters. We find we have no occasion to touch upon them, and we feel wonderfully relieved. We have enough else to do ; we have enough else to say. We direct men to their own hearts and to the Bible. And just as soon as any one is brought to read the word of God with a serious spirit. he is convinced of all, he is judged of all,' so that we have no need to say any thing. Indeed, he is generally disposed to break away from his church long before he has religion enough to carry him through the opposition he will have to encounter.

" Nor do we make any attempts to establish a new church to raise up a new party. We disclaim every thing of the kind. We tell them frankly, You have sects enough among you already, and we have no design of setting up a new one, or of pulling down your churches, or drawing away members from them in order to build up our own. No ; let him that is a Greek be a Greek still, and him that is an Armenian be an Armenian still. We have come to do all the good in our power, and to assist in raising your whole population from that state of ignorance, degradation, and death into which you are fallen.

" To be sure, the time is coming, and it is certainly drawing on apace, when there will be a tremendous breaking up of those churches, and when they will have to be entirely remodelled ; and then our counsel and advice will be wanted, and we may have to devote much thought and time to this particular subject. But in the mean time let it be our great concern to bring men to an acquaintance with the Holy Scriptures and to a knowledge of salvation, and thus prepare materials for something better in church and state."

Many years later he expressed his views on this point in a letter to a missionary at Trebizond : —

" No person should be, in the least degree, encouraged to break away from his church till there is good reason to believe that he is no longer a servant of sin, that his feet are on the immovable rock, and that he has a faith that will overcome the world. If we take any other course, we bring our friends into great trouble, and do them a lasting injury. There is danger of their being prejudiced and hardened. To quarrel with their own church, or to oppose it, is one of the very last steps they should be allowed to take. It should be absolutely frowned upon. They should be made to quarrel with themselves and oppose sin in themselves; and if they cannot be brought to do this, let them remain where they are. I would not, in ordinary cases, even discuss ecclesiastical matters and church abuses with them. Preach the pure, blessed Gospel; and if they will not receive it, they will perish, whether their own church be corrupt or pure."

The following passage occurs in his journal:—

"We feel it to be an occasion for devout thankfulness that we have never been drawn aside from our work to engage in any controversy with the Greeks. Notwithstanding all the books that have been published against us and our operations, we have never written one syllable or said one word in reply. We have had enough else to do; and we have kept about our own work as though nothing had been said or written against us, leaving them to fight on alone, 'as one that beateth the air.'"

So clear was his conviction of the truth that Christ's kingdom is not of this world, and that it is not to be advanced by worldly authority and power, that he was exceedingly averse to obtaining firmans for carrying on any missionary operations, or seeking official interference and protection from the government whenever it could be avoided. To one of the missionaries at Smyrna, who had urgently requested his influence with Commodore Porter, as United States *Chargé d'affaires*, to obtain some official protection of the schools, he counselled quiet prosecution of the work, without creating disturbance or invoking aid from any civil power, and especially a foreign power:—

"*January* 24, 1834. The fact is, our strength consists in being as quiet as possible. The less that is said and known about our operations so much the better. A great deal can be done in a silent, harmless, inoffensive way in these countries, but nothing in a storm. I do deprecate a storm far more than any of our consuls or worldly wise men do. If Mr. O. talks to you of prudence, you may go all lengths with

him, and a great deal further, unless he is different from any
consul I have ever seen.   Be frank with him, and ask his
advice whenever you know it cannot but be exactly in accordance with your own views ; ask it, too, whenever you are in
any real doubt as to our relations with the Porte, &c.   We
did not come here to quarrel with governors and pashas, nor
with patriarchs and bishops.   And, as to the Catholics, pray
let them entirely alone, and neither curse them at all nor
bless them at all."

To another missionary at Smyrna, who had asked the same
kind of interference, he wrote : —

" From a remark in Mr. T.'s letter, I find you are still
expecting I should endeavor to obtain a firman for the
restoration of your Turkish schools, and wondering why I
should have been so long silent on the subject.   I had in
numerous letters expressed my views and feelings so very
fully on this whole subject, in the case of Bishop Dionysius,
that I supposed all the brethren at Smyrna perfectly understood that the thing was, in our view, impracticable.

" Pray, how is such a firman to be obtained ?   Who shall
apply for it ?   No ambassador can do it officially, without
transcending the powers vested in him.   And to urge him to
do it is to urge him to do what is not his duty, what is a violation of the treaty, and what, of course, his own government
will not bear him out in doing.   Ought he, then, to do it?
I answer unhesitatingly, he ought not.   His official conduct
ought to be strictly conformed to the treaty, as it is mutually
understood by the parties.   If the treaty be defective, that is
no concern of his, except with his own government at home ;
all he can do is to represent its defects to them, and in the
mean time to abide by the existing one till his government
can or will form a new and better one with the Porte.
Should he happen to be on familiar terms with any distinguished Turks, he can, of course, as a private individual, ask
and obtain favors of them, such as they are able to grant.
But firmans are official documents ; they proceed from the
Reis Effendi, and bear the signature of the Sultan ; and,
besides, with the Reis Effendi the ambassadors are seldom on
terms of intimacy.   Indeed, they seldom have much intercourse with any of the high officers of government, except what
is strictly of a diplomatic or official character.   In this char-

acter they are not in general backward : but, on the contrary, are forward. This is especially true of all consuls, so far as I have known them. At Beyrout they were petty kings; they were disposed to go far beyond what existing treaties would allow, or their own governments at home would sanction, and instead of a spur they rather needed a curb. Ought they, then, to be urged and goaded and fretted, when their own inclination already leads them to interfere beyond what existing treaties give them any right to do? Manifestly they ought not.

" Near two years since one of our own little schools in this place was broken up. And although it had been visited and was patronized by the Russian and Spanish ambassadors, and more particularly so by the American minister, yet no one of them interfered. In the first place, they could not interfere lawfully, and of course had no right to do it. And in the second place, I did not wish them to do it. Such interference, had it succeeded, would have done more hurt than good. It would have alarmed the fears and awakened the prejudices of the whole community; their worst passions would have been excited; the misrepresentations would have been endless; and, instead of there being numerous Lancasterian schools in this neighborhood, as at present, there would probably have been but that one, and that one sustained only by civil authority and force, and thus, by shutting up other doors of usefulness, proving a curse rather than a blessing."

In such a world as this, however, and especially in such a part of it as the Turkish empire, and more especially among the adherents of the corrupt Oriental churches, " it must needs be that offences come." The breaking out of opposition could not long be stayed. Accordingly, he writes : —

September 9, 1834. During the Greek Lent, a monk, who formerly lived in one of the Ionian Islands, and who, it is said, was banished thence by the English government for his officious meddling, or seditious conduct, preached in the principal church of Constantinople, and before the patriarch, a most furious sermon against the schools, the books, and the new translations of the Scriptures into Greek, accusing the priests, the bishops, and even the patriarch himself, of being polluted with heresy, and of conniving at a monstrous evil, which was

8*   L

bringing ruin upon their church and nation. Many of the people left the church, and the patriarch sent a man into the pulpit three times to pull the skirt of the preacher's cloak; but he paid no attention to these hints, and continued to rave like a madman. The same sermon he preached also in Galata and in other places. And his influence was the greater, as he was almost the only individual at the capital at all capable of making a sermon, and as he could at least pretend to speak from his own experience of the tendency of this system of missionary and Bible means, and also from his personal knowledge of the motives and designs of those engaged in the work.

"In consequence of all this, there was an immediate interference in all the schools: every thing had to undergo the strictest scrutiny; the books were subjected to the most rigid examination; and, though they had the patriarch's own seal in their favor, though nothing appeared against them, yet it was resolved that poison must be concealed somewhere in them, and that therefore they must cease to be used as school-books, and the old church prayers and Psalters must be introduced in their stead. The teachers, one and all, resisted these measures for some time; but they were finally compelled to make at least a show of submission, either in whole or in part.

"Blessed be God, whether His beloved Son shall see of the travail of His soul, and whether He shall come and reign over the hearts of men or not, does not depend on princes or patriarchs. And as we endeavored to publish the laws of His kingdom, and to prepare the way for His coming to take possession of it under the former patriarch, so do we resolve in the strength of the Lord to labor still more abundantly to do this under the latter."

At the opening of another year there were evidences that the truth was taking effect, and that the good Spirit was moving upon the hearts of the people. He writes in his journal:—

"*February* 28, 1835. The state of things among the Armenians continues interesting. Almost every day, for a long time, there have been little assemblies in Constantinople for reading the Bible, God's own blessed word; almost every day some go to Peshtimaljian with questions; and very frequently some one comes to us for a solution of such as Pesh-timaljian cannot satisfactorily answer. A short time since they sent over to us to know what they were to do for a church. We replied, Be in no hurry at present. You are now going on well; your numbers are daily increasing; your influence is extending. Be content for a while to break your bread from house to house. Perhaps, by and by, the patriarch himself will give you a church, where you can worship God in spirit and in truth, and where the law and the prophets, with the glorious Gospel, can be read and expounded every Sabbath day. At any rate, have no fear but that the Lord will build you a sure house. The next day, they sent to know what they were to do for priests. We sent word back to them to pray that 'a great company of the priests might become obedient to the faith.'

" The excitement has been certainly great, but it has appeared to be rather a deep and earnest and sincere inquiry about the truth, and the way of salvation, than anxiety about a personal interest in its blessings. It has existed principally among the more sober and respectable of the people, and has been promoted by means judiciously selected and applied; and, what is truly wonderful, scarcely any opposition has been heard of from any quarter. It is difficult to account for this except from the fact that the bishops are really more enlightened than the people. Should the latter begin to take the lead, and the former to fall in the rear, then it will 'be impossible but that offences should come;' and, according to human view, there is but one way to prevent it, and that is by endeavoring to enlighten equally the clergy and the laity, and to bring them all forward together. When I first came into these countries, I laid hold of individuals, and endeavored to pull them out of the fire; but my aim is now to take hold of whole communities, and, as far as possible, to raise them all up to 'sit together in heavenly places in Christ Jesus.' The Lord grant that not one may be left behind!

" We are careful to say nothing which shall inflame the people against the priests, or the priests against the people; and we take as much pains to avoid an open rupture with either as General Washington ever did to avoid exposing the lives of his few hardy but ragged half-accoutred soldiers by risking a general battle. Washington rendered himself unpopular by so doing; but he manifestly did right, and posterity has given a verdict in his favor. He might have obtained for himself momentary glory and renown, by rushing into battle and dying like a brave man, but — our country would have been lost! He fought for his country, and not for himself. His plans and his efforts had in view the good of his country, and not his own reputation. And thus we should labor for the salvation of these people, and not for a martyr's crown. The ranks of the enemy are now thinning out daily, by desertions to the standard of truth, and we hope to come off victorious, without entering the arena of controversy ; yet we would not forget that the 'foolishness of God is wiser than men, and the weakness of God is stronger than men.' When, therefore, the providence of God evidently calls us to the field of battle, by the grace of God we will fight, sure of the victory. At present we need, more than any thing else, not the spirit of controversy, but the Spirit of God, the Spirit of Christ, the spirit of love, of holiness, of forgiveness, tenderness, long-suffering, and patience. May this be poured out upon us abundantly ! "

The Greek patriarch at Constantinople, having shown an enlightened zeal for the improvement of the people by encouraging the establishment of schools, and by favoring the course of the more evangelical among his clergy, was removed by the Synod. The new patriarch entered upon his office with a display of bigotry and zeal against the truth and against all that was calculated to enlighten and elevate the people. He applied to the Porte for authority to dismiss from the schools all the teachers who were not forward to carry out the views of the Synod against the heresy that was beginning to spread. He sent a priest to preach in the churches, who denounced the former patriarch as a Protestant, and declared that, had he continued in office but three years longer, he would have made the whole Greek Church Protestant by means of the Lancasterian schools. In regard to these proceedings Mr. Goodell writes : —

" *March* 6, 1835. The effect of all this has been very different from what the patriarch expected and intended, for the reaction was tremendous. The preacher had to stop preaching, and the patriarch was insulted to his face. The fact is, there have been so many examinations into this system of school operations, and all without discovering any thing treasonable, that the people are heartily tired of it, and seem determined to submit to no more vexations of the kind; and they have taken a stand, which looks very much like the attitude of defiance. I am perfectly astonished at the advance they have made, and the degree of influence and independence they have acquired, while the dignitaries of the church have lost in the same proportion. It appears to me that the latter have lost full fifty per cent since I first came to Constantinople, nearly four years ago. Every struggle they make shows more and more their weakness instead of their strength.

"The above-mentioned priest came over to Pera, and preached a whole sermon against our Greek school, uttering the most furious exclamations, and raving like a maniac. But every little girl comes just as before; not a single child was frightened away for a single day, and the school goes on as prosperously as ever. Besides all this, two new schools for boys, on the Lancasterian plan, have gone into operation in the interior.

April 2, he writes: "The good work goes on among the Armenians without any abatement. The change that has taken place among them within the last fifteen months is truly astonishing, and almost surpasses belief. Three of those who are most active in the reformation, and who talk and read and preach in all companies and on all occasions and with all boldness, are members of the great Synod, by which every thing relative to the affairs of the church or of the nation (the Armenians) is regulated. Almost every day, too, I am visited more or less by Mussulmans. I could very profitably devote my whole time to them."

Under the above date (April 2, 1835), he makes mention of the death of several eminent missionaries in different parts of the world: —

"The letter which brought us the intelligence of the death of Dr. Dodge, at Jerusalem, informed us also of the decease of the Rev. Dr. Morrison, in China, and of the Rev. Dr. Carey, at Serampore. And it was only a few days previous that we heard of our brethren Lyman and Munson being devoured by cannibals in the Island of Sumatra. This last

seems to us particularly shocking and awful, because it is an
event so uncommon. But in reality what difference does it
make whether our bodies be devoured by cannibals or by
worms? Our blessed Lord will in either case know where
to find us at the resurrection of the just."

In his correspondence at this time he speaks hopefully and
confidently of the blessing which was coming upon the people for whom he was laboring and praying. In a letter to a
friend in Boston, dated Constantinople, Oct. 13, 1835, he
writes : —

" Your kind letter of May 7th was received July the 4th,
together with the penknives and razors, with which, indeed,
you have kept me well supplied these thirteen years. But
for the former I should not have written so much nor so
well; and but for the latter I should not have made so
decent an appearance when I went abroad. Oh, how pleasant it is to belong to the kingdom of Christ, and to use
razors, penknives, scissors, and, indeed, every thing, under
His spiritual reign !

" As you already know, we erected His standard at this
capital four years ago, and I am happy to report that it is
now seen from afar. Many eyes are directed towards it,
and not only so, but there is really a gathering round it.
Instead of attempting to teach the Bible as heretofore, there
is a willingness on the part of many Armenians that the
Bible should teach them. They sit down at the feet of
Christ to learn of Him, and are, I trust, becoming wise unto
salvation. I have never before seen so much tenderness of
feeling since I left America, unless perhaps at times in our
English congregation at Malta. It seems like the coming
over of a cloud, and the first fresh droppings of the rain after
a long-continued and most distressing drought. It is like the
coming back of the Holy Spirit to dwell with men on the
earth, and to fit them to become subjects of the spiritual reign
of Christ.

" But I was going to tell you of a conversation I had with
an Armenian, a friend of ours, who lives in one of the villages on the beautiful Bosphorus, and who can scarcely be
less than fourscore years and ten. His limbs shake like
those of one afflicted with the palsy, and he cannot even take
his coffee without drawing his knees up near to his chin, and

grasping the cup between them with both hands. But, strange as it may seem, he is always found working at his trade, and his mind is vigorous and active. As he is sensible that he cannot continue long in this world, his thoughts are much directed to that world of which he is soon to be an inhabitant ; and, whenever I visit him, he always has many questions to ask about the momentous concerns of that world, and he always asks them with a serious and tender spirit. It is pleasant to talk with him, and tell him of the fulness and freeness of salvation by Christ. In the last interview I had with him, something was said of 'our conversation,' or, as it should be rendered, 'citizenship, being in heaven.' I told him that during the Greek revolution many respectable families fled to Malta. They lived there several years, but they did not become citizens of Malta. They did not build houses there, nor make any arrangement for a permanent residence there. They did not intermarry nor amalgamate with the people there, but, on the contrary, they retained their own customs and manners, and formed a class by themselves. They were citizens of Greece. They were interested in the affairs of Greece, and read every thing which was published about the state of things there. They laid out their money for houses and lands in Greece, and were making preparation to remove thither with their whole families. They hailed as a brother every one who was a friend to Greece, and they had a time of rejoicing whenever they heard good news from that country. In fact, they carried on a brisk correspondence and trade with Greece ; all their thoughts and desires and aims and endeavors had some reference or other to Greece ; they lived in Malta, but their citizenship was in Greece ; and they were known and acknowledged everywhere as the citizens of Greece. Every one of them could say, 'That is my country ; that is my home ; there my best friends and kindred dwell.'

"Just so should 'our citizenship be in heaven.' Every thing we do or say should have special reference to heaven. And whenever we are at a loss to know what is meant by 'our citizenship being in heaven,' we should think of these citizens of Greece. And oh, may our thoughts always dwell in heaven with a thousand times more delight and interest than theirs did in Greece ! "

The extracts from his journal are continued : —

"*Wednesday, October* 28. I was visited to-day by three Armenian bishops. One of them was Bishop of ——, near Aleppo ; the other two were from the party of the patriarch here, one of them being his chief secretary. The conversation turned on what was moral, and what merely ceremonial, in the institutions of religion. They all agreed with me that in Christianity the mode. the outward form, was comparatively nothing. while the spirit was every thing. Every thing in the institutions of Christ which pertained to the ceremonial part was, I told them, left unprescribed, to be accommodated to the customs of different countries, and the changed state of society of different periods. In the Lord's Supper, for instance, not a word was said at what hour it must be observed, whether morning, noon, or night ; in what way, whether standing, sitting, or kneeling ; how often, whether once a year, once a month, once a week, once a day, or several times a day ; in what place, whether in a 'large upper room' or on the lower floor. In fact, every thing ceremonial about the institution was left altogether undefined. The great thing required was to do it in remembrance of Christ.

"So of prayer. We are required to make known our requests unto God; but we are not told whether we are to do it standing, kneeling, or lying prostrate on the ground. Every thing outward and ceremonial about it is entirely overlooked. as not worth a straw in comparison with the inward and the spiritual frame of the worshipper.

" But how different from this are the requirements of the Koran ! and how different every false religion in the world ! In all false religions the mode, the form, is in general every thing. Every ceremony is defined with as much minuteness and accuracy as though, like a medical prescription, it had some intrinsic efficacy in itself; and, instead of being regarded as means designed merely to produce a moral effect, was regarded as efficacious in proportion to the precise and punctilious exactness with which the external rite should be performed.

" So in regard to the etiquette of the royal palace. The forms of behavior are prescribed ; there must be a punctilious attention to exactness ; ceremony is every thing ; for the Sultan looketh only on the outward appearance, and can command nothing further. But God is a Spirit who looketh on the heart, and the service He requireth is spiritual ; and it may be observed in general that whenever this truth is forgotten, and the moral effect of any institution of Christ is lost sight of by men, the ceremonial part is in exact proportion magnified by them.

" I afterwards conversed with them on the importance of their doing just what John the Baptist did, when he called upon the people to repent of their sins and forsake them, that they might be ready to welcome the spiritual reign of Christ. They must do what Moses did, when he enjoined upon the people to sanctify themselves and be ready, that the Lord might come down and do wonders among them; for it was very evident to me that the darkness was fleeing and the true light beginning to shine among them, and that God was about to visit and bless them.

" *November* 14. Received a letter this morning from the Bishop of Rhodosto, addressing me as ' the honorable Father,' the illustrious preacher of the Gospel,' &c. He begs me to overlook and forgive a misdemeanor in one of the young Armenians in the high school (he had stolen books from us), as he now appeared penitent, and the bishop would himself be a guarantee for his good behavior in time to come, if we would take him again into our service. Another instance of the confidence and kind feelings of these high dignitaries of the church towards us and our objects.

" *November* 30. The good work among the Armenians has been steadily advancing from week to week, and it now seems to be carrying bishops, bankers, every thing before it. And what is still more glorious, the work of regeneration has absolutely commenced, and is following right on after the work of reformation. God's blessed word was the first in order, and now it is God's blessed Spirit. We have seen nothing like this, nothing to be compared with it, since we left America, now almost thirteen years ago.

" *December* 9. At Hass-Keuy called on Der Kevork, the learned priest of whose ordination, together with that of fourteen others, I have made mention. The evidence he gives of being truly ' a man after God's own heart' is becoming more and more decisive. This priest has the charge of a school consisting of three hundred and seventy-five boys, with some half a dozen under-teachers. A class of twenty, the finest boys in the school, were attending, under his more immediate direction, to the critical study of the New Testament. After hearing them read, construe, and explain, I expressed the great gratification I felt in seeing them have in their own

hands, read with their own eyes, and endeavor to understand
with their own judgments, the words of eternal life. I then
added that I had read the whole New Testament through
five or six times in Ancient Greek, several times in Turkish,
Armeno-Turkish, and Modern Greek, several times in Italian,
Latin, and Arabic, and between fifty and sixty times in English; all this not carelessly, but with thought and reflection,
and not only with attention of the mind, but with a sincere
and prayerful desire of the heart to understand it, and that
the more I read it the better I liked it. It was truly a light
to our feet and a lamp to our path. It was my delight to
read of the Lord Jesus Christ, God's beloved Son; to read
of His miracles, of His doctrines, of His love and power and
tenderness and compassion. And when I was reading about
Him, how delightful to stop and think of Him, trust in Him,
learn of Him, pray to Him, and love and praise and serve
Him! How delightful to belong to His kingdom, to obey all
the laws of His empire, and to observe all His institutions!
And to think that when we are removed from this dark and
distant and rebellious province of His domain, we shall go to
the capital city, where He lives and reigns and shows the
glory which He had with the Father before the world was.

"*April 5, 1836.* Our helpers have been in jeopardy. One
of the boldest and strongest of them, who talked a great
deal, and whose arguments no one could confute, was accused
by a priest of being an infidel, and was publicly denounced
in the church. All Constantinople, in consequence, was in an
uproar; the noise was prodigious, and the patriarch appointed
a commission consisting of two bishops, several priests, and
several of the principal laymen of that church, to examine
the accused person. We were all extremely anxious for the
result, as a blow struck at this one would be a blow for all
our helpers. But this special commission not only pronounced
him orthodox, but declared the priest who had accused him
of infidelity of being an infidel himself. One of the bishops
afterward patted him on the shoulder, and told him to be of
good courage, for he was not alone, but many others were
talking and still more were thinking just like him on these
subjects. But while the matter was under investigation, the
enemies were very busy in ascertaining the number of these
'evangelical infidels,' as they were called, and they had
already written down the names of eight hundred persons.
The Lord add to their number a thousand-fold."

A letter to the Rev. William S. Plumer, D.D., then at
Richmond, Va., contains an interesting account of a conference of missionaries at Smyrna, to which he was called in the
spring of 1836. The object of the conference was to look
over the past and see where mistakes had been made or de-
ficiencies had occurred, and to inquire of one another, and
together of the Lord, what more could be done to give free
course to the Gospel and secure its influence in the hearts of
the people. The meeting was one of great religious enjoyment, and all present received a new impulse in the cause in
which they were engaged, and new encouragement to go forward. The letter is given entire: —

CONSTANTINOPLE, April 4, 1836.

REV. AND DEAR SIR, — I am indebted to you for several
letters, — the last bearing date " Washington City, Sept. 14,
1835," and though I cannot at present pay you so much as
even the interest, yet it may be some satisfaction to you to
know that I acknowledge the debt. Let me say, too, that
all your drafts in favor of those recommended to my hospitality have been duly honored at sight, nor do I anticipate
the necessity of ever protesting any such bills of yours, in
whose favor soever they may be drawn.

I returned a few days since from the meeting of the " General Assembly " at Smyrna, and a most interesting session we
had. We were all of the same mind and the same judgment,
and the most perfect unanimity, of course, prevailed. Scarcely
a dissenting voice was heard on any subject. This was the
more remarkable, as we have occupied different and distant
stations, and were in general ignorant of each other's particular views as to the best course to be pursued in our efforts
to regenerate these dead churches. Our meetings for business commenced usually at nine o'clock in the morning. At
six o'clock almost every morning I met the children of the
mission and other families, and endeavored to bring them all,
every one of them, into the kingdom of Christ. Almost every
evening we had social prayer-meetings, which were truly
precious. Much of the conversation was about Christ and
heaven. Whatever subject was introduced, it was almost
sure in the end to run into heaven. And frequently, when
the meeting was declared to be finished, we would all sit

down, and go to talking again, till some one would say, " Arise, let us go hence."

What gave peculiar interest to the occasion was, that four of the oldest missionaries of the Board in these countries, who have not all met before for many years, were present, viz., the Rev. Messrs. King, Temple, Bird, and myself.   Mr. Bird was my fellow-student at the Theological Seminary, my fellow-passenger from America, and my fellow-laborer for several years in Syria, but I had not seen him or his family before for six years.   Mr. King was also with us, both at the Theological Seminary and in Syria ; but since either of us had had an opportunity before of bowing the knee with him at the throne of mercy, his fellow-traveller and companion in labor, our beloved brother Fisk, had gone to bow with the ten thousand times ten thousand round about the throne above, near eleven years ago.   Mr. Temple was my classmate at the academy, at college, and at the Theological Seminary, — in all nine years, the last seven of which he was my room-mate. We ate at the same table, and slept in the same bed, and prayed in the same closet ; twice, also, we had been fellow-laborers at Malta ; but five years had elapsed since our last meeting.   We had no expectation of all meeting together again, till we should meet in another and very different part of the empire of Christ, even the capital of His glorious kingdom.   And as — excepting the Rev. Mr. Lowndes, of Corfu, who is of the London Missionary Society — we four were the oldest missionaries this side of India of any society whatever, we could not but feel that the time for putting off this tabernacle was in all probability, at least for some of us, drawing nigh.   You can easily imagine, then, that the season throughout must have been one of most tender interest to us. At the close of all, we united in celebrating the love of Christ at His table, and then parted, hoping to see each other again in that world where our hearts will rejoice, and our joy no man can take from us.

I ought to add that, in addition to this renewing of old acquaintances (among whom should be included the Rev. Messrs. Arundel, Lewis, and Jetter, with Mr. Barker), I had the happiness also of forming some new ones, among whom I must not omit to mention Mr. and Mrs. Adger and Mr. and Mrs. Houston, all of whom are from your section of the country, and the two latter from your own State, and all of whom are exceedingly dear to us.   We had also with us, to assist by his counsels and prayers during the whole session, the Rev. Mr. Paxton, who must be known personally to many of your good people in Richmond, and who appears to be truly a man of God. Oh, I love to see 'the North give up, and the South not keep back,' in more senses than one.

Speaking of the South reminds me that I have recently read the memoir of your good Dr. Rice. With his views on most of the absorbing subjects of the day I must say I am delighted. He is always sober, practical, and not afraid to follow the Bible, wherever it may lead him. This is what I like. May the great Head of the church raise up many such!

But I must close. I do not know that I have any acquaintances in your part of Virginia, unless Captain Skinner may be in your vicinity, of whom we cherish a grateful remembrance. But you can, if you please, "salute every saint in Christ Jesus," and say that " we are members one of another."

The Lord bless you, my brother, and finally bring you and, through your instrumentality, many with you to His eternal kingdom! And thus also may He bring,

Yours most truly and affectionately,
W. GOODELL.

His views in regard to the qualifications of a missionary's wife having been asked by the Board at home, he communicated them in full. Only one particular is here given, as not inappropriate to the discussion of some points that occupy public attention at the present day, and as having universal application.

" The very highest qualifications which a married woman can possess are those which fit her to discharge the duties of a wife and a mother.

" The exceptions to this rule are so rare, that the Bible takes no notice of them. On the contrary, it everywhere teaches that her first duties belong to her own family. Her place is in the centre of domestic cares; and her attention to public duties is always to be regulated by a due regard to her domestic claims. Such is the rule; and if there be an exception to it, the wife of the missionary in this part of the world is not likely to be the one. In these countries, where so much more can be done by living than by preaching, a missionary family is, or ought to be, the very nursery of heaven. His house is necessarily large, to accommodate translators, teachers, and inquirers. He has apartments consecrated especially to prayer and praise, to reading the word of God, and to preaching the glad tidings of the kingdom. He is visited by all sorts of persons, from all parts of the country, at all hours of the day. And ought not his family to be a pattern of whatsoever things are lovely, honest, and of good report? Ought not his family to exhibit all that comfort, and order, and neatness, and harmony, and purity, and frugality, and punctuality, and wisdom, and piety, and good sense, and well-formed habits, for which the domestic constitution is so happily designed? In short, should not his family be such that it may be referred to by the whole community as a specimen of what a Christian and well-regulated family ought to be? But whether such a beautiful example be exhibited in the family of the missionary, or not, turns chiefly on the point whether 'she looketh well to the ways of her household.' Nor can she procure the assistance of any one to divide with her the care and responsibility of all this. With you the thing is easy; with her, beyond the bounds of possibility. Poetry and eloquence in America may sing a rapturous song and tell a thrilling story about her future labors, but she will find, after all, that her most important duties are those which are too common to be celebrated in song, and too humble to procure renown.

"And, besides, she comes to a country where the customs are Oriental, where the sphere of woman has from time immemorial been much more limited than with us in America, and where she will get little credit to herself by going out of what even the Bible itself seems to recognize as her proper sphere. The people of the country are quick-sighted. They are by no means unapt at quoting Scripture, whenever they can make it answer their purpose. And they will not be able to see how her zeal is according to knowledge, if she neglect her own in providing for others. They will not be able to see how she is fit to be trusted with the children of others, if she does not appear to know how to manage her own; nor how she can be capable of teaching them their duty to God, if she fail in teaching them how to conduct themselves in the presence of their fellow-men. And you must know that much more attention is usually paid to dress and manners here than in America."

To a lady in the United States, who had written to him asking for Oriental curiosities, he wrote:—

" Had I received your letter a few hours sooner, I could and would have sent you a few curiosities from Jerusalem, for I was then making up a parcel for various friends in America. But now I have not so much as an olive leaf from the Mount of Olives, nor a pebble from the Brook Kedron, nor a wild-flower from the Garden of Gethsemane, nor a thistle from the Plains of Bethlehem, nor a petrifaction, of which there are some beautiful specimens, from Mount Carmel, nor a branch from the stately cedars of Lebanon, nor a single bit of asphaltum from the Dead Sea. No; the only thing I now have from Palestine is a small stick which was cut on the banks of the Jordan. And this, if you please, you can have made into something which, without one atom of superstition, you may keep, in order to help give a freshness and reality to the history of all those interesting scenes which took place on the banks of that sacred stream. Indeed, you can, if you please, suppose that our blessed Lord Himself stood by the parent stock when at His baptism He prayed, and a dove came upon His head, and from the opening heavens a voice broke forth in the hearing of the astonished multitude, ' This is my beloved Son, in whom I am well pleased.'

" Indeed, my dear friend. no Biblical scholar or enlightened Christian can visit Palestine without a feeling more deep and vivid than before, that every word of the Bible is true. Not only is the country the same, the mountains and valleys and rocks, but the customs are the same ; and the allusions to these which abound in the Scriptures have a beauty, a force, and a pertinency which none but an Oriental is fully capable of appreciating, and which, in some instances, none but an Oriental can understand at all."

To one of the missionaries at Broosa he wrote in a time of peculiar trial and anxiety, occasioned by opposition to the truth and to the missionary work :—

CONSTANTINOPLE, July 4, 1836.

MY DEARLY BELOVED SISTER, — I received yours of the 18th ult., and I do not wonder you have felt disconsolate. But "hope thou in God, for thou shalt yet praise Him, who is the help of thy countenance and thy God."

By the letter from Mr. Temple, which I sent for your

perusal last week, and by the copies of a defence of the missionaries, written by a Greek, which I sent you to-day, you will learn how matters are going on in that quarter.

It calls, I think, for special thanksgiving to God that this collision with the Greek ecclesiastics at Smyrna did not take place at an earlier period of the mission there. The missionaries have now done so much, and got such a foothold, established so many schools, made so many acquaintances, secured so many friends, conveyed a knowledge of the Gospel to so many minds, and are, moreover, now able to make themselves heard so extensively through the public press, that it is thought the priests will "prevail nothing," but will themselves be evident losers by the controversy.

But at Broosa, on the other hand, you will, I fear, be misrepresented, condemned unheard, and your influence for the present be curtailed. Not that you are to be blamed for the course things have taken; for I know of no missionaries of the Board in whose discretion I have greater confidence than in that of the missionaries at Broosa; and you have certainly succeeded in the good providence of God in parrying this blow much longer than I expected you would. But "it is impossible (even after we have done our very best) but that offences should come;" and, when they do come, we must look to God for light and direction, and endeavor to turn them to the best account possible. We are not to take it for granted that they will certainly promote the good cause; for they may hinder it. They call to fasting, humiliation, and prayer; and, at any rate, they may always, and should always, be improved to our own growth in grace. I have been led to think they are sometimes designed especially for our own good, — are sent on purpose to make us more humble and more heavenly minded, and to quicken us in our way to heaven. And though it is exceedingly humiliating to think that the people must remain still longer in ignorance, and die in their sins, in order that the missionary may "not perish, but have eternal life," yet these views I expressed to my brethren in Smyrna at the general meeting last spring; for I saw evidence that they had all been benefited by the various trials and afflictions through which they had been called to pass, — each one tried in the very point where his character needed most refining.

But whoever may be the instruments, or whatever may be the particular design of Providence, they may, as I said before, always be improved to our own good, — frequently also to the benefit of some others, — while sometimes they are manifestly overruled, as well as intended, for the good of the cause. One thing is certain, viz., that the great Head of the church has no less authority and control in the kingdom of providence than He has in the kingdom of grace, and that our trials are no less the appointments of His wisdom than our salvation is the fruit of His love. In each case it is He Himself, acting in His own official character as King in Zion. The hand that weighs and portions out to us the former is the same kind hand that dispenses so freely the blessings of the latter. And, however bitter the cup we have to drink, we are sure it contains nothing unnecessary or unkind; and we should take it from His hand with as much meekness as we accept of eternal life with thankfulness.

In fine, our disappointments and trials are not to be regarded as a chapter of accidents, but they are to be looked on, and looked for, as dispensations which are suited to our particular state, and by which God will either mend us or ruin us.

Be assured you have the prayers and sympathy of us all; and, as I have had more of such experience, perhaps I may say, especially of your friend and brother,

W. GOODELL.

He records in his journal, under date of Oct. 1, 1836, some striking coincidences: —

"It is a very remarkable circumstance that my brother Joel, in Ohio, and myself, in Constantinople, both of us, on the 10th of May, 1835, the very day of our sister Lydia's death in New York, preached from this text, 'There remaineth therefore a rest to the people of God,' — both of us thinking and preaching and praying about heaven at the very time of our sister's entrance there, as our hope and trust is.

"It is very remarkable, too, that of our disjointed family three should be ministers of the Gospel, in three different countries; and that all the rest, with all those connected with them in marriage, should be members of the church of Christ. 'Bless the Lord, O my soul, and forget not all His benefits.'"

With all his calmness and self-possession, there were times when he became excited with earnest desires for the success

9   M

of his work, and the triumph of the truth.   This desire only
became more intense as he saw the day approaching.   To a
missionary at another station he wrote, under date of Jan.
14, 1837 : —

"Light is kindling up here and there.   Truth is prevailing.   Priests and people. in some cases, sit up all night to
talk about the glorious Gospel.   I am sometimes quite fever-
ish with excitement.   I want to jump ; I want to fly ; I want
a thousand tongues to proclaim the unsearchable riches of
Christ.   We are unable to do the ten thousandth part we
want to do.   We do little more than stand and see the salvation of God."

To the Rev. Mr. Houston, who was considering the question of duty in regard to remaining at the island of Scio,
or seeking a more promising field of labor on the mainland
in Greece, he wrote, Feb. 4, 1837 : —

"MY DEAR BROTHER, — It is my decided opinion, and
it is the opinion also of some of my brethren here (I have
not had time to consult them all), that you would be justified. should you 'enter into a ship, and pass over to the other
side,' though not to your ' own city.'   And even your very
departure might be a greater blessing to the people of Scio
than your presence has been.   They might blame themselves, and blame one another, and deeply regret the
privileges they had lost; and thus be prepared better to
appreciate and improve those they might enjoy in time
to come.   But, in shaking off the dust of your feet, be
careful to do it in the most Christian manner possible.   It
should be a very solemn season, a season of great tenderness and prayerfulness.   In taking your final leave of
your neighbors and acquaintances, you should endeavor
to give them the decided impression that you love all the
people of the island, and feel most kindly towards them;
that you had no object in coming but to do them good;
that you leave them, having great sorrow in your heart,
but that you go for the sake of carrying the blessings they
undervalue to others who call for them, and will gladly
avail themselves of them.   And when you 'have gone over
Greece, and have no more place in those parts,' come to
Constantinople.   We need a helper exceedingly, and have
recently written for one expressly for the Greeks here."

The extracts from his journal are continued : —

" *March* 5, 1837. Some time last week one of the hermits put up a paper on the door of the Greek church in Pera, calling upon all the people to rise and utterly exterminate the corrupter of their youth and the destroyer of their religion. One of the principal citizens, passing by, saw it, and informed the bishop, in order that it might be immediately taken down; for, said he, should it come to the ears of the Sultan, as no individual is specified, he will very naturally think himself intended. But, though the paper was forthwith removed, yet it produced so much sensation that many protected Greeks went to church on Sunday, prepared, in case priest E. should denounce any individual as a heretic, to drag the preacher from the pulpit, and turn him into the street. The Sublime Porte also subsequently took cognizance of the paper, interpreting it, of course, in the very natural way suggested above; and the Greek patriarch found it very difficult to give a satisfactory account of the business. Some of the Greeks were for accusing our own quiet selves as the authors of the paper, but no one dared to do it openly and formally.

" *March* 17. Met in the street an Armenian teacher, who occasionally visited us last summer, and who had so much to say against superfluous worship. He asked whether our high school had commenced since the plague. I told him that our school no longer existed, but that there would be another and better one at Hass Keuy. He expressed surprise, and asked me to explain myself. As he appeared to be perfectly ignorant of all that had transpired, I began by saying, ' You are doubtless aware that the chief men of the nation became a little alarmed about our high school, not knowing what might grow out of it, and therefore ' —

" ' Aman ! Aman ! ' (Alas ! Alas !) he interrupted, ' I understand it all. Aman ! Aman ! '

" ' But stop a moment,' said I, ' and you will see that it is all ordered right, and has turned out well. You do not underst ' —

" ' Aman ! Aman ! ' he again interrupted. ' I understand it all ; my worst fears are realized. Aman ! Aman ! '

And thus he left me, crying, as long as I could hear him, ' Aman ! Aman ! ' which, for aught I know, he is repeating to this day.

"*April* 4. Being in the city to-day, a beggar, sitting by the wayside, asked charity for the sake of the mediation of Christ. I do not recollect of ever hearing a beggar use this plea before. If Christians, they generally ask for the sake of the Virgin, or some of the saints. In the present instance the poor man's plea was not in vain; for I stopped at once, and gave him something, and I resolved to give something, if in my power, to every beggar who asked in the name of Christ, recollecting that blessed promise of His, that 'whatsoever we ask in His name, it shall be given us.' And if His name had influence with me, how much more influence does it have in heaven! I treat it with some respect, but in heaven it is regarded and treated according to its infinite worthiness.

"*May* 20. I was visited to-day by a lady of the papal Armenian Church, who wished to change her religion and become Protestant. She could read, and appeared intelligent; had heard much of our dwelling in love, without ever quarrelling and fighting with one another, and many other wonderful things; and she begged to be admitted to our communion, and unite all her interests, temporal as well as spiritual, with ours. After assuring her that our kingdom was not of this world, and that we were building up no church here, nor forming any ecclesiastical organization whatever, I entered into conversation with her at once on the great and fundamental doctrines of the Gospel, — on our being justified by faith; our being united to Christ; His dwelling in us; manifesting Himself unto us as He does not unto the world; drawing our hearts away from earthly vanities; and enabling us to live in His kingdom, and to eat bread in His kingdom, even though all around us belong to the kingdom of darkness and the kingdom of sin. There was something suspicious about the woman; but whatever was her motive in coming, she heard many things which seemed to surprise and impress her, and which may be the means, under the Holy Spirit, of bringing her to Christ and heaven."

To the Corresponding Secretary at Boston he wrote, May 9, 1837 : —

" The sweet influences of heaven still descend upon us, gently, indeed, but constantly, and, as for the last four years, uninterruptedly; and this, perhaps, is better than a heavy shower of short duration to soften the dry and parched earth, which has been baked for centuries. Several Roman Catholics have become hopefully converted; but, strange to tell, we hear not a word of opposition from any quarter. Every thing betokens a great revival of pure and undefiled religion in this mighty city; and we bespeak the prayers of the churches, both for ourselves and the people. Let it be known, too, that more apparently can be done now by prayer than in any other way. Whoever prays most helps most. What a privilege to the widow and the orphan!"

In the month of June, 1837, he made a visit to the mission families at Broosa, of which he gave an account in a letter to Oliver Powers, Esq., father of one of the missionaries:—

CONSTANTINOPLE, June 20, 1837.

MY VERY DEAR SIR,—I have just made a visit in person to Broosa, and am happy now to make another by letter to Phillipston, and acknowledge your kind favor, written on the fifty-fifth anniversary of your birth, and received one year ago to-day. It was only yesterday I returned from one of the most interesting visits I ever enjoyed, having spent a whole week with the beloved families at Broosa, and feeling all the time as though I were on the Mount of Transfiguration. We talked and sung and prayed together. We walked out and rode out and visited together. We sat together in heavenly places in Christ, and ate and drank together at the table of our Lord. And —

> " What peaceful hours we then enjoyed!
> How sweet their mem'ry still!"

Both of those dear families, I am happy to assure you, appear really to be living a heavenly life upon earth. They love one another, and dwell in God, and God in them. Their homes are still, clean, quiet, peaceful, pleasant, and happy; where the blessed Saviour loves to dwell, and where, I trust, He will always dwell, till He takes them up to dwell always with Him. They pray a great deal for one another, for their dear friends in America, and especially for the poor, perishing people around them; and they are exerting all about them an influence as gentle, yet refreshing, as the dews of heaven. They have erected the standard of the cross at the foot of Mount Olympus, which is seen afar off; and, though the wicked have clapped their hands in derision, yet I do verily believe it will never be taken down. No; thousands and tens of thousands shall yet flock around it, and enjoy the happiness of Messiah's reign.

I spent the first night in one family, and the second in the other, and so on during my whole stay, and we were all together every day excepting one. They gave me apple-pies made from American apples; pumpkin-pies made of American pumpkin; bread spread over with American butter; cakes fried in American lard; boiled corn with molasses, after the American fashion; together with American cheese, American currants, and American spruce-beer, — all "sanctified by the word of God and prayer;" and we felt that we were indeed "eating bread in the kingdom of God."

For the dried-apple sent me by your beloved daughter, from the old farm in Templeton, will you return her my warmest thanks? I brought it with me on my return from Broosa, and wish to assure her that it was very acceptable.

Will you remember me also to your new minister? I once saw him, though he may not recollect me. May he have an unction from the Holy One, and his labors be greatly blessed!

I almost forgot to say that while at Broosa I rode out to see the spot where your beloved children will probably find their last resting-place. It is very retired and romantic, away from the noise of men; and a sweeter spot one need not desire to lie in till the bright morning of the resurrection.

Mrs. Goodell unites in Christian love to all your dear family. Will you remember us and our six little ones in your prayers?

Yours truly and affectionately,

W. GOODELL.

In a communication to the Board, he related some of the incidents of his journey, which are inserted as showing the condition of the interior and the character of the government: —

"*Constantinople, July* 25, 1837. I left this for Broosa on the 7th of June, and returned on the 19th. Broosa is about twenty miles from Mondania, which is a seaport town, situated on the southern shore of the Marmora; and, as the Sea of Marmora is here, including the gulf, full sixty miles across, Broosa cannot be less than eighty miles from Constantinople. I left home at five o'clock in the evening in an open boat, and arrived at Broosa on horseback before the middle of the following day.

"The return from Broosa to Constantinople is often a more serious matter; for, as the north are the prevailing winds, it is necessary in such cases to row all the way back; and, should the wind be strong, a detention at Mondania, or at some place (perhaps an uninhabited one) on the way, may be the consequence. This has happened to myself more than once; and it requires all the patience one can command to keep himself quiet in a place where he can do nothing, enjoy nothing, and perchance find nothing to eat.

"On the present occasion I was detained from a cause of a still more serious nature. An order had just come from Constantinople to Moudania for a hundred Greeks; and, as it appeared they were designed for the Sultan's navy, they were particularly sought for from among the boatmen. As might be expected, therefore, the boatmen fled in every direction, and, as they were all Greeks, not a boat could, of course, be found. I went to the governor; but he only exhorted me to patience. The plague was raging in the place, and every hour seemed to me as long as a day. The miserable coffee-shop where I was staying, and where nothing save thick, muddy coffee could be obtained, was filled day and night with filthy, lounging Turks. The impressment of young Greeks was going on, and the mothers and sisters were assembled before the governor's house, weeping and lamenting the fate of their sons and brothers. As I passed by repeatedly, I said unto them, 'Weep not;' but my sympathy was impotent. Oh, how unlike His who could dry the mourner's tear!

"At length, on the third day, the governor, not being able to seize any more, put them all, forty in number, into a small craft of the country to send them to Constantinople. There were, besides, two criminals, who had been taken up for counterfeiting money, and who were expecting nothing less than the gallows. Several Armenians and Turks, similarly situated with myself, also took passage. And, not knowing when there might be another opportunity for leaving the place, I thought best to take passage with them, although I feared, on the one hand, that the plague might break out among us, and, on the other, that the prisoners might mutiny, kill the guard, take possession of the boat, and carry me I knew not whither. We were in all sixty souls, crowded close together. But I secured a place for myself in the aftermost part by the tiller, where, although I had not sufficient room to stretch myself, I was in some measure isolated.

" I was on board when those who had been impressed were brought from the prison. They were pinioned and chained two together. Their mothers and other female relatives rushed to the water's edge to give them the last embrace. Their cries rent the air. One mother fainted away; another tore the flesh with her teeth from off her own arm; another threw herself into the sea, and was pulled out by the soldiers. Some of the prisoners, too, sobbed and wept like children, and some danced and sung, while the tears were still streaming down their cheeks. As I sat there, I literally ' groaned in the spirit and was troubled.' I was 'pained at my very heart.' I tried to speak some word of comfort, but my voice faltered, and I wept freely. At last I was able to say to the young men, ' Fear not. Put your trust in God. Commit all your ways to Him. Cast all your cares upon Him. In all the kingdoms of this world there is more or less of oppression and wrong and suffering; but in the kingdom of Christ there is none. Let us all belong to His blessed kingdom, and we shall be happy for ever.'

" We left Mondania about the middle of the day on Saturday, and within three hours all the fresh water on board was consumed. As we were then tacking to double the Cape of Boor-Boornoo, the captain ran ashore with the boat to take in more; but by the next morning this also was spent, together with all the bread. All that day we were without water, and the poor men had nothing but olives to eat, and I myself but little more.

" Early on Monday morning we reached Constantinople, and preparations were immediately made for presenting the young men before the Capudan Pasha. Whether they were to be employed in the Sultan's service for life ; whether they were to receive any adequate pay ; whether they would ever be permitted to visit their friends ; whether they would be tempted by hard treatment, or by kind offers, to become

Mussulmans, — were questions which none present could answer. One of them was recently married; one was betrothed; one was the son of a priest; and one 'was the only son of his mother, and she a widow.' Oh, what misery has sin brought into this world! Oh, this ill-fated country! When 'one woe is past, behold another woe cometh quickly.' God is desolating them with judgments, which follow each other in quick succession. But they repent not; they turn not from their evil ways; there is scarcely one that understandeth, or that asketh the cause of their sufferings; they 'go on still in their trespasses.' This is the general character of the present generation. And the high probability is, that they will never see the good land, but that the greater part of them will be swept off by the desolating judgments of heaven; and that it will remain for their children to live in 'the new heavens and new earth, wherein dwelleth righteousness.'"

9*

CHAPTER XII.

FOR a long period that terrible scourge of the East, the plague, seemed to have its home at Constantinople. Like nearly every other destructive pestilence that has swept over any considerable portion of the earth, it had its origin in Central Asia, from whence it began its westward march about the middle of the fourteenth century. Under the name of the "black death," it passed over into Europe, and became, as it were, domesticated on the shores of the Eastern Mediterranean. True to their belief in fatalism, the Mohammedans allowed it to come and go, without lifting a finger to prevent it. "What Allah wills must be," was one of the prominent articles of their creed. The Turkish government, until within the last few years, steadily refused to establish any sort of quarantine; and when the plague appeared, no effective measures were taken to prevent its spread. The consequence was, that it seldom prevailed anywhere on the Mediterranean without coming to Constantinople, and sometimes it remained for years.

The Greeks, Armenians, Jews, &c., of Constantinople were far from regarding it with the stoical indifference of the Mohammedans. The disease was considered in the highest degree contagious, and its horrors were often aggravated by the terror and dread of each other, that seized upon these people whenever it made its appearance. If a person were attacked with the disease, neighbors and friends would remove to a distance, and not unfrequently he would be left to die unattended. When a death occurred, public porters, who were secluded from the rest of the community, came and took up the body, and cast it, uncoffined and unattended, into a common pit.

As a consequence, during the greatest prevalence of the disease all missionary work among the people was suspended, the schools were closed to prevent its spread, and all ordinary intercourse was broken off. Even the missionaries established a rigid quarantine among themselves. None but the heads of the families were allowed to go into the street, lest in some unguarded way the infection should be brought into their homes. Each house had its closet or box in the yard for fumigating every one that entered. Not a parcel of any kind was handled until it had been thoroughly smoked. Letters were received from the hands of the courier with a pair of tongs, and disinfected in the fumes of sulphur, or by some other process, before it was considered safe to open them. At such times, to the missionaries and their families, there seemed but a step between them and death. Mr. Goodell once said, " When the plague is very bad, we always read the ninety-first Psalm." In his annual letter to his friend, Judge Cooke, in January, 1837, he gave the following account of the pestilence: —

CONSTANTINOPLE, Jan. 6, 1837.

MY DEAR SIR, — It is now near, or quite, six months since the plague passed beyond its ordinary limits, and full three months since it became truly frightful ; nor have its ravages yet entirely ceased, though I am thankful to say that it has received a check. Could you look in upon us at such times, you would see our schools suspended, our meetings broken up, our intercourse with the people cut off, our plans of usefulness interrupted, our domestics confined closely to the house, and every being and every thing admitted within doors either fumigated or made to pass through fire or water. You would see us in want of clothes, but not daring to purchase them ; our families requiring air and exercise, but unable to go abroad for the purpose, except at particular times and under certain restrictions ; our children destitute of shoes, and obliged to wait till we can send to Russia and get a whole box of them, having to pay some-

thing extraordinary, if not exorbitant, at the custom-house
in order to save the box from being opened and its contents
exposed to contagion. You would see one of the family
taken ill, perhaps from a mere cold, and immediately separated from all the others, no one feeling it safe to come in
actual contact, till it can be ascertained that it is not the
plague. You would see those of us who have to go abroad
put on cloaks. made of oil-cloth, which are said to be plague-
proof, and which make us look more like walking in the
midst of death than in the midst of life. But withal you
would see us generally cheerful and happy, attending to our
translations, having our own little precious meetings together,
and sometimes feeling that we were probably within a day
or two of heaven.

The number of victims cannot be ascertained with any
degree of certainty. For a considerable time the number
reported averaged from six to ten thousand a week. Some
say one-fifth of all Constantinople has perished. This, no
doubt, is an exaggeration; but it is agreed on all hands that
there has been no such plague here before, since the memorable one of 1812. I have never before seen the streets so
deserted and the places of public concourse so thinned.
Thousands of faces I used to see, I now see no more. In
one rich and influential family twenty-one individuals were
swept away in a few days, the father "only having escaped
alone to tell" the melancholy story. Oh, how many tens of
thousands have been hurried away from the land of the living! Oh, what a world that other world must be! But,
blessed be God, among all these multitudes I am happy to
report one individual who, it is believed, was a Christian.
This was Frans Müller, a young German, who was a constant attendant on Mr. Schauffler's German service. He is
the only one we love to call to mind, the only one we think
of with satisfaction, as being a follower and disciple of Christ,
and as belonging to His everlasting kingdom. And I have
therefore given you his name above, for "the righteous shall
be in everlasting remembrance."

The plague has come nigher to us this time than it ever
came before. Several of our acquaintances — some with
whom we had but a day or two before had money transactions; some who had been in the habit of visiting us, and
with whom we had conversed on the great subjects of eternity — are gone to render up their account to God. Had I

known that they would have been summoned away so soon, I should have besought them with more tenderness and earnestness to be reconciled to God.

Most distressing cases of suffering have come to our knowledge; but I have not time for particulars. Let it suffice to mention one poor German woman, who, on being seized with the plague, was cast out into the open street. She begged here, and begged there, but no one would receive her. She staggered out to the burying-ground, and lay down between two graves, where she continued two days and a night. At length a Mussulman passed by, "and when he saw her, he had compassion on her, and went" and took her to a hospital, and demanded admittance for her. And the woman lived; and she is now in one of our families, receiving Christian instruction.

I have introduced this subject, my dear sir, in order to bespeak your prayers, and the prayers of your church, that God would be pleased to restrain the vials of His wrath, and instead thereof to open the windows of heaven and pour out upon us blessings like a flood. You see how our labors are interrupted by these direful judgments. And as to the people, "why should they be stricken any more? They will revolt more and more." Their hearts appear to be hardened, and not softened; and their insensibility has become like that of the brutes which perish. It is not common for the Turks generally to ask, or speak, or even think, of plague and death. I have seen them pass by or step over the dead body of a man, as they would pass by or step over the dead body of any brute animal. It is like the unconcern of the blind, or rather the insensibility of the dead. But let the still, small voice of Christian instruction and the whispers of the Holy Spirit be only heard, and men's hearts are softened, melted, changed; and "there is joy in the presence of the angels of God."

Mrs. Goodell unites in Christian salutations to all your dear family.

Yours affectionately,
W. GOODELL.

In the summer of 1837, the plague prevailed in its most virulent form; and this time the mission was not spared. Mr. Goodell remained with his family at Pera, directly opposite the city, but the other mission families removed to the distant suburbs. Mr. Dwight was at San Stephano, on the Sea of Marmora, about ten miles from the capital, a place often selected for temporary residence during the visitation of the pestilence, on account of its remarkably healthy location. Commodore Porter had made it his permanent residence, and the seat of the embassy, for this reason. While they were dying by the thousand daily at the capital, even this chosen spot was not now to be exempt. One of Mr. Dwight's children was seized with the plague, and died within forty-eight hours. Mrs. Dwight was attacked at the same time, and, after lingering several days, died on the 8th of July, in complete separation from all Christian friends, excepting her husband. Of the sad scenes attending her death and burial Mr. Goodell wrote to his brother Temple, then at Smyrna : —

CONSTANTINOPLE, July 2, 1837.

MY DEAR BROTHER TEMPLE, — I hardly know where or how to begin. You know we have a precious concert for the children. Last Thursday was the day for little Johnny, and last Thursday was little Johnny's last day. He lived till, we may suppose, the last prayers were offered for him by any of those here or at Broosa who observe the concert, and then "he was not, for God took him." He died of the plague about half-past ten on Thursday evening, after forty-eight hours' illness. Our dear sister, Mrs. Dwight, then lay at death's door of the same terrible disease ; and thirteen others in the family all exposed, besides two of our German missionary brethren, who had gone down on a visit to San Stephano. On Friday, Mr. and Mrs. Schauffler, with Mr. Dwight's babe and its nurse, left and came to Mr. Dwight's house in Pera ; and all the domestics, except a pious German and his wife, went into a tent at San Stephano with Mr. Dwight's two eldest children. This German and his wife (the latter was the one who had the plague last autumn) stopped with Mr. Dwight, the former to cook, &c., and the latter to assist in taking care of Mrs. Dwight. Brother Dwight, with this German, carried the body to the grave, and buried it alone ; and the German said he never heard such a prayer before in all his life, though he did not understand a word of it, as it was in English, and was poured only into the ears of his heavenly Father. It is a great grief to us that we cannot be with him in this extremity; but his God forsaketh him not. Christ is nigh; heaven is nigh; and the peace of heaven is actually there.

Our dear sister. We are waiting with impatience the return of the courier; but we suppose we have also offered our last prayers for her, and that she is now free from all the imperfections of mortality. In addition to the exposure of all the others, my own family are also compromised, as I received several letters from brother Dwight without fumigating them, not having any suspicion at first of its being the plague. The Farmans were also down on a visit to San Stephano after Mrs. Dwight and John were attacked. So there is not a missionary here, not even the travellers, who may not be considered as compromised fully. How many of us, or who of us, may be alive after another week no man can tell! But you will lift up your heart in prayer to God for the remnant that may be left.

Your Brother,
W. Goodell.

Some extracts from his journal, written during the prevalence of the disease, show that he was walking in the midst of death : —

" *May* 20, 1837. Heard to-day of the death of an interesting young man, Tchelebi Diamond, from Broosa. He was a friend of our missionary brethren and sisters there. They had conversed with him, read the Scriptures with him, prayed with him, wept over him, and sometimes thought him not far from the kingdom of God. He brought from Broosa a parcel and a letter for me, which, on his arrival here, he sent to me, with the message that he was too ill to call himself. The next day he died. It was the plague. As I took the parcel and the letter without fumigating them, I was of course compromised. Indeed, in one way and another we are often much exposed. This is the second with me within a few days, to say nothing of the thousand exposures which never come to our knowledge. Thus by an unseen hand we are preserved from dangers seen and unseen. Some risks seem unavoidable, if we would not shut ourselves up entirely. Our Greek girls' school is now stopped on account of the whole school having been most fully compromised by a case of

plague in the adjoining house, where several of the girls of
the school were lodging.

"*July* 21. I read the burial-service at the grave of the
only son of Sir P. Malcolm, who died of the plague at Mr.
Cartwright's, the English consul-general.   He was on his
way from India to England, and arrived sick from Trebizond
on the 16th inst. Mr. Cartwright's house adjoins my own,
and the unfortunate gentleman occupied a room which corners on our own bedchamber. We have placed chlorine in
all the rooms that were particularly exposed; but we are
certainly · in deaths oft,' and are made to feel that, ' except
the Lord keep the city, the watchman waketh but in vain.'
Most of the English merchants have been compromised in this
instance, as well as the physicians, for the disease was not at
first suspected to be plague. I myself received letters which
he brought, without fumigating them, although I fumigate in
almost every instance. And it is very remarkable that in
those instances in which I have neglected to take this pre-
caution, I have been exposed in a very unusual degree.
Truly there is but a step between us and death."

In writing to his friend, Judge Cooke, at the beginning of
the following year, he took up the record of the pestilence
just where he had left it, giving further accounts of the perils
through which he and his family had passed in the inter-
vening year.

CONSTANTINOPLE, Jan. 1, 1838.

MY DEAR SIR, — And the plague did not stop there, — I
mean where I left it last year. No; it came on still nigher to us.
It entered some of our own families. And not only were all the
fifteen souls of those two families within the walls of that one
house compromised, but my own family was compromised
most fully, for we were daily receiving letters from them,
without taking the usual precautions.   And not ourselves
only, but Mr. Farman, the English missionary here, and his
whole family, were also exposed, and likewise three German
missionaries, one with a wife and two children, who were all
passing through the place at the time, and two of whom, as
well as the family of Mr. Farman, visited at Mr. Dwight's,
some of them spending the night there, after the pestilence
had already seized upon his two victims.

Thus every missionary, and every missionary family, of

whatever society, as well those that were only tarrying in the place as it were for the night. as those stationed here, were all exposed to the contagion in a very unusual manner and to a very unusual degree. It was truly marvellous. God seemed to be saying to us that He could dispense with all of us entirely, and carry on His work without us. We all kept quarantine, not only family with family, but, as much as possible, individual with individual. We felt that we might be living our last days on earth. When we walked abroad, and looked upon the beautiful sky, and upon the beautiful scenery around Constantinople, we felt that we might be walking the streets and beholding the beautiful prospects of this world for the last time. And, though they never appeared more beautiful than now, yet I believe most of us could say, " Farewell, all ye beautiful prospects ! There are infinitely more beautiful ones in the bright world above !" Whomever we met in the streets, we felt kindly towards him, and prayed for him. And in the family, oh, how kind were our looks, and how tender were our tones, and how sweet were our words, and how fervent were our prayers ! In fine, we tried to live together, as we hoped to live together for ever in heaven. And it was no bad way of living, I assure you. No; there was no sadness, no melancholy, no unhappiness whatever in this way of living. Would that we could always live so ! Yea, and a thousand times better !

The sequel you know. I therefore only add, to those that died we believe it was gain, infinite gain ! While those that survived lost nothing, nothing ! On the contrary, they received a thousand-fold. I do not think Mr. Dwight ever had so much real enjoyment before in his whole life, put it all together, as he has had within a few months. His peace is like a river. His feet are on a rock, or rather The Rock. And his head is far above all the storms and tempests of this temporary scene. Oh, what a Saviour is this of ours ! Oh, what a glorious Gospel is this of our Lord and Saviour Jesus Christ !

> " His worth, if all the nations knew,
> Sure the whole world would love him too."

Is not this my fifteenth letter to Catskill ? Shall you, my dear sir, live to receive fifteen more ? or shall I live to write them ? Neither the one nor the other is at all probable. But no matter, I trust we shall have eternal life, through Jesus

N

Christ our Lord.   And instead of saying to you, as all my neighbors are saying to me on this new year, "Many happy returns to you," I would say, "May you live for ever!"
And so may yours truly,

W. Goodell.

He writes in his journal at this time of these and other trying scenes through which he and his associates were called to pass: —

"The missionary families in and around the Mediterranean have been afflicted in a very uncommon degree, and not only by sickness and death, but also by opposition of a peculiarly trying nature.   Men have persecuted them for being so much like Christ, and God has chastised them for not being more like Him.   But of whatever nature the affliction, the fruit of it, as there is good reason to believe, has been to take away sin.   Though not in itself joyous, but grievous, it has yielded some of the peaceable fruits of righteousness.   Oh, what deadness to the world it has in some instances produced!   What lively hopes of heaven!   What acquaintance with Christ, and with the power of His resurrection, and the fellowship of His sufferings, and the preciousness of His Gospel!   And what near and strong views of those things which are unseen and eternal!

"And, 'if the Lord were pleased to kill us,' would such have been the effect of His chastisements? and such the manifestations of His grace, and the visits of His love?   No; 'it is good for us that we have been afflicted.'   However mysterious our afflictions may appear to others, they are all plain to us.   'We know, O Lord, that thy judgments are right, and that thou in faithfulness hast afflicted us.'   We needed these chastisements.   And the evidence is clear that they were not sent in judgment, but in mercy; that they came not from an enemy, but from a friend; and that they came fraught with distinguished blessings.   The Lord is not doing us evil, but doing us good.   He is, we trust, fitting us for more eminent services in His kingdom.   He is preparing us to sympathize with Christ, to breathe more of His sweetness, love, and tenderness in our conversation, and more of His faith and fervor in our prayers, and thus to learn how to preach His blessed Gospel to the poor, and to bind up the broken-hearted.

"In this way, also, may it not be that the Lord is making us a sign to the people? They have never before seen men walking about as calmly in the furnace of affliction as the three children in the furnace of fire. This is the first time they have ever seen men 'glory in tribulation also,'— being not merely patient but joyful, not merely submissive and resigned, but exceedingly filled with comfort. And thus 'death worketh in us, but life in them.' Their sympathies are in many instances awakened; their admiration is called forth, and they learn what all the preaching in the world could not make them see, viz., the power of the Gospel. They see that God is with us of a truth; that we have not followed cunningly devised fables, but that the truth we have proclaimed to them is God's everlasting truth,— truth which He honors, and which is not only sufficient to live by, but abundantly sufficient to die by.

"And what if it should 'please Him, for whom are all things, and by whom are all things, in bringing many sons and daughters unto glory, to make' us, as he did 'the Captain of our salvation, perfect through sufferings'! Shall we complain of this, and say with the disappointed prophet, 'I do well to be angry'? When we were contemplating a missionary life in America, did we never pray that God, in building up His kingdom and gathering His outcasts, would make just such use of us as He pleased,— would make us any thing or nothing, as might be most for His glory? Yes; I remember such prayers. And lo! God is pleased to take us at our word, and to make us appear, at least, very small. And what if He should go a step farther, and make us nothing, or even, as it were, less than nothing, both in our own estimation and in the eyes of all the people here, in order that He may appear to be something, in order that He may be seen, that He may be praised, and that He may be glorified, and not we, and that thus He may be, as He deserves to be, 'all in all'!

"*November* 15. To-day I removed from the house I have occupied for the last three years to another I have secured for two years to come. In no other house, since I left America, fifteen years ago, have I lived so long, or enjoyed so many comforts, or felt to such a degree 'the powers of the world to come,' as I have in this; and in no other have there been more important missionary operations going on. Here my translations in Armeno-Turkish have been carried forward, and the meetings in Turkish generally held. Here from Sabbath to Sabbath have been two distinct chapels opened for two distinct services, viz., in English and German. Here began and flourished our high school in both its branches. Here were our philosophical apparatus, our room for public lectures, and our chemical laboratory. Here, for the most part, we held our Sabbath school, our Bible class, our singing meetings, our communion seasons, our monthly concerts, and our daily concerts, and our special days for fasting or thanksgiving. And what is more and better than all, we trust the Lord will count, when He writeth up the people, that this and that man were born there.'

"My present house is a new one, but is not so well situated as the former, and, being built of wood, its end doubtless 'is to be burned,' for such is universally the fate of all wooden houses in Constantinople. But, while we occupy it, may we enjoy more of the divine presence and blessing than we have ever done before! May every room be consecrated to Christ! May the Holy Spirit find a mansion in every heart, and be always cherished, and never grieved away! May all who shall enter our religious assemblies learn to worship God in spirit and in truth! May all who come to inquire concerning the truth become wise unto salvation! May all who dwell beneath this roof dwell in love, that they may dwell in God and God in them! And whenever we take our last remove, may 'we have a building of God, an house not made with hands, eternal in the heavens'!

"In removing, and I have already removed some dozens of times, I always find that a great deal of rubbish has accumulated, which is not worth carrying away, and is fit only to be burned. And when we take our last remove, I fear we shall find that a great deal which we called religion and which we were at the trouble of lugging about with us through our whole pilgrimage, is perfectly worthless, fit only to be burned, and we shall never think of taking it with us to the other world. Oh that we might no longer burden ourselves with such wretched furniture; but might empty ourselves entirely, and trust to our blessed Lord to make all the necessary preparation for us in those mansions above!"

The following, from a letter to the Corresponding Secretary of the Board, shows his readiness to retrench expenses in a time of need. It also expresses the confidence with which he was anticipating an answer to prayers and labor, in the spiritual reformation of the people by whom he was surrounded, and the wisdom with which he was directing his efforts toward such a result: —

" We sympathize with the Board in their present distresses; but we trust it will in the end prove a great blessing to the cause, to the churches, and to all the missionaries. We find many little things, yea, and some great ones, which can be easily dispensed with, and that without seriously affecting the interests of our mission. And so long as we are not required to make retrenchments in prayer, in faith, and in making known a knowledge of Christ and salvation, I verily believe we shall live and grow. Your circular, instead of leading us to despond, has in fact led us to 'thank God and take courage,' and we feel that now emphatically is the time to labor and pray in earnest.

" I see in your letter to Smyrna that, since reading Mr. Boggs's letter respecting the church missions among the Syrian Christians in India, you feel some doubts as to the correctness of the sentiments you advanced in the instructions to Messrs. H——, L——, &c. But it should be borne in mind that the people of India are very different from the people here. There, it is almost impossible to excite them; here, it is difficult to prevent excitement. There, they will never make one change of themselves; here, as soon as their eyes begin to be opened a little, they are all for change at once, and the only danger is that the external changes will go on at a much more rapid rate than the internal ones. For the present, it does appear to me that our great concern is with the latter. The former will follow of course, and when we can prevent their taking the lead, and, in fact, becoming the all-absorbing topic, we are glad. Again, in India, as the papal missionaries long ago said, they are not capable of managing their own ecclesiastical matters. But in these countries, there is energy enough, and there will be no occasion for the churches to be subjected to English bishops or American presbyters. Our advice and assistance will, of course, be wanted, when the church comes to be reformed externally; but do let it be our first and great object to get the materials for such a reformation.

" Again, I think we ought to be careful not to mark out beforehand the form which the reformation shall take. We can no more do this than we can prescribe the way in which sinners shall be converted. None of the great reformers, though some of them had prodigious influence, probably a thousand times more than any of us will ever have, were ever able to give just that shape which they wished to the new organization of the church. They took things as they were, and did what they could. And so we must do here, and so they must do in Syria. and so they must do in Abyssinia ; and so also in India, in Greece, in the Presbyterian Church in America. &c. There is not the least probability that, among people so very different in character and circumstances, the work will everywhere take the same form. The glorious reformation under Luther was by no means such as he wished it to be. Had it been possible for him, by cutting off a right hand or plucking out a right eye, to have separated church and state in the new organization, he would doubtless have done it with the utmost cheerfulness ; but it was not possible. We can never control God's providences, nor can we always control even the pope and the devil."

A letter to his life-long correspondent, Mr. Temple, dated Feb. 10, 1838, alluding to a paper he had prepared for distribution among the Oriental Christians, contains a striking argument on the subject of the worship of saints : —

" Our blessed Lord was always infinitely more kind and gentle than His own disciples were. Their hearts were like adamant compared with His. Their hearts were frozen compared with His. His own mother and brethren would interrupt Him in His preaching. His own disciples would drive away the little children that were brought to Him. His own disciples marvelled that He should give instruction to the woman of Samaria. His own disciples would have sent away the woman of Canaan, and not allowed her a crumb. His own disciples, and the very best of them, would have commanded fire to come down from heaven. They had a little gentleness, kindness, benevolence, and condescension ; but He possessed all these in an infinite degree. Had all they possessed and all the saints have ever possessed been united in one heart, that heart would, after all, be cold and dead compared with the Heart of Infinite Kindness. What encouragement then have we to come boldly to such an High Priest, rather than to any of His saints."

In June, 1838, Mr. Goodell made a visit to Trebizond, near the south-eastern extremity of the Black Sea, the spot where Xenophon, in the memorable retreat of the ten thousand, struck the sea. Being the principal port of ancient Armenia, and an important point of communication with the Armenian race, it was early selected as a mission station. The object of this visit was to strengthen the hearts of the brethren who were laboring there, and also to partake of their joy in the work of grace which had already begun, of which he writes in his journal : —

"At four o'clock on the 8th of June, left Constantinople for Trebizond on the Austrian steamer, Prince Metternich. Reached Sinope, celebrated as the birth-place of Diogenes, at half-past nine o'clock on the morning of the 10th, Samsoon at half-past seven the same evening, and Trebizond the next day at three, P.M.

"Trebizond is so very seldom visited by the Christian traveller, that the mission families there may be said to be almost entirely alone in the wilderness; being scarcely ever cheered by the countenance and voice of any of 'the household of faith.' But though alone, yet they are not alone, for He is with them 'who giveth songs in the night,' and whose Spirit 're-viveth the hearts of the contrite ones.' Nor is there wanting evidence that He has thoughts of mercy for the poor, perishing people around them, for already is the blessed influence of His Spirit beginning to soften the hearts of some of those with whom they have intercourse. And this influence, though it be at first like the gentlest dew, yet how precious and how encouraging is even this!

"The country around Sinope, Samsoon, and Trebizond is strikingly beautiful. Indeed, of natural scenery I have never seen any thing more charming. Even Constantinople must yield the palm in this respect; for though the beauties of the Bosphorus are confessedly great, and all the views in the neighborhood of the city are varied, rich, and magnificent, yet they are wonderfully set off by the groves, the shaded avenues, the kiosks, palaces, and other public edifices, which Mussulman pride, taste, or piety have made to start up everywhere as if by magic. The former, on the other hand, are like Nature herself, 'when unadorned, adorned the most,' and instead of being limited, as those at Constantinople, to a few bright eminences with their retired recesses, alcoves, and lovely retreats, they are on a far more extensive and grand scale, — sometimes stretching off as far as the eye can reach. Indeed, the whole extent of hill and dale, pastures covered or that might be covered with flocks, and fields waving or that might wave with corn, spread out before the eye at one view, is sometimes prodigious.

" On our return from Trebizond, we had near four hundred passengers, among whom were ' Parthians, and Medes, and Elamites, and the dwellers in Mesopotamia, and in Judea, and Cappadocia, in Pontus, and Asia, Phrygia, and Pamphilia,' together with Europeans, Circassians, Kurds, and devil worshippers. The moment they set foot on deck they all come under new and the same laws ; they are brought in direct contact with European skill and superiority ; they are compelled to see and learn new customs. Warriors have to throw off their armor, executioners to deliver up the instruments of death, and officers to cease giving commands. They have to learn punctuality. When we reached Sinope, the passengers were told to a minute how long the boat would stop, and they were repeatedly warned of the danger of not being punctual. Still, some were left behind, and lost both their passage, and, what was still more grievous to them, their passage-money ; and the captain told me that there were such cases almost every voyage. Some would go to the Bath, no more thinking that the steamer would dare to stir without them than that the sun would stand still in the heavens. And thus haughty, imperious lords, who never knew it could be twelve o'clock till they gave orders for it to be so, now learn for the first time in their life that ' time and tide wait for no man.'

" So also activity and enterprise in business are promoted. The Turks have been squatted down here for ages, smoking their pipes with all gravity, and reading the Koran without being once disturbed ; when, lo ! a steamer dashes right in among them, and they have to scramble out of the way. And hardly have they time to get down again upon their hams and heels, with their pipes well lighted, when, lo ! other steamers, with more power than the former, come on, running round them and over them, and in such rapid succession that they must either remain on their feet and keep their eyes wide open like other men, letting their pipes and Koran all go, or move entirely from the ground, and give place to those of a more active and enterprising character.

"It struck me more than once on the voyage, that some of these steamboats would, occasionally, make an excellent missionary station. On going on board I found myself in immediate contact with people of different nations, languages, and religions, many of whom were eager to engage in conversation with any European who could communicate with them. Here were Armenians from five hundred miles in the interior, who had seen our brother Hohannes and his high school, and who knew something and were glad to hear more about the evangelical party at Constantinople. Here were Greeks, who asked me for tracts and Testaments, and Persians and Turks, who urged me to decide the great dispute between them, whether we shall see God in the future world,— as the latter affirm and the former deny. The former never united with the latter in their devotions, but expressed a great abhorrence of them, and repeatedly asked me whether their prayers were not an abomination, — assuring me at the same time, with all the self-complacency imaginable, that their own prayers were acceptable; and requiring me to say if I did not think they prayed better than the Turks. I told them that the Being with whom we had to do in prayer was not like a man, who looked only on the external appearance; and that they could not impose upon Him as they could impose upon Sultan Mahmoud or the Shah of Persia, by lying lips and hypocritical or heartless prostrations. They said that the Persians were good and the Turks bad. I replied that travellers gave a very different account of them. They would not admit this as any evidence, because I had not been in their country and seen for myself. I told them that I had seen a Persian dictionary, and that on almost every page I found the names of very bad practices and things, which showed that they must be a very corrupt and wicked people; that the names of things never exist unless the things themselves exist. Their own dictionaries, therefore, testified against them. In answer to my questions they afterwards admitted that there were prisons throughout all Persia; that every house was barred, and every trunk that contained any thing valuable was furnished with a lock and key; and thus their own confession furnished proof that they were a nation of thieves and robbers, and that, although they knew one another's characters better than foreigners could know them, yet, in all their daily transactions, they plainly showed that they had no more confidence in one another than travellers had represented them as deserving. The Turks were all awake to these arguments, and gathered round, while I demanded further of the Persians whether they did not wish to live long in this world, even a thousand years if they could, notwithstanding all the evils they suffer here; and whether their countrymen did not wish the same; and whether all, universally, did not consider it a great misfortune to die, and especially to die early. This too they were forced to admit, although their own sacred books declare that paradise, to which all faithful Mussulmans go, is an infinitely better place than this world,—thus proving themselves to be a nation of infidels. For if you believe not your own sacred books, I added, pray tell me what is there that you do believe?

" When the Mussulmans, whether Persians or Turks, rose up to their prayers, I felt that it was a special call on me to attend to mine. I knew it did not enter into the nature of their devotions to pray for me, nor had I any reason to suppose they had any knowledge of the characteristics of acceptable prayer. And if they could say their prayers five times a day without a Mediator or any Holy Spirit to help their infirmities, surely Christians, with such helps, such encouragements, and such an High Priest to aid them in all their approaches to God, should be ready to 'pray always with all prayer and supplication in the spirit.'

" The Mussulmans on other occasions as well as this have been frequently pointed out to me by Europeans as being a most sincere, devout, and praiseworthy people in respect to their devotions; and their punctilious observance of them, anywhere and everywhere, has been held up as an example for Protestant Christians to imitate. And yet these same Europeans would call us bigots, fanatics, hypocrites, and more names and worse than could be found in any dictionary, were we to pray in that way in the streets, in the coffee shops, in the public places of resort, in the midst of our business, or wherever we might happen to be.

" ' But see! they are not ashamed to pray anywhere.'

" Yes, I see. And so a man in America is not ashamed to wash his hands anywhere. Why should he be? He would be ashamed not to do it. It is the custom to do it. Everybody does it. No one could be admitted into good

society without doing it. And for a man to wash his face
or hands, does not imply that he fears God, keeps himself
unspotted from the world, leads a conscientious, heavenly life,
and acts constantly in view of eternity. If it did, worldly
men would be as much ashamed to be seen washing their
hands, as they are now ashamed of prayer, or of Christ's
ordinances. But it is not done out of regard to Christ, nor
does any one ever suppose it to be so done. It implies
nothing of this kind, expresses nothing of this character.
And just so of the prayers of these people. Everybody
prays. It is the custom to pray; it is the law to pray; a
man would be ashamed not to pray. He would, in fact, be
hissed out of society, if nothing worse, should he refuse to
pray. And his prayer implies no more as to his moral character than the custom with us of washing one's hands, or
shaving one's beard. Nobody here ever expects to find
a man more heavenly-minded, more benevolent, more
hospitable, more honest, because he prays. Nobody ever
feels that his life and property are in any degree the more
secure because he has fallen into the hands of those who
have just risen up from their prayers. No one is ever supposed to be the less covetous, the less selfish, the less impure,
the less a cheat. a gambler, a liar, a defrauder, a murderer,
because he prays. Nothing is farther from his own thoughts,
or the thoughts of the bystanders, than that his prayer
should exert any transforming influence upon his character."

He continues his journal after returning to Constantinople : —

"*May* 7, 1838. To-day we received interesting intelligence from T., in Persia, of the work of the Lord on the
minds of some English residents there ; from Nicomedia, of
the spirit of inquiry and seriousness awakened among some
of the Armenians of that place ; from Smyrna, of 'the times
of refreshing' in the mission and other families ; and from
Odessa, of the continuance of the revival, which was commenced a year and a half ago in that city. Showers all
round us ; and truly 'there is a sound of abundance of rain.'
Oh, may the whole of this dry and thirsty land be refreshed !

"*May* 18. Our Christian brother, Hohannes, called and
spent the whole afternoon with me in reading the Holy

Scriptures, and asking the meaning of various passages. The following incident which he related to me, shows the change which is taking place in the feelings of Mussulmans: —

"H——p, who teaches geometry in this high school, had a quarrel, a few days since, with the Turkish boatmen he employed, and, in an unguarded moment, he reproached the religion of Mohammed. He was forthwith seized and carried before the proper tribunal, where he was tried, and found guilty of death; but the punishment was immediately commuted for the bastinado and the bagnio. His mother, who had a short time before prescribed with success for the Sultan's son, when sick of the scarlet fever and almost given over by his physicians, now hastened to the royal gate, and informed the prince of the eunuchs of the situation of her son. This officer immediately sent and took him from prison, and, after admonishing him to beware in future of getting into any quarrel with Mussulmans, set him at liberty. As soon as it came to the ears of the Sultan's son, he sent for him, and told him that he understood he knew many things, and was able to teach geometry, astronomy, and the sciences, and that he must not, therefore, expose himself to the rage of Mussulmans, but let them entirely alone. As if he would say, they are illiterate, bigoted, and vulgar; keep out of their way, and have nothing to do with them. H——p promised to take heed to his ways in future, and came away proud of the acquaintance he had formed with the young prince, the heir-apparent to the throne."

Among the more remarkable records of the wonders of divine grace, wrought through the instrumentality of Legh Richmond's " Short and Simple Annals of the Poor," the following must have a place: —

In May, 1838, two Armenian priests, strangers, came to Constantinople from the interior. They had already become humble followers of the Saviour while ministering in their own church, and they came to make the acquaintance of the missionaries from America, that they might have the way of God expounded unto them more perfectly. It appeared also in the course of their sojourn at the capital, that they had a special object in view, which was to ask the prayers of the mission in behalf of their patriarch, to whom they were personally and strongly attached, and whom they were expecting on a visit at their home in a short time. They had together resolved to have an earnest conversation with him on the need of a revival of spiritual religion in the Armenian church, and they came to ask that prayer might be offered by the brethren at Constantinople for the gift of the Holy Spirit, to make their conversation instrumental in beginning such a revival in the heart of the patriarch himself.

While Mr. Goodell was engaged in his mission work at Beyrout, several years before, he had translated into the Armeno-Turkish language two of Legh Richmond's tracts, "The Dairyman's Daughter" and "The Young Cottager," which were printed at the mission press at Malta. On his first journey to Broosa, in company with Commodore Porter, in 1832, the year after his arrival at Constantinople, he carried with him, for distribution on the way, several copies of the New Testament in Armeno-Turkish, and of the tracts which he had translated. Some of these he distributed at the door of a church in Nicomedia, as he was passing through the city. One of the tracts, "The Dairyman's Daughter," was carried to a priest by the boy who received it at the hands of the passing stranger. The priest read it attentively, and it was a message from God to his heart, revealing to him the way of salvation. He went to another priest with the glad tidings, and he also received the truth, and rejoiced in the salvation of Christ. Without communicating with any foreign missionaries, they became missionaries themselves. They gathered their friends together, and told them of the true light that had shined into their hearts. Others soon embraced the truth and rejoiced; and now, after several years, these two priests had come to Constantinople, not so much to tell what God had done for them and for their brethren and friends at Nicomedia, as to ask that prayer might be offered for those who were still in darkness.

One of these priests spent a night at the house of Mr. Goodell, and communicated to him the first tidings he had received of the work of grace that had been so quietly going on at Nicomedia, and of the means which God had used for its commencement, — the tract he had once given to a boy on the street. It was the first time also that this Armenian priest had learned by whose hand God had sent the message to his city and to himself. A great part of the night was spent by the priest and the missionary in joyful communion on the things of the kingdom of Christ. In noting down these facts, Mr. Goodell wrote in his journal : —

"What a sweet comment on the text, ' Cast thy bread upon the waters; for thou shalt find it after many days '! and on this also, ' In the morning sow thy seed, and in the evening withhold not thy hand '! Oh, how many beautiful plants may, with the blessing of God, hereafter spring up unobserved from the good seed which is scattered here and there ! May I be encouraged in future to ' sow beside all waters '! "

These two priests, Vertanes and Harûtûn, afterward removed to Constantinople, and were placed over a church in one of the villages on the Bosphorus, where they were permitted to publish the true Gospel of Christ. And when the time of trial came and they were called to suffer for the truth, they cheerfully took the spoiling of their goods, and endured persecution, even to stonings and imprisonment, for the sake of Christ, "rejoicing that they were counted worthy to suffer shame for His name."

Two letters from Mr. Goodell, both relating to the tract which was instrumental in the revival of true religion at Nicomedia, are here inserted. One was written about two years subsequent to the visit of the two priests at his house in Constantinople, and inclosed the copy of a letter which

Mr. Goodell had written while at Malta, in 1829, but which had never reached its destination.   They were both addressed to the biographer of the sainted Legh Richmond:—

CONSTANTINOPLE, June 18. 1840.

To the Rev. T. S. GRIMSHAWE, *Rector of Burton-Latimer,* &c. :

REV. AND DEAR SIR,—In looking over some old papers this morning, I was happy to find a copy of the letter which I addressed to you several years ago, but which, as you informed me in your late visit to this city, was never received. I should not have thought of making a copy of it to send to you now, at this late day, had you not taken such a lively interest in that blessed work which the spirit of God has commenced in these parts, and with which one of those tracts which were the occasion and the subject of the letter had an important connection.   For a particular account of this work, so far as it relates to Nicomedia, I must refer you to the " Missionary Herald " for December, 1838, Vol. 34, and also to Vol. 35, the number for March, 1839.   This publication you will find at the house of the Church Missionary Society, and also at the offices of the London Missionary Society, and of Wesleyan Methodists.   In addition to what you will find published, let me add, that the Rev. Messrs. Dwight and Hamlin have just returned from an intensely interesting visit to this little company of believers at Nicomedia.   One of their meetings with them was seven hours long.   The brethren there are increasing in numbers and strength, and the work is extending silently, but surely, on every hand, even into neighboring villages.   The account of this visit will soon be published in the " Missionary Herald," and will be within your reach, so that I need not now enlarge upon it.

The two tracts which accompanied the original letter I am unable to procure, either at this place or at Smyrna, they being now out of print; but I am not without hopes of being able to obtain them from Dionysius, the Armenian bishop at Beyrout, who was my assistant in correcting the press at the time they were printed, and who was the author of the prayer at the end of " The Dairyman's Daughter."   The translator, whose aspiration is on the seventy-first page of " The Young Cottager," was another Armenian acting bishop, then in my service, who is since dead, but who died " in faith, giving glory to God."   Should I find the tracts at Beyrout, or in any other place, I will forward them to you without delay. In the mean time, will you present my Christian salutations to any of Mr. Richmond's family with whom you may meet? As I formerly ventured to ask for their prayers, that a blessing might accompany the reading of these tracts, so now I would venture to ask for their thanksgivings; for that which is worth asking for in prayer, is, when obtained, certainly worth a grateful recognition. The preparation of these tracts in this difficult language was very imperfectly done, for we were then but novices in the work of translation. But we see that God can bless the feeblest means; that even His "foolishness is wiser than men, and His weakness stronger than men." From the success that has so manifestly attended "The Dairyman's Daughter" in Armeno-Turkish, Mr. Dwight is encouraged to translate it into Modern Armenian; and we should all be encouraged to a great increase in the fervor and frequency of our prayers, that it may be attended with even still greater success in this language than it has been in the other. It is intended for the same class of people, and, when completed, I will see that you are furnished with a copy of the work.

Your visit to this city, dear sir, we remember with very great pleasure. It was refreshing to our spirits. And I trust, through the grace of our Lord Jesus Christ, that we shall be permitted to meet at last in another city, under a different government, and with infinitely better regulations, together with "a great multitude, which no man can number, out of every kindred and tongue and people and nation," the select from the whole universe. The Rev. Mr. Leeves has returned to Athens. Dr. Bennet is now ill, and Mr. Farman supplies the chapel. All your friends here often speak of you. Mrs. Goodell and the children, and all our families, join in affectionate salutations, and in commending ourselves to your prayers, and to the prayers also of the good people of your charge.

Yours most truly,

W. GOODELL.

The following is the original letter to which he refers · —

MALTA, May 5, 1829.

To the Rev. T. S. GRIMSHAWE, A.M., *Rector of Burton-Latimer*, &c.:

REV. AND DEAR SIR, — We have just read, with no ordinary interest, and I hope I may add with no ordinary profit, the memoir (American edition) of that "man of God," the Rev. Legh Richmond. And to the family once enlivened by the presence, but now afflicted by the departure, of that dear man, I take the liberty of sending through you "The Dairyman's Daughter" and "The Young Cottager," in Armeno-Turkish, *i.e.* Turkish with Armenian characters, recently published at the American press in Malta, under the direction of the American Board of Commissioners for Foreign Missions. In the memoir it is said that "The Dairyman's Daughter" had been published in nineteen languages; I suppose, therefore, that the Armeno-Turkish makes twenty. I have seen Little Jane read in manuscript by Armenian ecclesiastics in Syria, with tears flowing down their cheeks, and with their eyes occasionally raised towards heaven, as if they would say, "Oh for such grace and such enjoyment as Little Jane possessed!"

These tracts, in the same style of execution with those I now send, have already been read, or will probably soon be read, in Egypt, at Jerusalem, on "that goodly mountain Lebanon," in the cities "where Antipas was slain" and Polycarp suffered martyrdom, where Daniel prayed and made supplication to the God of heaven, and where Rebekah and Leah and Rachel spent their youthful days; and even "upon the mountains of Ararat," in "the land of Uz," and in countries still farther east. Will not then those to whom the amiable and interesting writer of these tracts sustained the most near and tender relations lift up a prayer to God that His blessing may attend them in Palestine, Asia Minor, Mesopotamia, or wherever they may travel, rendering them as useful in Turkish as they have been in English?

This intrusion of a stranger into the family of sorrow, and the entrance at such a time of these old acquaintances in a foreign garb, will I trust, be excused, for he to whom I had, before I heard the news of his death, anticipated much happiness in introducing them in their present habit, lived not to himself, nor for his friends alone, but to Christ, and for the church. Nor is it kindred nor private friendship alone that weeps, for to almost all those who have become "par-

10*　　　　　　o

takers of the divine nature," of whatever sect and in whatever country, he was known, and was dear, as "a beloved brother, and a faithful minister, and fellow-servant in the Lord."

Will you, dear sir, accept for yourself our Christian salutations? and have the goodness to convey to the afflicted the assurance of the condolence, sympathies, prayers, and best wishes of all our little American missionary circle now at Malta?

Yours affectionately,

W. GOODELL.

P. S. — The text under the cut in "The Young Cottager" is, "O death, where is thy sting?" The last two sentences before the poetry on the seventy-first page are an aspiration of the translator, first for himself, and next for the reader, that the peace of Little Jane may be theirs. On the last page is the Lord's Prayer; and on the cover is the story of the Roman servant who clothed himself in his master's garments, and thus suffered death in his stead.

The text above the cut in "The Dairyman's Daughter" is, "Hath not God chosen the poor of this world, rich in faith?" and under the cut, "I have fed you with milk." At the end of the tract is a prayer of Dionysius, the Armenian bishop with us, that every reader may become a partaker of the grace of God, and, like the Dairyman's Daughter, be "clothed with humility." On the cover is an extract from Young's "Night Thoughts."

The influence of this single tract, dropped casually at Nicomedia in 1832, has been spreading wider and wider. The work of grace then begun extended to neighboring villages, and the fruit of this handful of corn, scattered as it were upon the top of the mountain, will continue to shake like Lebanon, until the great harvest of the world shall be gathered.

While preparing these memoirs, and since penning the above, the writer has met with an incident relating to this very matter, which strikingly illustrates the declaration that "the foolishness of God is wiser than men." An American traveller, Dr. J. E. De Kay of New York, whose name has been previously mentioned, who was in Constantinople in 1831, and was intimate with the family of Mr. Goodell, published, on his return home, a volume entitled "Sketches of Turkey," in which he made the following criticisms upon the character of the publications prepared by missionaries for the religious instruction of the Orientals : —

"According to an official statement, it appears that from the year 1822 to 1829 there were issued from the Malta printing-press 250,000 copies of various religious works, containing more than ten millions of pages in Greek, Italian, and Turkish, with Armenian characters. It is a subject of regret that such benevolent efforts should in some instances have taken a wrong direction. Nearly forty thousand dollars have been expended upon works which are as unintelligible to the Greeks or Turks as a Pelham novel would be to ' Split Leg ' or 'The Black Hawk.' The remedy, however, is easy. Instead of translating ' The Dairyman's Daughter,' and other tracts of a similar character, let the missionaries be instructed to compose on the spot short stories filled with local allusions, and naturally arising out of the scenes and manners around them. Let them write something in the style of the ' Arabian Nights,' always, however, with a moral end and aim, and they will be read with avidity." — *Sketches of Turkey*, p. 287.

The very tract here specified as unsuited to accomplish any good among the Orientals was the one which God had chosen to employ in the conversion of these two priests, and which was instrumental in inaugurating, without any other apparent means, a religious revival and reformation in the interior of Turkey.

In his journal he makes the following reflections upon the death of a daughter of the Sultan : —

"*July* 3. The Sultan's second daughter, who was married two years ago to Said Pasha, died last night, and was buried early this morning. I feel reproved for not having prayed more in time past for the Sultan and his family. We enjoy protection and great peace and quietness under his reign, and in what better way can we repay him than by remembering him and his sons and daughters in our intercessions? They suffer pain and affliction, and they must die as well as others; and, in a dying hour, where can they look for comfort if they know not the power of the Gospel? It is affecting to visit the mausoleums of former Sultans, where their whole families lie buried in stately sepulchres, corresponding to the age and rank of each individual. Their tombs are covered with large and splendid cashmere shawls; candles burn before them by night; Imams (Mohammedan priests) are there, chanting the Koran at all hours. But their dust is like common dust. Their glory is departed. The festivities at their birth, or at their marriage, or at their investment with the insignia of royalty, or in commemoration of the victories they achieved, as well as the solemnities of their funeral, are all ended. They have gone to that other world, of which they probably thought little while in this; and if they went unholy, they are 'unholy still.'

"*July* 21. In returning early this morning from San Stefano in a boat, when we were just opposite the Sultan's powder manufactory, a part blew up. The cloud of smoke that went up was tremendous, and a shower of saltpetre afterwards came down upon us, although we must have been near a mile from the shore. We have since learned that five persons were killed.

"*July* 27. A terrible storm of thunder, lightning, hail, wind, and rain. Many boats were destroyed, and about a hundred lives lost."

CHAPTER XIII.

THE opening of the year 1839 marked a new era in the history of the American mission at the Turkish capital. It was the commencement of the first severe persecution which the evangelical Armenians were called to endure. Hitherto there had not been wanting manifestations of bitter hostility on the part of the ruling powers of the Armenian Church. Efforts had been made at different periods to arrest the progress of evangelical principles, by breaking up the schools which had been established under missionary auspices; by prejudicing the minds of the people against the foreign teachers, and circulating slanderous reports against them; by warning the people against their doctrines; and by threatening with excommunication all who should give any heed to their teachings. Thus far, however, the rage of the Armenian leaders had been expressed chiefly in words. None of those who embraced the principles of the Gospel had been visited with civil pains and penalties, and few with excommunication. But the end of this comparatively peaceful state of things came at last. The storm broke suddenly, and those who had renounced the superstitions and idolatries of their church were almost overwhelmed by its violence.

In order to understand how the leaders of a nominally Christian community could inaugurate and carry on a systematic, high-handed persecution against their former brethren, under the government of a Mohammedan power, and inflict upon them actual punishment, it will be necessary to refer again, and more minutely, to the peculiar constitution of things under which the various nations were living in Turkey. This system of government was established when the

Ottoman Turks took Constantinople.   It seems to have been adopted to relieve the Sultan and his ministers of the trouble of looking after the various classes of people that were under the control of the Porte.   It is a marvel that it worked even as miserably well as it did ; but it opened the door for a vast amount of oppression and misrule.

The Turkish government, of which the Sultan was the despotic head, was supreme ; but only the Turks and other Mohammedans were directly amenable to its authority.   All other nations, such as the Greeks, Armenians, and Jews, had each its own head and its own government, which was literally an *imperium in imperio*.   By the fundamental law of the empire, each nation was a distinct community, and attended to its own affairs very much as if there were no other government existing in Turkey.   The Armenians, for instance, had their patriarch, appointed by the Sultan and ranking with the higher Turkish pashas, who was held responsible for the government and the good conduct of that nation, and who was invested for this purpose with almost unlimited authority over his people.   Though nominally and really subject to the Sultan, his acts were seldom interfered with, however arbitrary or oppressive they might be, so long as they did not affect the Mohammedans.   He was both civil and ecclesiastical head of his nation, and had authority to inflict both civil and ecclesiastical penalties.   One form of punishment, dreaded almost as much as death, that of banishment to distant parts of the empire, he could not inflict; but an order of banishment was easily obtained from the Sultan, especially if the application for it were accompanied with a suitable bribe.

Every Christian or Jewish subject of the country must necessarily be connected with some one of these communities, and must be regularly enrolled ; nor could any one, of his own choice, transfer his connection from one to another. To do so was an offence, — a kind of rebellion against the supreme authority, the Ottoman Porte.   And not only

this, each community or nation was divided into a variety of
guilds, each trade or occupation forming a sort of caste, and
every member of the community must be enrolled in one of
these, and no one was allowed to change from one to another.
He was known in the community as belonging to a particular
guild, and must have his certificate, and be prepared to exhibit it to the Turkish officials whenever it was demanded.
This social police was administered with great strictness.

The wealthiest class in the whole Turkish empire were the
Armenian bankers. Even the Turkish pashas and other
officials were dependent upon them for money in securing
their appointments, and for advances on which to live and
maintain their positions; and their wealth gave them a controlling influence among their own people. The bankers in
reality were more powerful than the patriarch himself; for,
in addition to their pecuniary influence, they had the making
and the unmaking of the patriarch. He was appointed by
the Sultan on their nomination, and usually, when they
demanded it, he was set aside by the same authority. Prac-
tically they controlled the administration of affairs in their
own community, their views and wishes being carried out by
the patriarch. With very few exceptions, they were exceedingly bigoted in their religious opinions, being violently
opposed to the new doctrines and the spiritual worship
which threatened to supersede the superstition and mummery
of the ancient church. In the peculiar social as well as
religious organization of the Armenian nation, the patriarch
and his priests, who themselves were generally the tools of
the bigoted bankers, had absolute control over the Armenian
people. Not only could they cast them out of the church,
but whenever they chose to put a ban upon any man, they
could break up his business, cut him off from all intercourse
with others, even friends and neighbors, deprive him of the
means of subsistence, and reduce him to the condition of the
dogs in the streets, and all this without the fear of interference on the part of the Turkish authorities.

Just at this period, too, the Armenian patriarch having shown some degree of leniency toward the evangelical converts, if not a decided leaning toward evangelical doctrines, the bankers secured the appointment of an assistant patriarch, who, according to custom, took the reins into his own hands, and proved himself an uncompromising bigot.

There was still another class of the Armenian race, the most bigoted of all, from whom sprang a great part of the opposition which the missionaries and their disciples had to encounter. A small part of the nation were subject to the pope in religious matters, in communion with the Church of Rome, and breathed the true spirit of popery. They were intensely hostile to evangelical truth, and used all their influence, openly and by intrigue, to stir up the whole nation against the missionaries and their work. Not that they loved the Armenian Church, but they hated the Gospel more. Nearly all the interference that the American missionaries met with in prosecuting their work in the Turkish empire had its origin with these emissaries of Rome, or was sedulously fostered and promoted by this universal enemy of the truth.

Such was the state of things at the commencement of the year 1839, when the assistant patriarch, sustained by nearly all the Armenian clergy, and urged on by the bankers, determined upon decisive measures for extirpating the novel heresy. How many had adopted it was not known, for none had actually left the communion of the Armenian Church; but it was evident that the leaven of the Gospel was beginning to work, and the rulers thought that a few decisive blows would strike terror into the hearts of all, and arrest the progress of the evil. The bigoted leaders knew nothing of the power of divine grace in the hearts of men, nothing of the might of the Holy Spirit that was moving upon the minds of many of the people.

On the 19th of February, Mr. Sahakian, an evangelical Armenian, who had been in the employ of the American mission, and who was then at the head of the most important school, was arrested, and, without even being informed of the charges made against him, was thrown into prison. He was a man of the purest and most inoffensive character, and the only accusation that could with truth be brought against him was that he had renounced the superstitious rites and ceremonies of the Armenian Church, and become a humble follower of the Saviour. Other charges, indeed, were made. He was accused of sorcery, and of having the power to bewitch others.

Soon after, another man of the same character, Boghos Fizika, was seized and thrown into the patriarch's prison. Within four days an order was obtained from the Turkish government for sending them into exile, four hundred miles from the capital; and they were hurried away under charge of officers who treated them with the greatest cruelty. A banker also, who had been on friendly terms with the missionaries, was arrested and confined among lunatics; and a bedlam in Turkey is a more shocking place of confinement, even for a lunatic, than in any other part of the world. The following month, Der Kevork, the pious priest already mentioned, was cast into prison, and, with other leading men who had embraced evangelical sentiments, was banished. The patriarch, who had previously promulgated an order forbidding all intercourse with the missionaries, or even reading their books, and requiring all who had any in their possession to deliver them up to their bishop or confessor, now issued a bull, threatening with terrible anathemas all who should have any thing to do with the foreign teachers. The Greek patriarch, too, sent forth his bull, excommunicating all who should sell, buy, or read the books of the Lutherans or Calvinists, as the missionaries were called. Many persons were arrested on mere suspicion of having adopted heretical opinions, their business was broken up, and their families were in distress for want even of the necessaries of life.

At the breaking out of this persecution, Mr. Goodell wrote to Mr. Temple at Smyrna, Feb. 24, 1839: —

"This is, indeed, a day of rebuke and blasphemy. Many are our adversaries, but we give ourselves unto prayer. Many there be that rise up against us, but we have much confidence that He is with us, who will count for more than the whole world beside. Hohannes and Boghos Fizika are both of them sent into exile, each a distance of forty days' journey. Others are called up, and it is said there is a list of five hundred names, including bishops, priests, bankers, &c., who are known to be evangelical, and who are to be examined. Our friends appear remarkably well. Instead of being disheartened, they appear cheerful and happy, full of peace and courage. They really seem to have got hold of something which they think is reality, substance, worth possessing, — better even than life. Oh, what a blessed Saviour! and what blessed promises! worth living for and worth dying for."

April 22d he wrote: —

"I have just learned that five or six more individuals are sent into exile, among whom are Der Kevork and two bishops. They have gone in various directions, and will, I trust, do much good. If the Lord go with them, it is better to go than to stay without Him. If they have His presence, they will have life and peace. And wherever they go, may they kindle such a fire as, by the grace of God, shall never be put out! It is rather a strange thing here to have people taken out of their beds at midnight and sent off into exile, without even the form of a trial; no questions asked; no opportunity given any one to recant. May He who appeared unto John in Patmos manifest Himself also unto these, as He does not unto the world!

"I find, on inquiry, that only four are sent into banishment, viz., that godly priest, with a teacher in the school at Orta Keuy, into European Turkey; and a bishop at Orta Keuy, with the former Bishop of Tocat, into Asia. Every heart is smitten with terror, for no one knows where the next blow will fall. No one knows, when he lies down at night, but he may be on his way to some place of exile before morning. May the Lord come down as in days of old, and make the mountains melt at His presence."

In the midst of these scenes of trial and persecution Mr. Goodell makes this characteristic record of a new arrival at his home.

" On the 20th inst. a new missionary joined us. He came without a partner, and without any outfit; and, as is usual with all new comers, he boards for the present in my family, till he shall become acquainted with the languages and customs of the country; so that, what with his entire ignorance, and what with his entire dependence on us for even his ordinary clothing, we are full of business these days. In other words, a week ago yesterday morning, a third son and seventh child was added to my family; and we pray that they all may be like the seven lamps, which burn for ever before the throne of God. I had looked forward to this event with more than ordinary anxiety, but the Lord was better to us than our fears, and instead of diminishing our numbers hath added thereto; and if Job could say, ' Blessed be the name of the Lord,' how much more should we! He hath not dealt with us after our sins, nor rewarded us according to our iniquities.

" The children have looked through the whole Old and New Testament, with all history, ancient and modern, for a name, but without success. This, however, is not our greatest trouble. Our principal concern is, that he may have that new name which no man knoweth, save he that receiveth it; and that his name, whatever it may be, may be written in heaven. May the day of his death be better than the day of his birth ! "

June 24th he writes : —

" Our friends do not appear to be discouraged, or to feel that all is lost. We receive from time to time most unequivocal assurances of their confidence and good feeling. Some, who do not dare to visit us, have sent us their Christian salutations, and assure us that the people generally have no sympathy in these violent measures, and that the storm may be expected soon to pass away. Some of them represent the patriarch as holding a little taper in his hand to light them along, which, while the darkness continued, answered a good purpose; but now, the sun being up, the taper cannot be seen, while the patriarch still insists that they shall all turn away their eyes from the sun and walk by his taper, as heretofore. But a light from heaven, brighter even than the mid-day sun, may yet shine round about him, as it did about Paul, and bring him to renounce all the sparks of his own kindling for ever.

"The Turkish book, of which much use has evidently been made against us, was published many years ago, and, I believe, at Astrachan. We have none of us ever seen it, though we have often heard of it. It is the same book which our enemies made use of with the Sultan in obtaining a firman against the Scriptures and all our tracts, fourteen or fifteen years ago, while I was in Syria. So the book, which has evidently contributed to stir up the Armenians, came overland all the way from India. Missionaries must remember that they are acting for those afar off as well as those that are near, and for future years as well as for the present time. Books may be useful in one place, while they would be very dangerous in another; nor can missionaries or their helpers always judge aright as to what is most important to be published to the world. As missionary operations are extended and multiplied, and opposition to them is organized and strengthened, greater care than ever will be necessary in this respect; and the church should give her agents a special remembrance in her prayers in reference to this very thing. No missionary 'liveth unto himself,' in a most emphatic sense. I am persuaded that we at Constantinople could at any time do that which would endanger every mission of every society in the whole Turkish empire; and all this without its seeming to our patrons at home that we had been guilty of any indiscretion.

"Every thing is, to appearance, now hushed respecting our friends, and the attention of all these rulers, civil and ecclesiastical, has for several weeks past been directed almost exclusively to ourselves and our brethren at the other stations, their aim being nothing less than to effect our entire removal from the country. Whole kingdoms are moved against us for this purpose, and the ferment is sometimes so great that all the elements seem to be in motion. The very 'mountains smoke, as though God himself had come down and touched them.' And, if He has indeed come to set up His glorious kingdom, we may expect to see 'the hills melt like wax at the presence of the Lord, at the presence of the Lord of the whole earth.' And, in the mean time, we would lift up our hands and say, 'He that dwelleth in the secret place of the Most High shall abide under the shadow of the Almighty.'"

This severe persecution, after continuing for several months, instead of abating, only waxed fiercer and fiercer. It threatened not only to harass to the bitter end all who should give heed to the gospel of Christ, but to break up missionary operations, and to sweep away all the work of years. The missionaries were formally accused before the Turkish authorities of having made proselytes from the Armenians, an offence against the Sublime Porte, and it was evident that a strong influence was brought to bear upon the government to secure their banishment from the country. When the storm broke out, they were nearly all providentially absent. Mr. Schauffler had gone to Vienna, Mr. Dwight was in America, Mr. Homes had gone to Mesopotamia; only Mr. Hamlin with Mr. Goodell remained, and they awaited the order to leave, determined, since they had committed no offence against the government, that they would leave only when compelled by the government to do so. But for this they were prepared, and, in anticipation of it, Mr. Goodell carefully secreted in different places all his papers, journals, and correspondence, lest they should fall into the hands of the enemy and be destroyed during his banishment.

Just as the excitement was at its height, and the apprehension of the native Christians and of the missionaries themselves was most aroused, God Himself suddenly interposed, and by a series of striking providences arrested the hand of persecution. The war between the Sultan and Mohammed Ali of Egypt having been renewed, a demand was made upon the several patriarchs to furnish recruits for the army, always an unwelcome mandate to the Greeks and Armenians. Each nation or community at the capital was required to furnish several thousand men. This levy of troops turned public attention from ecclesiastical affairs, and the persecuted Christians for a time were left to themselves. An army of eighty thousand men was speedily raised and sent to meet the Egyptian army, but on the 24th of June the Turkish forces were completely routed near Aleppo, and the soldiers from Constantinople were scattered in all directions.

The news of this great disaster never reached the ears of

the Sultan. Before the tidings were received at the capital, a proclamation was issued announcing the death of Sultan Mahmoud; and his son, Abdul Medjid, a youth of sixteen years, was proclaimed his successor. Mr. Goodell recorded in his journal these two events: —

"*July* 1, 1839, *Monday.* To-day Sultan Mahmoud, who has been lying at the point of death for several days, was proclaimed dead, and his son, Abdul Medjid, born April 20, 1823, was proclaimed king in his stead. He died at seven o'clock, A.M., having been insensible from yesterday afternoon. Dr. Millingen, an English physician, who informed me of his death, was with him since Friday. No one of his wives or children came into his room. His two sons-in-law were present, and also the old Seraskier Pasha. He said nothing about his kingdom, his successor, or his departure.

"*July* 5. Sultan Abdul Medjid spent last night at the seraglio, and, it is said, will live there. His aunt, sister to the former Sultan, sent him a present of half a dozen wives. To-day he went to the mosque with much pomp and ceremony. The old Sultan is sincerely lamented by many, especially the Christians. Many of the Christians wept, as, indeed, they had reason to, for all his measures were for their good. But he will soon be forgotten."

The ceremony of girding the sword on the new Sultan, his formal inauguration, took place on the 11th of July, and a few days later came the tidings that the Capudan Pasha, the chief admiral, had ignominiously surrendered the entire Turkish fleet to Mohammed Ali. But for the intervention of the Allied Powers the government of the Porte would have been annihilated. As it was, the utter exhaustion of the treasury rendered it impossible to raise another army and rebuild the navy.

Upon the very heels of these disasters came another of those fearful conflagrations with which Constantinople has been so often visited. On the 9th of August, nearly if not quite half of Pera, where Mr. Goodell was living, was reduced to ashes. The fire broke out in the morning in the midst of wooden buildings, which, owing to a long-continued drought, had become like tinder, and before night between three and four thousand houses were heaps of ashes, and not less than fifty thousand of the inhabitants were without a home or a shelter.

In addition to these public calamities, the Armenians were visited with severe personal afflictions. In the sudden reverses of the government and the country some of the wealthiest bankers were reduced to poverty, one of them in the extremity of his misfortunes committing suicide. The hand of God was laid heavily upon many of those who had been leaders in the persecution, so that it became a common remark that God was taking the side of the persecuted and vindicating their cause.

In the shadow of all these public and domestic calamities a council of the Armenian leaders was called, at which it was resolved that those who had been sent into exile should be recalled, and that the rigorous measures against the evangelical converts should be suspended. There was no real change in the feelings of the leaders, but they were awed. They seemed to realize that the hand of God was lifted against them, and that it was best to stay the persecution. The old patriarch, who was friendly to the missionaries, was reinstated, and the assistant, who had been appointed to the office for the purpose of carrying out the most rigorous measures, was dismissed. One after another of the banished returned; those who had embraced the simple truths of the Gospel had their faith confirmed; intercourse with the missionaries was resumed; their own labors among the people were taken up; and the work of God appeared to receive a new impulse.

Another gleam of light broke in upon the darkness which was overspreading the mission work in Turkey. It came from above, for while in the imperilled condition of the Turkish empire there were state reasons which led to the action of the Sultan, we are compelled to refer directly to the leading hand of God this first decisive act, in a series of remarkable documentary concessions by the Ottoman Porte.

In opposition to all the traditions of Mohammedanism and of Turkish rule, Selim III., who came to the throne in 1789, had commenced the work of reform, but the power of the Janizaries was too strong, and he fell a victim to their hostility. Mahmoud II., almost single-handed, took up the work, and, finding that either he or the Janizaries must perish, just at the moment when they were counting on success he gave the order that they should be put to the sword, and they were literally exterminated. Still the whole army of officials, with very few exceptions, were in favor of sustaining the ancient abuses, and the death of Mahmoud was the occasion of scarcely concealed joy on the part of the bigoted Mohammedans. He was succeeded by his son Abdul Medjid, a youth of only sixteen years, who, on the 3d of November, 1839, four months after his accession to the throne, assembled the nobles of the empire, not only the Mussulmans, but the deputies of the Greeks, Armenians, and Jews, together with the ambassadors of foreign powers, and ordered his grand vizier to read to the august assemblage the first formal Bill of Rights, the Magna Charta of Turkey, and himself set the example to his officials, by taking the oath of fidelity to the new instrument.

This charter is known as the Hatti Sherif of Gûl Hané,* so named from the garden of the Seraglio, in which it was promulgated. It did not touch the question of religious liberty which was considered in later firmans, nor, indeed, the subject of religion in any form, being confined to these three points: 1. Guaranteeing to all the subjects of the Porte security of life, honor, and property; 2. A regular

* For the full text of the Hatti Sherif of Gûl Hané, and other imperial decrees relating to civil and religious liberty, see the Appendix.

system of levying and collecting the taxes; and 3. An established system of recruiting the army and defining the period of service. But this was the first step in a series of constitutional guarantees, which afterward took the form of charters of religious freedom, culminating in the celebrated Hatti Humayoun of 1856.

There are few events in the history of nations more remarkable than these attempts at reform, and these constitutional guarantees, emanating not from the demands of the people, but from the throne of one of the most despotic governments that has ever existed, and steadily carried forward in opposition to the wishes of the official force of the empire. Europe, it is true, demanded concessions in favor of freedom, especially of religious freedom, but not in the precise form in which they were first made; and one cannot fail to recognize a higher than any human power in securing guarantees so opposed to the genius of Islam and to all the traditions of the empire.

Mr. Goodell's mission at Constantinople was specially to the Armenians, but he had more or less intercourse with those of all nationalities. In his journal he has the following account of a movement among the Jews, and of an interview with one who came to tell him that he had found the Messiah, the one "of whom Moses in the law and the prophets did write:" —

"*February* 8, 1840. There is at present some stir among the Jews of this capital. Their chief rabbies had led them to expect that, according to their books, the Messiah must absolutely appear some time during the present year; but several months of *their* year are already gone, and still there are no signs of His coming. A learned rabbi, who assisted Mr. Schauffler in his translation of the Scriptures, occasionally visits me, and almost the first, sometimes the very first question I always ask him, as he enters the door, is, 'Has He come?' 'Not yet,' has always been his reply, till his last visit a few days ago, when, laying his hand on his heart, he said in a low and solemn tone, 'If you ask me, I say He has come; and if you will show me a safe place, I will bring you ten thousand Jews to-morrow, who will make the same confession.'

"I replied, 'The apostles and prophets had no safe place shown them to confess truth in; but they made the confession in the very face of stripes, imprisonment, and death. If you believe the promise made to the fathers has been fulfilled, and the Messiah has come, then receive Him with all the honor of which He is worthy, submit to Him, acknowledge Him, follow Him, and let the consequences be what they may. Act like Abraham, like Moses, like the prophets, like all the holy and good of your nation, though like some of them you be sawn asunder, though you be slain with the sword.'

"But, alas! they know too little of Christ, and feel too little interest in the subject to venture all consequences for His sake. How can men believe whose hearts are altogether worldly! Only let them be as much in earnest about salvation as they are about the perishing objects of time, only let them be as much awake to things eternal as they are to things temporal, and they will no longer ask for a safe place to confess Christ in. And only let the churches pray as they ought for these perishing people, and who can tell but more than these ten thousand will be so baptized with the Holy Ghost, that in the face and to the utter astonishment of Jews, Turks, and infidels, they will come forward as one man to be baptized in the name of the Father, and of the Son, and of the Holy Ghost."

Mr. Goodell's truly catholic spirit, his indifference to mere forms and modes as compared with the reality and substance of religion, his willingness to lay aside his own preferences in things non-essential when he could thereby edify any member of the body of Christ, are exhibited in the accompanying extracts from his journal: —

" *October* 19, 1840. One has to become all things to all men. Who is there that has not his preferences so strong as to amount to prejudices? This is not confined to the people of these countries. It is universal. New England itself is not different from other countries in this respect. In the baptism of children I have to conform to all these prejudices. In some instances I must put on the gown, and in others leave it off. In some I must wear a white cravat, and in others a black is preferred. In some two or three cases I have made the sign of the cross; in others, I am told to have no popish ceremonies,' as they call the sign of the cross. Some are afraid I shall do too much, and others are afraid I shall do too little; while each one thinks his own views of the subject are a perfect standard. One wishes it to be done exactly in the New England fashion, and another as it is done in Old England, while the former I have forgotten, and the latter I never knew. As for myself, forms are alike to me, because I can use them all in a manner to instruct and edify; and no form is of any value in my estimation any farther than I can make use of it to impress the observer or hearer.

"I always precede the ordinance of baptism by some remarks on its nature and importance, such as I love to make, and such as I could make on no other occasion so well as on this. So when I make the sign of the cross, it gives me an opportunity of speaking some things which I love to say in the presence of a congregation when they are all awake to listen. In baptizing my own children I dress as when I preach. I have an utter abhorrence of forms as forms, whether it be a New England form or any other. Form is nothing, the substance every thing. When another baptizes my own children, it never enters my mind to prescribe how he shall baptize it, what dress he shall wear, &c. I wish him to take his own way, and to render the service as profitable to the parents and children, and as edifying to all, as possible.

"Some of my brethren in these countries always wear a black cravat when they preach, and disdain to wear a white one, being as much set in one way as some of their hearers are in another. As for myself, I would disdain nothing but sin. I would even wear an Armenian *kalpach* (a high, black head-gear), if that would obtain for me a better hearing; though if wearing that were made indispensable to salvation, and the time were come to take up the subject in all its length and breadth, then I would no more wear it than I would perform a heathen ceremony."

The letter of consolation and reminiscence which follows was written to his friend, Professor Haddock, of Dartmouth College, on seeing a notice of the death of his wife in an American paper:—

CONSTANTINOPLE, Dec. 11, 1840.

MY DEAR BROTHER, — I learned yesterday by the "Boston Recorder" that you have been visited with affliction; while another of those favored ones, who twenty-five years ago were visited by infinite grace, has now gone to the land of everlasting peace and love. I carried the paper into our weekly prayer-meeting last evening, and read the account, and you had a special remembrance in our prayers. I also made some remarks on the commencement and progress of that great and marvellous work of God at Dartmouth, which had such an influence on the college and on the church of Christ. I have never known a revival the influence of which appeared to me to be more important and more extensive. All those interesting scenes, — Oh, how fresh and sweet they are in my memory still! I remember, dear brother, the first prayer you ever made in public. It was in the evening, and in that memorable school-house (does it stand there still?) " where prayer was wont to be made ; " and Damon, who himself soon after " began to call upon the name of the Lord," intimated to me, in walking home, that he felt it was high time to attend to the eternal interests of the soul. I remember when Spaulding first raised his spectacles and wiped away the "rivers of waters that were running down his eyes," and, lifting up his hands and his voice, addressed the overflowing house in that peculiarly strong manner which had been so natural to him on other subjects, and which was now consecrated to the great subject of salvation. I remember when those fine scholars in your class and mine and the next after, who have since become presidents and professors in so many of our colleges, were quickened and first began to breathe the breath of spiritual life, and to live for eternity. I remember that evening meeting where all the young ladies of the Plain were assembled at Mrs. Chapman's, and God was there, and almost all of that lovely circle, if not every one, ultimately became willing to welcome the reign and live under the government of Christ for ever. I remember when the room of Brother Temple and myself was filled from morning to night with our classmates and other students, who were anxious to learn what is most important for a sinner to know, but which colleges cannot teach, viz., how the righteousness of God's beloved Son could become theirs? and when from day to day we laid aside the demonstration of mathematical problems to attend to the more clear and more important demonstrations of the Spirit.

Nor have I forgotten when that interesting young lady, who subsequently became the partner of your joys and sorrows, and who has now gone to join "the general assembly and church of the first-born" above, was examined for admission into the church here below, with the various questions proposed to her by different individuals present on that occasion. Oh, what delightful meetings we had in college, and on the Plain, and in all the region round about!

> "Those were golden, happy days,
> Sweetly spent in prayer and praise."

In Mr. Lang's family I spent many pleasant hours, the remembrance of which is pleasant still. And though, at first, an involuntary sadness begins to steal over the mind in the reflection that the whole family, root and branch, is plucked up and removed for ever, yet the sadness immediately gives place to joy, in the thought that it is an unbroken and a happy family still, and that its removal from all these earthly scenes is not into a darker state, but into one of infinitely greater light and purity and blessedness. Here, to be sure, they enjoyed much, but there they will enjoy incomparably more. Here they inherited a little, there they will "inherit all things." Here they had a pleasant abode and many sincere friends, but all these were nothing in comparison with what they find in that "better country, even an heavenly."

Why, then, should we ever think or speak of them as being dead, when it is we who are dead, and they — they now have begun to know in reality what it is to "have life, and to have it more abundantly"! Oh, what thanks shall we render to Him who came down from heaven for no other purpose but to take us up with Him to His own glorious kingdom above! And how should the departure of one and another of our friends, and their happy entrance into that blessed kingdom, quicken us in our way thither! What a place heaven must be, where all that is worth preserving from this world, and all that is worth seeing and knowing and loving from any other world, is there collected and made perfect! While, then, you have my sympathy in your loss here below, you have also my hearty congratulations on the increase to your friends above. If those that love us most are diminishing in number here, they are increasing in number there; and how could we have it better?

Present my very affectionate and my Christian salutations to any of my friends whom you may see, and who may inquire after me. In the prosperity of the college I ever feel the liveliest interest. The portrait of President Brown I have framed, and it hangs in my parlor with Worcester, Evarts, Wisner, and Cornelius.

Eighteen years day before yesterday since we sailed from New York; and what was then outside of that city is now, I suppose, about the centre. Should we ever return to our native country, we should neither know nor be known, recognize nor be recognized. Eighteen years! but I feel that I have during this time been an exceedingly unprofitable servant, and must confess my utter unworthiness, and look for pardon, where all the perishing of our race have to look, if they would obtain the forgiveness of their sins, and an inheritance among the sanctified ones. You will rejoice to hear that the severe persecution we have suffered has now ceased, and that the scattered converts are recollected with an increase of faith and zeal. The Lord seems to be turning our captivity as the streams of the south, and we are hoping for times of refreshing from His presence.

Mrs. Goodell unites in kind regards and, although it will come late, Christian sympathy for you and yours. May we hope in due time to be cheered by receiving an answer to this! I have written more than I intended, but I do not know that I need ask you to excuse it, as it comes from your ever affectionate brother in Christ,

W. GOODELL.

In a letter to a fellow-missionary, dated March 8, 1841, he makes mention of some of his minor trials, and of the occasion he had to exercise his own good judgment in regard to the mode of prosecuting his work: —

"Many thanks for your long letter, which was as full of kindness as of explanation. I regret that I was able to see so little of you while you were within our little circle; but, in order to enjoy a visit, I must go from Constantinople, the hurry and distraction here are too great. Mr. Evarts once told me he had neither made nor received a visit of friendship for many years, and had no expectation of ever being able to have such a pleasure again. I remember I thought at the time it was very hard, and could hardly persuade myself it was his duty thus to deny himself. Now let me tell you some of my own troubles and sorrows, that we may the better sympathize with one another, bear one another's burdens, pray for one another, and feel that we are not alone in trouble and sorrow, but that the same, or similar ones, are suffered by others.

" Some letters which I receive have constant reference to my family, as though I were specially deficient in my duty to them, and needed to devote more time and thought for them. Others have constant reference to my translations, as though I needed to be stirred up to the importance of prosecuting the work with vigor, and not suffer my translator or the press to stand idle through my neglect. Others leave every thing else out of the question, as of no comparative importance, and urge it upon me to *preach, preach, preach.* Others, again, from the various missionary stations, and from all parts of America, are calling for letters, and blaming me for not answering theirs. Many, many of my friends are offended with me, and some of them say hard things about me, while all the time I feel that it is I, and not they, who suffer from the want of this correspondence. Now what to do I know not. I would most gladly give my time to my friends ; I would give it all to my family ; I would devote it all to the great work of translating the word of God ; and I would with all my heart spend it in publishing the good news. But to devote the whole of it to each one of these objects is an impossibility. Only a certain portion can be given to each, and as one may receive more, another must receive less. Now, if any one could tell me exactly how to proportion the amount to be given to each, I should be thankful. But, while everybody seems to feel that I am very deficient somewhere, nobody seems to agree with his neighbor as to where the deficiency lies ; and I seem to myself to be like the poor man who tried to please everybody, and pleased nobody, and accomplished nothing for himself. I must try more to please my blessed Lord, and let the whole world go."

CHAPTER XIV.

THE year 1841 was a year of severe domestic affliction in the family of Mr. Goodell. Mrs. Goodell, who more than once before had been very low with sickness, was again, in the spring of this year, brought to the borders of the grave, and several members of the family were prostrated by the same disease, — a malignant and prevailing fever. So repeated and protracted were these visitations, that, toward the close of the following year, Mr. Goodell wrote: " It is now more than two years since the voice of health has been heard in our habitation."

But the hand of God was laid yet more heavily upon the stricken household, and one who was peculiarly dear to their hearts, the child of promise and of hope, the first-born of Americans in the city of the Sultans, the one who had received his name from the city of his birth and the land of his fathers, Constantine Washington, after a very trying illness, was removed beyond the reach of earthly love. He was the first of Mr. Goodell's children from whom he was separated by death, and the only one whom he found waiting for him at the heavenly gates, when his work on earth was done.

We do not recall any thing more touching and tender than the record which the father made in his private journal of the boy's illness and protracted suffering; of his own prayerful solicitude, not so much for the recovery of the lad to health, as for his eternal life; of the quiet submission, mingled with almost broken-hearted love and sorrow, with which he gave up his beloved son, when it became evident that the separation must come. That journal, written from day to day, filled with the outpourings of a fond father's heart, containing all the little details of parental anxiety, hope, fear, sorrow, submission, trust, is too sacred to be transcribed. But a letter, which Mr. Goodell wrote with chastened feelings to his own aged father, a few weeks after the angel of death had visited his home, contains all the record of those scenes that needs to be made here.

CONSTANTINOPLE, April 17, 1841.

MY DEAR AND HONORED FATHER, — I wrote you as usual on February the 14th.   Since that time we have been visited with affliction, and Constantine Washington, our fourth child and second son, has been taken from time and probation at the age of nine years and seven months.   His disease was the gastric typhoid fever, which has been very prevalent here this spring, and which, though it has not generally proved mortal, yet in his case set at defiance all medical skill.   Day after day, during the space of three weeks, the physicians came and looked upon him, and declared his case hopeless.

On the 27th ult., which was the twenty-fourth day of his illness, and while his life was hardly expected from one hour to another, Mrs. Goodell had a violent attack of the same fever, and was immediately removed to another apartment of the house, where she has been confined ever since.   That night we had our dear boy's grave-clothes lying ready in the chamber; but there was a little change for the better, which during several succeeding days gradually increased, and gave pleasing indications of a recovery.   But the inflammation had continued so long, that, quite unexpectedly to us, ulcers or gangrene suddenly finished the work on the morning of the 8th inst., after thirty-five days of intense suffering.

For several days I had forgotten to pray for his life, unless when praying by his bedside, nor did I always remember it then.   Whether he were to be removed from us by that disease, or to be lent to us a little longer, seemed of comparatively little consequence.   And the idea of having my family broken in upon in that way was as nothing.   I have for many years been looking for it, and endeavoring from day to day to live in reference to it.   Temporal life seemed a trifle in comparison.   Eternal life, oh, that was every thing!   It was this which occupied all my thoughts and called forth all my prayers.   In regard to the other, my language and my feel-

11*

ings were just these: If thou seest it will be best for the child, and best for the family, and best for thy cause, that he live still longer on earth, restore him in thine own good time; if otherwise, I have not a word to say; "*Thy will be done.*" But for the blessings of salvation I felt that I might be importunate, and that I might take right hold on everlasting strength, and say, "I will not let thee go, except thou bless me." I took him up and carried him to the Lord Jesus, and placed him in His hands, and said, "He is no longer my child, but he is thine. I can no longer provide for him and take care of him, but thou canst. He will no longer remain in my family; receive him into thine, and let him belong to thy blessed household. Wash him, cleanse him, make him whiter than snow, and fit him for thy holy presence and service."

I then turned to the child, and said, "You can no longer live with me; will you now live in the blessed family of Christ? Will you honor and obey Him? Will you conform yourself to the rules of His house? Will you now give Him your hand, and let Him lead you and guide you and provide for you for ever?" He answered with great composure, "Yes, papa."

I felt a good degree of confidence that I had placed and left our dear boy in the hands of the Lord Jesus. I felt assured that He would not refuse to take what was thus given to Him, nor throw from His arms what was thus confided to them. But would the child be willing to stay with Him? Would he have confidence in Him? Would he go with Him? I then remembered for my encouragement that Christ Himself makes His people willing in the day of His power; that it is His work also to inspire with confidence, faith being His own gift; and that repentance, too, as well as forgiveness, He is exalted as a Prince and a Saviour to give. This, then, formed a new subject of prayer, and I laid hold of it and used it accordingly, with very great comfort and satisfaction to myself, for here was every thing I had occasion for.

In the former part of his sickness, I had asked him if he thought of God, and he replied, "Yes, papa, and I pray to Him." When I told him for the first time that he could not live, but must soon die, he very composedly closed his eyes for a few moments. On his opening them, I asked him if he was praying, and he said, "Yes, papa." This way of closing his eyes was striking, and he did it frequently when addressed on serious subjects during his illness. When afterwards I repeatedly asked him about his dear mamma, — if he knew she was sick, if he wished to see her, &c., — he always closed his eyes in the same composed manner, but never answering a word, as though he felt more than, through great weakness, he was able to express, and therefore chose to be silent.

One morning I began to repeat one of his hymns, which I thought suitable to his state, when he took it out of my mouth, and went on with it two lines, but was too much exhausted to proceed, and I finished it for him. Mrs. Goodell had previously repeated to him a very appropriate hymn, with which he was unacquainted. He lay a few minutes in apparent thought, and then said, "Mamma, what was that hymn?" and she repeated it to him again.

Dr. Gerstman, a Jewish missionary, who was much interested in him, and had previously given him lessons in Hebrew, kindly watched with him several nights. On one of those occasions he said to him, "You know the Lord Jesus loves little children?" "Yes." "Do you love to have the Lord take care of you?" "Yes." On his offering up various short petitions for him, the child always added "Amen" at the close.

For prayer he always seemed ready, and frequently I offered prayer by his bedside eight and ten times a day. I also frequently repeated passages of Scripture to him, or let fall some remark of a spiritual nature, when I gave him drink, or ministered in any way to his wants.

Some days after the change for the better, and when, though exceedingly reduced, he appeared to be returning to dwell among the living, I asked him if he remembered my telling him that he could not live, and he answered, "Yes, papa." As he was so very low, I said no more; but I anticipated great pleasure in recurring to these scenes as returning health and strength should enable him to bear it.

Two days before his death he repeatedly asked me for "David Brainard's Life," that he might read it. I finally carried it to him, and suffered him to pass his eye over a sentence or two of that good man's experience, promising him he should read the book as God should give him strength. I, however, put into his hands some Scripture cards, which he looked at for a few moments, and then laid aside for ever. During that day his little strength became still less; but as

I attributed it to the operation of some medicine which the physician had ordered, I felt little alarm. An unexpected repetition of the same the next day reduced him yet lower; but I still thought that it was only weakness, and that time and patience, with God's blessing, would restore him.

But on the following morning the watchers spoke to me a little after four o'clock, and said there was a change in him for the worse. I arose, and found his eyes fixed. I spoke to him, but he gave me no answer. I took his hand, but he returned no sign of recognition. We succeeded in giving him what seemed best suited to restore him, but he was evidently sinking fast. I offered a prayer by his bedside, and then hastened to the sick chamber of my dear partner to inform her, that, if she had any more petitions to offer for the beloved child, she must do it without delay. I prayed with her, and then, calling up the children, I returned and offered prayers at short intervals by the dying child. Mr. Dwight's family was sent for, and he and I by turns prayed at short intervals, till the dear object of so much intense interest was no longer a subject of prayer. As the last breath was quivering on his lips, I committed his departing spirit into the hands of Him who gave it. We placed him in the faithful hands of our blessed Lord, and we left him there. As I put my hands upon his eyes, and closed them on all things below the sun, I prayed that he might open them on an eternal day. I arose, kissed his yet warm forehead, and was retiring when Isabella, who stood weeping by, ran to me, and said, " Is it all done, papa?" " Yes, my dear, it is all done." She clung to me, and sobbed, as if her heart would break. I said, " Will you go and kiss your beloved brother once more?" She did so, and was quieted. The other children did the same, and I then immediately assembled them around the bedside of their mother, and we all bowed down together before Him who is alike good when He giveth and when He taketh away. It was Thursday, and the very day when Constantine has for several years been particularly remembered in the daily concert for the children of our families, it coming round to him in turn once a fortnight. This was his day, and it was God's day. And he died just about the very time when I have been accustomed to hold the concert, viz., at seven o'clock. Blessed day! and, as I would hope, an infinitely better day to him than the day of his birth!

During all that day I was enabled to view the dispensation as coming from the hand of God, and I felt satisfied with what He had done. At three o'clock, P.M., our friends and neighbors assembled, and we sang, —

> "Friend after friend departs:
> Who hath not lost a friend?" &c.

Mr. Dwight made some remarks, and prayed, and I added a few remarks myself. At four o'clock Dr. Bennet, the English chaplain, came, and we "took up the body and buried it, and went and told Jesus."

But the next day I wilted down, and I could not join my children in singing at family worship. The thought would come over me now and then with such power as almost to make me faint. "Perhaps the dear boy went alone into eternity! His probation is ended; his day of grace is over; and perhaps the great work of preparation for eternity was not done!" But I recollected that my concern was not with the dead, but with the living; that God had done perfectly right in removing the child at the time and in the manner He did; that I had left him in His blessed hands, and had no right to interfere; and that I should be guilty of undervaluing His mercies, did I not bless Him for all His kindness to him, and for whatever reason there was to indulge hope respecting him. I felt, too, that I had asked for him all the blessings of the everlasting covenant; that, if the Lord should give me another day to intercede for him, and should say to me, "Ask what I shall do for him," I could not ask for any greater or other blessings than I had already asked for him, nor pray with more fervency than I had already for several years prayed for him, nor could I think of any thing I wished to tell him which I had not already told him. I thought this also, — had he recovered, we should one and all have said that it was certainly in answer to prayer. But we prayed far, far more for the salvation of his soul than we did for his restoration to health. And our heavenly Father is infinitely more ready to hear us for spiritual blessings, than He is for temporal blessings.

Perhaps so many prayers have never been offered in the same space of time in Constantinople for one individual, as were now offered for him, — prayers in public and in private, sometimes also in social circles appointed expressly for the

purpose; prayers offered by Greeks, Armenians, Germans,
English, and Americans.   Most of those who assisted in
watching with him, or attending upon him, were persons of
prayer.   Special prayers were also offered for him by our
friends at Smyrna. Broosa, and Trebizond.   And when he
lay a dying, I said, perhaps some of the children would like
to offer up one prayer more for their dying brother; let us
all bow our heads and offer up each a silent petition for him.
We did so.   But the last prayer is now offered.

That Constantine had for many months been conscientious
in observing his own seasons of devotion, I have reason to
believe.   I often questioned him about them, as I did also
the other children, and I seldom found him a delinquent.
At the concert for all the missionary children on Sabbath
evenings, he frequently retired with his elder sisters to join
with them in prayer.

He was very affectionate to his sisters, often sitting with
them, bringing them flowers when he walked out, and considering it a great treat to be allowed to remain in their chamber with them to read some good book.   During his sickness,
whenever his little brother was brought into the room, even
to the last day of his life, he always beckoned to have him
come and receive a kiss.

He was a child of truth.   If I so much as hinted my fears
that he had not told me the whole truth in any instance, he
would often burst into a flood of tears.

On the Sabbath he was generally reading through the
whole day, when not attending any public service.   And
frequently, if he found something that pleased him, or with
which he thought we should be pleased, he would ask if he
might read it to us.   Frequently also would he rise from his
seat and come and sit on my knee, when I have been addressing the children on Sabbath evenings.

He was a child of great simplicity and good-nature, readily
accommodating himself to the wishes of others in play, and
yielding in case of any dispute.

His was a fine form.   He was as straight as an arrow,
well-proportioned; and to see him play, or throw off his
clothes and work, you would think his flesh was of brass.
But he is dead!

He was a good scholar; learned with facility; and, considering his advantages, had made very satisfactory progress
in his various studies.   He had also committed to memory

from seventy to one hundred hymns, "The Child's Daily Food," the Assembly's Catechism, all the Gospel of John, and the Gospel of Matthew as far as to the middle of the tenth chapter.

He always told me that he would preach the Gospel of Christ. But he can preach only by his death. And oh that his early death might be the means of life to all his young friends, as indeed we hope it has been to some of them!

During his sickness he never appeared in the least degree agitated with the fear of dying, nor elated with the hope of living. His frame of mind was composed, and, I would hope, resigned. What money he had, amounting to more than two dollars, mostly given him at different times by friends, he, at my suggestion, requested me to put into the missionary box at the monthly concert.

His sufferings were great, very great; but his patience was remarkable. I often turned away to weep at beholding it. His principal physician repeatedly said that he had never seen such patience, and that as for himself he was sure it was not possible for him to exercise so much of it. I saw no reason to doubt then, nor in looking back do I see any reason to doubt now, but that he was by the grace of God conscientiously patient. One of my missionary brethren, who had enjoyed some opportunity of witnessing it, has since written me, "I only pray that, if ever I am called to suffer what he suffered, I may have grace given me to endure it as patiently as he did." Sweet sufferer! and He in whose kind care we left thee did suffer every thing for thee.

I have many more similar reminiscences of the beloved child, which are very, very precious to me, and on which memory dwells with great fondness. He was always obedient; and he was "obedient even unto death," submitting to whatever his physicians prescribed, however unpleasant or nauseous it might be, if I told him it was necessary.

Not long before he was taken sick, I told the children one Sabbath evening that, if they had any hymn which particularly pleased them, they might read it to me. He said at once he knew what he should read; and he immediately turned to it and marked it, till it should come to his turn to read. He then immediately turned to another in another book, which he told Isabella was a good one for her. His own hymn was, —

> "Lo! at noon 'tis sudden night!
> Darkness covers all the day,
> Rocks are rending at the sight:
> Children, can you tell me why?" &c.

The one he selected for his sister was, —

> "Behold the Saviour at thy door!
> He gently knocks, has knock'd before ;
> Has waited long, is waiting still :
> You treat no other friend so ill," &c.

The whole of this beautiful hymn, I have found since his death, he had copied into his scrap-book. The following, which I also found copied by him in the same book, I have ordered to be inscribed on his tombstone : —

> " Time was, is past, thou can'st not it recall ;
> Time is, thou hast, employ the portion small ;
> Time future is not, and may never be;
> Time present is the only time for thee."

Perhaps even my own father will feel that I have already said too much respecting the child. But " God maketh my heart soft." He is come nigh to us. He is visiting us. He is speaking to us. He is touching us where He knows we shall feel His hand. He is, so to speak, taking special pains with us for our benefit. And we beg your prayers that we may not receive the grace of God in vain, nor remain un-profited by His paternal corrections.

When Mr. and Mrs. Powers came into my family last autumn, I never expected she would leave it, till she should be carried to the house appointed for all the living. And the idea of her coming to spend her last hours with us was to me a pleasant thought, as I hoped it might be a blessing to the family. But God's thoughts are not like ours. He permits her to depart for her native country, and takes my own child away instead of her, as though He would teach me not to expect to be benefited at the expense of others, but to be willing to bear the expense myself.

When this beloved brother and sister left us, a few days before Constantine was taken sick, I prayed that the blessed Saviour who, I felt assured, had dwelt with them might not leave the house, but now come down to our apartments and take up His abode with us. Little did I think He would come in this manner, But we would cherish His visits how-ever made, we would welcome His presence though He come to us in the midst of darkness and storm. Let us but see His steps, though it be on the highest billows, and let us but hear His voice saying, "It is I, be not afraid;" though it proceed from the raging tempest, we will gladly receive Him. Though He slay us, yet will we trust in Him. God's blessed word has seemed to us like the Rock of Ages, on which one may stand unmoved amidst the howlings of the storm, and the roaring and dashing of the billows.

Mrs. Goodell has been supported and comforted beyond my expectations; but you, dear father, know from your own blessed experience that God always keeps in perfect peace those whose minds are stayed on Him. She is now able to sit up an hour at a time, several times in the course of the day. But E., who has had much to do in nursing the sick, has now the same fever.

Since I commenced this letter I have heard through the "New York Observer" of the return of my beloved cousin from the Sandwich Islands, and of the decease of her dear Lucy. Assure her of my love and sympathy and prayers.

All my family join in love to you, and in commending ourselves to your prayers.

Your ever affectionate son,

WILLIAM.

Though in contrast with this expression of parental sorrow, we turn to other scenes of a domestic character. Having in his own family and around him a large circle of little ones, Mr. Goodell took the most lively interest in all that tended to make them happy. His own uniformly cheerful and even mirthful disposition made him always the welcome friend and companion of children. He had the happy faculty of adapting himself to their years and thoughts and tastes, and in their society he was ready to be regarded and treated as if he were the youngest of them all. Some letters are subjoined showing the interest he took in all that related to his own children. The first was written to his aged father, to whom the previous letter was addressed, and was his own way of announcing the birth of a child : —

MY DEAR AND HONORED GRANDFATHER, — As I was not born till the 12th inst., it cannot be supposed that I should know much of letter writing. But having heard my parents speak of giving you some information of my little self. I thought it would be better for me to give it myself, even though my thoughts should be very crude, and I should have to employ an amanuensis to express them, than to leave it entirely to those whose acquaintance with me has been so short. And, besides, if what I hear is true, I have but one grandfather in the world, and he an old man, perhaps not much farther from the end of his time than I am from the beginning of mine, and therefore I should not lose a moment in commencing a correspondence with him, both for the sake of giving him some token of the respect and love I bear him for all his kindness to my father and to my paternal uncles and aunts, and also to request that he would give me some of the results of his experience during his long sojourn in this world.

You will doubtless expect that I should express my views and feelings in regard to this world; but really I have been an inhabitant of it so short a time, that perhaps the less I say the better. I may say to you, however, in confidence, that my first impressions were very unfavorable; and I felt so much disappointment, that, though it was Sunday, I could not refrain from immediately lifting up my voice and crying aloud. My friends did what they could to soothe my feelings, but I must confess it was some time before I could endure the horrible sights and sounds which came rushing into my eyes and ears, like the cold air into my tender lungs, and which led me at first to suppose that every object in nature was intended to give, and every one of my senses designed to convey, pain rather than pleasure. And, though a residence of four days has some-what modified my first impressions, and I am becoming in a manner reconciled to my situation, yet it seems impossible that I should ever love this cold, selfish, vain world so much as, it is said, many persons do. My parents, however, tell me that those who now have the greatest attachment to it were at the first sight filled with as great a horror as I was myself, and that therefore they entertain strong fears for me, lest by and by I should, like many others, think of nothing, and care for nothing, and love and desire nothing, but this vain world. I hope that their fears will not be realized; and I am sure that you, who know the dangers that surround me better than I do myself, will offer the most fervent prayers that during my whole sojourn here "I may use the world as not abusing it."

All my brothers and sisters seem very fond of me; but I see plainly that they love themselves best, and are willing to give up but little for my comfort; and that I shall in general have to yield my wishes to theirs, or have many very close rubs with them. They talk, indeed, about instructing me, setting before me good examples, and so forth and so on; but it is easy to see that, however good their intentions may be, — and I hope I am not disposed to be uncharitable, — they are certainly very forgetful of their promises and resolutions, and need to be reminded often of their duty; and, to tell the plain truth, I begin to fear that I shall not be much benefited by any of their efforts in my behalf. I am, however, disposed to make every reasonable allowance, remembering what I must have once heard or read, viz., "that in this world *talking* is much easier and much more common than *performing*." I do not know whether I have quoted it quite correctly, as my memory has not yet become very tenacious, but I believe I have expressed the idea.

You will be gratified to hear that, according to the customs of New England, and, I suppose, of the United States generally, I have a bath every morning; and, though I am not altogether pleased with the custom, and sometimes cannot refrain from shedding tears, yet I consider it far preferable to that which prevails among the Armenians of Constantinople. These, on the birth of a child, immediately scarify its arms, back, legs, &c., with a lancet, put on salt, and swathe it close, and thus let it remain for days, weeks, and I do not know but months, without unswathing. Whether they salt down the child in order to preserve it, or whether the object is to get all the old Adam out of its blood, I must confess my ignorance; but, at any rate, a daily purification by water must, it appears to me, be unspeakably better.

I wish to be properly remembered to all my uncles, aunts, and cousins in the land of my forefathers. Would it were in my power to tell you my name, but really I am not so rich as to possess one; and whether I am to be Jemima, Keren-happuch, or something else, I have not the least idea; and all my friends here seem to be at as great a loss about it as I myself. But though my name is not yet written on earth, I hope it is already enrolled in heaven; and oh, may it never be blotted from the book of life!

And as to yourself, I presume you will know perfectly
well who I am, and for whom you must pray, when I subscribe myself

THE LITTLE DAUGHTER OF YOUR SON W. G.

Another letter was written by Mr. Goodell, as amanuensis
for a son just born, to one of the officers of the American
Board, whose name had been given to the child : —

MY DEAR SIR, — I joined this mission on the 20th ult.,
and, though I was not wholly unexpected, yet I arrived at
so early an hour in the morning as to take some of the missionary circle by surprise. For the present I board in Mr.
Goodell's family, which seems to be the case with all new
missionaries, till they have learnt something of the language,
with the manners and customs of the people; and this whether
they are to remain permanently at Constantinople, or whether
they are to pass on after a while to the regions beyond. I
make more trouble than I could wish, and increase the cares
and burdens of the family, instead of doing much to lighten
them. In short, I for the present require a great deal of
attention from others, without being able to render any in
return. I came, too, without any outfit whatever. To have
seen me on my first arrival, a stranger might have concluded
naturally enough that I had suffered shipwreck, and had not
a friend in the world, so entirely destitute was my condition.
I lifted up my voice and wept aloud, and my situation excited
universal sympathy. I was received as a beloved child, and
I have had every possible kindness shown me. I assure you
nobody could have done more for me than Mrs. Goodell and
her eldest daughter. For a whole month they devoted their
attention almost exclusively to me ; they wiped away my
tears, anticipated my every want, and have so comforted me
that, though I was weak and helpless as an infant, I already
begin to look up and smile. Indeed, the whole family are so
abundant in their caresses and attentions that it will be well
if I do not become wholly selfish, and think, with the Princess
Amelia, —

" That all the world is made for me."

True, I joined this mission without any appointment from
the Board ; but I assure you I should not have done so had
I not been under a higher appointment than any that could

emanate from the Prudential Committee. I came not of myself, and the authority which sent me I presume no one will question. Certain it is I have no right to return, except at the bidding of the same authority; nor is there any power on earth which can lawfully set that authority aside. It is also true that living here is very expensive; but, as I came unattended, and as I have no thought at present of seeking a partner, especially without the advice of my friends, a suitable maintenance from the funds of the Board will doubtless be allowed me.

There is one other subject on which I must touch before I close, as it perhaps concerns you more than any other I have mentioned. I was unknown by name to all the missionary circle. Without doubt I had a name recorded where I received my appointment, but it was not put in my passport. I was, therefore, absolutely nameless, except as I was called by a common name. But it is said that grammarians here divide all names into common and proper, and insist upon it that every individual who has the former should also be furnished with the latter. Being myself ignorant of the customs and unacquainted with the grammar, I just let them do as they saw fit, though I assure you it was very amusing to listen to all the odd names they from time to time called over me to see how they would sound, and which would best become me. Suffice it to say that, after the younger members of the family had looked through the whole Old and New Testament, with all history, ancient and modern, they at last, without one dissenting voice, united with the older ones in giving me the name of —— ——. This is the name by which I am known in this world; it stands thus on the records of the baptized ones; and this, therefore, must be the one which was previously recorded on high, and which would have been inserted in the passport had such an insertion been customary. The motive of my friends in calling me after your own name was to secure your prayers for me; and that such also was the original design in the records of eternity is so evident as to justify you in acting accordingly. Will you also sometimes remember those whom I am taught to call brother and sister in this family? We are now seven, which in Scripture is a perfect number. And may we "be perfect, even as our Father who is in heaven is perfect"! Like the seven lamps of the golden candlestick, may we be burning continually before the throne of God, with hallowed fire from off the altar!

With my love to all your children and to their excellent mother, in which my best friends join, I subscribe myself,

YOUR VERY LITTLE NAMESAKE.

His first resort to artificial means to aid his sight he mentions in a letter to his brother Temple, Sept. 11, 1841 : —

"My sight begins to fail, and I this day procured some spectacles. This looking upon so many books of different languages so rapidly and so intensely, as is necessary in the work of translating the Scriptures, is very trying to the eyes. For the year past I have found it difficult to read small print in the night; and the difficulty so much increased that I thought I ought not to use my eyes any longer in the night without the aid of glasses.

"But I have no reason to complain. On the contrary, I would be unfeignedly thankful that I have seen so long and so well. My eyes were naturally weak ; but, though I have always favored them, they have served me well. I must confess I have also used them in gazing upon objects upon which they should have been for ever closed. When I can no longer see with them, not even ' through a glass darkly,' may ' the Lord be my everlasting light.' "

About the same time he makes another characteristic allusion to a loss he had sustained : —

"*December* 17. For the last week have been quite ill, confined to my couch most of the time, from a cold in my head, teeth, and throat. One who has been a grinder in my household for forty-six or forty-seven years, and who has done me a great deal of hard and important service, I have had to expel for ever. For some time past he has been disabled from doing any kind of service, and the latter part of the time he gave me constant annoyance from his peevish habits, and had begun also to make disturbance among the other servants. Whether, at the time of the restitution of all things, he will be found in his place again, I cannot say. Some of my children think he will, and others not. However, it does not depend at all on our reasonings."

In a letter to the Rev. Dr. Anderson, Secretary of the American Board, he gives an encouraging account of the prospects of the mission, — an earnest of the great work that the Spirit of God afterwards wrought in the hearts of many of the people.

CONSTANTINOPLE, Sept. 17, 1841.

MY DEAR BROTHER, — Last Sabbath was our communion season. We sat down at the Lord's table, being representatives not only of the Church of England and of the Presbyterian and Congregational and Methodist churches of Scotland and America, together with the Lutheran Church in Germany, but also of the three ancient Oriental churches, viz., the Armenian, the Greek, and the Nestorian. We were gathered out of many nations and kindreds and tongues, and raised up to sit together in heavenly places in Christ.

Yesterday was the monthly concert of prayer, and, as usual, one of the services was held expressly for our native brethren. They always take a lively interest in this meeting; and, in conducting the exercises, Mr. Dwight and myself generally alternate. The present occasion was peculiarly interesting, from the fact that a bishop, a priest, and a deacon of the Nestorian Church were present, and a large room was filled at an early hour. Five prayers were offered, one by Mr. Hamlin, in Armenian; one in Turkish, by my translator; one in Turkish and one in Armenian, by the two pious priests so often mentioned; and the last in Armenian, by that native brother "whose praise is in all the churches." And could you have been present, though you would not have understood a word these brethren said, yet, from their tones of voice and serious, earnest manner, you would have felt at once that they had "an unction from the Holy One, and knew all things;" that they had "received the Holy Ghost, as well as we;" and that they had been taught from above to "pray with the spirit and with the understanding also."

Mr. Dwight continues his regular meetings twice a week. These are generally small, there seldom being more than about fifteen present at any one time; but then these fifteen are only a part of some seventy or seventy-five persons, who come as often as circumstances will permit. You will recollect that they come a distance of from two to three, five, and even ten miles; that they come in the middle of the day, and in the very midst of business hours; and that, belonging as they mostly do to the various trades, and being men of thrift, they have to shut up their shops in the midst of all the worldly around them, when they come to hear the Gospel.

They pay their own boat-hire for the sweet privilege of hearing the Gospel. By coming to us they have nothing to get but the Gospel. They hope for nothing else. They do not even look to us for protection, or for any other earthly favor. Excepting four or five, they have no temporal connection with us whatever, but are altogether independent of us. They are all men, the customs of society not permitting them to bring their families with them. They belong generally to the middling class, — that class now rapidly rising in importance, becoming the nation itself, and taking hold of the management of its affairs with a giant-like grasp.

Those who attend these meetings are not the idle, or the dissipated hangers-on, or busybodies in other men's matters. Not one is known to go away to mock, or to dispute, or to plunge into the follies or cares of this life. On the contrary, it is confidently believed that, in almost every case, they retire to pray, to commune with their own hearts, to bless God for the glad tidings of the Gospel, and to resolve in the strength of the Lord to lead a life of faith, of deadness to the world, and of preparation for eternity. If they are not all of them "spiritually minded, which is life and peace," they are at least "sober minded." As a general thing, we may say of them that they are either already "in Christ Jesus, and walk not after the flesh, but after the Spirit," or they are of that class of persons usually found at the seat of the inquirer in the revival scenes of America.

Nor is the work confined to these seventy or seventy-five, of whom we have been speaking, but there are others of both sexes in the same state of mind, — persons of like character and spirit, but whose circumstances or the customs of society forbid their attending the meetings. These are more particularly looked up and looked after from day to day by our native helpers. To say nothing, then, of the interesting state of things in the interior, there are perhaps not less than a hundred persons in the very neighborhood of the capital who are serious inquirers, and to a goodly number of whom, should they be present at our communion seasons, and ask for the privilege of partaking with us, we should not hesitate to say, in the name of Him who spreads the table, "Eat, O friends; drink, yea, drink abundantly, O beloved." Perhaps it would be difficult to find anywhere a body of Christians who understand better than these that it is "not by works of righteousness which we have done, but according to His mercy, He saves us, by the washing of regeneration and the renewing of the Holy Ghost."

I say nothing here of the great increase of enlightened Armenians, who may now, I suppose, be computed at some thousands. But, in the character of the work described above, is there not something very peculiar and striking, calling for special thanksgiving to God? It is not confined to children in school, who are out of the way of temptation and out of the way of present usefulness, and of whose future exposures and apostasies there is just cause for apprehension. But the subjects of this work are men of present standing in society, already stemming the entire force of this world's dreadful current; already placed in their respective neighborhoods as so many distinct lights that burn and shine; already, like the angels to the wandering shepherds, reporting to their neighbors and friends the glad tidings of a great salvation for all people.

Nor is the work confined to those who are in our employ, or who are expecting some temporal advantage from us, and are thus willing to hear something about Christ for the sake of the loaves and fishes. But, on the contrary, as I have already said, it is almost exclusively confined to those who expect nothing but the Gospel, with persecution; who are known to us in no other way than as those who are ready to count all things but dross for the excellency of the knowledge of Christ; who always have to give, instead of receiving, not being able to come even once to us without making a sacrifice of time and money.

You would naturally suppose that the meetings on the Sabbath would be the best attended; but just the reverse is the case. The reason is that our hearers have nearly all of them turned preachers on that day. As it is a day of leisure with their friends and acquaintances, they improve the opportunity for making them acquainted with the Gospel; and in this work of faith and labor of love they have the divine blessing.　　　　　　Yours,

W. GOODELL.

12

CHAPTER XV.

ON the 6th of November, 1841, Mr. Goodell completed the translation of the Old Testament into Armeno-Turkish, having finished the New Testament before coming to Constantinople. This may be regarded as the great work of his life, especially as he devoted many subsequent years to its careful revision and perfection. This translation has been, and will long continue to be, the lamp of life to the millions of the Armenian nation. On the day that he completed this labor, he wrote to the Rev. S. H. Calhoun, then in the Levant, as the agent of the American Bible Society, under auspices of which this translation was given to the people of the East: —

CONSTANTINOPLE, Nov. 6, 1841.

MY DEAR BROTHER, — Through the kindness and blessing of God, the translation of the Old Testament into Armeno-Turkish is at length completed. This I had hardly the least idea of living long enough to see, when I commenced the work; but the divine forbearance towards me has been great. I came in course this morning to the last verse of the last chapter of the last book, which I corrected "with shoutings, grace, grace unto it." At the bottom of the page I wrote, "Bless the Lord, O my soul, and forget not all His benefits." I then arose and shut up all the books that have been lying open before me these many years, and fell on my knees to give thanks unto the name of the Lord, who " hath not dealt with us after our sins," who hath given us His blessed "word to be a lamp unto our feet," and whose wondrous love permits us to hold it up to "lighten every man that cometh into the world." Oh, may the nations " no longer have to walk on in darkness," but may they all be speedily furnished "with the light of life "!

082,

The preparation of this work has been a great and difficult one; and it has employed nearly all my strength and time for several years. After I came to Constantinople, I tried my utmost to carry it forward at the same time with other missionary and more active labors; but I found that I accomplished next to nothing in it. It was necessary that my room should be a study, and not a church; that my mind, instead of being distracted and disturbed, should be composed, like that of the prophet Elisha, and like that of the other inspired writers, whose words I was endeavoring to translate; and that my attention should be strictly devoted to this, and to nothing else. It is not like giving the Scriptures to the destitute heathen, where haste is required rather than extreme accuracy, and where, the idiom not being supposed to be perfectly understood, a more critical examination of difficult passages may be reserved for a future edition, when the language itself may have to be revised and made more idiomatical. Nor is it like giving the Scriptures to the ignorant and unenlightened, who will never of themselves find out any of those mistakes and defects which the translator can himself correct in some future edition, when more time may be devoted to the work, more experience acquired in it, and better helps obtained for it. But it is preparing the Scriptures for those who are comparatively enlightened; who as a nation have access to them in at least two languages already, though neither of them generally understood, and the learned and influential of whom have in many cases become great pedants in criticism, and captious beyond endurance, — being much more inclined to compare for the sake of finding discrepancies than to read with a prayerful desire to understand the meaning, and be guided into all truth.

But as nearly all can read the Armeno-Turkish, and very many thousands among them can read nothing else, the translation of the Bible into this language is imperiously demanded. It was strongly urged upon me eighteen years ago by the Rev. Pliny Fisk, one of the first missionaries of the Board to Palestine. I have had my eye upon it ever since; Providence has furnished me with the means by raising up instruments, and I have spared no pains or labor to have it as perfect as possible, otherwise I might have completed it long ago. In some instances I have spent more time on the examination of a single passage than I should have felt justified in employing on a whole chapter, had I been throwing it out upon a starving population, who had never yet tasted this Bread of Heaven. It is not a version, or a revision of a former translation, for no such ever existed. The whole has been taken fresh from the Hebrew. And may it in some humble way prove to be like the "pure river of the water of life, clear as crystal, proceeding out of the throne of God and of the Lamb." May hundreds of thousands of the perishing come and recline on its banks, and drink, and live· for ever!

One adventitious advantage which may be hoped from this translation is, that it will render it less difficult at some future time to bring back their ancient Armenian Scriptures to the original Hebrew, from which they have more or less widely departed. It is preparing the way for this, inasmuch· as it makes them familiar with a translation professedly of this character.

To me this work has been, next to preaching the Gospel, the most delightful employment. The land through which I have passed has not been a wilderness to me, — a land of drought and barrenness, but it has been a country of fertile vales, and hills of the richest mines, abounding with such beautiful prospects and refreshing shade and cooling fountains, that I have often stopped to enjoy the scenery, to listen to the sweet songsters of the grove, to "drink of the brook in the way," and thus to "go on from strength to strength." My feelings have gone along with those of the sacred writers to such a degree, that often when alone in my study I have been reading a page perhaps for the seventh time, I have had to stop in order to wipe away the fast flowing tears, or to offer up such prayers and praises, as the subject called forth. And then, only think of such a song as that of Deborah's! Having in such perfection all the softness and delicacy and minute detail and lively description of female composition! Who could translate it without feeling his very heart dance within him! I could almost wish that all the Lord's people were translators, as Moses wished them all prophets, in order that they might see with their own eyes the very words and the very manner, often inimitable in translating, in which the great God expressed His thoughts to man, and might thus enter more readily into all the scenes and circumstances and feelings of those "holy men of God, who spake as they were moved by the Holy Ghost." God's word is, indeed, a great deep; who can fathom it? It is divinely beautiful; who that once looks upon it can help gazing for ever with ever increasing delight? It is fraught with the riches of eternity; who shall not prize it "above gold, yea, above fine gold"?

My helps have been Robinson's Gesenius and Simoni's Lexicon, Michaelis' Hebrew Bible, with critical notes in the margin, Rosenmüller's Scholia, Barnes's Notes on Isaiah, Keiffer's Turkish Bible, Leeves's Greco-Turkish, and the Septuagint, with the English.

My translator, who, as you know, is a pious Greek, and a fine scholar in Greek and Turkish, to which, through our instructions, may also be added English and Hebrew, had for helps Robinson's Gesenius, Leeves's Modern Greek and Greco-Turkish Bibles, Keiffer's Turkish, the English, and the Septuagint.

On certain passages we have both of us consulted various Hebrew scholars; and I trust we have both of us availed ourselves of the privilege of asking the assistance of that same blessed Spirit, through whose inspiration the Scriptures were at first indited.

Dionysius, the Armenian bishop, formerly in my employ, first translated the work with the help of the Arabic and Ancient Armenian Bibles, together with Keiffer. Nearly or quite half of this translation was burnt at the time of the great fire here ten years ago; and the bishop had to translate it again. My present translator, Mr. Panayotes Constantinides, had the advantage of this translation, and made his first corrections upon it, or at least upon a part of it, and then rewrote the whole. He always translated directly from the Hebrew, with the helps above mentioned.

This translation, as small portions of it were from time to time completed, I took and examined every word with the Hebrew, in the most careful and conscientious manner. And I herewith send you some of the notes I made, by which you will see that I had various inquiries to make, or various alterations to propose, in regard to almost every verse. To the examination of these we sat down together, and devoted on an average a day, or a day and a half, in a week. It is, however, but justice to him to say that we sometimes concluded to let the text remain as he left it, without adopting the changes I had proposed. These papers are marked No. 1. Some of them are of course destroyed; for I had no thought of preserving them longer than I had use for them myself.

These portions of the translation would now be laid aside till near the time when they would be wanted for the press at Smyrna, — sometimes a year, and generally several months. When called for at Smyrna, Mr. Panayotes would take and read them over carefully, to notice any error in orthography or grammar or punctuation, or any thing that appeared not idiomatic in the language; and No. 2 are some of the papers, showing the changes he made. These papers and the manuscript were then given to me, and I read it over for the same purpose; and you have the result in No. 3, which we of course again examined together. Very few, however, of Nos. 2 and 3 remain, as I had no motive in preserving them.

In translating the New Testament into this language several years ago, I had the help of Bishop Dionysius. It was new work for us both; and, when he began to learn from me the peculiar shape of the Greek, he began to try to conform his Turkish to the Greek idiom, as he said the Ancient Armenian was thus conformed; and, being absent as he was from the people who would read the work, this error increased upon him from day to day. My present translator has been more exposed to the same error, than to any other, as I presume every young and conscientious translator of the Bible would be. But I have had a special eye upon it, and have kept asking, "Is this Turkish? Is it Turkish or Hebrew?" Moreover, we are now among the people for whom the work is intended, and some parts of it have been put into the hands of various individuals of different standing in society, to ascertain whether the style would be comprehended. Some parts, also, have been read by the best masters here, and a due regard paid to their criticisms. I say a due regard, for the style of the best masters would in general be above the comprehension of the common people. Of the general acceptableness in this respect of those portions of the work which have been put in circulation among the people I need not now speak, as some of the facts have already been communicated to the Bible Society.

The printing was done at Smyrna, and with neatness and despatch, and the proofs were read there. But in every instance the last proof was sent to me, that I might see whether it were entirely conformed to the manuscript. This I have had for the most part to do alone, as my translator was much of the time in Greece for safety. When he was here, he examined the proof first, and I afterwards, but in no instance, even after he had read the proof, have I found one entirely correct. Accuracy is not in him, nor indeed in any other native I have found, except Bishop Dionysius. He was remarkably accurate, and his services would have been to me invaluable in this respect, and would have saved me many, many months of hard labor; but it was not safe to bring him from Beyrout. A great deal of my time has all along been devoted to those niceties of the language, which it is the province of a native to attend to, and not of a foreigner. I have done the best I could; but, with all my attention to the subject, minor errors have doubtless crept in through inadvertence. Nor, to speak of the work in general, is it to be supposed that the meaning has in every instance been truly apprehended by us, or that the words used have in all cases been the most judiciously chosen to express what may have been rightly understood. All these things are but approximations towards what is required. We do what we can, and leave it for those who come after us to do better.

I would still suggest, however, though the suggestion might come with more grace from another, that translations which have once obtained, and which are not radically defective, had, like our own English Bible, better remain altogether untouched, than be too often meddled with, or be made to undergo more than partial changes. The history of translations in India is full of instruction on this subject.

And now may the blood of the everlasting covenant be sprinkled upon the book, upon those who have had any thing to do in preparing it, and upon all who shall read it! May it be made use of by the Holy Spirit in softening and sanctifying the hearts of men, and in bringing many sons and daughters unto glory! Already is God pouring out His Spirit upon this people, and your society is at the same time sending among them the very "words which the Holy Ghost teacheth." What a wonderful coincidence! what an encouraging fact! Let it excite our gratitude, and awaken us to more prayer and faith. Tell your society that the blessings of many ready to perish will come upon them. Tell them "not to be weary in well-doing; for in due season they shall reap, if they faint not." Tell them not to wait for a vote of thanks, or for a formal expression of obligation and lasting gratitude, from this great community, — these hundreds of thousands the objects of their bounty; but in this respect to be " perfect, even as their Father in heaven is perfect, who sendeth rain on the just and on the unjust."

With Christian and affectionate salutations to yourself, and through you to them, I remain

Your brother in the faith and work of the Lord,

W. GOODELL.

A few days later he wrote to his first preceptor, John Adams, LL.D. of Phillips Academy, for whom he ever cherished the warmest affection and the most profound respect:—

CONSTANTINOPLE, Nov. 19, 1841.

MY VERY DEAR PRECEPTOR, — Very kind, indeed, it was in you to remember me among so many hundreds of your disciples. I say disciples; for verily I believe we learned not only under you, but of you. The impressions I received at Phillips Academy were more vivid and more deep and lasting than those I received at college or at the Theological Seminary. And I feel that I have more of your character impressed on my own than of any other teacher. Perhaps one reason was, that I had just come out of the woods, and every thing was new to me. I was living in a new world. Thus new and wonderful does it often appear to a person when he is first translated from the kingdom of darkness into the kingdom of God's dear Son.

It is nineteen years to-day since we were married, and in a few days it will be nineteen years since we sailed from New York for the East. More than half a generation has, during this time, gone to the other world. More than four hundred millions have done with time and probation, and have commenced their eternity. To my own family God has in His great mercy to the unworthy given an unusual degree of health and domestic comfort. To many daughters and sons do we sustain the relation of parents. But all are not now under our poor guidance and direction, for one, a beloved and promising boy of nine years and a half, ceased to be the object of our prayers, but not of our love, the 8th of April last, when " he was not, for God took him."

I have within a few days completed the translation of the Old Testament into Armeno-Turkish. The New Testament I had finished before. I have thus opened fountains of living waters here in the desert, and for the perishing people, or, as Mr. Temple says, "set wide open to them all the twelve gates of the New Jerusalem." This good brother, as you know, is stationed at Smyrna, about two hundred and fifty miles from the capital. We correspond every week with great regularity, and as he becomes more cheerful in his old age and I more sober, we are of course getting to be somewhat more alike than when we occupied the same room and slept in the same bed for seven years at college and the Theological Seminary. Were we not indebted to your own barn for the straw? yea, and for the mouse withal, which we happened on one occasion to put into the bed with the straw, to our great annoyance the following night, when we had to throw off the bed, not knowing what in the world was the matter with it.

With the history of your own beloved family I am not unacquainted, having been informed from time to time of all the principal incidents, whether they respected yourself or your dear children. To all who are on this side heaven I send my Christian and most affectionate salutations, from Mary the eldest, down to Phebe the youngest. When I heard that dear Elizabeth had met with a watery grave, I felt that one of my most precious friends was in heaven. If there were no blessed Saviour, who would take care of our friends in the other world?

Mrs. Goodell unites in kind and Christian regards to yourself, to Mrs. Adams, to Betsy Cleveland, and all, and, commending myself and family to your prayers, I remain

Your much obliged and very grateful quondam pupil,

W. GOODELL.

On the completion of his fiftieth year he wrote to his brother Nathan: —

CONSTANTINOPLE, Feb. 14, 1842.

MY DEAR BROTHER, — This day completes half a century of my life. Some of my friends have remarked that the changes that have taken place in the world during these fifty years are greater than during almost any other equal period of time. And is it not so? God has certainly been doing great and wonderful things in the earth, both by His providence and by His Spirit.

. . . .

Did you ever take particular notice of God's first command to our race, —" Replenish the earth and subdue it?" Now, instead of subduing the earth, and turning the very elements to the greatest and best account, by ascertaining the numberless uses to which they could be applied, our whole race, from the beginning of the world, have been subduing one another. All their strength, all their ingenuity, all their resources, have been employed for the destruction of each other. The history of the world is only one black disclosure of the designs formed, the means used, and the projects executed or attempted, to subdue one another. The historian finds hardly any thing else to mention. This has been the great vortex which has swallowed up all the wealth and the strength and the thoughts of nations from generation to generation.

But within the last fifty years the minds of a few persons in a few countries have been turned to the subject of subduing the earth, and ascertaining what they could make out of it. The experiments have been numerous, splendid, and the results astounding. The very ends of the world are now brought together, and the moral effect of this among the nations is, that men begin to feel that they belong to one brotherhood. What, then, may we expect when all minds in all countries shall be waked up to this great subject, and the ingenuity of man be turned into this new and beautiful channel, as our benevolent Creator at first commanded! What improvements may we not confidently expect in the next fifty years! Long before the expiration of that period we may have done with steam, have found something much more useful. Who can tell what we shall yet make out of the earth, as we come truly to the task of subduing it. Who can tell but we may yet tame the volcano, or hitch on to the lightning, or ride above the clouds! Who can tell but we may yet turn icebergs and earthquakes to some public benefit!

When our race departed from God, and we were cut off in a great measure from intercourse with one another, perhaps we were then cut off from all the intercourse we may have heretofore enjoyed with the inhabitants of other worlds, and confined to our own narrow limits, that we might not corrupt others by our example ; but as missionaries are sent forth, and the nations return to God and to duty, who can tell but we may yet be permitted to find the means of holding intercourse with our neighbors in other planets, or our fellow-beings in the stars. But you will probably prefer to let your neighbors go, till you hear something of your own relatives at Constantinople.

.   .   .   .

Dear brother, let us live for eternity, for time will soon be no more. Let us pray for each other, and for each other's families.   Your brother,
                                    WILLIAM.

He writes in his journal : —

"*February* 18, 1842. On account of the encroachments of the Turks on the Frank burying-ground, I had to remove the body of our beloved boy. The grave, contrary to the custom of the country, had been dug deep, and the coffin was scarcely damp. Every thing was sweet and still. The new grave which we have prepared a few rods distant was also deep and dry ; and there we laid the body, to rest in its quiet bed till the resurrection morning. Beloved child, farewell !"

Mr. Goodell was original in almost every thing that he did or said or wrote. The following letter of introduction is characteristic. It was superscribed : —

"To the Rev. Messrs. Temple, Adger, Riggs, Van Lennep, and Calhoun, Smyrna, introducing one of those that resemble the children of a king :" —

                              PERA, March 5, 1842.

DEAR BRETHREN, — I have much pleasure in introducing to you and to your good families Mr. Marshall, a fellow-countryman of ours, " a fellow-citizen of the saints," one of the royal family, born to a great estate, even "an incorruptible inheritance," and possessing, also, no inconsiderable portion of comfort and convenience, on his way to the " better country." Having said thus much, I need not say more to bespeak your attentions and civilities to one of such high and noble extraction, and of such boundless prospects for eternity.

And with Christian salutations I venture to subscribe myself, by the grace of God,

                  A fellow-heir,
                         W. GOODELL.

P. S. — Brother Temple will remember our old classmate

Alva Woods, since made President and D.D., — he married a sister of Mr. Marshall.

The extracts from his journal are here continued: —

"*April* 27, 1842. An Armenian youth came to me for money, which was due to his family; and I, as usual, gave him an order on our banker, an English merchant in Galata. He took the paper and looked at it a moment, and said doubtingly, 'But he does not know me.' 'No matter,' I replied, 'he knows *me*; and whatever you ask in my name he will give it you. If you go to him in your own name, you will of course get nothing; but my name has so much influence with him, that whatever I endorse for you will assuredly be honored. If I give you my name to carry to him, he will, without asking whether you are a prince or a beggar, give you just as much as he would give me, should I go in person and ask for myself.' He understood at once to what I alluded, and appeared much struck with it.

"Saw a Circassian offering his little boy for sale, and two Turkish women, whom he met in the street, treating with him about the price. He seemed not to have one thought about the poor boy, — into whose hands he might fall, or what his fate might be for time or eternity, but to be intent only on getting as much money by the sale as possible. '*Without natural affection.*' Oh, how little do those baptized children in America, who refuse to submit to the government of Christ, think of the temporal blessings and privileges they enjoy, by being made to live even near the borders of His kingdom! And what blessings they might enjoy through eternal ages, would they but pass over the line which for ever separates the two kingdoms of light and darkness, of benevolence and sin!

"Walking out in the country, I saw two Mussulmans, one saying his prayers and going through his prostrations with all apparent devotion, and the other sitting by and relating to him for his entertainment a story with all particularity. When the devotee had performed all the required ceremonies, and, finished repeating all the words to be said, he turned, and, as though he had only been cleaning his teeth, made the proper replies to the different parts of the story, to which he had evidently been listening with interest; and neither the one nor the other seemed to feel that he had been guilty of any impropriety. And, alas! how many in Christian lands, it is to be feared, are guilty of similar impropriety! How many in public prayer, instead of transacting business with heaven, are thinking their own thoughts, pursuing their own plans, following after their own wandering imaginations, and telling their own story to themselves!

" Several days since I passed by a blind man whom I have often met before, but, on account of the crowd, I had no opportunity of speaking a word to him. I placed in his hands, however, the third part of our Armeno-Turkish Old Testament, which has been recently bound up and ready for delivery. He smiled, pressed it to his lips, and put it into his bosom without uttering a word, though I saw his lips move for some time, as if addressing his own heart, or his God. Some young ladies, who were passing at the time, smiled more than he did, to see me give a book to a blind man,— the very last thing in the world to give him, they doubtless thought. But there is more real good sense in it than a superficial observer or thinker would be apt to imagine ; for the book has to be read aloud, and thus several may be benefited at once. On speaking to him to-day, he immediately began to tell me about the good man who was so roughly handled by Satan. I could not imagine at first whom he should mean, but I soon recollected the circumstance of the book, and perceived he was telling me of the Patriarch Job, — being so full of the subject that he had not thought it neces- sary to mention his name ; for of whom can the whole world be thinking but of that afflicted man ? He said he had, blind though he was, read the whole story over several times, and with great comfort to himself. This led me to bless God that I had been instrumental in putting His holy word into a language which the poor afflicted ones of earth can under- stand ; and it led me to think, also, that a tract on afflictions might be very useful for these poor people. They need something to comfort them ; especially something to teach them how to improve their afflictions, and to derive spiritual benefit from them."

June 4, 1842, he writes to his brother Temple : —

" Mrs. Schneider expressed her utter astonishment that she could converse as familiarly with you as a brother. She thought you were as an angel of God, so far above all human imperfection as to have little or no sympathy with mortals. But she found you could so far condescend to those

of low estate as to be able to speak words of comfort even
to her heart. I told her that the more any one grows in
grace, the lower, and not higher, he becomes, and the more
fitted he is to sympathize with those who are struggling
amidst many temptations and sorrows to keep on the way
that leads to life eternal. Christ had *perfect* sympathy.
Ours is at best imperfect; but the more we are like Him, the
better fitted we are to have compassion on the ignorant, and
those who are out of the way, and those who meet with trials
and afflictions. This seems a paradox. But the whole of
Christianity is a paradox. When I am weak, then am I
strong. When I die, then I live. When I am poor, then
am I rich. When I have nothing, then have I all things.

" The first time I saw Dr. Payson, of Portland, I was perfectly astonished to see him on the side-hill without his hat,
running after a stray horse, and throwing stones at him. I
was no longer afraid to come nigh him, and speak to him,
but I was afraid he might commit some sin by hitting his
horse with too big a stone."

When he had completed his translation of the Old and
New Testaments. giving to the Armenian population the
whole word of God in their own tongue, Mr. Goodell
commenced a systematic exposition of the Scriptures in a
course of lectures. For this service he had become eminently fitted by his familiarity with every line of the sacred
volume in the languages in which it was written, and by
having deeply imbibed its spirit while carefully and prayerfully studying its pages. This exposition proved highly interesting and edifying to all who had learned to prize the
word of God. Occasionally he noted down in his journal
the incidents and illustrations he had used, and their effect
upon his hearers. The following is a specimen : —

" *July* 22, 1842. Our meetings twice a week for a familiar exposition of the Scriptures have been continued to the
present time, and the interest in them seems unabated.
When I commenced the one on the Sabbath, I expected that
the other on Tuesday mornings, which was comparatively
small, would dwindle away, and become merged in this ; but
I am happy to say that this has not been the case. Some-

times half a chapter is commented on at a meeting, and sometimes only one verse, or even half a verse. When any fail to understand, or when they wish for more full explanations, they ask questions. Some of our more constant hearers are very shrewd and clear-headed men; and, when they get hold of the idea intended to be conveyed, which is often before we have completed the explanation, their very eyes sparkle, and they seem to 'rejoice as one that findeth great spoil.' I have often thought of that beautiful passage in Jeremiah, 'Thy words were found. and I did eat them; and thy word was unto me the joy and rejoicing of my heart.' They swallow down the truth by whole mouthfuls, like those who have been long famishing. And to open the rich treasures of the Gospel to such is like 'pouring water upon the thirsty, and floods upon the dry ground.' Not a drop seems to be wasted. Often does every ear seem open. every eye riveted, and every heart prepared by the Holy Spirit to receive the truth. The word is with power. It comes with all the authority of eternal truth. It comes with all the freshness of a revelation from God. It cuts every way, like the sword with two edges. It scatters all the mists and mazes of night, like the rising of the sun. It is 'perfect, converting the soul.'

Several of those who attend take notes, and especially of all references to parallel passages in the Old Testament. To find so much pure Gospel in the Old Testament, and such a wonderful degree of harmony between the Old and the New, and so much more of spirituality and of real evangelical religion among the patriarchs and prophets, than even the disciples appear to have had before their baptism with the Holy Ghost on the day of Pentecost, is altogether new to them. And those who thus take notes do it for the purpose of communicating to others what they hear from us. They 'gather up the fragments,' and retail them; and, as retailers, nobody in all Constantinople carries on a brisker trade than they do. They light their candle, not to conceal it under a bushel, but to put it on a candlestick, for the public benefit. And the water they drink for their own refreshment becomes a well of living water, springing up for the refreshment of all their neighbors and friends."

During the year 1842, the Gospel made silent but rapid progress among the Armenians. The Spirit was moving upon the hearts of the people with greater power than at any previous time. Many who had rested in the forms and ceremonies of the church, and who had trusted to the priests to negotiate with God in their behalf, learned for the first time that " God is a Spirit, and they that worship Him must worship Him in spirit and in truth," and that there is only " one Mediator between God and men, the man Christ Jesus." Some who had been stout opposers of the truth, taking part or rejoicing in the persecution of the followers of Christ, were humbled at the foot of the cross. The female part of the population, which, owing to the seclusion in which the women of the East are kept, and in part also to their ignorance, had been inaccessible, now began to feel the truth, and for the first time were among the attendants upon the ministration of the word. Having the whole word of God in their own familiar language, many of the people began to study it as did the ancient Bereans, searching the Scriptures daily, though not so much to learn whether these things were so, as to learn more and more of Christ and of His truth.

The believers at the capital had rest for a time, but the arm of persecution was not withdrawn in the interior. Many in the towns distant from Constantinople, who had heard the word gladly, were called to suffer as witnesses for the truth. At Erzroom, an enlightened and truly pious priest, who had begun to preach the Gospel in its simplicity, was seized by order of his bishop, bastinadoed until he swooned, and in that state was thrown into prison and bound with chains. At Nicomedia, and at other places nearer the capital, where the number of believers was multiplied, the enemies of the truth were restrained from using violence, but they did not at all withhold the tongue of hatred and slander.

In the midst of all the opposition, an incident transpired that was full of encouragement, in regard to the nature and depth of the work that was going on in the hearts of the people. It was found that during the summer of 1842, a number of pious Armenians, whose services had been broken up by their own ecclesiastics, resorted secretly to a retired spot among the hills, not far from Constantinople, where, of their own motion, or rather moved only by the divine Spirit, they organized a missionary society. They came to the conclusion that the time had arrived for them to send to their brethren in other parts of the empire the glad tidings which had brought life and joy to their hearts, and they actually set apart for this service one of their own number, who was sent into the interior to preach Christ to their benighted brethren, and his labors were greatly blessed from on high.

Two years after completing the translation of the Old Testament into the Armeno-Turkish, Mr. Goodell wrote to the Rev. Dr. Anderson, announcing the revision of the New. His letter is an eloquent tribute to the priceless value of the Holy Scriptures, and a fresh evidence that the writer had been drinking deeply at the fountain of the water of life, while drawing water for others.

CONSTANTINOPLE, Jan. 27, 1843.

MY DEAR BROTHER, — You will have as much pleasure in receiving the intelligence as I have in announcing it that the revision of the New Testament is now completed by me, and that it is nearly all printed. I had the same pious, able, and faithful helper that I had in translating the Old Testament, and, although the whole was rewritten by him, yet it was finished in just about one year. And it is in a style so much more acceptable than the previous edition, that I trust it can be said, " The former had no glory in this respect, by reason of the glory that excelleth." I have now put into the hands of that portion of the Armenian population who use only the Armeno-Turkish language the whole word of God, — all the information that has ever come from heaven for their instruction and benefit, — "and therein I do rejoice, yea, and will rejoice."

But with translations and revisions I have now done for ever, and "the poor remnant of my days" I hope to spend in pouring into the ears of men some of those great and glorious truths which I have been engaged for several years in spreading out before their eyes. But "which shall prosper, whether this or that, or whether they both shall be alike good," who but God can tell. This, however, is a matter which concerneth us not, and of which, indeed, we are incapable of judging. It is in the hands of God, and as He employeth whatever instruments it pleaseth Him, so in bringing men to a knowledge of the truth He useth whichever of their organs of sense He chooseth, whether their eye or their ear. The noble Bereans are specially commended for having made use of their eyes, and to this the sacred writer ascribes the great success of the Gospel in that place. And in the reformation in England, Tindall's translation of the New Testament was apparently more blessed in opening the eyes of men and convincing them of the truth than any other means whatever. What could the preaching of even one hundred reformed priests have effected without it? Such a translation was absolutely necessary to satisfy the minds and to quiet the consciences of men. Without this, how should they know whether to believe this priest or that? Every thing would depend, not on a solid foundation, but on the eloquence, or, rather, the influence of the speaker. In carrying forward all such reformations, the Bible must be the final appeal, and of this not a part, but the whole, because in such cases the part published would be rejected by the opposer, and the appeal be made to the part unpublished; and because, too, the whole must be very thoroughly examined before the mind can be convinced that none of the superstitions and errors which have crept into a corrupt church can be found in any part of the Bible.

Turn, now, to our labors among the Armenians. Our whole work with them is emphatically a Bible work. The Bible is our only standard, and the Bible is our final appeal. And it is even more necessary for us than it was for the reformers in England, because we are foreigners. Without it, we could say one thing and the priests and bishops could say another; but where would be the umpire? It would be nowhere, and all our efforts would be like " beating the air."

And we may ask, What could even the apostles have done without the Bible? Among the Jews they could have done absolutely nothing. They based their whole new revelation upon it. They appealed to it always, and they asserted it to be more sure and certain than any voice they had themselves heard in the holy mount. And so our Saviour Himself appealed to it. Instead of requiring the Jews to take His

mere word for the truth of any doctrine, He either confirmed
it to them by a miracle or referred them to their own Scriptures for the truth of it.

Among the Gentiles the case was, of course, different;
and so, among the heathen now, the case is different in this
one respect, very different. But among the ancient Jews, or
among the nominal Christians of the present day, the Scriptures are indispensable even at the very outset. Had the
ancient Jews — all except a few of their learned and bigoted
doctors — lost, as these nominal Christians had, the knowledge
of their own Scriptures, the apostles, in order to convince
them that Jesus was the Messiah, must first of all have
translated their Scriptures into a language they could understand. Without this they could not have advanced one step.
They could not have "shown by the Scriptures that Jesus
was Christ." And such was the state of mind among the
Jews, that there was no other way to show them this. But
the Scriptures were already translated to their hand, and
with these they "mightily convinced the Jews;" for whoever now rejected their testimony, rejected God Himself.

And so we ourselves, foreigners though we be, and thus
laboring under peculiar disadvantages, yet with the Bible in
our hands, and in the hands of these people, seem to be
standing on the Rock of Ages, and building for eternity.
But without it we are weak; we build on the sand, and our
house is exposed to be blown down by every storm that
sweeps by.

These remarks I thought it necessary to make as an apology, should any be deemed necessary, for having spent some
eight years of my life in this work of translating the word of
God. And it is also worthy of very special remark that this
work has been carried on when much of the time, on account
of the peculiar circumstances of our mission, I could have
been doing nothing else of any comparative importance. I
bless God that my attention was directed to so great and
good a work, and to Him be everlasting thanks that the
whole is now brought to a conclusion. I read over the last
chapter, I trust, with some gratitude and humility, certainly
with tenderness and tears, and, finding at the close that my
translator had set up a pillar, on which he had inscribed,
"To God be all the praise and glory," I added underneath,
"Amen and amen, and let every one that readeth say
amen!"

And thus I left for ever the rich and beautiful country through which I have been passing, — a land " flowing with milk and honey," that drinketh water of the rain of heaven, and hath fountains gushing out from every hill, and springing up into everlasting life.   And, blessed be God! that portion of the community for whose special benefit I have prepared these Scriptures in Armeno-Turkish have now no occasion in " passing through the valley of Baca " to " make it a well," for they will find it already made for them, and " the stone rolled away from the well's mouth ; " and thus they may now " with joy draw water out of the wells of salvation," for the refreshment of their souls for ever.

And am I yet alive, and favored, too, with a good measure of health and strength ?   Oh, what thanks shall I render to the God of all patience that, instead of now casting me aside as a broken vessel in which He hath no pleasure, He should still deign to employ me in His service !   I desire no other service but His, here or in eternity ; and I would, therefore, now consecrate myself to the work of missions, renewedly and unreservedly, as though I had never done it before. Let me now begin anew to serve God in the Gospel of His Son.   Let me now have an unction from the Holy One, that the word spoken by me may be with power, and that the dead may hear the voice of the Son of God and live.   Let me now tell the good news of salvation as news, and not as an old story.   Let me tell it as though I had myself just believed it for the first time ; or, rather, let me be as full of it as though I had just received it fresh from heaven.   Having set wide open to thousands of the perishing all the twelve gates of the New Jerusalem, let me now gird myself anew, and go out and compel them to come in.

It is now more than twenty years since I received the charge of the ordaining council at New Haven, and, although I would by no means consider that as having waxed old and lost its efficacy, yet I would now solemnly charge myself to come henceforward to my fellow-men as though I had the most important and cheering intelligence possible to communicate to them.   I would charge myself to take right hold with both hands of every child of mortality that comes in my way, and say to him, " My brother, I bring you the love of your Father in heaven, with the very richest present His beneficence could bestow, — a cup of blessings, overflowing with eternal life.   Receive it, and you shall live for ever."

" But who is sufficient for these things ? " and especially one who has in a measure unfitted himself for the work by previous habits ?   And, after all, where I shall with the living voice address hundreds, I shall probably by means of the printed word address thousands ; and, when the former is silent in death, the latter will, I hope, be guiding souls to heaven from generation to generation.   And " blessed is he that readeth," as well as " they that hear," these words of spirit and life.

Asking your prayers, that I may be faithful even unto death, I subscribe myself, as in the first days of our long acquaintance,

" Your brother and companion in tribulation, and in the patience and kingdom of Jesus Christ,"

W. GOODELL.

Mr. Goodell makes the following record of the death of Commodore Porter, who had continued to represent the government of the United States at the Porte from the time of his arrival in 1831 : —

" *Pera, March* 4, 1843.   The Commodore was attacked with pleurisy on Monday night.   Yesterday I went down to see him, at San Stephano, and found him insensible, and to all appearance dying.   I prayed with him, or, rather, *for* him, and he expired very soon after, before I left.   He had his reason very little from the first attack, but previous to it he seemed to feel that the day of life was drawing to a close.   About two months ago I informed him that he could not live, that he must look upon himself as a dying man, and must now let this world go, and turn his thoughts to another.   He was affected, but said little.   He said he was a sinner, and expected salvation by Christ alone.

" The funeral will be on Monday, and his body will lie for the present, according to his wish, at the foot of the flag-staff, but it will ultimately be removed to the United States."

In an early part of this volume Mr. Goodell relates how he found a wife for Mr. Thurston, one of the first band of missionaries to the Sandwich Islands.   The wife to whom Mr. Thurston was thus introduced was Mr. Goodell's own cousin, Persis Goodale.   In the year 1841 Mrs. Thurston came to this country to provide for the education of several of her children.   They landed at New York in the month of February, and, coming from and through a tropical climate to our shores at this inclement season of the year, nearly all were attacked with pneumonia.   One of the daughters, Lucy Goodale, died at the home of Mr. A. P. Cumings, soon after landing.   A sketch of her life, prepared by Mrs. Cumings, was published at the time in a volume, entitled "The Missionary's Daughter."   It is now among the publications of the American Tract Society.   The letter which follows was addressed to Mrs. Thurston : —

CONSTANTINOPLE, May 8, 1841.

MY DEAR COUSIN AND BELOVED SISTER IN CHRIST, — How much I would give to sit down by your side and mingle my tears with yours on the death of your beloved child! But, as this cannot be, let me at least assure you of our sympathy and of our prayers.   From my recent long letter to my father, you will learn that we also have been called to pass through the cloud and through the sea.   But, my dear sister, it was not a *dark* but " a *bright* cloud " that " overshadowed " you and us ; and, though we " feared as we entered into it," yet did there not come from it to our ears some of the sweetest accents we ever heard?   Yea, and let the cloud be ever so dark and terrific, yet, with an encouraging word from Heaven issuing from it, we shall come safely out of it, and see nothing " *save Jesus only.*"   Blessed sight ! and blessed fruit of sanctified afflictions !

> " And darkness shows us worlds of light
>   We never saw by day."

The letter to my father left my dear wife and our eldest daughter both ill of that same dreadful fever.   The latter soon afterwards became much worse, and our youngest child was also seized in the same manner.   The oldest physician of the place, too, was for pursuing a course quite unsatisfactory to me.   Then it was that my mind became exceedingly anxious and my feelings unsubdued.   One night I was so troubled I could not sleep.   God held my eyes waking, my flesh trembled for fear of Him, and I was afraid of His judgments.   The next day I was very low in body as well as in spirit. But at evening, Mrs. Goodell spake some words of comfort to me, and I was strengthened. And I was enabled to say, and, I hope, in some good measure to feel, " this family is not mine, but God's ; these children are not mine, but His; and He has the most perfect right to interpose, interfere, order, govern, dispose, give, or take away, according to His own good pleasure. Here am I, let Him do with me as seemeth good in His sight. Let Him correct me, but in mercy, not in anger, lest He bring me to nothing, and I be consumed by the blow of His hand."

But, though our heavenly Father cause grief, yet will He have compassion, according unto the multitude of His tender mercies. He is healing all our diseases, and restoring us again to health and comfort, though till this day we have not all been able to meet either at the family altar or around the table of daily bounty. One also is not. A month to-day since we imprinted upon his cheek the last token of affection. But, though out of sight, he is not out of remembrance, nor out of existence. We learn that the conduct of our dear boy in his sickness, and *our* conduct at his death, are topics of conversation in different circles among the Armenians in Constantinople. Even the patriarch exclaimed, " Who ever heard of such things." Some of our native brethren seem much strengthened by what they have seen of the power of the Gospel, though I feel that, alas! we have exhibited but a poor specimen of it. But surely we are encouraged to pray that this our affliction may prove a blessing to many, even to those of another nation and another language. And oh that we ourselves may all receive the full benefit our heavenly Father designed for us by this discipline !

The account of your beloved daughter, which was published in the " New York Observer," my family read with melancholy interest. May the Lord Jesus, who knows your sorrows, and every minute circumstance of your affliction, make all grace abound towards you, and towards your surviving children, and towards your far-distant husband ! The world can do nothing for us. But Christ can do every thing. Philosophy can only steel our hearts, and brace up our souls with stubbornness, and render us just what we should not be, viz., *insensible.* But the grace of God is all-sufficient. It can soften our hearts on the one hand, and sustain and elevate them on the other. Let us be more than ever encouraged to pray that His blessed will may be done. In our own families, *our* will is done, and not our *children's*. We cross *their* wills every day, and often without assigning a reason for it; and, if they are very small, we cannot make them understand a reason. Should *their* wills be done, our families would be in a state of utter confusion. So in God's great family, let *His* blessed will be done, and not our foolish wills; and this, whether we can at present understand the reasons of His conduct or not. Indeed, the time will never come when we shall fully comprehend all the ways of God. We shall have to trust Him for ever and ever, as the angels have to do now; for who by searching can find Him out? Let us begin to confide in Him *now*, and go on increasing in this confidence for ever.

Mrs. Goodell unites in Christian love. Remember us all to your children.

Your truly sympathizing friend and brother,

W. GOODELL.

In a letter to Mrs. Cumings, written several years later, he acknowledged in his own peculiar style the receipt of a copy of "The Missionary's Daughter," which she had sent to him at Constantinople: —

My good Sister, Daughter, or, what shall I call you?

I suppose, however, it makes but little difference what I call you now, for long before I shall see you, you will be "called by a new name, which the mouth of the Lord shall name." I wonder what that name will be! Gentleness? Charity? Patience? Hope? Zeal? or what? I fancy we shall recognize Abraham at once. As far off as he can be seen, CONFIDENCE IN GOD will be seen inscribed in such bold characters on his whole being, that he will at once be "known and read of all men." So when we meet with one whose character is throughout and throughout developed in *meekness*, we shall know at once it is Moses.

Now I can form no idea what your new name will be, nor, indeed, what will be my own, unless it be, *Unworthy to have a name*. But in the many mansions our blessed Saviour has prepared for His friends, I hope that yours and ours will not be so far apart but that we can see each other occasionally, without being under the necessity of taking a sea voyage. I am thankful that my precious Sandwich Island cousin has put me in communication with you, and that through a daughter of mine and a brother of yours I am brought into almost veritable relationship, while through Jesus Christ, our common head, the connection between us is still nearer and more precious, and it will continue as long as our connection with Jesus Christ will continue.

But let me not forget — for that is, indeed, the object of this note — to thank you for the Memoir of my cousin. I shall read it with double interest now that I know you to be the writer. And, commending ourselves to your prayers, I remain, in Christ,

Yours affectionately,

W. GOODELL.

February 14, 1843, he makes this brief record: "I am this day fifty-one years old. Abide with us, blessed Saviour, for the day is far spent."

The Rev. Jonas King, of Athens, having visited Mr. and Mrs. Goodell at Constantinople at the time of the birth of their youngest son, playfully promised to give them a cow, on condition that the child should be named Jonas King. On his return to Athens, having heard that the name of Edward was likely to be substituted for Jonas, in making the boy a King, he wrote to Mr. Goodell: —

ATHENS, Sept. 26, 1843.

DEAR BROTHER GOODELL, — I arrived here last Saturday, and found the people rejoicing in a Constitution. Such excitement and such enthusiasm I seldom ever saw. I verily believe if any man in the streets were to say a word against the Constitution he would be torn in pieces. There is so much steam up, and such a fire burning, I am sometimes afraid the boiler will burst, and that we shall some of us be terribly scalded. However, I am on board with them, and must take whatever happens. I have a good life-preserver in the protection of Him who is the giver of life, in whom we live and move and have our being, without whom not a sparrow falls to the ground, and by whom even the very hairs of our head are all numbered.

How is Mrs. Goodell, and how are all the children? What have you called the little boy who made his appearance at

13   8

your house the first time when I was there? If you have called him Jonas King, I suppose I shall have to send him a cow. But if he is only called King, half my name, I must send him only half a cow. It seems that the name of the disobedient prophet who fled to Tarshish is not in great repute with you! But to tell you the truth, I believe he was quite as good a man as his namesake, who has been sent to preach in Greece! I feel that my life has been full of disobedience, and I often wonder at the mercy of God in permitting me to labor in His cause by preaching His holy word.

Pray for your unworthy brother,

JONAS KING.

On the 4th of July, 1843, the venerable father of Mr. Goodell died at the home of his son in Copley, Ohio, whither he had removed a few years previous. The letter which Mr. Goodell wrote to his brother on receiving the intelligence was inserted at the commencement of these Memoirs.* It is not only a touching tribute of filial affection, showing that the heart of the writer was as fresh and tender in its love as in the days of his boyhood, but, as a specimen of epistolary composition, and for the spirit of glowing, Scriptural piety that it breathes, it will bear many perusals. The Rev. Dr. William Adams, in quoting it in his introduction to "The Old and the New," says, "We know not which to admire the most, — its purity of taste, its depth of pathos, or its simplicity of piety."

* See page 6.

CHAPTER XVI.

IN August, 1843, occurred an event which in its results
had an important influence upon the cause of religious
liberty in Turkey, and an important bearing upon the mission work in that country. The circumstances are detailed
as follows in an official despatch to his government by Sir
Stratford Canning, the English ambassador : —

"*Buyuk-Dèrè, August* 27, 1843. Within the last few days
an execution has taken place at Constantinople, under circumstances which have occasioned much excitement and
indignation among the Christian inhabitants. The sufferer
was an Armenian youth of eighteen or twenty years, who,
having under fear of punishment declared himself a Turk,
went to the island of Syra, and, returning after an absence
of some length, resumed his former religion. Apprehensive
of the danger, but resolved not to deny his real faith a second
time, he kept out of sight, till accident betrayed him to the
police, and he was then thrown into prison. In spite of
threats, promises, and blows, he there maintained his resolution, refused to save his life by a fresh disavowal of Christianity, and was finally decapitated in one of the most
frequented parts of the city with circumstances of great
barbarity."

During the month that he was in prison every effort
was made by the Turks to induce him to embrace Mohammedanism. He was offered a commission in the army, and
other inducements were held out to him to say, " There is
one God, and Mohammed is his prophet." He was several
times led out to the place of execution, and the sword of the
executioner was brandished over his head, as though his

last moment had come, but no word or sign of apostasy was extorted from him. Sir Stratford Canning exerted all his influence to secure his release, and, it was said, obtained a promise from the Turkish authorities that his life should be spared; but the law of the Koran, as interpreted by the Turks, was put in execution. The man was beheaded, and, according to custom, his head was placed between his legs, and his body exposed in a public place for three days.

This shocking occurrence led to a formal demand on the part of the English, French, Russian, and Prussian ambassadors for the abolition of the death penalty for a change of religion. There was a long and earnest correspondence with the Turkish government, conducted chiefly by the English ambassador, the result of which was that the Sultan, on the 21st of March, 1844, gave this written pledge: " The Sublime Porte engages to take effectual measures to prevent henceforward the execution and putting to death of the Christian who is an apostate." On the 23d of March, the Sultan, in an audience which he granted to Sir Stratford Canning, gave him personally this assurance: " Henceforward neither shall Christianity be insulted in my dominions, nor shall Christians be in any way persecuted for their religion."

The chief honor of obtaining these important concessions from the highest authority in the Turkish government belongs to that noble advocate of religious liberty and friend of Christian missions, Sir Stratford Canning, who, upon the successful termination of his protracted correspondence, declared that the giving of such a pledge by the Sultan seemed to him little less than a miracle, and that God alone could have brought it to pass.

The year 1843 was memorable for another movement in the cause of religious freedom, — the exodus of nearly five hundred ministers from the Established Church of Scotland, and the organization of the Free Church on the basis of

Christ alone the Head and King of the church. Among the many visitors from various lands at the Turkish capital about this time was the Rev. R. W. Stewart, to whom, after his return to Scotland, Mr. Goodell wrote, expressing his cordial sympathy with those who for conscience' sake had gone out from the Establishment, leaving all its emoluments behind them: —

CONSTANTINOPLE, Sept. 16, 1843.

To the REV. R. W. STEWART:

REVEREND AND DEAR SIR, — Your note from Malta, with the music-book of Scotch church psalmody, went by the way of Beyrout, and did not reach me till quite lately. As our eldest daughter has been at Broosa for a few weeks, we have as yet only tasted a *wee* bit of your sweet music; but we expect she will return next week, and then we intend to have a real feast, wishing you could be here at least for one evening to enjoy it with us.

Yours of August the 21st was received the 8th inst. And so, dear brother, the manse, that sweetest and happiest and most hallowed of all spots, is gone for ever! Well, you all have our tenderest sympathy, and, I may add, you all have our high veneration. Yes, we venerate those four hundred and seventy men of God who stood ready at the call of their Master to "provide the creels again;" and, leaving the manse, the glebe, the church. the stipend, *all*, to go forth, not knowing where they should erect their next altar or kindle their next hearth-fires. Everlasting thanks to the great Head of the church that there are so many of this stamp in Scotland! — men of noble birth, who are born from above and belong to the royal family, and are jealous for the royal prerogatives, and who, suffering with their Prince here, shall soon sit down with Him on His throne, and reign with Him for ever. That memorable 18th of May will never be forgotten. The world has seen nothing like it for at least two hundred years. With what a great cloud of witnesses your Free Church must have been surrounded, composed of those ancient, noble martyrs, confessors, and covenanters, of whom the world was not worthy! It does appear to me that the Lord is about to bless all Scotland with such a revival of pure and undefiled religion as has never yet been known there, and that the influence of this mighty movement of yours will be felt, not only in every part of England, but even to the uttermost parts of the earth. It is intimately connected with the light and liberty and glory of the Gospel of Christ, and the missionary spirit seems in a wonderful manner to pervade and sanctify it all.

Do you remember that little, cold, upper chamber in my house ? We regretted that we had no better to offer to one " of the household of faith," and he, too, an " ambassador of Christ ; " and, had we not considered it a sort of discipline and preparation for what was to follow when driven out from your own pleasant habitation, with all the comforts and precious recollections of thirty years, we might have regretted it the more. We rejoice that Providence has assigned you so interesting and important a post as the one you now occupy. And who knows but the great Head of the church took away your voice on purpose that you might employ your pen for Him in this new situation !

Mrs. Goodell and our daughters (for since I commenced this letter the one at Broosa has returned) unite in the kindest regards to Mrs. Stewart, whom we shall all be most happy to see with you, and to whom we will give the very best room in the house, should Providence ever direct her steps with yours to the city of domes and minarets. Of my " Sermon to Mothers " she is at liberty to make any use which she may think will promote the cause of the blessed Redeemer. I feel that I could make it better in some respects, but perhaps I should make it worse, and at any rate I have no time to make the experiment. May prayer and the Lord's blessing accompany it !

All our families unite in sending Christian salutations. Remember us very kindly to Drs. Chalmers, Keith, Black, and Wilson, should it be convenient for you to do so, not forgetting our good friend and brother, Dr. Rich. And say to Mr. Bonar that I received his books, that I love him as my very dearest brother, and that I congratulate him on the recovery of his Bible from Jacob's well.* The Lord bless him and all the four hundred and seventy prophets who have not bowed the knee to the image which has been set up in Scotland.

---

* Mr. Bonar's pocket Bible, which he accidentally dropped into Jacob's well, near Shechem, was subsequently recovered by another traveller, and restored to him.

My address is, Rev. William Goodell, Constantinople, Turkey; but in subscribing myself, I am always and only,
Your very affectionate brother in Christ,
W. GOODELL.

In October, 1843, Mr. Goodell was elected a member of the American-Oriental Society, and a diploma, officially signed and forwarded to him at Constantinople, is found among his papers, together with an acknowledgment of a copy of the first edition of his Armeno-Turkish Bible, which he presented to the society.

An occasion of much interest to the American missionaries in Turkey occurred in the course of this year. Up to this time they had never enjoyed the privilege of joining with the people at home in the national festival of Thanksgiving. The mode of communicating with the United States was so tardy, that they had never before received notice of the appointment of the day until after it had passed. But this year the proclamation reached them in season, and Mr. Goodell thus records the observance of the feast: —

"*Constantinople, December* 1, 1843. Yesterday was the first Thanksgiving (I mean New England Thanksgiving) I have kept for twenty-one years. We have never known before when Thanksgiving came till the day was past; but the increased facilities of intercourse gave us this year timely information. We all enjoyed our meeting much. It was at two o'clock, P.M., and Mr. K. left his business, and he and family, with a pious captain, came. Among the many causes of thankfulness mentioned were the following: God's love to this world, — a thing never to be lost sight of by us; that wonderful grace which has saved us from sin and hell, and raised us up to be co-workers with God, — what an unspeakable mercy! the continued tokens of the presence of the Holy Spirit among the people; though we have had sickness in our families, yet no one of our public labors has ever been interrupted from this cause, and no one of the male members of this mission has ever been laid up by sickness; during all the years we have lived together, and amidst all the various scenes through which we have passed, there has never been any misunderstanding between any of us, and our harmony has continued up to the present time unbroken. Harmony has never been restored, because it has never been impaired. A great blessing this ! "

The missionaries at Constantinople, in common with those at other stations in the Levant, were greatly cheered, near the close of the year, by a visit from the Rev. Rufus Anderson, D.D., Corresponding Secretary of the American Board, who was accompanied by the Rev. Joel Hawes, D.D., of Hartford. Dr. Anderson came officially, to study the character and to see the extent of the work that was going on, and to consult with the members of the various missions in regard to plans for the future. Dr. Hawes, though not commissioned by the Board, had a similar errand, and his presence and counsel were no less acceptable and cheering. They spent several months in the eastern part of the Mediterranean and at Constantinople, arriving at the capital on the 24th of December.

The visit of this deputation was peculiarly refreshing to Mr. Goodell, who had been personally intimate with Dr. Anderson before going to the East. After the latter had returned to this country, Mr. Goodell wrote to him: "It is twenty-two years since we sailed from New York, and during all this time I can think of but few events, if, indeed, of any, for which, as it appears to me, I have greater cause for gratitude than for your visit." A letter of reminiscence, addressed to Dr. Anderson after his return to the United States, shows what progress had been made in the mission work since Mr. Goodell reached Constantinople in 1831, and also what prospects were opening before the mission : —

CONSTANTINOPLE, March 7, 1844.

MY DEAR BROTHER, — Whenever I look back to the year 1831, when my own family first arrived at Constantinople, and contemplate the great and wonderful changes which have taken place since that period, I always feel that I am myself not half awake to the reality and importance of that work of grace, which God is carrying on here with such power. *Then*, not a single European in the place knew fully how to sympathize with us; nor, during a whole year, was there, except our Greek brother, Mr. P., a single native found, whose heart seemed at all moved by the Spirit of God. *Then*, all direct access to the Armenians seemed closed against us; nor did it appear possible to reach them, except in a very circuitous way. We had, in fact, to commence operations among the Greeks, in order thus to introduce ourselves among the Armenians.

But God hath "remembered us in our low estate; for His mercy endureth for ever." He hath helped us by His providence, and He hath helped us by His Spirit; and in the wonderful turn things have taken, His hand is most clearly seen. For "He that hath the key of David, that openeth and no man shutteth, and shutteth and no man openeth," has fast closed the door among the Greeks to the amazement of everybody; while, among the Armenians, He has "set before us an open door, which no man has been able to shut," although the very mightiest ones in the whole empire have once and again conspired together for the express purpose of closing it for ever.

Less than twenty years ago, the question was asked by some one at Constantinople, whether a Protestant service, except in the palaces of the foreign legations, could be held on the Sabbath in any language. And the opinion expressed was, that it would not be tolerated. But lo! a few Protestant missionaries have come; and, without power or influence, or even *permission*, they have quietly seated themselves down in the very "city of the Sultan," under the very eye of high-priests and patriarchs, and in the midst of all the grandees of the empire, and the emissaries of Rome; and they have opened chapels in their own private houses, where the Gospel has been preached without molestation in the English, German, French, Spanish, Italian, Greek, Armenian, and Turkish languages. And our right to do so will now never be likely to be questioned. Those times have gone by; and custom here has all the force of law. There has, indeed, been great indignation against us; but it has been strangely impotent. Kings and princes have taken counsel together against us; but their "counsel has been carried headlong," and has come to naught. Bribes, the never-failing resort and the mighty engine of all these

13*

Oriental hierarchies, have not been spared; but "the devices of these crafty ones have been disappointed, so that their hands could not perform their enterprise." And I know of no other reason than this, that "*The Lord of Hosts has been with us, and the God of Jacob has been our refuge.*" From Him cometh wisdom. But He has not given it to the opposers of His truth to carry out their plans; or He has "destroyed and divided their tongues;" or He has furnished them with other and more pressing work to do; or in His providence there has been all at once an entire change in the Turkish ministry; or the very individual, who was entrusted by them with the execution of the whole business, was unexpectedly turned out of office; or else, in their blindness and rage, they have been left so to transgress all bounds and trample on all laws and usages, as to leave us real and substantial ground of complaint to our country's representative, which he could lay hold of, and use with power to our advantage. And thus has the Lord "not once nor twice," "shown us His marvellous kindness in this strong city," and given us fresh occasions of encouragement to place all confidence in His power and wisdom, His goodness and faithfulness. And, though we have always "feared as we entered into the dark cloud," yet have we, I trust, learned in some measure the important lesson, that there is after all "*no one there save Jesus only;*" and that His hand, and His alone, is to be seen and felt and acknowledged everywhere.

Ten years ago, "the strong man armed kept his palace and goods in peace," and no one dared lisp a syllable against the prevailing superstitions and corruptions of the times. "But a stronger than he has come," and broken in upon this death-like quiet, and "set a man at variance against his father, and the daughter against her mother," in all parts of the city. An individual, who came to us some ten years ago for the express purpose of conversing on the great things of salvation and eternal life, and who spoke freely all that was in his heart, said, on passing out of our door, "On quitting your house, I must close my lips, and not suffer a word on these subjects to escape them." But now the whole city is filled with these new doctrines; and they are publicly discussed in the khans and coffee-houses, and at all the chief places of concourse.

Much of the time, indeed, we have ourselves been scarcely able to walk round this great "valley of dry bones" in an open and public manner, or to prophesy to them except in a whisper, or to only one at a time; and yet, from our retired corners we have heard "a noise and a shaking" among these "dry bones;" and, in regard to not a few of them, we have the most consoling evidence that "the Spirit of life from God has entered into them." The voice of the Son of God has broken the slumbers of death, and they live. They have been breathed upon by the Holy Spirit, and they have "become living souls." And these may now be seen every day walking abroad in the streets of this great city, *living, breathing men;* men who, like all those that have been quickened and made alive, and that will live for ever, are calling on every side to their neighbors and kindred, "Awake, thou that sleepest, and arise from the dead, and Christ shall give thee light." There is certainly a great deal of life and activity among them. Look abroad in almost any direction, and you will see some Andrew bringing his brother Simon to Christ; or some Philip persuading his friend Nathanael to come; or, peradventure, over the very house-tops, and "through the tiling," and greatest difficulties, you will see "one sick of the palsy," who is "borne of four." Blessed sight! who would not be a missionary to see such "*visions bright*"? But truly "this is the Lord's doing; it is marvellous in our eyes."

I close this communication with a remark, which I recently made to our native brethren, whom, as you know, I am accustomed to meet alone by themselves every Tuesday morning, "If this work of God go forward in the same proportion for ten years to come, as it has gone for ten years past, there will be no further occasion for any of us to remain here, unless it be to assist you in bringing to a knowledge of these same precious saving doctrines of the Gospel the Greeks and Jews and others around you."

But, dear brother, reverses are to be expected. And may you and we, and the churches at home, and all concerned, be prepared for them.

Yours most truly,

W. GOODELL.

In the spring of 1844 Mr. Goodell experienced a great trial in the recall of his beloved friend and brother, Rev. Daniel Temple, with whom he had been on terms of intimate fellowship almost from boyhood. They had occupied the same room in the academy, in college, and in the Theological Seminary for the space of nine years, and although separated in their missionary life in the East, Mr. Temple being stationed at Smyrna, they had exchanged letters and interchanged their most sacred sentiments every week since coming to the Orient. The trial was the more severe because the giving up of the missionary work was so painful to Mr. Temple. One of the results of the visit of Dr. Anderson to the East was the discontinuance of the mission to the Greeks, for whom Mr. Temple had been exclusively laboring; and as the Board concurred with him in the opinion that he was too far advanced in years to commence the acquisition of a new language and enter upon an entirely new mission, he reluctantly decided to return to the United States. Before he left, Mr. Goodell wrote to him: —

"We all sympathize with you deeply in your being called to give up your work and return to the land of your fathers. It seems to me that such a blow would well-nigh kill me. But it is true, for the word of God declares it, 'As thy days so shall thy strength be.' And the question is not, what is painful? but, what is duty? Fear not; your poor ship will find a safe harbor at last."

After his return, Mr. Goodell wrote to him in his usual strain: —

"By the way, I see one of the papers calls you Dr. but whether it was tormenting you before the time, or whether you are actually a D.D., I do not know. At any rate, I have no doubt you are the same Daniel Temple, whatever affixes or prefixes, augments or increments, you may have to your name. If it would but cure you of the awful habit which your dear wife complains you are guilty of, viz., of being advanced in years beyond the wishes of most parishes, perhaps you would no more object to the title than to any other bitter medicine."

At the same time with the departure of his friend Mr. Temple, a more severe trial was laid upon the family of Mr.

Goodell. This was the separation from his household, of his two eldest daughters, who came to the United States to enjoy advantages of education which could not be had in the lands of the East. From an extensive and intimate acquaintance with missionary families in different parts of the world, the opinion is confidently expressed that, as a class, no children are more accurately and thoroughly educated than the children of missionaries; but, at the same time, it is often a matter of great importance, if not a necessity, that they should have some measure of training in the midst of a Christian community, in order to become better fitted for their work in life, wherever their future lots may be cast. After long and prayerful deliberation, it was decided by Mr. and Mrs. Goodell to send their daughters to America, in company with Mr. and Mrs. Temple. A brief extract from the father's journal depicts a scene of heart-breaking sadness, which has had its counterpart in hundreds, if not thousands, of families in the far-distant fields of missionary life: —

" *May* 23. Our beloved daughters left us yesterday. My last prayer with them was with tears and sighs. Our parting was a silent one, — an affectionate embrace, but not a word spoken on either side. We gave them up to our Father. May He be their Father, and they His children. Our other children at night wept themselves to sleep. No one could read; no one could sing at our worship this morning. May the Lord comfort all our hearts."

An incident that occurred about two years later may be mentioned most appropriately in this connection. At various intervals, and for long periods, the missionaries in Turkey lived in great apprehension of personal danger, owing to the violent hostility awakened by their presence and their teachings. Not only did they sympathize with the native Christians in the persecution they endured; they had a share in it themselves. Against open violence they were protected by their nationality, but often did they have reason to fear secret assaults instigated by Moslem fanaticism, Armenian and

Greek bigotry, and Jesuitical intrigue.   The compiler of these Memoirs has, in his own private correspondence with the missionaries in Turkey, and especially at Constantinople, the evidence that they often lay down at night under the apprehension that, by insurrection, or the secret hand of violence, they might be called to end their labors and their lives before the dawn of another day.

Just at the time referred to, Mr. Goodell had received special intimations of personal danger, when one evening, as he returned home from a meeting, there was handed him a strange-looking package, addressed to him, and marked, " Favored by the Rev. Dr. Beshiktash." It had been left at the house by a stranger.   What it could contain, or who the Rev. Dr. Beshiktash might be, no one was able to divine. The circumstances all had an air of mystery, and a slight examination of the package made the affair appear still more suspicious.   Thoughts of the Patriarch and his people, and of other agents of evil, passed through the mind of Mr. Goodell ; and the mere imagination that it might be some infernal machine induced him to lay it carefully aside until the family should have retired for the night, in order that he might open it without exposing any member of his household but himself.

Accordingly, when all had retired, he took the mysterious box to his study, and, before proceeding to open it, kneeled and commended himself, his household, and the mission, to the care of the covenant God.   With trembling hands he then removed one envelope after another in a long succession, until he reached and removed the last ; when his eyes fell, not upon a deadly weapon, but upon the faces of his beloved daughters, who were far over the seas.   They had chosen this method of forwarding from the United States their daguerreotypes, as a surprise to those at home, sending the package by the hand of the captain of a ship, with an injunction that it should be delivered without any intimation of what it contained, or of the source from which it came.

The father's tears of love and thankfulness fell thick upon the familiar faces, and the whole family were immediately aroused to share in his joy.

During the latter part of 1844 and the following year, the fierceness of actual persecution on the part of the Armenian ecclesiastics was stayed, but their hostility toward all who manifested any tendency to evangelical principles was not in the least abated. They took another method of expressing it, described by Mr. Goodell, under date of Oct. 27, 1844 : —

"All fiery persecution has now ceased. The policy of the present patriarch is more in accordance with civilized usage. The aim is to wear out the patience of the brethren, by depriving them of business in the most quiet and effectual way possible, and thus to reduce them to subjection by reducing them to poverty in a more genteel way than by prison and exile. This is really, as our brethren confess, harder to bear, because it does not, on the one hand, rouse up the mind of the sufferer to such a spirit of determination, nor, on the other, does it secure so much sympathy from others. But, to the praise of God's grace be it spoken, they all hold on their way, and the Lord is adding to them continually of such as shall be saved. The papists are still popping away at us with missiles drawn from the " Missionary Herald," but nobody seems now to care any thing about it. In fact, I have heard of no one being shot, or even wounded.

"All our various meetings have continued to the present time, and the interest in them appears unabated. The brethren still ' have life,' as formerly, and even, we believe, ' have it more abundantly.' Among others, however, there is not at present so much of ' a noise ' and ' a shaking,' with so many signs of coming to life, as we have witnessed in times past, and as we now hear of in the interior. Some sixteen villages in the vicinity of Broosa have been recently reported to us, in each of which the Holy Spirit is breathing upon a few individuals, making them living men. They are waking up to a life and happiness which belong exclusively to the children of light and the children of the day."

The spirit of the one who is the subject of these Memoirs has been abundantly indicated in the extracts that have been made from the most familiar and unrestrained expressions of his heart, as that of one who had an almost singular simplicity of purpose to live for nothing but the advancement of the kingdom of Christ and the glory of His name. One secret of this singleness of heart, or one form of its expression, was, that he seemed always to feel and to act as if he were in the immediate presence of Christ; and living under His personal reign. The kingdom of Christ was to him a reality, and the ground of his confidence, especially in regard to the success of the work in which he was engaged. This is expressed in an extract from his journal, bearing date Jan. 31, 1845 : —

"There is now a very interesting state of things among the Armenians at the capital, and many new instances of awakening. At the monthly concert this week it was stated that there was probably not an evening in the week in which there was not a prayer-meeting held by the native brethren at some place in Constantinople proper, for the outpouring of the Holy Spirit. At our public services on the Sabbath the congregation is large, and the word is with power; and although all the ingenuity and wisdom and influence of the very mightiest ones among both Armenians and Turks are most actively employed from day to day to arrest the work, yet it is carried forward by a hand unseen, and a power not to be resisted. And who can stop the progress of that which is invisible, and 'cometh not with observation'? Who can banish or confine or prohibit that which is spiritual, and which can, of course, be touched by nothing material? The kingdom of Christ knows nothing of territorial divisions and geographical lines, and our brethren here may take all their meals, make all their visits, perform all their journeys, and transact all their business in this blessed kingdom, however despotic their own temporal government may be. They may live in it every day, and sleep in it every night; and no power on earth can forcibly carry them out of it. They can have daily access to the great King himself, and lay their petitions at his feet; and no police that ever existed, however terrible its character, could ever find means to prevent it. And the progress of this kingdom is itself like the silent stealing of light on darkness, which none of the potentates of earth can interrupt."

In October, 1845, in order to exert a more decided influence upon that part of the population which in all Oriental lands is most difficult of access, a female boarding-school was opened at the house of Mr. Goodell, and eight Armenian young ladies were received into his family. Mrs. Goodell had previously made herself familiar with the Italian language, which was chiefly spoken at Malta; with the Arabic, which she had made use of at Beyrout; and with the Greek, which was extensively spoken at Constantinople. But to qualify herself for usefulness in this new charge, she now commenced the study of the Armenian. Her health, which for many years had been feeble, was quite established, and, with the new responsibilities which she assumed, it was like entering afresh upon missionary life and service.

The catalogue of the school, in the handwriting of Mr. Goodell, is a curiosity. The history of each scholar is recorded, and, with the name, its signification. Names in the East are more significant than with us; whether the name is always appropriately bestowed is another matter. The first on the list of the school is Armaveni, which signifies *Palm-tree*. She was a young lady about twenty years of age when she entered the school. She afterward became the wife of the evangelical pastor at Trebizond, where she flourished literally like the palm-tree, living a life of great usefulness. Another bore the name of Soorpoohi (*Holiness*). Another, Aroosiag (*Morning Star*). She has since been very useful as a teacher among the Armenians. Still another was Sophik (*Wisdom*). She became the wife of an Armenian bearing the name of Avedis (*Glad Tidings*), who has been a Christian pastor at Constantinople. This school, as will hereafter appear, enjoyed to a remarkable degree the blessing of God in the presence and gracious influences of the Holy Spirit, and it was a nursery in which many precious youth were trained up for lives of usefulness.

Miss Harriet M. Lovell, who afterward became the wife

T

of Mr. Hamlin, joined the mission at this time, taking the principal charge of the school, and finding also a home with Mr. and Mrs. Goodell. Her correspondence, which may be seen in the memoirs of "The Missionary Sisters" (Mrs. Everett and Mrs. Hamlin), is filled with expressions of her great happiness in finding in a distant land, among those who had been strangers to her, a circle of devoted and beloved friends, and in Mr. and Mrs. Goodell a father and mother, to whom she became tenderly attached.

To Rev. E. E. Bliss, at Trebizond, he wrote, in reply to a letter asking advice : —

CONSTANTINOPLE, June 2, 1845.

MY DEAR BROTHER, — What persecution your friends suffer from their own neighbors and families cannot be helped. Many of our friends suffer the same here, and have for years. Some of them for a long time have been excluded from the paternal roof; but this kind of persecution is suffered at the present day in France, England, and even in America; and no law can prevent it. So your bishop can excommunicate as much as he pleases, and nobody out of his church has a right to interfere. But if he makes use of the civil arm, if he throws into prison, sends into exile, or uses the bastinado, then there is ground for interference. If your people would be saved, they must endure to the end. If they are unwilling to suffer with Christ, they are unworthy of Him. But this, by the way, teaches us the importance of not encouraging any to oppose their bishop, or to take any strong stand against the errors of their church, till we have good reason to believe that they are the Lord's people, and have a good deal of faith; for otherwise, it is very certain they will not stand in the day of trial.

If the bishop goes on excommunicating and casting out of the church those who have received the Gospel, after we have suffered patiently long enough, we shall be fully justified, in the view of the whole world, in gathering them into a congregation by themselves. But it is well to have on hand a good many cases of our great forbearance in order to justify this step, showing that we were not over-greedy for it, snatching at the first opportunity, but were literally forced into it.

Your brother,

W. GOODELL.

The year 1846 opened with marked spiritual prosperity, but it ushered in the most severe persecution which the Armenian converts were ever called to endure. The Gospel was so evidently making progress among the people, and was so plainly in conflict with the dead formalism and idolatry which prevailed in the ancient church of the Armenians; the teachings of the missionaries, and of the converts who had become preachers of Christ to their own nation, were so decided a rebuke to the ecclesiastics of all grades, from the patriarch down to the humblest priest, whose lives and ministrations were utterly opposed to the spirit and the letter of the word of God, that their hostility could not longer be restrained; and having the power, as they supposed, to suppress the new religion, they determined to attempt it once more.

Accordingly, on the last Sabbath in January, "the lord archbishop and patriarch of the great metropolitan city of Constantinople" issued his anathema, which was ordered to be read in all the churches on that day, excommunicating an evangelical priest, Vertanes, and consigning him over to Satan as an enemy of all righteousness. He was described as "a vagabond fellow, going about through the metropolis babbling out errors; an enemy to the holy church, a divider of the members, a cause of scandal, and a seducer of the people; a traitor and murderer of Christ, a child of the devil, and offspring of antichrist," &c. The bull of excommunication continued: —

"Wherefore we expel him, and forbid him, as a devil and a child of the devil, to enter into the company of our believers; we cut him off from the priesthood as an amputated member of the spiritual body of Christ, and as a branch cut off from the vine, which is good for nothing but to be cast into the fire. By this admonitory bull I therefore command and warn my beloved in every city far and near not to look upon his face, regarding it as the face of Belial; not to receive him into your holy dwellings, for he is a house-destroying and ravening wolf; not to receive his salutation but as a soul-destroying and deadly poison; and to beware with all your households of the seducing and impious followers of the false doctrine of modern sectarists," &c.

This anathema was nominally aimed at only one who had renounced the errors of the Armenian Church and embraced the truth of the Gospel, but it was intended as a warning to all who gave heed to the teachings of the missionaries. Its proclamation at once stirred up the fiercest bigotry and hatred on the part of the Armenian clergy, who entered immediately upon a crusade against their evangelical brethren. Their pulpits resounded with denunciations of the most precious truths of the Gospel, and of all who gave an ear to them. The patriarch no longer had power to imprison and otherwise punish with civil pains and penalties, but he made the most of his ecclesiastical power by inflicting church censures and exciting the people to visit with social martyrdom all who gave countenance to the missionaries or followed their instructions. A second anathema against Vertanes was promulgated, including with him all who were of like sentiment: —

"Wherefore, whoever has a son that is such an one, or a brother, or a partner in business, and gives him bread, or assists him in making money, or has intercourse with him as a friend, or does business with him, let such persons know that they are nourishing a venomous serpent in their houses, which will one day injure them with its deadly poison, and they will lose their souls. Such persons give bread to Judas. Such persons are enemies to the holy faith of Christianity, and destroyers of the holy orthodox church of the Armenians, and a disgrace to the whole nation. Wherefore, their houses and shops also are accursed; and whoever goes to visit them, we shall learn and make them public to the holy church by terrible anathemas."

Nothing more was wanting to arouse the bigoted Armenians to a fierce social persecution of their brethren. Persuasion having failed to bring the converts back to the ancient formalism of the church, they assailed them with bitter hostility. They broke up their business; they refused them employment; they drove them to the verge of starvation, and would fain have starved them literally; they stoned them in the streets; they brought against them charges of debt and had them cast into prison, while their families were in distress and want. The words of the Saviour were often verified: "A man's foes shall be they of his own household." Brother was arrayed against brother, father against son, and even tender mothers cast off their own daughters, and husbands became the persecutors of their wives, and wives of their husbands. Bigotry overcame all natural affection.

"Nearly forty persons in Constantinople," wrote one of the missionaries, "had their shops closed and their licenses to trade taken away, and were thereby prevented from laboring for an honest livelihood. Nearly seventy were obliged to leave father, mother, brother, sister, husband, wife, or child, for Christ's sake, and were forced by the patriarch's orders from their own hired houses, and sometimes even from houses owned by themselves. In order to increase their distress, bakers were ordered not to furnish them with bread, and water-carriers to cut off their supply. As multitudes of families in the metropolis depend entirely upon the latter for all the water they use, and the greater part of the water-carriers are bigoted Armenians, this measure operated with great severity."

In a letter written to the Secretary of the Board near the commencement of the following year, Mr. Goodell describes the severity and the continuance of this persecution: —

CONSTANTINOPLE, Feb. 27, 1846.

To the Rev. Dr. ANDERSON, *Cor. Sec. A. B. C. F. M.,*
    Boston:

MY DEAR BROTHER, — You will have heard of the wrath of the enemy, and of the desperate efforts made to "swallow up the inheritance of the Lord." The aspect of the two parties was, and is still, one of great moral sublimity. On the one side were all the power, influence, wealth, and numbers of a great nation; on the other, fewness, feebleness, and poverty. On the one side were age, wisdom, experience, cunning, craft, and dissimulation; on the other, youth, inexperience, and utter simplicity. On the one side stood up the whole Armenian hierarchy, excited to the utmost pitch of hate and fury, and armed with all the sacredness of antiquity, with all the authority of the entire nation, and with all the panoply of civil and ecclesiastical despotism; on the other was neither Urim nor Thummim, neither tabernacle nor ark, neither priesthood nor church; nothing sacred, nothing venerable, nothing to inspire terror, nothing to attract notice, nothing outward to encourage the least hope of success. On the one side were falsehood and cursing and blasphemy; the thunders of anathemas, the threatenings of annihilation, the cutting off of bread and water, the driving out of families and individuals from their inheritance and their homes, from their shops and their business; the wresting by force from them of their necessary protective papers, and thus the exposing of them, without the possibility of redress, to all the insults and frauds of the most unprincipled and villanous of "the baser sort," and consigning them to a filthy Turkish prison, where some of them are now lying.

On the other side sat patience and meekness, peace and truth. There was serenity of countenance, and there was joy in tribulation. There was the voice of prayer and praise. The New Testament was in their hands, and all its blessed promises were in their hearts. There was no haste, no perturbation. They wrote a very appropriate and manly letter to their patriarch, making fully known their faith; and, when their letter was not received by him, they sent copies of it to all "the mighty men," and they have since lithographed it, and scattered it through the nation. They sent to the Sublime Porte, to give notice of their situation, a document drawn up with so much care and judgment as to secure the immediate attention of the whole Turkish divan, and to command the admiration of some of the very ablest diplomatists in the political world. To individuals known to be friendly, to this and that priest or vartabed, they wrote a long letter, calling upon them either to stand up in their own church and protest against the superstitions and wickedness of the times, or else to leave at once, and take their open stand with the persecuted friends of truth, choosing rather to suffer affliction with them than enjoy all the pleasures of sin and the honors of the world, with the divine indignation resting upon them. They had days of public fasting and prayer, and the spectacle was an affecting one. Their songs of praise from the whole congregation went up like the sound of many waters, and reminded me of the singing of the ancient Bohemian brethren amidst the raging fires of persecution. And, indeed, to see them stand from day to day with such firmness on the Rock of eternal ages, unmoved and undismayed; to see them manifest such unshaken confidence in the power and wisdom and faithfulness of Christ; to see them take joyfully the spoiling of their goods, knowing that they have in heaven a better and an enduring substance; to see them called up, one after another, from time to time, even women and children, and going alone, single-handed, cheerfully and fearlessly, into the presence of the greatest and craftiest of their enemies, and there witnessing a good confession, to the utter confusion of their inquisitors, — was a spectacle for angels and for men.

Thus far I have used the imperfect tense, and said " *was*," but I now use the present, and say " *is* ; " for the end is not yet. On the contrary, the night is every moment growing darker and darker, and the storm is raging more and more furiously, and there is not a single gleam of hope to be seen from any quarter of the horizon. Every outward ray is now entirely extinguished; and those who have not eyes to see far enough to discern the " rainbow round about the throne " must remain in utter darkness. In short, the combination of all nations and kindreds and tongues against the truth is so formidable, nothing now remains for its friends to hold on to but the power and faithfulness of Christ. With Him all is light, all is plain; " *all things are possible.*" Here may our persecuted brethren continue to cling with both hands! And will not all the beloved churches at home, if they have never done it before, for once try the full efficacy of prayer in their behalf? I have myself for several days been holding on to Judges xiii. 23; for surely, if the Lord were pleased to kill us, would He have sent here His word, His Spirit, and His converting grace, and shown us so much of His love and mercy in quickening the dead in sin?

Your brother in the Lord,

W. GOODELL.

They who had been the honored instruments in the hands

of God of effecting that religious reformation which had brought about this persecution were not left without the evidence that God smiled upon them and upon their work. In regard to the school that had been opened at the house of Mr. Goodell, he wrote a few days later : —

"*March* 4. Our female boarding-school, instead of being scattered to the four winds by this tempest, has been increased. The parents of two of the girls were so hard pressed by the patriarch that they took them from the school; but they left their beds and books as a pledge of their return as soon as the indignation should be overpast. In the mean time four new ones have joined the seminary, so that, instead of eight, which was as large a number as we thought we could possibly take, we now have ten, and when the absent girls return we shall have twelve. At the commencement of the storm the little girls manifested much fear, and some of them wept lest their parents should not remain firm. But as they heard from time to time of the excommunication of their parents and guardians, their fears were hushed, and they ' shouted aloud for joy.' It was exceedingly interesting to see how all the sympathies of their little hearts were enlisted on the side of ' grace and truth.' Many, I doubt not, have been the prayers that have gone up from day to day, ' out of the mouth of these babes and sucklings ; ' and prayer, by whomsoever offered, 'moves the hand that moves the world.' One of the eldest was publicly excommunicated and cursed by name last Sabbath. On my informing her of it, she remarked in her own quiet way, ' I have not been of that church for a long time. Let them curse, if God do but bless.' One of those in prison is her brother.

"*March* 17. The persecution continues with great severity, and we are brought very low. Three successive Fridays have been observed by us with our Armenian brethren as days of public fasting, humiliation, and prayer, and from little circles here and there prayer is offered continually. But the work of desolation has been dreadful, and hundreds, including their families, are in a suffering condition. Many are driven from their homes, and denied a shelter or a drop of water from any sect ; refused a place to live in, a place to die in, or a place to be buried in ; unable to flee to a mountain or a cave for want of a passport ; unable to work, for whoever employs them shares their fate; thrown into the filthiest prisons for want of security, and whoever offers himself for security is thrown in with them."

Through the interference of some of the foreign ambassadors, conspicuous among whom was Sir Stratford Canning, the evangelical Armenians were, by the authority of the Turkish government, delivered in a measure from the oppression of the patriarch; and, on the basis of the pledge of 1843, which guaranteed a sort of religious liberty, they were authorized to pursue their former occupations under Turkish license, and were promised protection by the Turkish police. But this was a precarious reliance, and ineffectual to secure them even in the enjoyment of their former means of subsistence, and many became dependent on the charitable assistance of foreigners. The state of things Mr. Goodell describes a month later : —

"*April* 17. Thirty-five shops remain shut. The Turkish rulers decide with all authority on the one hand that there must be no religious persecution, and with equal authority on the other that not one of these shops can be opened, unless the occupant submits his conscience to the patriarch's rules. Thus the excommunicated and their families are still dependent on charity. To put them in prison, or destroy them by fire and sword, would be persecution, and would not be tolerated; but to prevent them from laboring, and thus virtually to starve them to death, is in their estimation a master-stroke of policy, such as Nero and the Jesuits never thought of. Much more sympathy has been awakened in this vicinity for the sufferers than we had dared to hope. Messrs. Hanson & Co. promptly gave us one thousand piastres for their relief, Mr. Ede gave us two thousand, and Messrs. Van Lennep & Son one thousand, to say nothing of many smaller donations. 'But what are they among so many?'

"The patriarch has excommunicated no new persons for several weeks. He seems to have become suddenly alarmed at the numbers he was separating from his own church, and at the daily decreasing prospect of their ever again being united to it, and at the constantly growing importance attached to their interests. For the last few weeks he has

14

314 FORTY YEARS IN THE TURKISH EMPIRE.

contented himself with excommunicating afresh different parties of those already excommunicated, as though the first excommunication had lost its efficacy. Thus some of them have been excommunicated by name a dozen times or more.

" We read in Acts that ' the persecution which arose about Stephen ' scattered all the disciples abroad except the apostles. But what is very remarkable, *here* the persecution has brought them all together. *There* they had all been living together for some time, had become acquainted with one another, had often prayed and conversed together, and it seemed good to the great Head of the church that they should be scattered abroad. But *here* the brethren scarcely knew each other, many of them had never met excepting at the chapel, and had perhaps never exchanged a word with each other, and many of their families had never even seen each others' faces. It was therefore a kind and wise providence that brought them together in such close contact, in order that they may become acquainted with one another, may pray with and for each other, may learn to feel an interest in each other's welfare, to love as brethren, and to help one another on their way to a better world.

" Their intercourse with us and with each other is now uninterrupted, and our meetings are frequent and solemn. Every Friday we preach to a congregation of some twenty-five or thirty females, many of whom also attend the chapel on the Sabbath. In the evening we from time to time visit the families that occupy the two houses we have taken for them in Pera, when thirty or more individuals assemble to unite in conversation, reading the Scriptures, and prayer. These are precious seasons, which we feel we must improve while we have the opportunity, for the persecution cannot be expected to last always. There is now less prayer offered for the persecuted, and more for the persecutors and for the timid and wavering. Some, without waiting to be excommunicated or molested, have already come over to join the little flock of Christ; and in this time of ' rebuke and blasphemy ' why may we not be looking for some striking displays of ' grace and glory '? Why may we not hope to be ' baptized with the Holy Ghost, not many days hence ' ? "

This hope was speedily fulfilled in an abundant outpouring of the Holy Spirit, which was followed by the most decisive and important results.

CHAPTER XVII.

THE time had now come for taking a step to which the various members of the mission, and most decidedly of all, the patriarch of the mission, Mr. Goodell, had been averse from the very beginning; but it was a step to which they were called alike by the grace and the providence of God. By the extracts from his journal, and his correspondence on this subject, it has been seen that Mr. Goodell was the farthest possible from indulging, or encouraging in others, a spirit of proselytism, and that he did not even desire to have the Armenians leave their own church, in which they had been born and educated. He was anxious that not only the people, but the priests, and all the ecclesiastics of the Greek and Armenian churches, should see and feel that the missionaries, in coming among them, were not actuated by any desire to gather around themselves a company of followers, but that they simply wished to persuade men to become followers of Christ. So fully did he act upon the principle enunciated by the great apostle to the Gentiles, though in somewhat different circumstances, " Christ sent me not to baptize, but to preach the Gospel," that he steadily refused to baptize the children of Greek or Armenian Christians, or to encourage members of the Greek or Armenian church to forsake in any way the communion of those churches, lest the attention of the people generally should be drawn away from the great object of his mission, which was to lead souls to Christ. His desire was to have the leaven of the Gospel, of true spiritual religion, diffused among the masses of the Oriental churches ; to see them revived and renovated, rather than to organize a new church, which might become the occasion of controversy and opposition to the truth. The fact that from time to time priests as well as people became obedient to the faith, and then preached a pure gospel to their brethren, encouraged the missionaries more and more in the course which they had pursued.

When the Armenian patriarch began to hurl his excommunications at all who had adopted the new opinions and entered upon the new life, and when he forbade his people to have ecclesiastical or social intercourse with them; when those who believed were driven out into the wilderness of the world, like sheep without a shepherd, and had no one to break to them the bread of eternal life or to administer to them any of the ordinances of the Gospel ; — when to all these privations there was added, on the part of their own church, bitter, relentless persecution, there was no longer any question as to whether it was duty to gather them into another fold, and watch over and feed them in the name of the great Shepherd.

The patriarch set the seal upon the movement that was in preparation among the evangelical party of his community, by issuing, on the 21st of June, 1846, a new excommunication, directed against all who still adhered to the principles of the Gospel, ordering that it should be read publicly in every church in the Turkish empire at each anniversary of the day on which it was issued. There was no longer any hope of their being recognized again as members of the church in which they were born, or of their being admitted to any of its privileges, if privileges they could be called.

The evangelical Armenians had, for a long time, met together for mutual counsel and comfort, but they had no separate ecclesiastical organization. Driven, therefore, to the last extremity by persecution and excommunication, they resolved to unite as a branch of the true catholic church of Christ; and with the advice of the missionaries, who prepared for them a platform or constitution, on the 1st of July, 1846, they entered in solemn covenant as the First Evangelical Armenian Church of Constantinople. Of this event Mr. Goodell wrote:—

"'Tis done! On the 1st inst. an evangelical church was organized upon the foundation of the apostles and prophets, Jesus Christ Himself being the chief corner-stone. It was a most interesting occasion. The meeting continued four hours and a half, and was one of great solemnity. Forty persons, of whom three were women, voluntarily entered into covenant with God and with each other; and we, in the name of all the evangelical churches in Christendom, rose and formally recognized and acknowledged them as a true church of Christ. They then chose by ballot a pastor and two deacons, together with three others, who are to hold office for the term of one year, and who with the pastor and deacons form a standing committee or church session, for the examination of candidates, the bringing forward of cases of discipline, &c. To this church some thirty or forty more will probably be added by profession just as soon as time shall be found to examine and propound them.

"I did not expect to live to see this day, but I have seen it and am glad. 'This is the day which the Lord hath made, and we will rejoice and be glad in it.' When I removed to Constantinople fifteen years ago, I felt assured either that this day would come, or that the Armenian Church as a body would be reformed; and I never had any anxiety as to the result. I always felt that we were engaged in a great and good work, so great and so good that I would without any impatience have labored on in the same way fifteen years longer, had it so pleased the great Head of the church.

"This has been a most marvellous work of God, and so evident is this, that the nations around say one to another, 'The Lord hath done great things for them.' Even the Mussulmans have said, 'This is the miracle of 1262' (1846). It is all wonderful. I often walk the room, and lift up my hands and say to myself, 'Wonderful! Wonderful!' And what language more suitable for us to use than that of the Psalmist, 'Not unto us, O Lord, not unto us, but unto thy name give glory, for thy mercy and for thy truth's sake.' He has in this great work condescended to make use not so much of our wisdom as of our folly; not so much of our strength as of our weakness. And more than this, He has made use of the strength, the pride, the high looks, the malice, the evil intentions, the 'violent dealings' of opposers, and thus has He 'stilled the enemy and the avenger,' and covered their faces with confusion."

The pastor-elect of this new church, Mr. Apisoghom Khachadurian, an Armenian, was ordained July 7, 1846, all the American missionaries and the Rev. Mr. Allan, of the Free Church of Scotland, taking part in the services. Of this occasion Mr. Goodell wrote: —

"Although the ordination was kept secret on account of our straitened accommodations, yet as many as one hundred and eighty or two hundred must have been present, filling every seat and every passage, and standing around the doors. Perfect stillness reigned during the whole, and the attention was profound and solemn. The hearts of the brethren seemed stirred up from their innermost depths. One said the whole place seemed full of the angels of light; another, that his very flesh trembled for fear of the Lord and for the glory of His majesty, so sensibly did he feel the divine presence."

The evangelical Armenians who united in this organization adopted a paper containing the reasons which induced them to take this step. It was signed by the pastor, deacons, and committee of the church, and was addressed, "To the much respected and honored members of the society of the American Board," and is as follows: —

"We, evangelical Christians of the Armenian nation, believing that the true foundation and perfect rule of Christian faith is the Holy Scriptures alone, have cast away from us those human traditions and ceremonies which are opposed to the rules of the Bible, but which our national church requires. And, furthermore, without having had the least intention of separating from it, we have been united together for the special purpose of enlightening and reforming this church. And since we receive entire the Nicene creed of the church; and also since, up to the present time, no creed embracing particularly these human traditions has been framed and enjoined upon the members of the Armenian Church as necessary to be received, we could be considered as regular members of the national church by simply receiving the ancient (Nicene) creed. But in the year 1846, Bishop Matteos, patriarch of the Armenians, has invented a new creed, embracing particularly these human traditions, a copy of which is found in the tract called 'An Answer,' &c., printed in Smyrna, and he has insisted upon our accepting and subscribing it.

"But we, obeying God rather than man, have not received it; on account of which he has cast us out of the church, and anathematized us particularly and publicly by name; and, according to his ability, he has also inflicted upon us material injuries. We had indeed, previous to this, suffered persecution of different kinds for our religious opinions; as, for instance, about seven years ago several of us were sent into exile; and also within about two years some have been banished, some put in prison, some fined, some bastinadoed, &c.; yet, since the present patriarch rejected us by excommunication from the church, he has inflicted on us generally various additional bodily penalties. Thus, for several months all the shops of the evangelical Armenians were closed; some were unwillingly separated from their homes and parents, and some even from their wives and husbands; bakers and water-carriers were forbidden to bring either bread or water; and to the extent of his ability he strove by every species of bodily infliction to compel us to receive and sign his new confession of faith.

"And although by the interposed protection of the powerful Ottoman government he has been prevented from continuing this severity of persecution, he has to this day, every day on the Sabbath, repeated the command to the Armenian people not to receive us into their houses or shops, or even to look upon us. And, finally, after all these things, he has issued a new bull, and caused it to be read in all the churches on the day of the Catholic Church festival; which bull of excommunication and anathema is also to be read in all the churches throughout the Ottoman empire, every year successively at the same festival. Thus he cuts us off and casts us out for ever from the national church, by the standing order and high authority of this bull.

"And now, it being evident that we cannot be in fellow-ship with the Armenian Church without receiving human traditions and rites, which, being contrary to the Holy Scriptures, we cannot receive, we therefore, by the grace and mercy of God, following the doctrine of our Lord Jesus Christ, and obeying the Gospel, and consequently being members of His one catholic and apostolical church, do now rightfully and justly constitute ourselves into a church with the following confession of faith."

To this was appended a confession that is strictly in accordance with the faith of the reformed churches generally.

In regard to the wisdom and propriety of the course which had been pursued by the mission, in abstaining heretofore from all attempts at effecting a separate organization of the Armenians, Mr. Goodell wrote at this time: —

"We could not have attempted it without descending from the high and holy ground we occupied, and coming down, or appearing to come down, to the low earthly stand of mere sectarianism. We could not have attempted it without endangering our very existence as a mission, and thus exposing to infinite hazard this blessed work of the Lord. It was first necessary, in the providence of God, that the Armenian renegade should be beheaded, the sympathies of the whole Christian world awakened, and the death-blow to despotism given by extorting that wonderful pledge from the Sultan. Most manifestly for the first years of this mission Christ sent us not to baptize, but to preach the Gospel; and I, therefore, thank God that we were enabled in this respect to do our duty, though hard to flesh and blood, and that we absolutely baptized no one, not even Crispus and Gaius. But blessed be the name of the Lord, these more than Chinese walls are now broken down. 'The former things are passed away,' and 'there is no more sea.'"

Of the circumstances and the reasons which led to the change of policy on the part of the mission in the organization of churches, Mr. Goodell subsequently wrote: —

"When I came to Constantinople in 1831, having learned something from experience in other places, I was fully convinced that we ought to stand as far aloof as possible from any connection with bigotry, and to be altogether free from any policy that was narrow and contracted; that from our peculiar circumstances, being thrown among persons of all religions, we ought to consider ourselves as belonging rather to the universal church of Christ than to any particular section or denomination of that church. Accordingly, being often called upon by Europeans of different nations and communions to officiate at funerals, baptisms, marriages, &c., in the absence of their respective chaplains, we endeavored to conform ourselves as far as possible to their forms, — those for which they had predilections, — thus not seeking our own profit or pleasure, but of many, for their edification.

"In our intercourse with the natives of the countries, for whose good our labors were specially directed, we endeavored to act in the same liberal manner. It was not to pull down their churches and build up our own that we came here, and we have not from the first day until now so much as hinted to any one that he should leave his church and join ours. Our efforts have been directed rather to enlighten, improve, and elevate the whole community by means of books and schools, and in our earlier efforts we had the sanction of these ecclesiastics, and had intercourse with their patriarchs and bishops. But as the people became enlightened, and some of them began to take a lively interest in the things they were learning, persecutions began to take place. In these persecutions no question was asked the accused by their accusers, no opportunity given them to explain the reason of their faith or conduct, no creed offered to them to subscribe. They were seized and thrown into prison or sent into exile without form or ceremony, and when they were released or recalled, as they had never been excommunicated, they still retained their connection, both civil and ecclesiastical, with their ancient church.

"But this persecution has been different. The people were called upon to recant their opinions. A creed was presented for them to subscribe, — not a creed of the church, but a creed prepared for them by the patriarch, with special reference to their principles, and which no enlightened, conscientious man could subscribe. The consequence was, many were excommunicated, cut off from their church, were persecuted, and the sufferings of many were great.

"As excommunicated persons they were, of course, deprived of the sacraments and ordinances of the Gospel. But

14*   U

these were not men of careless lives that they should continue willingly deprived of these sacraments and ordinances.
They were not infidels.   They were serious men and women,
who prized the Sabbath, the house of prayer, and all the
institutions of the Gospel.   After waiting some four or five
months, they applied to us to assist in organizing them into
churches.   This we have accordingly done, for 'who could
forbid water that they should not be baptized?'   Who could
forbid bread and wine that they should not commemorate
the death of Christ?   And who could forbid their having
pastors to feed them with knowledge?   We assisted in
organizing them into churches at Constantinople, Nicomedia,
Ada Bazar, and Trebizond.   These churches are not ours,
but theirs.   We have no control over them.   They are not
formed exactly according to the model of any of our churches
in America.   We went directly to the New Testament for
our model.   These are all Protestant churches, and their
articles of faith are such as are acknowledged by all the
great branches of the Protestant church in America, England, and the continent of Europe.   And these churches we
present to you at this time as members, and I hope worthy
members, of the great Protestant family."

Before the close of the year two aged members were called
from the ranks of the church militant to enter upon the rest
and reward of the church triumphant.   Mention is made of
these cases, not only because they illustrate the power of
God's grace, and the genuineness of the work which had
been wrought among the Armenians, but also as showing the
extent to which the spirit of persecution was carried on the
part of their former brethren.   These aged saints, who died
in the faith and triumph of the Gospel, were hounded to
their very graves by their persecutors.

One of them was an old man, who had learned the way of
life in the very evening of his days.   His previous history
had been remarkable.   He had been once saved from the
sword of the Janizaries when they ranged the city altogether
without law.   When a comparatively young man, as he was
going home one evening from the bazaars, he passed two of
the Janizaries, who sat in front of a coffee-shop admiring a

new yataghan, or sword, that one of them held in his hand. Seeing the Armenian, he ordered him to come to him, and then told him he had just bought a new yataghan, the metal of which he was going to try by cutting off his head; which he would have done with as little compunction as he would have cut off the head of a dog, and with as perfect impunity, so abject at that time was the subjection of the Christians to the Mohammedans. It was only by humbling himself at the feet of the blood-thirsty Janizary, and pleading, not so much for his own sake as for that of his family, dependent on him for daily bread, that the Armenian's life was spared at the entreaty of the other Janizary, who said, "Let the hog live." When the first evangelical church was organized, this Armenian, now an old man, was one of its original members, having been brought to a knowledge of the truth as it is in Jesus. He was present at the ordination of the pastor, and was then ready to say, "Lord, now lettest thou thy servant depart in peace, for mine eyes have seen thy salvation."

He was soon called to join the church triumphant. As he was drawing near his end, some one asked him how he regarded the step he had taken in forsaking the church of his fathers, and in turning his feet into a new path that had been pointed out to him by strangers from a strange land. His reply was, "It is the Gospel that I have received in the place of human inventions." To one of the missionaries, who called to see him, he said, in great weakness of body but in firmness of spirit, "I am going to leave all my brethren and friends here, but I am going to join other equally dear friends elsewhere." On the occasion of his burial an immense mob of hostile Armenians assembled at the cemetery, shouting and hooting at the company of evangelical brethren who attended his remains, assailing them not only with abusive and filthy language, but with stones. Mr. Dwight and many of the native brethren were struck with the stones.

The other case was that of a shopkeeper, who had formerly been an opposer. When he received the Gospel, he was called to take the spoiling of his goods, and to suffer violence. He was driven from his father's house, and never permitted to return. He was once attacked in the streets, knocked down and beaten. As he was seated one day in his shop, he was assailed by one of the patriarch's men, who had previously threatened to take his life. The assault brought on a hemorrhage of the lungs, which soon after proved fatal. As he was about to die, he exclaimed, " Glory to God that He has condescended to call me into the light of His glorious Gospel ! Blessed be His name that I have been made acquainted with my former errors in time, and that the true Gospel has been made known to me ! Glory to Thee, O Lord ! Glory to Thee, O Lord Jesus ! " When he could no longer speak, he looked upward, and pointed toward heaven as the home to which he was going.

The pastor of the church, Mr. Apisoghom, was not long in following these first-garnered fruits. It was thought that the injuries he received from the mob at the funeral of the aged disciple who was first called home were among the immediate causes of the attack that resulted in his death. He passed away giving glory to God. His peace and joy at the last called forth expressions of sympathetic triumph on the part of his friends who were present, even in the midst of their grief at his death.

The number of members of this church was speedily doubled, and similar organizations soon followed at different places in the interior, no hindrance being offered by the Turkish government. The Spirit of God was poured out upon portions of the Armenian community, and scenes of awakening and conversion, such as have been witnessed in Christian lands, were vouchsafed to the infant church of Christ in Turkey. A special visitation of the Spirit was enjoyed in the boarding-school at the house of Mr. Goodell, several of the girls giving the clearest evidence that they had been born again. In the elevated, we might say the excited, state of his feelings, produced by these manifestations of the power and grace of God, Mr. Goodell wrote, on the 7th of December, in the same year : —

"He who has saved His people here 'from the lion and' the bear,' from the fury of the patriarch, the prison and the bastinado of the civil and ecclesiastical rulers, has now come to command still greater deliverances for them. In the former case He employed inferior agencies, but He is now employing His highest and greatest and best. Yes, His Holy Spirit has now come to save, not the body, but the soul, not from the power of man, but from the dominion of sin and Satan.

"It was on the Sabbath, the 22d ult., that something unusual in the Female Seminary was first noticed. Two of the pupils came to Miss Lovell, and asked, with tears, how they could obtain new hearts, saying they had been praying for it for several weeks, but the more they prayed the worse their hearts appeared to them, and they were entirely discouraged. Others in the school were almost immediately brought under the convincing power of the Spirit, and in a few days the seriousness was general. Individuals would have to leave their studies and the school-room to give themselves unto prayer. Many were the little circles of prayer held at odd moments during the day, and every evening the whole school had a prayer-meeting among themselves. On the following Friday the state of feeling was such that, contrary to our intentions, all study throughout the whole school had to be given up."

As the result of this awakening, of the fifteen pupils all but two were soon rejoicing in hope, and gave good evidence of conversion; and the spiritual influence also pervaded the minds of the students in the seminary at Bebek.

After this work of grace had commenced in the school, the whole congregation of evangelical Armenians (or Protestants, as they now began to be called) observed a day of fasting, humiliation, and prayer, with reference to this display of God's presence and power. The chapel was crowded; and from this time onward many others were heard asking what they must do to be saved. One of the Armenian women, who had never before had any conscious knowledge of what it was to be moved by the Holy Spirit, said that, at the chapel on the day of prayer, she felt impelled to go out of the meeting and bring in all her nation. Several were hopefully converted on that very day.

Near the close of the year 1846, Mr. Goodell received an urgent invitation to join an American family, with whom he was on terms of intimate friendship, and who were then at Constantinople, to make the tour of the Holy Land. But he declined the invitation, and, in a private letter to a friend, written at the time. gave the following reason for not accepting it: " Though I have never yet seen Jerusalem, I did not feel that I could leave my work, especially as my health did not seem to require any relaxation." His course in foregoing this opportunity to fulfil the long-cherished desire of his heart to " stand within thy gates, O Jerusalem!" is a simple illustration of the spirit of the man, of the self-sacrificing devotion with which he had consecrated himself to the service of Christ in the missionary work. When he left the United States, and, indeed, when he was first taken into the service of the Board, it was with the full expectation of going to labor on the spot where his Master had lived and taught and suffered for the salvation of men. He had no romantic ideas of the missionary work, but he cherished the most sacred associations with the scenes of the Saviour's life and death. When he reached Beyrout, it appeared best that he should remain there, for a time at least; and there he spent five years on the borders of the Holy Land, without actually entering it. He had no time that he could take from his Master's work to devote to his own personal gratification, even in a matter of such sacred interest as a visit to the Holy City. And now, after more than twenty years of unrelaxed toil, because he felt no special need of relaxation, he declined the most favorable opportunity he was likely to enjoy, and the only opportunity, in fact, that ever did present itself in the same inviting form.

In June of the following year he made a brief trip to Smyrna, his health in the mean time having become greatly enfeebled by his incessant labor, and by the anxiety and joy he had experienced in connection with the special religious interest that prevailed in the school and among the people. During his absence, one of the girls of the seminary under his care, about thirteen years of age, had died of consumption; but she was fully prepared by the grace of the Saviour for her departure. For many days before the end came, her face was shining like that of an angel, and her peace was like a river. She fell asleep at last, like a child upon its mother's breast. So general and deep was the interest felt in this young convert, that more than a thousand persons gathered around her grave, where the funeral services were held, — an unprecedented sight at Constantinople, in connection with the death of a young girl.

The first marriage, according to the simple rites of the Protestant Armenian Church, was celebrated on the 4th of November, 1847. Hitherto all marriage ceremonies had been performed by the clergy of the old church; but now that the Protestants had a separate organization, they had no occasion to go back to the old ecclesiastics, nor could they obtain from them any official service. They were excommunicate. The bride, in the marriage alluded to, was a pupil of the Female Seminary, of whom Mr. Goodell gives the following sketch: —

"She was in school a little more than a year, but it was to her the year of jubilee. She came poor and ignorant, and it was necessary to assist her with clothing. She had no bed, and expressed her willingness to lie on the floor. But she was diligent in her studies; she waked up to a new life; she sat daily at the feet of her heavenly Teacher, to learn of Him; she had much to learn, and she learned much; she joined the church of Christ; and the poor ignorant girl, whom we at first hesitated to receive, has become wise unto salvation, and rich for eternity. She is now married to one of our native helpers, who was employed by us to distribute the word of God, and point dying men to the life-giving efficacy of atoning blood."

CHAPTER XVIII.

WE have had occasion more than once to speak of the catholic spirit which Mr. Goodell manifested toward all who loved our Lord Jesus Christ, to whatever church of Christ they belonged. All were his brethren, truly and well beloved, who loved and served the same Master. This characteristic marked his whole life, and appears in all his writings, as they have been transferred to these pages. It is a pleasure, also, to record that he was generally received in the same spirit, even by those who might be supposed to differ from him in regard to important ecclesiastical matters. He was called to act as a sort of chaplain to the English embassy from time to time, during a great part of his residence at Constantinople, and in the families of English and American Episcopalians he was often invited to officiate as a minister of Christ in the most sacred services. To them he was a true minister of Christ, accredited not only by his standing in the church, but by his life of faith and holy service, and by the evidence that the spirit of grace was upon him. The following extract from one of his letters will show what feelings were cherished toward him by the members and representatives of the Church of England : —

CONSTANTINOPLE, April 7, 1847.

"The Rev. Dr. Bennett, who was chaplain to the British embassy here, departed this life on the 26th April, 1847, of disease of the heart. At his request I visited him often during his illness, and prayed by his bedside. The consolations of religion, which he had so often been called in the course of a long ministry to give to others in their last hours, I endeavored to administer to him; and though the prayers I offered were probably the first extemporaneous prayers he ever heard, they appeared to be a comfort to him.

"Of his situation as a dying man he was perfectly aware; and he made all his arrangements, and gave his parting counsels to his friends with as much calmness and composure as though his removal, instead of being from time to eternity, was to be only a removal from one apartment of his house to another. His end was peace. He often remarked, 'I die in peace with all men. I feel no ill-will towards any person, however much he may have differed from me.' And, 'although I have endeavored to perform with fidelity the duties of my station, yet I know I am a sinner, and I do not expect salvation for any works of my own, but only through the merits of Jesus Christ our Lord.' His spirit was truly a catholic one; and, instead of that exclusiveness which 'separateth very friends,' his was that charity which embraces all the good, of whatever name or denomination. Rarely, if ever, did I visit him during the last few weeks of his life, when he did not send his love and blessing to all the missionary brethren, often to each one by name. At the request of his family, at the request also of the English residents, and of Mr. Wellesly, the English ambassador, I performed the last sad offices at the funeral on the 29th. On the following Sabbath I endeavored to improve the occasion by an appropriate discourse, and to stir up the people to prayers that another pastor may be speedily sent to them, one who shall be a man after God's own heart. And as this is a subject which concerns not only them, but also this mission, let prayer be offered for them by all the friends of the missionary cause."

Of the successor to Dr. Bennett in the chaplaincy of the English embassy, he subsequently wrote: —

"The Lord in answer to prayer has sent to the English residents here a worthy chaplain and lady. They both seem to be very pious and excellent persons, as far removed from Puseyism on the one hand as from indifferentism on the other. He preached a thorough-going sermon on the new birth, in our chapel, the first Sabbath he spent in Constantinople."

Up to 1847 the Protestants had no recognition before the Turkish government apart from the Armenian nation to which they belonged. They were still nominally subject to the patriarch, although they had enjoyed a measure of protection from the Turkish officials. Their separation being complete, it was absolutely necessary for their comfort and convenience, and almost for their existence, in the order of things that prevailed under the government of the Porte, that they should have their independence distinctly recognized. In the temporary absence of Sir Stratford Canning, who had been the steadfast friend of the missionaries and of the persecuted Christians, Lord Cowley negotiated the matter with the government, and on the 15th of November, 1847, the grand vizier issued a firman, declaring that the "Christian subjects of the Ottoman government professing Protestantism" should constitute a separate community, with all the rights and privileges belonging to others, and that "no interference whatever be permitted in their temporal or spiritual concerns on the part of the patriarch, monks, or priests of other sects." *   This firman was so worded that converts from among the Greeks and Jews who joined the Protestants might enjoy the same immunities. This decree was sent to all the pashas in the interior; and upon the basis of it a head to the new community was chosen, occupying in civil matters the same position as the patriarch among the Armenians or Greeks.

The missionaries of the American Board united in sending to Lord Cowley a letter expressive of their sense of the important service which he had rendered in securing to the Protestant Christians liberty of conscience and the enjoyment of the same civil rights with other Christian subjects of the Porte. The reply of the British ambassador was alike honorable to himself and to those to whom it was sent. Addressing Mr. Goodell as the senior, and representative of the mission, he wrote: —

* See Appendix.

"Permit me also to take this opportunity of publicly stating how much the Protestants owe to you and to the society which sent you here. I gladly give my testimony to the zeal, prudence, and patience which have characterized all your proceedings in this country, and to which I attribute much of the success that has crowned our joint endeavors.

"We, however, are but mere instruments in the hands of a higher power; though perhaps to you, reverend sir, it ill becomes me to make the observation. To that same power, then, let us recommend the future interests of the emancipated community."

Another letter, to his friend Judge Cooke, of Catskill, is here inserted: —

CONSTANTINOPLE, Jan. 1, 1848.

MY DEAR SIR, — Henry's Commentary of the Bible, which you gave me some seventeen years ago, as a balance for not writing me as often as you should, I gave yesterday to Baron Harûtun, who was recently ordained as pastor over the evangelical churches at Nicomedia and Ada Bazar. I think a small balance must again be due me on the same score. It is difficult, of course, to state the amount with much precision, when from the nature of the case not even algebraical terms can be used; but suppose I give you a receipt in the following manner: —

Received of the Hon. Thomas B. Cooke, one copy of "Message from God, or Thoughts on Religion for Thinking Men;" one copy of "Tale of the Armenians," by MacFarlane; and one copy of "Life of Caspar Hauser," — being an equivalent for balance due me for default in correspondence since 1831.   W. GOODELL.

Though I have acknowledged in the above to have received the equivalent, yet this is only for form's sake, to make the document legal, and thus secure you from all fear, or possibility even, of further molestation. But should you add one or two sets of the American Tract Society's publications for some of our native pastors, and various other things which may suggest themselves to your fruitful and benevolent mind, I do not think that even then the whole would be any thing more than the legal interest for one year, and much less a full equivalent for the whole, principal and interest. But as

I never intend to injure you or any of your family on account of this debt, I have given you a receipt in full, and I hope you will take no advantage of my having more confidingly than prudently placed my signature to it.

Both the pastor at Constantinople and the one at Nicomedia understand English, and so also does the one about to be ordained at Trebizond. The first pastor of the church at Constantinople died last March, and was succeeded by his brother. At every communion, which is once in two months, there have been additions to this church. It now numbers ninety-three, of whom thirty-four are females. All the members of the church can read, and all except a few females can write. This new community is indeed by far the best educated of any native sect in the whole country. They are poor; but, if the richest man in the empire had joined them two years ago, he would have been as poor as any of them, for so violent was the persecution, that they were called to suffer the loss of all things. They are now acknowledged by the Ottoman empire as a distinct and separate community, having a Turkish officer of high rank for their civil head, and all their ecclesiastical and spiritual matters being managed by themselves without interference from any quarter. This was effected through the influence of the English ambassador.

The Female Seminary now contains twenty-three pupils. During the year one left on account of ill-health, one died in the triumphs of faith, and one, a professor of religion, was married to a native brother, who has gone to be a helper in the work at Broosa. The Boys' Seminary at Bebek contains forty.

Our eldest son, William, left us last spring, and is now a member of Williams College. Mrs. Goodell is as great a student as ever, and next to the Bible prizes her Turkish and Armenian Dictionaries. Every morning at the breakfast table she and Miss Lovell repeat their verse of Scripture in Armenian, the elder children in Greek and French, the three younger children in English, and myself in Turkish.

January 3. This is the great monthly concert, and a glorious day it has been in Constantinople. Think of a great union prayer-meeting, consisting of English, Scotch, Americans, Germans, Greeks, Armenians, Jews, and Catholics, — and all sitting down together at the table of the Lord; Episcopalians, Presbyterians. Congregationalists, Lutherans, Baptists, Methodists, baptized Jews, and Protestant Armenians. Prayers were offered in three languages, Turkish, English, and Armenian. Addresses were made in four languages, German, English, Armenian, and Turkish, and hymns were sung to the same tune at the same moment in three different languges, Armenian, German, and English. There was no confusion, no discord. No one was out of tune, or out of time. The harmony was perfect, while each with the spirit and with the greatest power and might was singing, in his own tongue wherein he was born, the high praises of our God. The effect was overpowering. It was the voice of a great multitude, and rose up like the sound of many waters. Our chapel was crowded with communicants, and our hearts with thoughts too big for utterance. Had Fisk and Parsons lived to see this day, they would have felt like the aged Simeon, when his eyes had seen God's great salvation.

It is now more than a quarter of a century since we have seen the good land of our fathers. Shall we ever see it again? It is not probable that both of us will ever set our eyes upon it, but I hope that both will at length see "a better country, even an heavenly." My own health has failed the last year, and I am forced to consider myself an invalid. I am thankful that I have been able to continue preaching, to superintend the Female Seminary, and perform the duties of chaplain, but I have done much less upon my Commentary than I had hoped.

I am, as ever,

Yours truly,

W. GOODELL.

To two of his former fellow-students he addressed a letter, which has in it much of personal interest, — personal alike to the writer and to those to whom it was written: —

CONSTANTINOPLE, April 7, 1848.

My dear brethren, Spaulding and Winslow, greatly beloved and longed for:

I remember one of you at Andover, the other at Dartmouth and Andover, and both of you at Salem. I have a daughter at Norwich, and Brother Spaulding has a daughter there, and I have just been reading for the fourth or fifth time (and this last time with more tenderness and tears than ever before) the memoirs of that blessed woman from Norwich, who was Brother Winslow's companion in the faith and patience of the saints. It is now nearly thirty years since we met. I am growing old, and so must you be. I said, I will take my pen and write my good brethren, I will say to them, Be of good courage, the night is far spent, the day is at hand; let us be laying entirely aside what will answer in the dark, and be putting on the garments which the light and the day require.

I have learned several things since I saw you: —

1. That a great deal of the religion that I used to carry about with me I had received from man, and not from the Spirit of God.

2. That sin is a more awful thing, and leads man infinitely farther from God and goodness, than I had supposed possible.

3. That the direct influence of Satan over the minds of men is incomparably more powerful and destructive than I had been taught to believe.

4. That human suasion, human argument, human eloquence, human efforts, education, civilization, have in themselves no more efficacy to raise dead sinners to life than they have to call the dead out of their graves. Oh, how impotent we find all these in lands unvisited by holy influences!

5. That the Gospel is all-powerful, all-precious. What language can express its power! what words can tell its worth! You have seen in India, we have seen in Syria, what it can do when preached with the Holy Ghost sent down from heaven. And not even all the glowing poetry of Isaiah exceeds the sober reality.

I am now writing a Commentary, I will not say on the Bible, for I have no expectation of living to complete even one-half of the New Testament. May I be assisted by that same unerring Spirit of Truth, under which the Scriptures were written. I lay hold without any ceremony of all the thoughts and helps I can find in any quarter; but still, should any one on reading ask, " Whose is this image and super-scription ? " I presume the universal answer would be, " It is Goodell's." It is to be published in both Turkish and Armenian. In preaching, I use only the Turkish, and most of my brethren use only the Armenian. They are both of them mighty languages, when the Holy Spirit puts power into the word; otherwise, they are insipid enough. Mrs. Goodell in her old age is learning both these languages. She had previously learned the Italian, Arabic, and Greek, but of these languages the Holy Spirit uses only the last in these parts, and therefore for the last two years, since she has had the temporal charge and I the chaplaincy of the Female Boarding-school, she has with the vigor and success of youth set about to acquire these two new languages.

Since I saw you I have prayed with the ardent Byington in the woods among the Choctaws ; I have seen the beloved Fisk close his eyes on all below, and go to the bright world above ; and from my good brother Temple, with whom I studied nine years and with whom I roomed seven years, I am at length separated. The providence of God called him to return to America, and he returned, though hard for flesh and blood. He is a good man, full of the Holy Ghost, and in whatever manner the prince of this world comes to him, he never finds any thing in him.

May we all meet above ! May we be for ever employed in the service of the King of kings, here and hereafter, in time and eternity ! Amen and amen.

Thus prays your affectionate brother,

W. GOODELL.

If Mr. Goodell had been called to devote his life to such a service, he would have been the prince of beggars, to use a word which is too often applied to those who present the claims of Christ's cause to His people. He never felt that he was asking a personal favor in asking help for the work in which he was engaged. He asked with as much dignity as could be exercised in conferring a gift, and yet he neither made a demand, nor presented any request in an offensive manner. He had the happy faculty, without using deceit or artifice, of so stating what was wanted as to confer a pleasure in making the application, and of causing any one to whom he applied to feel that he was embracing a privilege in giving what was asked. The following letter was written to a clergyman in this country : —

CONSTANTINOPLE, June 1, 1848.

MY DEAR BROTHER, — Immediately on the receipt of this, please call together a few of the " mighty men of wealth " in the city, and say to them, " Hear now, ye rich men ! this commandment is for you." God, your benevolent Creator, says the silver and the gold are all His ; but for reasons known only to Himself, He has entrusted some of it for a short time to you. Your own Redeemer placed it as a sacred deposit in your hands, and whenever He calls for the whole, or for any part of it, He expects, and has a right to expect, that His drafts will be cheerfully honored. Whether the call be now from Him, whether the bill now presented really bear His signature, you yourselves, who must already have had many transactions of this kind with Him, can easily determine, especially after reading the following letter of advice on the subject.

There are now seven evangelical churches in Turkey, and, before you receive this, there will probably be eight. These churches of the living God have nowhere to assemble but " at the door of the tabernacle of the congregation," in a private house, or in a room rented for the purpose, no house of prayer having been yet erected for any of them. The church of Constantinople was organized nearly two years ago, with forty members, and sixty have since been added to it, there having been additions at every communion. The number of those that belong to the congregation is at least four times as large as the number of those that belong to the church, and no private house is sufficiently large to accommodate them. " Your servants for Jesus' sake," whom you have sent here to invite " as many as they find " to the Gospel feast, can no longer say to those that come, " And yet there is room ; " but, in direct opposition to the whole spirit of Christianity, our straitened circumstances declare to them more plainly than words, You must go away ; there is no more room.

A house of God, then, is imperiously demanded. A lot for the purpose has already been purchased. The contract for the building is already made. The house will absolutely be built. The cost will be ten thousand dollars. The money *must* and *will* be forthcoming. You will see the bills are drawn at *sight*. Should you honor them, the honesty and the reward will be yours. Your own precious Redeemer, who poured out His own soul unto death to save yours, has such confidence in your punctuality and uprightness that you have the honor of His first call. His first drafts are on you; and surely not for worlds would you have His confidence in the stability and integrity of your house shaken.

Should it be asked why the people here do not build their

own church, the answer is, they have suffered the loss of all things for Christ, and taken joyfully the spoiling of their goods. Some of them are not even yet able to earn their own bread, so vigilant are their enemies to distress and ruin them. "Now at this time, then, let your abundance be a supply for their want, that their abundance may hereafter be a supply for your want," beyond the Rocky Mountains, in Oregon, or California.

One word more. *Satan* has a house of worship building here, — a magnificent theatre, — which will cost at least one hundred times as much as this contemplated church of the Redeemer. Some scores of men have been employed on it for many months, and they will be employed for months more. This also is built by subscription. But all Satan's drafts for this object are duly honored. We have not heard of a single bill of his being protested here, although he really has no funds in any house.

Now, my dear brother, we have no more words to say. If any more are necessary, *you* must say them. But we fully expect to hear that those on whom these bills are drawn sat down immediately and wrote "*Accepted*," and said at once, " Rise up and build." And thus all that any future historian of these transactions will have to add will be, " So they strengthened their hands for this good work."

Alleluia! Amen! Farewell.

In behalf of the station,

W. GOODELL.

To this were appended a number of drafts for various amounts, to be signed with the names of the cheerful donors of the several sums.

From his very entrance upon his work at Constantinople, Mr. Goodell had aimed at calling forth the energies of the people in sustaining pecuniarily the various operations that were undertaken for their benefit, and this not merely as a matter of economy, but in order that they might appreciate their privileges. What costs nothing is little valued; and it is equally true that those who have expended time and labor and money on any enterprise will naturally look for some return from the investment. The first year that he was at Constantinople, he encouraged the Greeks and the Turks to

15   v

establish their own schools, while he furnished the plans for carrying them on, and, as far as possible, books and teachers, for which they were expected to pay. In this way they were made altogether responsible for keeping up the schools.

So, when churches began to be organized, he felt that it would be no charity, but a positive injury, for the mission to assume the entire control, or become responsible for the expenses, any farther than was absolutely required by the necessities of the case. Native pastors, instead of missionaries, were placed over the churches; the people took part in their government; and they were encouraged to contribute according to their ability to the support of the pastors, and to other needful expenses in maintaining the institutions of the Gospel. Soon after the organization of the first church, Mr. Goodell says : —

" Recently their pastor was in straitened circumstances, and applied to us for relief. We told the church it was their duty to see that their pastor did not suffer, and we informed them of the donation parties in New England. They immediately took up the subject in a business-like style, and appointed committees to receive contributions for the relief of their pastor. One member of the female seminary was appointed to receive what the pupils were disposed to give; and, to our great surprise and gratitude, they brought forward of their own accord between three and four dollars. The next day I spoke to them on the privilege and duty of their doing something regularly to maintain the institutions of religion among themselves. I told them that after this year the pastor would not probably look to us for any part of his salary, but would look to his church and congregation for the whole, and that they must be ready to do their part. In the evening they all came running to me with money in their hands, — their first payment for this object. I afterwards told the deacons of the church that, if they would now undertake to support their own pastor, I was sure these poor girls could with their needles, even while members of the school, raise one-thirtieth, if not one-twentieth, of the funds necessary."

Having made a visit to the interior, where churches had been organized, he wrote : —

"In this visit we labored to impress on the minds of the churches the importance of supporting entirely their own pastors; and not only so, but of themselves contributing also to send the Gospel to those who were more destitute than themselves. We told them how the ladies in a certain town in Connecticut once built a meeting-house by raising onions; and we charged every husband who owned a garden to give his wife a corner of it, that she might at once begin to work in it for Christ. We told them of a town in Massachusetts, in which the good people in a time of great distress contrived to support their pastor by sharing with him whatever they had for themselves, one and another sending to him three candles, thirty nails, some beans, a few hops, two quarts of milk, cloth for a shirt, a broom, half a dozen pigeons, &c. We told them that, if there should be an increase of fifteen or twenty to their families 'by ordinary generation' during the year, they would be able to support them all without asking for the charities of their brethren; and could they not therefore support one whom God had now sent them?"

On the still more important branch of this subject, that of educating the people to an independence of foreign direction, by withdrawing that control as speedily as possible, he wrote to the Secretary of the Board, in reply to a communication on the subject:—

CONSTANTINOPLE, Oct. 7, 1848.

MY DEAR BROTHER,—I hope you may not find it necessary to curtail us in our expenses next year; but, should you have to do it, would it not be better to leave it to *us* to decide in what particular department of our labors this curtailment must be made, than for the committee to do it at such a distance? It is of course for them to name the sum, if in the providence of God a sum must be named; but ought it not, of course, to be expected that we should be more capable of knowing than they, where the reduction will appear likely to produce the least possible injury to the cause?

With the drift of your letter to the mission I was much pleased, and I hope you will follow it up with others, urging us not to keep native helpers in the background for the sake of rendering ourselves apparently indispensable to the work, nor to delay settling native pastors, lest we ourselves should be found to be no longer necessary. Even though in a given place and for a given time we ourselves should do better than a native pastor, still, there is no doubt but Christian economy requires that a native pastor be immediately settled; and that, instead of managing things in such a way as to stay there ourselves as long as we can, we should bring forward the pastor in such a way, and put things in such a train, that we may safely leave them in the shortest time possible, and go somewhere else. Instead of acting as though we were to be the pastors and have the control of these churches, we are to feel that our work is to prepare others to sustain the pastoral office, and assume all its responsibilities. There is danger, I think, of our not taking this view of the subject, and acting with sufficient distinctness in reference to it. At any rate, we all need being reminded of our duty, and being quickened in it.

As old as I am, I hope I should be willing, and not only willing, but ardently desirous, to leave my present situation as soon as my work here is done, and go where duty calls. And this, I doubt not, is the feeling of every brother of the whole mission. But still we may all, without special care, be too slow, and I think we *are* too slow, in shaping and driving our labors to such a consummation.

I hope to be able to write you next week of various events that are transpiring here, and of changes that are passing over us.

Yours most truly,

W. GOODELL.

The promised letter, which was written near the close of the month, relates principally to changes in the *personnel* of the mission. It is as follows: —

CONSTANTINOPLE, Oct. 25, 1848.

MY DEAR BROTHER, — A great change has come over us, one which deeply affects our families. Those of us who in the providence of God have been thrown together in Pera for so long a time, and who have passed together through so many thrilling scenes of joy and grief, who have so often been called to weep and pray together, and to observe the days both of fasting and thanksgiving, are now in the same good providence thrown apart. Our prayer-meetings, our singing-meetings, our maternal meetings, our family gatherings, our social interviews, and all other such pleasant and profitable seasons as we have enjoyed together these many years, are now interrupted. The special providence of God has separated us. His eye and His hand seem to be specially upon us in this change, for we ourselves made every effort to prevent it. Mr. Dwight's family has been forced, by reason of ill health, away to Malta; Messrs. Home and Schauffler's by fire to Bebek; and only Mr. Everett's and my own (the eldest and the youngest) are suffered to remain at Pera. Nor is there any apparent probability that we shall ever again be associated together in Pera, as we have been in times past. For,

A great change has come over the place. In consequence of the frequent and dreadful conflagrations (and we call no conflagration dreadful which does not burn over some ten, fifteen, twenty, or more acres of compactly built houses at a time), and in consequence of the rapidly increasing population, from the great influx of the rich and of the higher classes to this quarter, house-rent in Pera has become enormously dear, and there is a great scarcity of water. The reservoirs are altogether inadequate to supply water for such a multitude, and were never intended to do it.

"A great change, too, has taken place in our relations with the people. Formerly we could not meet them at their own houses without exposing them to the severest persecution, nor preach to them in a public manner, except in Pera and Galata; but those times are now happily passed away. All who wished to hear the Gospel preached had formerly to come to us at Pera, however great the distance, however bad the weather, however feeble their health, and however inconvenient it might be for them in other respects; but now they can have meetings in their own immediate neighborhoods, throughout all the city and suburbs.

"But still further. When that dreadful persecution commenced, near three years ago, it drove all the persecuted to Pera, and brought them near to us, and to each other. Here they had an opportunity of becoming more intimately acquainted both with ourselves and with each other, than would have been possible in other circumstances. Here they prayed and wept, and suffered and fasted, and rejoiced together; and it seemed a special Providence that compelled them, men, women, and children, to be not only ' of one accord,' but also ' in one place.' But in the providence of God they are all now separated; both from us and from each other they are scattered, and even more widely than before; but we hope that, like salt, it is for the preservation of many in their respective neighborhoods. It is now almost an impossible thing for them all to come together, even on sacramental occasions. The consequence is, that many are denied the privilege of hearing the Gospel preached statedly; that some of the poor widows are almost necessarily neglected in the ministration of the word and of charity; and that there is danger of mutual mistrust and clashing interests arising out of these circumstances. The providence of God seems to be forcing us all to the full impression that we must immediately have more churches and more pastors. One of these will, doubtless, be in Hass-Keuy, where more than twenty members of the church with their families already reside, and where there is a great waking up of a spirit of inquiry among their neighbors. Another will, of course, be in Constantinople proper. But I need not anticipate events before they are fully developed. Suffice it to say, that, instead of regretting these changes, we are the rather to rejoice in them, and to hope that we may soon have a dozen evangelical churches and pastors in this great city, even though the more they be multiplied the less our services shall be needed.

I am myself expecting to be soon laid aside; and I work as hard as I can every day, under the full impression that "the night cometh." To labor in this holy cause I feel to be a great privilege; and for the uncommonly long opportunity I have enjoyed, and the great forbearance and patience of my heavenly Father, I desire to be unfeignedly thankful.

Yours most truly,

W. GOODELL.

Fire and plague and persecution had surrounded the mission families at Constantinople from the beginning, and only from the latter were they personally exempt, while even in this they suffered more intensely by sympathy than in all the other calamities. The plague had now been stayed, but not the flames. On the 14th of October, Mr. Goodell writes: —

"Soon after midnight, on the morning of the 12th, we were again alarmed by the cry of "fire!" The wind was very high, and the fire raged terribly for four or five hours; but through God's great mercy the chapel and boarding-school were again preserved. This is the fifth great confla-gration we have had immediately around us, within about a year, — the fifth time it has been shouted in the camp of the enemy at Constantinople that the Protestant chapel was in ashes; the fifth time an unseen hand has been stretched out to arrest the raging element, and hold it back from devouring us. And now we have, almost literally, 'a wall of fire round about us for a defence;' that is, we are, humanly speaking, much more safe from conflagration than though these terrible devastations had not been made about us. 'The Lord liveth, and blessed be our Rock; and let the God of our salvation be exalted.'"

The following passage occurs in a familiar letter to one of his fellow-laborers: —

"I have just made a discovery. In reading the second chapter of Genesis, in Hebrew, I was struck with the fact that four different words are employed to express the work of bringing the world and mankind into existence. In the third verse, the two words employed are 'created and made.' In the seventh verse, the word employed in reference to the formation of man is one peculiar to a potter's business. The work, you know, is all done without tools. The potter takes a lump of clay, and presses it with his hands, pushing out a protuberance there, and making an indentation here, taking off a little in one place, and sticking on a patch in another, dipping his hands frequently in water, and thus working up the clay into the shape of something. But in the twenty-second verse, the word used is one that belongs to an archi-tect, who takes his fine-edged tools, — his plane and handsaw and gauge and chisel and adze, — and erects a splendid palace. Thus, from 'the rib, which the Lord God had taken from man, He *built up* a woman,' — the last, the best, the finishing stroke."

The commencement of the year 1849 was marked by another special outpouring of the Holy Spirit upon the female seminary. There was a great increase of spirituality and of prayer among those who had professed themselves Christians, and among others an increased attention to the

concerns of the soul.   Mr. Goodell makes mention of the
state of things under date of April 5 : —

"Two of the pupils had just begun to express a decided
hope that Christ was theirs, when the news of the revival at
Oroomiah reached us, and greatly deepened the religious
feeling already existing.   The pupils from day to day petitioned for a day of fasting and prayer ; but so intense was
the feeling already developed, that we did not dare appoint
such a day.   And, indeed, while the Bridegroom was with
us, why should we fast?   In less than a week all our
beloved pupils, excepting five of the youngest, were apparently brought out into light as bright as the brightest day.
' God is my Father, and I am happy,' said one poor orphan.
' Bring all the school together, that I may tell them what
God has done for me,' said another orphaned child, a sister
of the former.   'Yes, yes, I know I love my Saviour,' exclaimed, with great earnestness, one sweet girl, who has always been very careful not to express more than she really
felt.   'The world cannot give, and the world cannot take
away, my joy,' said another.   ' Prayer is so sweet, I do not
like to leave that spot for any other,' said a fifth.   ' I prayed
for this, but I hardly belived it would ever again be,' said
one and another of those who were converted in the former
revival.

"Oh, what a blessed change do we now see and feel!   The
mountains have melted like wax in the presence of the Lord.
Every one of the scholars is made still and thoughtful;
every voice is subdued and kind ; every countenance is sweet
and pleasant, and the whole aspect of the school is most
heavenly.   The chills of winter are past, and the beautiful
spring has come.   The nightingale has begun its sweet notes
in our gardens, and all the trees of the field are putting forth
their green leaves and their fragrant blossoms.   The voice
of the turtle is again heard in our land, and from the earliest
dawn till late at night the joyful sound of prayer and praise
continually salutes our ears.

"Six of our pupils were professors of religion before this,
— all but one fruits of the former revival ; and six others
have now, in the judgment of charity, been quickened and
made alive by the Holy Spirit of God.   Three of them were
here in the former revival ; and the two who are mentioned
above as having begun a week ago to feel more assured of their

acceptance, we ourselves have always seen some reason to hope were converted in that revival; but their own hopes, never at any time strong, were in general so feeble that they were never received into the church. But, at any rate, they are received now; the church-members, too, are revived; all are revived; and, in truth, I believe we may say, that *we are all subjects of the revival.*"

Near the beginning of this year Mr. Goodell was chosen pastor of the mission church (comprising the missionaries and their families), of which he makes the following record : —

"*February* 17, 1849. Our missionary church organization has been recently remodelled, and to-day I was chosen pastor, and Messrs. Schauffler and Everett, deacons. On account of my age and infirmities; on account of my already crushing responsibilities and labors, from which I greatly needed relief rather than to assume additional ones; on account of having been nearly twenty-seven years absent from America, having never exercised the pastoral office, and having entirely forgotten all I ever knew about it, and being wholly unfit, — I begged the brethren to excuse me; but they urged me so much to take it, at least for a while, that I finally consented. May the Lord smile upon us and help us and bless us, in these our new relations and duties!"

In the month of May, 1849, in company with Mr. Hamlin, Mr. Goodell visited Ada Bazar, to assist in the ordination of a pastor. In passing through Nicomedia, where he had been in 1832, the circumstances of his first visit were forcibly brought to mind, in contrast with those of the present. He saw now the fruits of the handful of seed he then scattered by the way, not by the way-side in the sense of the parable. It was here that a copy of "The Dairyman's Daughter," which he had translated into Armeno-Turkish, and which he gave to a stranger, had been blessed to the conversion of many souls, and led to the founding of the church. He writes : —

"We went by steam to Nicomedia, and reached there early enough to attend the lecture at six, P.M., preparatory to the communion. Baron Harûtun, the pastor, addressed

15*

the members of his church on the theme appropriate to the occasion.   He called upon the teacher of the school to offer the first prayer, and upon Harûtun, the former noted priest there, to offer the last.   The tunes sung were " Hebron " and " Illinois," and the music was well performed.

" The next day was the Sabbath, and a beautiful day. With great impatience I waited for the hour of morning prayer, and when it came, ' I was glad when they said unto me, let us go into the house of the Lord.'   Being four ministers of the New Testament, and having Baron Vertanes and Baron Harûtun also with us, we attracted some attention in the street.   One boy could not refrain from running behind a tree at a considerable distance and crying out, ' Protestant, Protestant.'   I turned and looked after him, not to curse him in the name of the Lord, but to pray that the poor fellow might himself soon become a partaker of the blessings of the everlasting covenant.   During the day we had one exposition of the Scriptures and two sermons, the Lord's Supper was administered, five persons were received into the church, and three children were baptized.

" The church now consists of more than forty members, nearly one-half of whom are females, and all appeared to be ' walking in the fear of the Lord and in the comfort of the Holy Ghost.'   They have a good school of thirty-five children, boys and girls, the teacher being from Bebek seminary, and a great helper to the pastor in his work.   The whole Protestant community there numbers about two hundred souls, men, women, and children, and some of them are men of more age, experience, and character than I expected to find.

" I was at Nicomedia with Commodore Porter seventeen years ago, and spent one night and part of a day there; but I did not become acquainted with a single individual, and had very little opportunity of saying any thing to any one on spiritual subjects.   I however left for the priest who showed us the church an Armeno-Turkish Testament, which I had recently prepared at Malta, and to our guide and others I gave a few tracts in the same language.   These, so far as appears, were read without profit by those who first received them ; but they passed into other hands, were read with deep attention, and under God were the means of awakening such a spirit of earnest inquiry after truth and salvation, as no persecution has been able to hold in check.   ' And thus,' I said to them in my remarks at the communion table at this time, 'the seed that was sown in much weakness has sprung up, and my own eyes are this day permitted to see the fruit. And instead of now going, as in my former visit, to see the ruined temples and palace of the Emperor Diocletian, I came into this beautiful garden of the Lord, to regale myself with the buds and blossoms and fruits of these trees of righteousness.' I told them I felt greatly encouraged by what I had seen, and was resolved hereafter, wherever I go, to 'sow beside all waters,' and I hoped my present visit to them would be attended with as great a blessing as the former, though there was no probability I should live seventeen years more to come and see the results.

"On Monday we went to Ada Bazar, nine hours from Nicomedia. The pastor of the church at Nicomedia could not leave his family, but eighteen or twenty of the brethren of that place accompanied us, some on foot and some on horses, one man on an ass, the rest in an ox-cart. The country through which we passed is beautiful, and were it not for the insecurity of property and life, it would be teeming with population and full of activity and happiness. The villages now are few and very miserable, and the roads in many places almost impassable; but let Christ come and set up His kingdom there, and how will all those fields rejoice; these hills be joyful together, even to their very summits; these streams that rush down from the mountains lift up their voice with singing; these dense forests be filled with gladness, and the very rocks and woods clap their hands for joy! When Christ comes, all blessings come with Him; and the journey which now requires nine hours of great discomfort and fatigue, will then be accomplished in one hour, with all comfort and without fatigue. 'Come, Lord Jesus, come quickly, and take possession of this whole country,' begins now to be the prayer of not a few."

After a very interesting account of their arrival and welcome at Ada Bazar, of the prosperous condition in which they found the infant church, of the struggles and persecutions through which the Protestants had passed, and of the ordination services which were attended by a great congregation of the people, he proceeds:—

"No wonder, then, that the rage of the enemy should be excessive, and that in the usual way of bribes they should instigate the governor of the city to acts of violence. In the evening, after the ordination, we learned that all our brethren from Nicomedia were thrown into prison, and that all their horses and most of ours were seized and taken away, and that even the cafégee, a Turk who took care of our horses, was beaten and his feet made fast in the stocks for daring to harbor even the animals of such thieves and robbers as ourselves. It was only after repeated remonstrances to the governor, and strong representations of the sad consequences to himself, of this course, that we and our friends were able to leave the place at ten o'clock the next morning."

Still another great conflagration occurred at Constantinople, in June, 1849 : —

"*July* 5, 1849. Another terrible fire at Pera, which, on the morning of the 26th ult., consumed about four hundred houses. It did not sweep over any part that was burned last year, but it took all below, towards Tatavala. We were roused from sleep a little after midnight, and found the fire much nearer to us than any of the last year's great conflagrations were at their commencement. As the wind, though providentially light, was in the right direction to bring it upon us, we immediately began to move our effects. First, however, I retired to my room, and committed to the Lord, or rather gave back to Him, our houses, chapel, school, and all, and then went to work for the Lord with great presence of mind. A little after four o'clock, Mr. Everett's family and my own had secured every thing belonging to us and to the school. Just at this time the fire was checked, and just at this time the wind arose and blew fresh and scattered upon us and around us coals of fire, in such a shower that our houses for a short time were in much danger. But we and our neighbors threw water abundantly, and extinguished the fire wherever it caught, and thus by the good hand of our God upon us we were preserved from the devouring element.

Our houses, however, were in such a state that we had no place where to kneel down for prayer, and both our families repaired to the chapel, and gave thanks to God that our holy place of worship, where so many spiritual blessings had been bestowed, was not 'burnt with fire,' and that 'all our pleasant things were not laid waste.' Some of those who rushed by us at the time of the fire were overheard to say, ' These houses never burn.' But when the great Head of the church shall no longer wish our school and chapel to be here, these houses will be found as combustible as any others."

The inquiry made in the following paragraph, in reference to an earthquake "passing through the place," though at first view having the appearance of a jest, is a strikingly accurate description of the impression sometimes made by this occurrence. It is contained in a letter to a missionary at Smyrna :—

" *Constantinople, April* 20, 1850. Two shocks of an earthquake were felt here last night. Do the earthquakes at Smyrna seem to be right under you, or do they seem to be only passing through the place? How small one feels to be thus taken up and shaken by the Almighty! 'The pillars of heaven tremble, and are astonished at His reproof!'"

A case which he records, April 25, 1850, illustrates at once his own aptness and ingenuity in presenting divine truth, and the spiritual obtuseness and ignorance of those who are brought up under the sensuous teachings of the Oriental churches :—

" A few days since I was visited by an Armenian of decent appearance, who appeared to be about thirty years of age. He had heard, he said, a great deal of our benevolent deeds; and, after pouring out more than the usual profusion of compliments, and going round about rather more than the usual number of miles in coming to the point, he finally declared the object of his visit to be, that I would send him to America, and. educate him at one of our very best colleges. I told him that it was out of my power to do any thing of the kind; and that, if I had the power, I should still not have the disposition; for that, as a general thing, it was much better for persons to be educated at home than abroad. At this he expressed the greatest disappointment, and said, America was such a blessed country, had prospered so many years without a king, and had such liberty and such privileges, that he must absolutely go there.

"But there is a better country than that, I replied. America, good as it is, after all is not perfect; various evils exist there; some of the people there are proud, and some are selfish; briers and thorns grow there; the weather is sometimes too hot or too cold, too wet or too dry; there is more or less of poverty; sickness is found there; and there is a graveyard near every town. But in that better country of which I speak not a single one of all these evils exists; not a brier is found there; the inhabitants are, all of them, just as kind and benevolent as you could possibly wish them to be; no one there suffers want; no one —

"But I want an education; are there any schools there?

"There is not an uneducated person there, for every one is furnished with the very best of teachers free of cost, and, of course, can hardly fail of becoming learned in every department of knowledge. I was going to say that there is not a single pauper there; but, on the contrary, every one is rich; that no one there ever lies down and says, 'I am sick,' but on the contrary, every one enjoys perfect health the whole year round; that though it has been long settled, no grave has ever yet been opened there, nor has any sign of death ever yet been seen there; and —

"But where is that country? Is it beyond? — no, it cannot be beyond America, for that is Tchin me Tchin (China).

"No, it is not *beyond* America, nor is it exactly that way. But I was going to say that every man there is really like a king, and lives in a great palace, and abounds with every comfort.

"But where is that country?

"Have you never read any thing of it?

"Never.

"Have you never heard of it?

"Never.

"If I tell you where it is, will you begin to make immediate preparation to go there?

"To be sure I will, but how much will it cost to get there?

"Probably not so much as to go to America. To go to America will require, on the least calculation, from eighty to one hundred dollars; but I have known persons go to this 'better country' for less than half that sum. Indeed, the ruler of the country is so desirous to have emigrants come from every part of the world, that he offers to pay their passage, to take upon himself the whole charge of their getting there, and of making most handsome provision for them after their arrival.

"But where is that country? Pray tell me.

"After giving him various descriptions of it, and finding he had no more spiritual understanding than the woman of Samaria, I at length told him it was the 'better country, even an heavenly.' But even this Scripture expression he did not apprehend, and I had to tell him in plainest language that it was heaven itself. He immediately clapped his hands to his head in utter astonishment, as though the eyes of his understanding had been opened for the first time. After a few moments I continued, Will you go there? I have come to this country for no other purpose than to turn the attention of men to that, and to encourage and help them on their way by every means in my power. Will you go there, and be eternally rich and happy?

"He was still silent; and after a pause I added, When you lie down to-night, remember you have had an invitation to go to that blessed country, and the offer of having all your expenses paid. When you awake in the morning, let your first thought be on this subject; and delay not to make up your mind, whether you will go or not.

"He sat and thought, with his head down, and said little; and when he left he was followed by a prayer, that this strange conversation might be the means of waking up a new and sanctifying train of thought in the man's mind. And let all to whom this story shall be told pray for the same thing."

November 19, 1850, he writes: —

"It is twenty-eight years this blessed day since I took to wife Abigail, the daughter of Lemuel the Holdenite, who has borne me four sons and five daughters, and who has been my loving and faithful companion in all my removings and sojournings in the East. Almost half of my own life, and more than half of hers, has been Oriental. Goodness and mercy have followed us in all our Eastern pilgrimage. And such is the low estate of our mission at present, that were it not for seeing and blessing our dear children in America, I should at once give up all idea of ever again seeing my native home, and should set my face directly and for ever towards that 'better country, even an heavenly.' Well, let us do it now. Wherever we are, whatever we do, let us not forget

that we are on our way to the promised land.   May all our
children go with us."

Of a children's celebration of the 4th of July he wrote:—

PERA, July 13, 1850.

MY DEAR BROTHER,— We did not observe the fourth of
July this year.   I just recollect, however, that the children
at Bebek observed the day, and that I, happening by chance
to pass that way, gave them a speech on the glorious prospects of America, telling them that if the United States
should increase in population for the next one hundred and
fifty years, as it has for the last fifty, there will then be more
people in the United States than there are now in the whole
world.   The children, however, seemed so much more interested in increasing the number of their squibs, than in the
increase of the population of America, that I was very brief.
Mr. H. then tried to read to them a part of a printed oration,
but with no better success.   I do not think one of them
remembers the shortest word in it, not even *is* or *of.*   There
is, however, this to be said, that, though rather noisy, they
all seemed perfectly sober, and all got home in season without any of them being intoxicated.   I remember but one
toast, and that was given by myself, and drunk by myself
alone to a full bumper of Adam's wine, viz. : —

" The day we celebrate."

The rest were so intent on *celebrating* the day, they could
not stop to *drink* it.   The greater part, however, joined in
singing, " My country, 'tis of thee," under that very able
Germano-American chorister, the Rev. Mr. Schauffler.

Your brother,

W. GOODELL.

In November, 1850, a charter was granted to the Protestants by "His Imperial Majesty, Sultan Abdul Medjid,"
completing and confirming their distinct organization as a
civil community, and securing to them equal religious rights
with the older Christian organizations.*   The firman of
1847, having been issued only under the ministerial authority
of the Porte, was liable to be withdrawn on a change of
ministry, or by imperial command; but the decree of 1850

* See Appendix.

came from the Sultan himself, and was of supreme and permanent authority. It secured perpetually to the Protestants the right of choosing their own head, of transacting business, of worship, of burial, free from all molestation, and promised to them protection by the imperial government against persecution.

On the issuing of this firman, Mr. Goodell wrote: "I have seen Sir Stratford, and at his request gathered together the nobles of the Protestant community, and sent them to him to go to the Porte and receive their Magna Charta as a distinct community. May they be a holy nation, a peculiar people, zealous of good works."

CHAPTER XIX.

IN the spring of 1851, Mr. Goodell revisited his native land, accompanied by Mrs. Goodell and two of his daughters. This was a pleasure which he had scarcely ever anticipated during the thirty years that he had spent in incessant and arduous labor in the East. It was not of his own motion, even then, that he came, but at the invitation of the Prudential Committee of the Board, to whom he wrote in reply : —

"The idea of visiting my native land has hardly so much as passed through my mind for many, many years. I doubt whether the patriarchs ever thought less of returning to 'that country from whence they came out' than I have of revisiting my native country, and now 'what I shall choose I wot not.' Should the Spirit take me by the locks of my hair and lift me up between the heavens and the earth, as He did the prophets, and offer to carry me wherever I might please to go, I should beg Him to decide the matter for me, or else set me down again. 'Where He appoints I'll go,' and what He appoints I'll try and do."

To his friend Judge Cooke he wrote somewhat more freely in regard to the reasons which induced him to accept the invitation : —

"Should I not go to my Father's house above, I may return to see once more the land of my fathers here below. Suffice it to say, the Prudential Committee have invited me to return and show my face to my friends and the churches. This invitation I am disposed to accept, though not so soon by a year as they proposed. I cannot well leave this year, but possibly I may be able to do it the next. In the mean time, pray that if I come, it may be both to receive and to impart a blessing. I feel that I need a new fitting up, both in body and spirit. I need to have a new varnish, both on my mind and manners. I need an entirely new set of teeth, for I have preached and sung away almost every one of the old ones. I need to catch the spirit of the latter half of the nineteenth century, for I brought away with me only that of the former half. And more than all do I need an unction from the Holy One. I have also three beloved children in that land whom I long to see, that I may 'impart to them some spiritual gift, to the end that they may be established.' Two others we shall bring with us to leave there, and three we shall leave behind with our friends, who require them as a pledge of our return. But who knows what shall be on the morrow. 'Only let your conversation be such as it becometh the Gospel of Christ, that whether I come and see you, or else be absent, I may hear of your affairs that ye stand fast in one spirit, with one mind, striving together for the faith of the Gospel.'"

Not until he had formally asked the advice of the brethren with whom he was associated in the mission at Constantinople, nor until he was assured that in their judgment it was his duty to accept the invitation of the Board, did he come to a decision. Their concurrence was most cordial, and he received from all a hearty God-speed, in the expectation of his speedy return. From many of the brethren connected with the other missions did he receive the same expressions of affection, of interest in his anticipated pleasure of seeing once more the home of his fathers, and of earnest desire for his safe return.

As he was leaving he received, among other parting notes, the following from his beloved friend and associate, Rev. Mr. Schauffler:—

BEBEK, May 9, 1851.

MY DEAR BROTHER,— I suppose everybody wants to drop you a last line before you go. But I have a special reason and apology, as I have taken no formal leave from you on your leaving here. And now this "good-by" makes me think of my first visit in your house in Buyuk-Dèrè in 1832, in July. The many years that lie between *then* and *now* have passed like a vapor; and what will the rest be?

I desire to sit down upon this stone by the wayside and look back, and look forward, and look *up!* " There *is* a land of pure delight, where saints immortal reign." When I bade Mrs. Goodell farewell, and as I was leading her down to the boat, I had so many things to say, that I said nothing. In such circumstances I am a very poor manager. I can hardly think about seeing you again here, so little does it seem to be worth while, considering the brevity of our remaining journey. However, if it please God so, I shall greatly rejoice. May He be with you and with us, and with all our children East and West, and establish his covenant with each one of them, unto eternal life and glory!

And now, good-by! My love to Mrs. Goodell, and a thousand good wishes for her health, her cheerfulness, and her spiritual comforts. My love to your children in America; and may the Lord Jesus cause His blessed countenance to shine upon their souls, and make them happy in His love and fellowship. My love to *you.* Pardon all my sins and follies which I committed while under your observation, and when you come to the land of your pious father and ancestors, remember sometimes the poor Jews, and

Your sincere friend and brother,

W. G. SCHAUFFLER.

Among the letters that he received on the eve of his departure was one from his friend Bishop Gobat, of Jerusalem, whom he had entertained many years before at his home while at Beyrout : —

JERUSALEM, Feb. 5, 1851.

MY VERY DEAR BROTHER IN THE LORD, — Your two letters of Nov. 20 and Dec. 19 have both safely reached this, nearly at the same time, and have, indeed, as you say, made my heart glad, not only on account of the remittances, which I see you understand are very welcome for the carrying on of divers works in this country, but, I assure you, it is always a source of joy to hear of you, and especially to receive your kind letters. The Lord bless you abundantly for your kindness. I should be very glad, before you proceed, as you intend, to America, to see you and your dear wife in Jerusalem, and I think you would find some change for the better in the disposition of the people of this country since you left it. But whether you come or not, I pray that God may bless you abundantly on your visit to America.

Since I saw you at Beyrout in 1827, I have never been so long in one country as I have now been in Jerusalem, now above four years. Many sweet and many bitter blessings have we received at the hand of the Lord in our wandering life, and all is intended for our good.

You will hear with much pleasure that thirteen families, with sixty-one souls, at Nazareth have just declared themselves Protestants, several of whom, I hope, are under the influence of the Spirit of grace. Here among the Jews we see just fruits enough to keep up our courage, but certainly I do not yet perceive any important change among the Jews at large. Oh that the Spirit of life might be breathed upon these dry bones!

Please remember us kindly to your dear wife.

Ever faithfully yours,

S. Angl. Hierosol.

He left Constantinople May 3, 1851, and reached Boston just in time to go to the dying bed of his life-long friend and fellow-laborer, Rev. Daniel Temple, and to preach his funeral sermon at Reading, Mass. The sermon, which was published in pamphlet, besides being a striking comment upon the text, "There remaineth therefore a rest to the people of God," was a warm-hearted tribute to the exalted character of one whose conversation had long been in heaven.

Soon after reaching this country, he made his way to his native town, which he had left nearly forty years before, and had seen only in vacations while a student. He arrived at Templeton late on a Saturday evening. The next day, on going into the pulpit and looking round upon the congregation, he could not recognize a single countenance, not even among the hoary heads. The church itself, an orthodox society, had been organized and built up since he had left the place. His first call was at the burying-ground, of which he said, " I thought I should find there more whom I knew than anywhere else." But even the graves of many of his friends were obliterated. He wrote at the time, " The changes everywhere are very great, 'one generation passeth away, and another generation cometh.' All the former elders of

the land, the deacons, the selectmen, the school committee-
men, the town-clerks, the lawyers, the representatives, — all,
all are gone! 'The world passeth away and the lust thereof,
but he that doeth the will of God abideth for ever.' Oh how
blessed are all those who are connected with that which is
eternal!"

He visited the home of his childhood in a distant part of
the town, where he had left his aged father when he went at
the call of God, as did Abraham, into a far distant country.
But that too was gone. The site only remained. Near by
he found living an aged aunt totally blind, of whom he
wrote: "She said that sometimes when she lies awake in the
night the whole room seems as bright as day, and she thinks
she sees every thing, but when she puts out her hand and
waves it, she finds she 'can see nothing but the love of God.'
Blessed eyes that can see that!"

As extensively as possible he visited his relatives, especially his brothers and sisters, who were scattered over the
country, from Massachusetts to Wisconsin, and many were
the sacred and joyful, and sometimes amusing, scenes that
occurred as he made himself known to them in his own
humorous way. In every case they failed at first to recognize the family likeness in the aged man who called at their
doors and asked in the name of a disciple for a shelter, or a
cup of cold water. He had kept the fire of love for his
kindred burning bright on the hearthstone of his heart, during the many years that had separated him from all to whom
he was bound by natural ties, and as he joined them in their
family circles, and bowed with them at their family altars,
he felt as if he had not been absent a day. The account
which he gave of a visit to a brother in the far West, when
they laughed and wept by turns, but all for joy, is too
domestic to be here transcribed, although strikingly expressive of his genial, loving character.

The two years that he spent in this country were devoted
almost exclusively to hard work in the same blessed cause

for which he had gone forth to the Eastern world so long before. He was constantly going from place to place, from one part of the country to another, preaching and advocating the cause of missions, on the Sabbath, during the week, and on all occasions. During these two years, lacking five days, he travelled about twenty-one thousand miles, visited eighteen States of the Union, and the District of Columbia; he occupied two hundred and thirty-five different pulpits, preaching or addressing more than four hundred congregations, speaking on an average about an hour each time, and addressing, in addition, the students of colleges and theological seminaries, Sabbath schools, select schools, &c., all over the country. As he was leaving for the scene of his labors in the East he wrote: "Instead of being worn down by this service, I feel all the fresher and the better for it. What thanks are due to Him 'who giveth power unto the faint,' and what thanks shall we render to Him for all that cordiality, that truly Christian hospitality, with which He inspired the ten thousands of His dear people to receive us."

Mrs. Goodell remained more quietly among friends, a part of the time at a sanitary retreat, recuperating her health and energies, and preparing for her remaining labors in the missionary field.

During his stay in this country he was often called to address public assemblies on important occasions; at the anniversaries of our benevolent societies, at missionary conventions, ordinations, and other like occasions; and his quaint, original, sententious style never failed to arrest attention, while his whole-hearted devotion to the cause of his Master, for which alone he seemed to live and plead, gave his words an entrance to the hearts of all who heard him. While in this country he received an application from one of the missionaries at Constantinople for some needed supplies, to which he replied: —

NEW YORK, Feb. 21, 1852.
DEAR SISTER IN CHRIST, — Yours of the 7th ult. has been received, and I immediately sent an extract from it,

marked No. 3, with other documents, to the ladies in Rochester, with the following note: —

"To Mrs. ELY, Mrs. BURKE, Mrs. CHAPIN, Mrs. MILLER, and
to the rest of their companions on both sides of the river
at Rochester, ' Peace, and at such a time.'

"BELOVED FRIENDS, — From Nos. 1, 2, and 3 of the accompanying documents you will see exactly what is wanted,
and you have the great honor and the distinguished privilege
of furnishing, without loss of time, the outfit required.   · And
now if ye will deal kindly and truly with my master, tell me;
and if not, tell me; that I may turn to the right hand or to
the left.'   In short, if you desire with all your hearts to provide for your and our beloved daughter, Miss L , the articles
mentioned in No. 3, then send them to Pemberton Square,
Boston.   But if it be inconvenient for you, on account of your
being just now deeply engaged in other benevolent enterprises,
then drop me a line without delay, as I know well where to
make the blessed offer next, ' in the name and for the sake of
our common Master.'

                "Yours most truly,
                                    "W. GOODELL."

So rest assured tablecloths, blankets, bedsteads, &c., will
all come.   There are a great many good folks in America.
     In the greatest haste and with the greatest love,
                                    W. GOODELL.

Before returning to his field of labor in Turkey, he prepared a volume, which was published on the eve of his
departure, entitled, "THE OLD AND THE NEW; or, The
Changes of Thirty Years in the East."   The opening chapter contained his impressions on revisiting his native land,
from which an extract is here made: —

"After an absence of near one-third of a century from
our native land, where we once enjoyed to a high degree the
friendship of the benevolent and the good, we have been
permitted to revisit it.   About one-half of my own existence,
and more than one-half of Mrs. Goodell's, had been spent in
the East; and, when first invited by the Prudential Committee to return, we did not think of accepting their kind
invitation.   We had been so long away, and such great
changes had in the mean time taken place, both in our own
habits and among our friends at home, that we felt we should
' know not the manner of the God of the land,' nor the lati-
tude and longitude of any of the customs of this new genera-

tion. But the more we considered the subject, the more we deemed it our duty to make this visit, especially on account of our beloved children, three of whom, having already been several years in this country, we greatly longed to see; two others being ready to follow, we could bring with us, while our three youngest could be left with dear friends at Constantinople, who kindly offered to take charge of them as pledges of our return.

"This visit has been a very refreshing one to our spirits. We have loved to look out upon the greenness, the freshness, and the verdure of your meadows and pastures, so different from those of the East, which, in summer, are withered and dried from the scorching heat of the sun, and the long absence of rain; and to think what a good land it is which the Lord God of your fathers has given unto you. We have loved to look upon your godly-minded farms, as they might almost be called, that is, farms cultivated with honesty, industry, and economy, and in many cases, too, 'sanctified by the word of God and prayer,' so unlike the dishonesty and indolence, the shiftlessness and oppression, with which all land in the East is ploughed and every field is reaped. And after having for so many years seen scarcely a face which was not more or less distorted by arrogance or cringing servility, by intolerance, bigotry, selfishness, or unjust suffering,— we have gazed with delight on the tens of thousands of happy countenances in this happy land, which are lighted up with such bright expressions of kindness, benevolence, and Christian hope.

" Here my best friends and kindred dwell.'

"And how could we feel otherwise than at home among them? Most of the fathers, indeed, and many also of their descendants, whom we used to know and love, are gone. But the blessed promise is fulfilled: 'One generation shall praise thy works to another, and shall declare thy mighty acts.' And another rich promise has been thankfully remembered and often repeated: 'Instead of thy fathers shall be thy children, whom thou mayest make princes in all the earth.' That is, the children were to be so much better than their fathers and mothers had been, that they might well be called princes and princesses. So have we found it in regard to some of the present generation; and our fervent prayer is, that it may be so in regard to them all. And being received by all

16

of them, not as strangers but as fellow-citizens and joint-heirs, we have felt that all things were indeed ours: these pleasant fields and beautiful gardens, with all their fragrant flowers, and the cattle upon a thousand hills, — we have enjoyed them all.

"In all our travels through this good land we have met with the most hearty welcome, and have had the very best accommodations. We have had no taxes to pay, and no trouble with domestics, nor have we been burdened with any care or responsibility; and yet, during all our sojourn here, we have been like the possessor of a great estate, having 'servants and maidens, men-singers and women-singers, musical instruments, and that of all sorts,' for our special entertainment. The Bible promises a hundred-fold to those who suffer any loss for the truth's sake; but this good Bible always does better than it promises; and we here publicly acknowledge, for the encouragement of all others, that we ourselves, however unworthy to suffer, or to speak of suffering, have already received ten times nearer a thousand-fold than a hundred.

"From the West we now turn our faces again towards the rising sun. And 'I suppose you like living there better than you do here,' many have said to us. No, indeed, we do not go there for the liking of the thing at all; for if we sought our own comfort or pleasure, we should most certainly remain in this good land. No romantic views of missionary life beckon us back; for we have had too long and too much experience in all the sober realities of this kind of life to feel the influence of any such romance. No glowing speeches from venerated fathers in the church now inspire us with enthusiasm to return to the scene of our former labors; for 'the fathers, where are they?' Their voices are silent in death, or faltering with age. No, it is only a strong sense of duty that urges us to return. The ties which bind us here now are far stronger than those we were called to sever thirty years ago; for we now have children here unsettled in life and without a home; and to leave them in these circumstances is to us a trial so great, that the separation from parents and brothers and sisters thirty years ago seems as nothing in comparison. Ourselves, and those so dear to our hearts, we commend to your prayers; and to your prayers do we commend that great, good work in which we have been so long engaged. We have, by the grace of God, been permitted to see much greater things accomplished than we had ever expected, even in our brightest days of hope and anticipation; and we are encouraged to go back and resume our labors in the East. We are, indeed, now advanced in life, and we cannot reasonably expect to do much more active service anywhere; but what little we may be able to do, we are better fitted to do in that country than in this. It is also more needed there than it is here, and the influence of it will, if the future be like the past, reach much farther there than it would be likely to reach here. And oh, may the Lord of Life Himself 'abide with us, for it is toward evening, and the day is far spent'!"

On the return voyage he wrote to his beloved preceptor, Dr. John Adams:—

BARQUE "SULTANA," Aug. 9, 1853.

To JOHN ADAMS, LL.D., Jacksonville, Ill.:

MY DEAR AND HONORED SIR,—After many years of absence from my native country, I was, in God's great and good providence, permitted to return to it. It was to me a very pleasant visit, and I am glad, and I hope grateful, that I was permitted to make it.

I had intended and expected to visit Jacksonville, and I regretted not being able to do so. I had thought much of seeing again the venerable instructor of my youth, to whom more than to any other individual do I feel my obligations for those maxims and precepts which contributed so much to form my character. When I entered Phillips Academy I was already a *professor* of religion, and perhaps I *possessed* a little of it; but earnest and spiritual religion, benevolence as an active, living principle, and sympathy with Christ in self-denying effort to save men, were but little understood in my native place. The hints, therefore, which you dropped from day to day, the views you expressed, the exhortations and appeals you made to our consciences, together with the deep religious feeling you manifested in every thing, were all new to me. They were indeed spirit and life to my soul, and they waked up within me new thoughts and purposes, the influence of which I feel to this day. A blessed place was that academy to me, as it has been, I doubt not, to many others. To have seen your face, therefore, once more in the flesh, and, bowing the knee with you in prayer, to have joined in those fervent supplications with which many of your former pupils were so much edified, would indeed have been very gratifying; but it was not permitted.

I am now on my return to my field of labor in the East, and we have already passed the Western Islands. This our second departure from our native land was much more trying to us than was our first, for we had now to tear ourselves away from five beloved children whom we left behind. May this painful separation be greatly blessed both to them and to us. To your prayers do we commend them, together with ourselves and our work. And may your own life be long preserved, that you may still for many years be a blessing to your friends! and that in the important sphere you now occupy you may be as useful to ten thousands of the children's children as in times past you have been to the children themselves.

It is not probable that we shall ever meet again *here;* but no matter, for we are almost *there.* Time seems short, and eternity near; and this is just as it should be. May we daily feel the powers of the world to come, and be as strongly attracted thither as we are swiftly carried thither on the wings of time!

Christian love to all your dear children, and best wishes for all their children.

Your affectionate pupil,

W. GOODELL.

To the Rev. Dr. Anderson, Secretary of the Board, he wrote from the ship, on reaching Malta: —

MALTA, Sept. 5, 1853.

MY DEAR BROTHER, — To the day of our second departure from our native land we had looked forward with much apprehension; and we had long prayed that all the circumstances of it, and especially of our separation from our beloved children, might be ordered in great mercy and kindness. And God, "who is rich in mercy," heard our prayers, and sustained and comforted both their hearts and ours far beyond what we had expected. May He grant also abounding grace, that this separation, though now so painful, may be greatly sanctified both to them and to us, and to all our other dear relatives and friends, and thus prove a much richer blessing to us all than our presence with them could have proved. And in the same great mercy and kindness may He order all the circumstances of our re-entrance into our field of labor in the East, of our continuance in it, and of our final departure from it, together with our removal from all these earthly scenes.

Renewedly would we now consecrate our unworthy selves, and the poor remnant of our days, to the blessed service of Christ; and had we a thousand to devote, we would not reserve one of them for mere self-gratification.

To be connected with His great kingdom is to be connected with that which is not only great and good, but everlasting, and "of the increase of which there will be no end." And to be connected with it in this very way of extending its humanizing, saving influences among whole races and communities of men who "heretofore were not a people," and "had not obtained mercy," though it be attended with many privations and hardships, and much self-denial, is yet a work which the sons and daughters of the church should esteem as a privilege exceedingly great and precious.

We have excellent accommodations on board the bark "Sultana." Captain Watson is one of the kindest of men. Our passage has been longer than we hoped it would be, forty-five days to Malta; but we have had for the most part such gentle breezes and so smooth a sea that I have enjoyed the voyage more than I ever did any preceding one. Mrs. Goodell has suffered a good deal, especially from the long confinement. Her health is, I think, improved from this visit to America, but it cannot reasonably be expected that she will ever fully recover from the shock her constitution has received. The only wonder is, that she has survived all that she has been called to pass through.

For the various stores we found on board, expressly for the use of the missionaries, but which we shared with the other passengers, we are, I presume, indebted to yourself and your associates; and for this and every other act of your and their kindness, — the interest manifested in our welfare from first to last, — both you and they will accept our sincere thanks. Stores of grace and patience you did not provide for us, nor could you do it; nor did we attempt to make any such provision for ourselves. We have been taught by past experience that all such stores, like the manna laid up by the unbelieving Israelites for the morrow, are perfectly worthless, and that it is infinitely better to get these things fresh from day to day, according to our necessities. And since we can have them at any moment, fresh from heaven, whatever grace we need and will accept, why should we be burdened with a great stock of that which cannot be kept from spoiling, and which can be used only at the very time it is obtained!

Our past experience has also taught us that we need take no responsibility upon us in regard to the regulation of the wind, but that we may safely leave the whole management of this to Him whose province it is, and whose power and wisdom and goodness are fully adequate. So here we are at Malta, after a passage of forty-five days; and our voyage was no less prosperous, and certainly much more pleasant, than if we had been quarrelling the whole way with the wind. How much trouble we all might save ourselves by not meddling with any thing beyond our province.

Your brother in the Lord,

W. GOODELL.

He returned to Turkey with a deep impression that he had but a short work before him, and that what he had to do for his Master must be done quickly. This, indeed, had been his abiding feeling during all the years that he had spent in the mission, owing to his life-long feebleness of body; but the feeling was intensified as he went back to resume his former work. To a friend, who expressed a desire to hear from him by letter more frequently, he wrote not long after his return:—

"All my friends in Turkey, and I suppose, too, in America, complain of my neglect in writing to them. But the fact is, all my strength and all my time are given to my missionary work, and every day I become so exhausted wi'h my labors that I am hardly able at the close to write even a short note. My habitual feeling is that my time is short; that I have returned here not to live long, but to die soon; and that if I would do any thing more for Christ and the souls of men, I have no time to lose. And this feeling, being, as it is, altogether suitablé and proper, I would rather cultivate than check."

The year after Mr. Goodell's return, the honorary degree of Doctor of Divinity was conferred upon him, both by Rutgers College, New Jersey, and Hamilton College, New York. Of the former the Hon. Theodore Frelinghuysen was at that time President, who was also President of the American Board, and thus had abundant occasion to know on whom the degree was conferred. It was announced at both institutions the same day, July 26, 1854. In acknowledgment of the honor, he wrote to the Secretary of the Board of Trustees of Hamilton College, expressing a very sensible view of a distinction which he had never sought or desired: —

"The honorary degree of Doctor of Divinity, which they were pleased to confer upon me, I would regard in the same light in which they intended it, viz., as a mark of honor. And, although it is an honor, to which in my own consciousness I have no claim, and which perhaps it would be better should not be bestowed at all in any case, yet to decline it would only be to bring myself into unnecessary notoriety, and to show a disrespect to those venerable men whom I ought and would wish to honor."

The conferring of this honor was the occasion of the following correspondence with the Rev. William G. Schauffler, who soon after was worthily advanced to the same degree: —

Reverendo Domino GULIELMO GOODELLO, *Doctori Venerandæ Theologiæ:*

Intellexi te esse provectum, idque bis, ad gradum Doctoris Theologici, de quo certior factus maximopere lætatus sum. Istius honoris homo te dignior apud nostrates atque in tota hac civitate, imò hoc imperio non invenitur, ut jam omnibus tuis constat amicis, præsertim mihi, tibi tuisque semper sincerrimè faventi. Hæc cum ita sint, festino te gratulari, ex animo, de laureis tuæ fronti pariter sapientia et humanitate adornatæ impositis. Bisque (nam id mihi semper in votis) non bis tantum, sed terque quaterque beatus, atque faveas, velim, tuo fratri sincero devotoque in fide et caritate,

GULIELMO TH. SCHAUFFLORO.

BEBECI, Die Septembris aõ, 1854.

HASS KEUY, Sept. 8, 1854.

Rev. W. G. SCHAUFFLER, Bebek:

Alas! my brother, I know not whether those two **Alma Maters** should receive your sympathy, or their poor foster-child your congratulations.   At any rate, "the children should first be filled."   Of one of those institutions I know only the worthy president, and of the other I know not even the name of a single executive officer.

"That the soul be without knowledge, is not good."   And these literary institutions, however they may be in *appearance*, yet in *fact* are not pure fountains of knowledge; for had they known half as much of my brethren at Constantinople as I know of them, they would not have thus "erred exceedingly," but would have bestowed their favors in a much more unexceptionable manner; unless, indeed, they acted on the very benevolent principle of "bestowing more abundant honor upon the part that most lacked."   Could this "more abundant honor" bring up the weaker one towards an equality with his brethren, it would, indeed, be something to be prized; but, alas! it would take more of this "abundant honor" than all the fountains of honor in our land could send forth to effect this.   And I assure you I value more the good opinion of my missionary brethren and sisters, and of their sons and daughters, than I do all "the degrees" which all the universities in both the Old World and the New could bestow.

Who does not know that the moon shines not by its own light, but by reflecting that of the sun?   And who does not know that, as a general thing, "he who walketh with wise men shall be wise" himself, or, at any rate, will have the *appearance* of being so?   It is not strange, then, that one who has been so long associated with his brethren here as I have been, so long revolving near these bright suns in the firmament of wisdom and knowledge, should at length begin to reflect some of their light.   The only wonder is that this lesser light should, through some defect in the telescope, have been so strangely confounded with the greater.

For your affectionate salutatory in Latin, accept my thanks. I dare not attempt a reply in the same learned tongue, for I do not see that I know a bit more of Latin, or even of theology, than I did before.   And I should be very sorry to do any thing which would bring dishonor upon the reverend heads of those whose honest intention, I doubt not, was to do honor to "your brother and companion in tribulation, and in the kingdom and patience of Jesus Christ,"

W. GOODELL.

CHAPTER XX.

ON his return to Constantinople, Dr. Goodell took up his residence at Hass Keuy, on the Golden Horn, where he had a pastoral supervision of the Female Seminary, then under the care of Miss West, and where he preached regularly on the Sabbath, preaching also at the capital. He resumed at the same time his revision of the Armeno-Turkish Bible, in regard to which he wrote to the Secretary of the American Bible Society : —

"To aid me in the work, I have a Greek, an Armenian, and a Mussulman ; and as those who might escape the sword of Hazael were to be slain by Jehu, and those who might escape the sword of Jehu were to be slain by Elisha, so I hope that whatever errors may escape the notice of any one of my helpers will be detected by another. But, to put God's blessed word into Turkish is a very difficult work, and I feel my incompetency more and more. The language is not a religious language ; it has never been deemed fit by the Turks to be used for the sacred purpose of religious worship, and of course no written prayers or devotional books are to be found in pure Turkish.

"To my Turkish teacher it sometimes seems quite shocking to express the everlasting truth of the Bible by the ordinary words for eating, drinking, walking, sleeping, wrestling, conquering, buying, selling, losing, saving, &c. ; while such terms as ' justification, adoption, and sanctification, with the several benefits, which do either accompany or flow from them,' are still more difficult to be disposed of in a manner which shall be intelligible, and yet not contemptible. I have suggested to him that if the Turks had long ago translated the Koran into Turkish, and had thus used the very language of the people in their religious worship, it would have been

16*   x

of great service to us in translating the Bible, as many words and phrases would then have been familiar and at home in religion, which now seem awfully strange and incongruous. This he admitted; but said that no such translation of the Koran would be or could be the Koran itself; that nobody would or could receive it as such; that it would have no authority, and *could* have none; and that all their prayers and worship and religious expressions must absolutely be in the ancient language, whether understood or not. I told him that in this respect they were exactly on a level with the Jews, Armenians, Greeks, Coptics, Maronites, Jacobites, Roman Catholics, and even the degraded heathen in India, all of whom had their Shasters and Liturgies in ancient and unknown tongues; that while in business transactions with one another they always made it a point to understand and be understood, in all transactions with their Maker they used words without meaning, and that, in fact, nobody but Protestants even so much as pretended to offer unto God a ' *reasonable* service,' — a worship intelligible to themselves.

"The British and Foreign Bible Society have spared no pains or expense in their efforts to procure a good translation of the Scriptures into Turkish for the Mussulman; they have revised, and re-revised, and they are ready to make any further effort which may be required. But my own opinion would be, that they should now wait, and make no further change till the present editions shall be nearly exhausted, or till there shall be a waking up of the Turkish mind to the truth. When there shall be a class of Turks who desire to know, and to have their neighbors and friends know, exactly and fully what God's revelation is, it will then be comparatively easy, with *their* help, to prepare a translation which shall meet their wants and wishes; for it would then be adapted, and *intended* to be adapted, to the common mind. Learned natives could then be employed in the work, who, like Luther, would be all alive to the subject, from their own personal interest in it, and who, being fully capable of appreciating the common mind, would have all the stores of the Turkish language at command, to be used freely for the benefit of such minds."

To the Society of Inquiry in Andover Theological Seminary he addressed a letter on the great want of laborers in the mission field, which exhibits his absorbing interest in the

cause and his earnest desire to secure re-enforcements to carry
on the work more vigorously:—

"During my late visit to the good land which the Lord
God hath given us to inherit, I travelled very extensively;
but though I was greatly importuned by many to remain
there, and though far stronger ties bound me there than those
I was called to sever thirty-three years ago, yet I bless God
that I was permitted to return here. Never during my whole
missionary life have I preached the Gospel with so much
pleasure as since my return. Doors are opened, or are
opening, in every direction. Gladly would I, were it possible,
be every day in a hundred different places at once; but I
can be in only one place, and that one I shall occupy but a
little longer. Who of you will come to take my place here,
and to occupy these other hundred places, which we cannot
occupy? Most gladly would I go back, and serve in another
third of a century's campaign, that I might see the good of
God's chosen, and rejoice with His inheritance in those
mighty changes and wonderful moral revolutions which are
fast coming on through the feeble instrumentality of His
servants.

"Were the Saviour Himself to stand up in the midst of
all our theological students, and, looking them all in the face,
should say, as one who had authority, 'Go YE into all the
world, and preach the Gospel to every creature,' I do verily
believe that comparatively few of them would have the least
idea of its being their duty to remain at home. They would
as naturally take it for granted that they should go to the
heathen, as they now generally, indeed almost universally,
take it for granted that they are not to go, but are to remain
at home. And should every student now at Andover declare
his resolution to be a missionary, and should he at the close
of his term of study carry this resolution into immediate
effect, it would probably be a greater blessing to Andover,
and a greater blessing to the churches of our land, and a
greater blessing to our whole country, than if you should all
live and labor at home for half a century, — and all this, to
say nothing of the blessed influence of your direct labors among
the heathen. What a spirit of prayer would naturally be
awakened throughout the whole length and breadth of our
land! What copious effusions of the Spirit might be expected to be poured out from on high! 'God, even our own

God, would bless us.' And even the very feeblest of our churches in the far West, who now think their very life depends on *receiving*, might find a world of meaning in 'the words of the Lord Jesus, how He said, *It is more blessed to* GIVE *than to receive.*'

" In conclusion, let me say, I have written unto you, young men, because ye are strong, and the word of God abideth in you, and ye have overcome the wicked one. Then '*be* strong, quit yourselves like men,' and ' do exploits.' "

The following paper on " Aggressive Movements " was written for the annual meeting of the mission. His observations upon the condition of the churches in this country at the time of his visit are eminently just, and his suggestions are not inappropriate at the present day, although we may believe that the church has become more decidedly aggressive in its spirit : —

" In my recent visit to America, I was struck with the fact that the work there was not, as it appeared to me, sufficiently aggressive. In all the older churches and congregations, it did not in general seem to be the expectation of the ministers to do any thing more than to keep things along, without going backward. The additions which were made to the church or congregation were just about sufficient to counterbalance the removals. The Gospel was not carried to men, and urged upon them, as it is in a new enterprise, in a new place, or where a new society is just formed ; but, if they wanted it, they must come after it. The minister was ready to meet them at the appointed time and place, and preach to all who were willing to come and hear; and having done this, he felt that he had discharged his duty.

" But there are in every such place a multitude who never come, and never think of coming, to hear ; and, unless the Gospel is absolutely carried to them, they will never hear it. If the pastor himself cannot do this, his church must be active in doing it, or they must employ a city missionary to do it. When a church is full, or about full, it can prosper no longer ; it must remain stationary, or it must retrograde, or else it must colonize. If the church sends out a colony, there may be two churches that are living, growing, flourishing, instead of one that is dying. Very many of the older congregations

I did not find so large as I left them, thirty years before; and their state was such as to produce the conviction in some few minds that Christianity had proved a failure, and that a new dispensation must be expected. Whereas it is not in God, nor in Christianity, that they are straitened, but in themselves, — their own slothfulness. Like the Israelites, they have not the courage, the heart, to go and take complete possession of the land; but they let the Amorites live among them, as though the sword of the Spirit, which is the word of God. were never again to be drawn, except where these Amorites are never seen.

"Now let the experience of the churches at home be a lesson to ourselves. The moment we cease to be aggressive, we cease to prosper, we stand still, we grow dull, we retrograde. But the pastor and his session, and, indeed, his whole church, should be full of life in carrying the Gospel to their neighbors and friends. The time has been when the missionary in these countries could do little more than sit in his own hired house, and receive those that came to him; not because he feared danger to himself, but danger to those whom he might visit. He could do nothing more or better than sit still, and be thankful that he could do even that. But, blessed be God! that time has passed away. And sad, indeed, will it be, if we now indulge in the habits we were then obliged to form. Then we had to lay hold of our zealous young brethren, and hold them back. Now we would urge and push them forward; or rather we would run ahead ourselves, and beckon them to follow after. Then we had to write a whole book of '*hints and cautions*,' now *earnest exhortations* may more properly be substituted.

"Many of our churches have for several years remained as to numbers about the same. The increase has been scarcely perceptible. Are, then, our efforts sufficiently aggressive? Is the missionary or native pastor doing more than half his work, if he only think of meeting and feeding his own flock at stated times? Why should he not break forth on the right hand and on the left, and teach and train up every member of his church to do the same? not, indeed, with rudeness, but by seeking and improving opportunities. It might not be a bad plan to have a weekly or monthly churchmeeting, and ascertain how many persons each member had visited during the week or month, how many persons each member had brought or tried to bring to meeting, to how many persons each member had offered the Gospel, — the pastor or missionary himself setting the example by first tell-ing what he himself had done.   *Go*, preach the Gospel; not *wait*, and preach it.   We are, perhaps, more in danger of neglecting our duty in this respect, than in any other.   No missionary, unless his connection with schools, the press, or translations forbid it, can possibly be excused from this.   It is not simply or mainly to receive the stragglers who come along that we are sent here ; but it is our duty to go out into the highways and hedges, into the streets and lanes of the city, and ask and entreat and compel men to come in. Let every one. then, whose peculiar work or state of health does not forbid it, be careful to do the work of an evangelist, and to make full proof of his ministry."

The letter which follows was addressed to " The Children of America," and was published at the time in the " Youth's Day-Spring : " —

CONSTANTINOPLE, April 29, 1854.

MY DEAR CHILDREN, — Seven Marys now lie almost side by side in the Pera Protestant burying-ground.   Of these, six are from our own families, and the other, a Protestant Armenian, was a member of our female boarding-school. The last of these was Mary Benjamin, whom I baptized at Smyrna on my way to America, and who was the last child upon whom I ever sprinkled the baptismal water.   She died this week, of scarlet fever, after an illness of less than two days ; and she died in the same house, and in the same room, where little Mary Everett died almost six years ago.

There are, I presume, more by the name of Mary on earth, and more by that name in heaven, than there are of any other name.   And it was a name which, we may suppose, our Saviour spoke oftener than He spoke any other name, for several of His best and most intimate friends were Marys. Mary, too, it would seem, was the first person He addressed, and the first name He pronounced, and hers was the first heart He comforted, after His resurrection.

Mary Benjamin was but three years old, but she was so original in all her conceptions and expressions, her thoughts and words and ways, as to raise the highest expectations of her friends, and to call forth a frequent repetition of the passage remarked upon at her baptism, " *What manner of child shall this be?"* She could sing some twenty or more tunes, sitting on her father's knee, and carry her part alone, while he sung another part. She spent much time every day in singing, amusing herself, when alone, in singing some of her beautiful hymns. One of her favorite hymns was, —

> "I think, when I read that sweet story of old,
> When Jesus was here among men," &c.

One of the very last hymns she ever heard, and the first verse of which she had already committed to memory, was, —

> "A home in heaven! what a joyful thought!"

And she went singing it round the house, in her pleasant home on earth, till within a few hours of the time when she went to sing in her Father's house above, —

> "A home in heaven! what a joyful" PLACE!

This little Mary was of a most affectionate disposition. She loved with great strength. It almost seemed as though she had more love than her little heart could possibly hold, for it ran over on all sides. And who can doubt that she has gone to that bright world above, that heaven of love, which she talked so much about, not only when awake, but even in her sleep; and that she now dwells with that great and good Father, whose face, even months ago, and when in perfect health, she longed even with *weeping* to see, and in whose holy presence, in order to be prepared to dwell, she was already "purifying herself even as He is pure," correcting her own faults, and "waxing strong in spirit" to do right. Strange to say, that, though of a very inquisitive turn of mind, asking most prying questions about things that came under her observation, yet she never asked where the body is put, when the spirit goes to heaven; and thus, in blissful ignorance about the fearful passage over Jordan, she crossed it unawares, and found herself at once in the promised land.

On the marble stone that lies over the remains of one of these lovely Marys (Mary Homes) is this inscription: *"And Jesus called a little child unto Him."* This is taken from Matthew xviii. 2, and we there learn that Jesus had a special reason for calling this little child to Him; He had a special use for the child. And do you not think that this dear child ran with alacrity at the call of the benevolent Jesus, and stood close to Him, and looked into His kind face, and waited to know His blessed will? Now, the Lord Jesus is calling a great many children to Him, and He needs them all; He has a special use for them all, either in His kingdom below, or in His kingdom above. Will you not, then, dear children, run at His call, whether it be on earth, or whether it be in heaven, that He wishes to employ you? Wherever it may be, it will be a most blessed service.

The "little child" mentioned by Matthew (I wonder whether her name was Mary) "Jesus called to him," in order to teach His own disciples humility. And I should not be at all surprised to hear that He had called quite a large number of you to Him, in order by you to teach the world His love. "As obedient children," are you ready to come to Constantinople at His bidding, or to go into any other part of the world, in order to give to perishing men practical lessons of humility, faith, and love? Be sure and first learn well these lessons yourselves. One lovely youth, whose pleasant countenance I shall not soon forget, came to me in America, and to my first salutation, " Will you be a missionary?" the answer was most promptly given, "I will, if you will tell me *how*." Now, my dear children, if you are willing that the good Spirit of God should tell you how, you will learn very quick, and there will be no longer any lack of missionaries.

But why does Jesus call so many little children to Him in heaven? Because He has so much use for little children in heaven. Sometimes, indeed, His calling away of a single little child is made the greatest possible blessing to the parents, to the brothers and sisters, or to others, who survive here on earth; but to what unspeakably great, delightful, and blessed services He must have called them above, though we know not now, yet we shall know hereafter. If, then, any ask the reason why so many are called away in very early life, " Say ye, The Lord hath need of them." This is answer sufficient.

But will you remember in your prayers these sorrowing parents, with their weeping children, and pray that they, and all our families, may be profited by Jesus calling so suddenly to Himself this precious little Mary Benjamin?

"A child in heaven! what a glorious thought!"

From your aged friend,

W. GOODELL.

To the Rev. George W. Wood, D.D., of New York, formerly his associate in the mission at Constantinople, who had returned to this country, and was now acting as one of the Secretaries of the American Board, he wrote in regard to the prospects of the work at the Turkish capital:—

CONSTANTINOPLE, Sept. 27, 1854.

MY DEAR BROTHER,—This week the Sublime Porte summoned all the patriarchs and high dignitaries of church and State, and enjoined it upon them that they should not oppress their respective flocks, nor take a bribe to blind their eyes therewith. Who ever heard that Nero had any occasion to call up St. Paul and St. Peter for a similar purpose?

And is it to be supposed that the high-priest of the Jews, and the all-holy patriarchs of the Greek, Armenian, and papal churches, will tell one lie or take one bribe the less in consequence of this high command from the Grand Turk himself? Not at all. They will merely do the thing in another way, and not in so barefaced a manner.

And does any one imagine that these venerable men, who arrogate to themselves the title of All-holy, felt it to be a mortifying thing for them to be admonished in this way? Not in the least. It would not suggest the idea of shame; nor would it abate one iota from the high opinion they entertained of their own worthiness to sit in Moses' seat, or to be the only successors of St. Paul.

It is, indeed, very affecting to think that in these times of public calamity and suffering, occasioned by war, cholera, and famine, there is among all these various communities no such thing, even in appearance, as humbling themselves before God, turning from their abominations, or seeking after truth and salvation; but every one goeth on still in his trespasses, "neither repent they of their murders, nor of their sorceries, nor of their fornication, nor of their thefts." And let Pilate, Herod, Barabbas, no matter who, reign over them, what care they, provided they have full opportunity to deceive and oppress one another? But "away with this man!" we will not have Christ to reign over us; no, let His kingdom of truth and goodness be put far away from us, seems to be the unanimous vote of the country. And thus what was sufficiently evident years ago, is every day becoming more and more conclusively so, viz., that these communities, as such, will never be reformed, and that "their end is destruction." They seem, like the Jews before the entire extinction of their civil and ecclesiastical polity, to be given up to utter infatuation. But, blessed be God, there is now, as there was then, a new spiritual kingdom set up, which is daily extending, increasing, and gaining in influence, numbers, and strength.

Your brother,

W. GOODELL.

In the earlier pages of these Memoirs it is stated that, on leaving the seminary at Andover, in 1820, Mr. Goodell made, on behalf of the Board, a visit to the missions among the Cherokee Indians. Not only had he cherished the remembrance of that visit, through his many years of toil in a far distant and very different land, but it was remembered with deep interest among the Indians. He received more than one letter from the daughters of the tribe, containing donations for his work in Turkey. To one of these he sent the following reply : —

CONSTANTINOPLE, June 6, 1855.

MY DEAR CHEROKEE DAUGHTERS, — Many thanks for your letter, and for the beautiful " Cherokee Rose Buds." More than thirty-three years ago I was in your nation, at Brainerd and Creek Path, where I saw your sweet sister, Catharine Brown.* She had just given all the love and confidence of her heart to the precious Saviour ; and, as she had now no further use for her ear-rings, — very large they were, — she gave them to me, to dispose of for His dear sake. These I sold for $16.50, and paid over the amount to the Treasurer of the A. B. C. F. M., to send the bread of life to the perishing in Palestine, as she had desired me. She also gave me in addition three dollars for the same object.

This little rill from Creek Path was one of the tributaries to the great stream of benevolence which has since carried so much fertility, gladness, and salvation to every part of the

* The interesting story of the Christian life and triumphant death of this Indian girl has been preserved in a volume prepared by the Rev. Dr. Anderson, Secretary of the Board.

Turkish empire. And now there comes another rill from "near Tahlequah," springing out from amidst the "noble trees" that "lift their lofty tops proudly to the blue sky," in full view of that beautiful " range of green hills, rising one above another, the most noted of which is Park Hill."

Well, my dear Cherokee children, this little rill I did not suffer to blend with the other streams that flow to us from the far West; but I turned it off by itself to Nicomedia, where one of my Armenian daughters is cultivating a beautiful garden of choice flowers, that are never to fade. Acabe, for that is her name, has eyes as black and as bright as any of my Cherokee daughters can boast. She was educated at our female boarding-school in Constantinople, and afterward married and removed sixty miles to Nicomedia, where she at once opened a school for girls, which she has taught ever since.

But this little rill of yours, so refreshing and so pure, does not spend itself at Nicomedia; for the good Acabe has another garden, which she is cultivating with great care, and where she has already planted " the rose of Sharon and the lily of the valley." At Bagtche-juk, directly across the gulf from Nicomedia, is a large Armenian village, in which there is no native pastor and no native helper, and which we ourselves can very seldom visit for want of time. Here the people are wonderfully waking up to a new and spiritual life. And over here Acabe goes every vacation, and spends her whole time in visiting from house to house, and conversing, praying, and singing with the women and children. Her labors there are appreciated by the people, and we deem them highly important. But she is poor, and some means have always to be provided to defray the necessary expenses of her mission. What you have contributed is just about sufficient to cover these expenses.

And now, my daughters, read in the sixteenth chapter of Romans about " Phebe our sister;" about " Priscilla," so active and s good; about " Mary," together with " Tryphena and Tryphosa," so honorably mentioned by Paul; and about " the beloved Persis, who labored much in the Lord," — and consider Acabe your sister as worthy to be reckoned among them, leaving her home every vacation, and giving all her time to the work of the Lord at Bagtche-juk. She is also worthy to be called your sister; for she is as timid and silent, as modest and retiring, as any good Cherokee girl.

The meaning of Bagtche-juk is Little Garden. And re-joice, dear children, that this Little Garden is now watered by the stream that flows directly from " near Tahlequah," in the far West. And not only has this beautiful stream come from the far West, but — did you know it? — Miss West herself has come to help us, and is now the beloved teacher of the daughters of the East at Constantinople. She and all her pupils send their very affectionate salutations to you. Among her pupils are the Misses Queen, Miss Cleanliness, from Broosa, and Miss Eve, not Adam's wife, but one of his great-grand-daughters. They desire me to tell you that they were exceedingly interested in reading your paper, particularly with the account of " an Osage wedding," from the lively pen of Miss " Ka-ya-Kun-stah; " and the Misses " I Can't " — for I am sorry to say there are some of this name in our school as well as in yours — were greatly affected with " the Algebra Sum Soliloquy," and with the marked difference between their character and the character of Miss " Perse-verance." They wish you to inform them in your next what is the bill of fare in your seminary, whether you have many rules, whether you keep them all, and which ones you are most apt to break. And will Miss " Ka-ya-Kun-stah," — I wonder what it means — give us a description of a *Cherokee* wedding?

Remember us to your kind teachers, " Misses Avery and Raymond, from New England, and Miss Jane Ross, a Chero-kee." Remember us also to the fair " Editresses, Miss Cath-arine Gunter and Miss Nancy E. Hicks." In their devotion to " the good, the beautiful, and the true," we wish them all the patronage and success they so justly deserve. An affection-ate remembrance also to Dr. Butler, whom I knew at Brainerd, and who, if he has not been " in prisons oft," has been in a prison long, — " a prisoner of Jesus Christ for you " Cherokees.

In your next, please subscribe your own names, and tell me also the names of all your schoolmates, for I like to know all my children.

The Lord bless you and your school and your teachers, with your parents and your whole nation! May we all be saved from our sinful, ruined state, and meet at last in a world of purity and love, through Jesus Christ our Lord! Thus prays

Your aged friend,

W. Goodell.

The letter which follows, breathing the truly catholic spirit of the writer, was addressed to the First Baptist Church of Providence, R. I., in acknowledgment of a donation to constitute Dr. and Mrs. Goodell honorary members of the American Baptist Missionary Union. The pastor referred to was the Rev. James N. Granger, D.D., from whom they had received a visit at Constantinople, as he was returning from a tour among the Baptist missions in the East: —

CONSTANTINOPLE, Sept. 3, 1855.

DEAR BRETHREN AND SISTERS IN CHRIST, — Of the pleasant and profitable visit made us by your pastor on his return from India we often speak, and still oftener think. And that example of true Christian liberality you have recently furnished us has brought him and his visit again before us with great distinctness. It is gratifying to us in no ordinary degree to be thus constituted honorary members of your great and good and growing missionary society, so remarkably owned and blessed by the great Head of the church. Of some of your missionaries and their wives, of your Judsons and Boardmans and others, I have known so much, that, although I was not personally acquainted with them, they always seemed like my own dear brethren and sisters. And, indeed, they belonged not exclusively to your own branch of the Christian church, but rather to the whole general assembly and church of the first-born, in heaven and on earth. Some forty-three years ago I heard Dr. Judson preach one evening at the school-house in Andover from Isaiah l. 11, "Behold all ye that kindle a fire," &c. Of his earnest and serious manner I have a very distinct recollection. His discourse was most solemn and impressive, and a blessing followed it. — one individual, if not two, being hopefully converted by it I was also present at Salem, when he and his associates were ordained and set apart, amidst prayers and tears, to the sacred work of preaching Christ to the heathen.

May the Spirit be poured out abundantly upon all your missions, and upon ours, and upon all the churches of Christ at home! Why should we rest satisfied with drops, when we may have showers, yea, *floods!* For, saith Jehovah, " I will pour water upon him that is thirsty, and *floods* upon the dry ground." The ground is everywhere dry enough for floods.

Let us, then. greatly enlarge our desires and our expectations, in praying both for ourselves and for one another.   When we ask great blessings for ourselves, we need not feel that we are depriving anybody else ; and however great blessings we may ask for others, we need not fear that we shall receive in any degree the less ourselves.   Our Father is very rich, and nothing delights Him more than that we give Him an opportunity of imparting liberally to all the needy.   Nor does giving impoverish Him.   However many, and however rich blessings He may bestow upon one, He has none the less to bestow upon all others.   Let us, then, be encouraged to ask not for little, but for much ; not only for the churches at home, but for those planted in heathen lands ; and not only for those missions supported by our own society, but for those supported by other Christian societies.   So long as we are not straitened in God, why should we be in our own selves?

Additions have recently been made to all our three churches in Constantinople, and our female boarding-school has been again visited by the grace and spirit of God.   But in these times of war and desolation, of great overturnings and changes, we need divine influence of a most distinct and impressive, as well as extensive, character.   And to your prayers do we commend ourselves, and all these mingled, perishing people around us.

We have been spared to see great and wonderful changes, since Mrs. Goodell and myself came to this Eastern world, a third of a century ago.   But those who come after us will see still greater ; and herein do we rejoice ; yea, and we hope, by the mercy of our Lord Jesus Christ, to rejoice for ever, being sinners saved by grace alone.

Affectionate and Christian salutations to each and every member of the church, especially to those with whom we have the happiness to be acquainted, including your worthy and beloved pastor.   The Lord bless, comfort, strengthen, and establish you for ever.   Thus prays

Your unworthy brother in Christ,

W. GOODELL.

CHAPTER XXI.

A THREATENING cloud gathered over the missions in Turkey in the year 1853, and was the occasion of much anxiety to the friends of the cause throughout the world. For several years all things had been going on quietly and prosperously. The Protestant Christians had been made secure in the enjoyment of their privileges; the hand of persecution had been stayed, and the evangelical churches had rest; the missionaries themselves were prosecuting their work without molestation or interference. But a new cause of apprehension sprang up, and no human eye could foresee what would be the result. There were some who did not regard it with so much fear, who even hoped that out of it would come immediate benefit to the cause of missions; but for the most part the missionaries looked upon it with dark forebodings. This was the war with Russia, known as the Crimean War.

The immediate and ostensible cause of the war was the ancient dispute in regard to the Holy Places and the respective rights of the Greek and Latin churches; but the real cause was to be found in the ambitious designs of the Russian government upon Turkish territory. The acquisition of Constantinople, the dismemberment of the Ottoman empire, and its partition between different powers, if not its entire absorption by Russia, had unquestionably been the aim of the Czars. At the very outset Russia claimed the right of establishing a protectorate over the millions in the Turkish empire, who were in connection with the Greek Church, and proceeded to exercise it in the Principalities.

The Russian army, in July, 1853, took possession of the Danubian Provinces, and thus commenced hostilities, the Ottoman Porte making a formal declaration of war on the 1st of October.

Early in the following year the missionaries at Constantinople set apart a day for fasting and prayer with reference to this matter, and the day was observed with deep solemnity not only by those immediately connected with the mission, but by the friends of the cause from different countries, who were resident or sojourning at the capital. Special prayer was offered in behalf of Lord Stratford de Redcliffe (formerly Sir Stratford Canning), the British ambassador, that he might be endued with the spirit of wisdom in conducting his important negotiations, and that, in counselling the Sultan, he too might have counsel given to him from above. Never before had the position of this representative of the British government and devoted friend of the cause of Christ been so responsible, and never before did he hold such influential relations to the Porte.

In 1854, when the governments of England, France, and Sardinia made common cause with the Ottoman government for the sake of putting a check on the ambition of Russia, and sent their armies to Turkey and the Crimea, apprehensions of the disastrous effect of the war upon the missionary work were not dissipated, but rather increased. As these large armies came pouring into the capital, and its suburbs became as it were one great camp, it was natural to fear that such a state of things would seriously interfere with the work. But in the midst of war God spread a shield over His servants. At no previous period had they prosecuted their labors in greater quietness and peace, or with clearer evidence of the divine presence and blessing.

The war was still further overruled for the furtherance of the Gospel by becoming the occasion, if not the actual means, of securing another important concession from the Turkish government on the subject of religious liberty, a new Magna

Charta for the Christian subjects of the Porte. This is known as the *Hatti Sherif* (Sacred Edict), or *Hatti Humayoun* (Imperial Edict) of 1856,* and was issued on the authority of the Sultan himself. It was generally regarded at the time as a complete guarantee of religious liberty to all the subjects of the Ottoman Porte, of whatever creed, and an assurance that no Mohammedan who chose to become a Christian should suffer on that account. But it has always been questionable whether the Turkish government, whose dealings are so often marked by duplicity, the prevailing sin of Orientals, really intended that it should have such an unlimited significance. Events of more recent occurrence give greater strength to such doubts, if they do not prove that the Porte intended only to make more secure the rights and privileges of those who were nominal Christians before.

The *Hatti Humayoun* was recognized by the contracting Powers, Great Britain, France, Austria, Russia, Sardinia, and Turkey, whose representatives met to form the treaty of Paris the same year; and in the records of this congress it is distinctly stated that it was communicated by "His Imperial Majesty the Sultan," as "emanating spontaneously from his own will;" but a clause in this treaty states: "It is clearly understood that it cannot, in any case, give the said Powers the right to interfere, either collectively or separately, in the relations of his Majesty the Sultan, with his subjects, nor in the internal administration of his empire." This was leaving the Turkish government to put its own construction upon the document, and to administer its own domestic affairs in its own way.

The *Hatti Humayoun* was regarded by the mission, and by the friends of evangelical Christianity at the capital generally, as a real charter of religious freedom to all the subjects of the Sublime Porte, not excepting the Mohammedans. This is evident from their action at the time. On the 5th of March, 1856 (the edict was issued in February),

* For the full text of the Hatti Humayoun, see the Appendix.

17   Y

eleven missionaries of the American Board, together with four other missionary laborers and two British chaplains united in presenting to Lord Stratford de Redcliffe, through whose special agency the charter had been obtained, an address, acknowledging in the warmest terms the important service he had rendered to the cause of humanity and of Christianity in Turkey. The following are the opening sentences of this address: —

"The undersigned, Protestant missionaries, belonging to various Christian churches and societies of Great Britain and America, consider it their duty at the present important and auspicious period of this empire, signalized by the publication of the Imperial Hatti Sherif of the reigning Sultan, to give utterance to their feelings of gratitude to God, the giver of every good gift; to express to your lordship their entire satisfaction with the extent and the spirit of that document relative to religious freedom and the rights of conscience; and to congratulate you on the honor providentially and deservedly conferred upon your lordship of having become instrumental in accomplishing so great and so good a work for the millions of Turkey. While we would gratefully recognize the valuable services rendered by the representatives of several other countries to forward this praiseworthy end, we cannot but realize that the accomplishment of this work is pre-eminently due, under God, to the influence of the representative of Great Britain.

"From the beginning of the disastrous war, still pending between the great Western Powers and Turkey on one side, and Russia on the other, we have looked upon each passing event with painful and prayerful interest. We have prayed for the maintenance and triumph of right, and for the speedy return of peace, — a peace re-establishing justice among neighboring nations, and promoting truth and righteousness, and the temporal and spiritual prosperity of the various classes of society, and the different nationalities resident in the Turkish empire. We have always believed that such would be the result; and this has been our comfort amid the scenes of horror which surrounded us.

"Nor has our hope been disappointed. The Imperial Hatti Sherif, lately published, has convinced us that our fond expectations are likely to be realized. Turkey, snatched from the border of imminent destruction, will see a better day. The light will shine upon those who have long sat in darkness; and, blest by social prosperity and religious freedom, the millions of Turkey will, we trust, be seen ere long sitting peacefully under their own vine and fig-tree."

On the 1st of July, 1856, the First Protestant Church of Constantinople held its tenth anniversary; and a joyful day it was, in striking contrast with that on which the church was organized. The people were then just coming out from the hiding-places into which they had been driven by persecution; some had but just returned from exile; others were taken out of prisons and delivered from torture; they all came out of great tribulation to stand up before God, and enter into covenant with Him. Forty persons, three only of whom were females, subscribed with their own hands unto the Lord. Faith alone supplied the hope that this feeble band would become a great people.

But now, on this tenth anniversary, they recorded the names of thirty native Protestant churches that had been organized. The three churches at the capital, Constantinople, Pera, and Hass Keuy united in celebrating the day in the same place in which the first church was formed. Addresses were made by the native pastors and the missionaries. They joined in prayer and praise, and united in commemorating the dying love of the Redeemer in the ordinance of the Supper. To those who had seen the foundation-stones of this living temple laid, the day was one of great joy, and full of promise for coming decades.

Dec. 27, 1856, he writes in his journal: —

"About two months ago the Bishop of Hass Keuy commenced a Turkish service in the Armenian church here, precisely at the hour of my service. As the Armenians at the capital understand Armenian much better than Turkish, it is difficult to see what the object could be, except to prevent people from coming to our chapel. It was said that he preached evangelically; and that on one Sabbath he preached not only at the same hour, but from the same text I did, and, moreover, divided his subject precisely in the same way. As I preached the same sermon in another chapel on the previous Sabbath, it is supposed he must have had a reporter there to take notes; for my treatment of the subject was not such as an Armenian bishop would naturally fall upon. But however this may be, ' Christ is preached, and I therein do rejoice, yea and will rejoice.'   The text on this occasion was, ' The Master is come, and calleth for thee.' "

In March, 1857, Dr. Goodell drew up and forwarded to the Board an elaborate paper on " The Importance of Constantinople as a Missionary Field," as compared with some other fields on which a large amount of labor and money had been expended.   Only the heads of this paper can here be given : —

1. Constantinople is a great world in itself.   It contains, including its suburbs, more inhabitants than the whole Commonwealth of Massachusetts, and ten times as many as all the Sandwich Islands.   2. All the nationalities of the empire are represented at the capital.   Every sect and almost every clan in the empire has here its civil and ecclesiastical head; its court, to which all appeals are made, and where all its business of any importance is transacted.   3. All the pashas and acting bishops, or vartabeds, in every part of the empire, go out from Constantinople.   4. Constantinople is the great centre of Eastern and Western Turkey.   It stands on the margin where European civilization terminates, and where Asiatic barbarism commences.   5. There are at Constantinople not less than fifty thousand foreigners, from England, France, Germany, Italy, and, indeed, all parts of Europe; and the greater part of them are never reached by any evangelical influence.

These several points he enforced with strong argument, and in answering the objection to the thorough occupation of this stronghold on account of the expense, he wrote : —

" What if it does cost more to maintain a mission here than anywhere else?   So it cost the allied armies at Sevastopol an amazing amount of money and life to take the place; but who ever thought of raising the siege on that account? Constantinople is much the same to us that Sevastopol was to the allied armies. To get possession of Sevastopol was to possess at once more than the whole Crimea; and to possess Constantinople is to disarm at once every hostile organization throughout the whole empire."

The importance of these suggestions has not passed away, and never will, until the great stronghold of Mohammedan power and influence is brought under the power of the Gospel.

During the long residence of Lord Stratford de Redcliffe at the Turkish capital, as British ambassador, Dr. Goodell had enjoyed his intimate friendship and confidence; and on the occasion of his departure to England, at the close of his period of important service, an event which was deeply deplored by every Christian missionary in Turkey, Dr. Goodell addressed to him the following letter, expressive of his own personal regret and regard: —

CONSTANTINOPLE, July 1, 1858.

MY LORD, — I cannot let this opportunity pass without assuring your Lordship of the deep regret we all feel at the little prospect we have of seeing you again at Constantinople. But certainly we should be very ungrateful not to acknowledge the wise providence that brought you to this land, and that kept you here for so many years; and this, too, at a time when, in the changes called for, your influence was mighty, and mighty for good. In these changes your name stands connected with all that is worthy to rise and prosper, with all that is stable and enduring. Connected as it is with the great cause of civil and religious liberty, it stands connected with that which shall never pass away, for it is as eternal as the immutable purpose of Infinite Goodness can make it. And when this cause shall triumph in Turkey (and triumph it shall), and the future history of the country shall be written, the influence and important agency of your Lordship will not fail of a public recognition and a due acknowledgment. May all our unworthy names be found at last written in the Lamb's Book of Life! And may we all be eternally connected with that kingdom of truth and goodness, " of the increase of which there shall be no end"!

Mrs. Goodell unites with me in very kind regards to Lady Redcliffe and to your daughters. May the divine blessing, in all richness, attend both you and them.

I have the honor to be, &c.

To the corresponding secretary of a missionary society at Phillips Academy he wrote: —

CONSTANTINOPLE, Dec. 9, 1858.

MY DEAR FRIEND, — My daily walks lead me through a large Jewish cemetery, containing, I should judge, not less than a hundred acres of graves. Slabs of white marble cover the whole ground. From the days of Ferdinand and Isabella, when the Jews were expelled from Catholic Spain and found a refuge at the capital of the bigoted Moslem, this great field has been for the most part their place of interment. Here lie buried hundreds of thousands of that rejected race who, while they lived, spat at the name of Jesus, and died with curses on their lips. They generally lie with their feet towards Jerusalem, that, when they rise from their graves, their faces may be towards the holy city.

Some seventy or eighty thousand Spanish Jews, the descendants of those who lived in the days of Columbus, still reside in Constantinople and its suburbs; and among them all it is to be feared that not ten can be found who feel the need of any such Saviour as God has provided. Will you offer special prayer for these poor Jews? For unless the Spirit of the living God breathe upon them, the preacher might as well go into this great cemetery I have described, and call upon the past generations to come out of their graves, as to go into the families or into the synagogues of the present generation, and urge them to admit the claims of Jesus to be the Messiah, the Christ, the Lord's anointed.

But the Jews are one of the smallest of the communities here. The Greeks are much more numerous than they; the Armenians are much more numerous than the Greeks; and the Turks are more than all the others combined. And "what is the ratio of labor to the population?" you ask. I answer, about the same as ten ministers for all Massachusetts. Suppose that every thing in Massachusetts relating to morals, to education, and to religion were to depend upon ten men, and these foreigners, and for the most part mere stammerers in the language; that if any preaching was to be done, they must do it; that if a congregation was to be gathered, they must go round and collect it; that if they wished a place to hold their meetings, they must find it and fit it up; that if they would have a Sabbath school, they must establish and superintend it; that if there were to be any free schools, or boarding-schools, or seminaries of a still higher character, they must establish them, support them, and provide teachers for them, and also teach in them themselves; that if any school-books were to be used, they must prepare them; that if a stove, or fuel, or any thing else was necessary, they must procure it; that if the Scriptures or any other good books were to be read in all Massachusetts, they must translate and print them, and send persons round to put them in circulation; that if justice was to be administered in any of the courts, they must lie awake whole nights and think how they can exert a little influence here and a little there to secure so desirable a result; and, to mention but one thing more, if any good, sweet bread was to be eaten in all Massachusetts, they must show how it can be made, and, moreover, that it can be made without kneading with the feet; — suppose all this, and much more of a similar kind, do you not think these ten men, with very limited means placed at their disposal, would often find themselves at their wits' end? And would they not declare it to be your solemn duty to help them in Massachusetts, rather than to go West, where we will suppose the destitution to be exactly what it is known to be there?

Now, apply this to Constantinople, and, in fact, to this whole country, and you may see at once our necessities and your duty in relation to them. In the name of the great Head of the church, then, we cordially invite the members of your society to come and help us. In the name of all the perishing multitudes around us, we earnestly entreat that you will let nothing prevent your coming but a providence so special as not to be misunderstood.

Before I close, let me say that my recollections of Phillips Academy are very pleasant. It is almost forty-eight years since I went there to pursue my preparatory studies, and I have great reason to be thankful for the privileges I there enjoyed. May divine influence be every year richly enjoyed there! And in this blessing may all the members of your society largely share! You and they are at one of the very best academies in our highly favored country, and may your improvement correspond to your privileges!

Remember me very kindly to the principal, Mr. Taylor, and believe me to be
                    Yours most truly,
                                        W. GOODELL.

The following correspondence, though chiefly personal, will be read with no less interest on that account:—

                                        BEBEK, Feb. 3, 1860.

DEAR BROTHER GOODELL, — Do you remember February 3d, 1839? It had been a snowy day and night on the 2d. We cast anchor in the Golden Horn late in the evening of the 2d, and I went up on deck and could see nothing but straggling lights. Early in the morning I was up, and all the roofs were covered with snow, although it was not extremely cold. Henrietta came up and asked, " Is this Constantinople?" But after we had looked round in all directions we agreed that it was " beautiful for situation," — a truly glorious city.

Mr. Homes came in a caique, and we recognized him from his portrait, which we had seen at his father's. We came ashore with him. Oh what mud and slosh! We were glad to reach Father Goodell's house twenty-one years ago this morning. Belle and Mary were little bits of girls, and William and Constantine were little boys, and H. was only in the decrees. What changes of joy and grief! What heart-breaking sorrows, what long watchings, what days and hours of anxious suspense, what forebodings of coming ill, what anguish of heart at the bedside of suffering and death, and what peace and joy intermingled, have made this life a checkered scene! " I would not live alway," although I can sing of mercy as well as judgment.

Not less strange have been the vicissitudes of our work. Freedom of conscience acknowledged in Turkey! Mussulmans baptized and preaching the Gospel in safety! Churches formed, churches built! Protestantism an acknowledged element of the empire! Unwilling ambassadors compelled to protect what they hate! " Kings to shut their mouths!" God has truly done great things for us in these twenty-one years, since from that quiet room Henrietta and I used to look down upon Cassim Pasha and that part of the Golden Horn.

The next twenty-one years will see greater things than

these, but ere that shall have passed we shall all, I trust, look down upon the events of time from Mount Zion above. Love to Mamma Goodell and all.

Yours truly,

C. HAMLIN.

HASS KEUY, Feb. 3, 1860.

MY DEAR BROTHER, — Yes, I remember well the snowy morning you and your good wife came to us twenty-one years ago to-day. Isabella and Mary were then our youngest children. The others were not yet, except in the purposes of Him who calleth things that be not as though they were. One of our children, with whom you and William and myself used in stormy weather to roll marbles in the large hall, has been taken from us. Two of our children are happily settled in life, and two others are looking forward with bright anticipations to the same happy state. Their mother, who for some fifteen years was a great sufferer, is now through great mercy restored to as good health as could reasonably be expected by one of her age. Their father, who at his best estate was never more than half a man, is now encompassed with the infirmities of age.

But while my own powers fail, I rejoice to see the health, strength, and vigor, which is still granted to my brethren, some of the oldest of them entering or ready to enter upon new fields and new schemes of labor and effort, demanding all the activity and energy of manhood. May they long continue to increase, although I must decrease!

It is now more than thirty-seven years since I came to the East, and near twenty-nine years since I removed to Constantinople. Wonderful moral changes have taken place during this time, and though I find myself sinking, I rejoice to see evidence that the blessed cause is rising, and that greater things than I have seen will be witnessed by those who come after.

May your own life and health be long spared! the new enterprise which you undertake be greatly prospered! and your family, a second time scattered, and once more restored, be abundantly blessed! May your heart be made glad according to the years in which you have been afflicted, and the days in which you have seen evil! And at last may you and we cast anchor, not in the Golden Horn, but before the Golden City, and meet with a more joyful reception in our

17*

Father's house above, than you met with at Father Goodell's twenty-one years ago!

Your very affectionate brother in Christ,

W. GOODELL.

On the occasion of the death of his youngest brother in 1860, he wrote to his bereaved wife, then in Washington Territory: —

MY DEAR AFFLICTED SISTER, — Of the sudden death of my youngest brother, your own beloved husband, and the father of your dear children, I heard on the 6th inst. And be assured I have you and your fatherless ones in constant and tender and prayerful remembrance. The Lord comfort your hearts, and greatly sanctify to you and to us all this dispensation of His providence! Our heavenly Father in his dealings with us commits no mistakes. Too wise to err, and too good to afflict willingly, He always has the very best reasons for all that He does, although we in our childish weakness understand them not.

I wrote my good brother the 24th of last January, having just learned from our sister Phebe the place of his residence. Oh that I had learned it sooner, for, alas! he had already gone to that country with which our post-office regulations have no connection. But, blessed be God! it is not an unknown territory to which he has gone. It is "the better country," of which we have heard and read so much, and which is so accurately described in our great and good chart. And "there shall be no night there," no darkness, poverty, sickness, fear, oppression, no sin and misery, no grave-yard nor sign of death. What glorious negatives! We know something of the glorious King and His blessed government and His happy subjects. And may our thoughts often go up there! the whole strong current of our affections be turned thither! And may we all at last, through infinite grace, have an abundant entrance there.

Will you inform me how all your children are situated? Would that I could step in and inquire after your welfare, and ask in what way I could be of service to you! But though I cannot do this, yet by knowing your circumstances I shall know better how to pray for you and yours. The Lord God, not of the dead, but of the living, bless you and your children, and may they in early life give their love, their confidence, to Christ, who is worthy of all.

My dear wife and children unite with me in love and sympathy for you and yours. Will you remember me in your prayers? I am old and gray-headed, and shall soon follow my beloved brother.

Shall you remain in Washington Territory? If you remove, do not fail to give me seasonable notice, that I may know how to direct my letters. Though I know you not personally, yet I love you as having been the wife, and as having contributed to the happiness, of the dear departed one, and I subscribe myself,

Your ever affectionate and truly sympathizing brother,

W. GOODELL.

March 6, 1860, he wrote: —

"An aged woman was added to the Evangelical church last Sabbath. She is the very one of whom I once made mention as putting on three pairs of spectacles, so great was her eagerness in learning to read the word of God."

The record that he had made of the case, May 19, 1847, was this: —

"You can hardly conceive of the waking up of the female mind in our little community. Every female member of our church can now read, and this has been acquired in most instances from the impulse which piety in the heart has given to the intellect. This spirit is now extending from the church through the whole community, and even mothers and grandmothers are learning to read, in order that they may peruse the Holy Scriptures for themselves. You would be amused to see one grandmother with three pairs of spectacles, all without bows, and all stuck fast from the bridge straight on toward the tip of the nose, making it unnaturally sharp in appearance and not a little obstructive to the sound of the voice, and she occasionally peering over the top of the whole three to ask you a question, with a look of as much animation as any professor in a theological chair! Until the present year she appeared to feel no interest in eternal things."

The missionary circle at Constantinople were favored with the presence and the cordial sympathy of many residents from other lands who loved the cause in which they were engaged. There were not a few Christian men and Christian families, with whom social intercourse was a Christian privilege, and the moral aid they gave to the missionaries in their work of evangelization was by no means light. We have had frequent occasion to mention the important service rendered from time to time by Lord Stratford de Redcliffe in the various difficulties that arose as the Gospel was taking effect upon the different communities. The missionaries had still another warm friend and helper among the foreign ambassadors in Count de Zuylen, who represented the kingdom of the Netherlands. He was a warm-hearted, evangelical Christian, and his residence at the Turkish capital, where he did not hesitate to make himself known as of the same household of faith with the ambassadors for Christ who were beseeching men, in Christ's stead, to be reconciled to God, was in itself a benediction. The letter which Dr. Goodell addressed to him on the occasion of his promotion to a high position under his own government at home sets forth his character and the value of his presence as a man of God:—

HASS KEUY, CONSTANTINOPLE, March 12, 1860.

To His Excellency COUNT DE ZUYLEN DE NYEVELDT,
   Dutch Ambassador, &c.:

MY VERY DEAR SIR, — I was so taken by surprise to-day, that I did not once think to congratulate you or the good Countess on your elevation to a more desirable post. It was very selfish in me to think only of our own loss, and to express to you nothing but our regrets at the change which has taken place in your prospects. But God's great hand is to be acknowledged everywhere. It was His good providence that brought you and your family here, and we bless His name for it. So it is His good providence that now says to you, "Come up higher," and we offer you our hearty congratulations. You came here at the very right time, and you have greatly encouraged us in our work, not only by your influence in your official capacity, but by the high moral stand you and your beloved family have been enabled to take and maintain in this great and wicked city. May the grace of God be ever abundant towards you! and may His kind hand ever lead and guide you! May your new situation be

as much more pleasant and your influence and means of usefulness as much greater than before, as your post will be
more honorable! Be assured our prayers and best wishes
will ever attend you. We commend you to God and to the
word of His grace. And to your prayers do we commend
ourselves and our work.

Mrs. Goodell and all my family unite in the very kindest
regards to the good Countess, and to Miss Nixon, and to all
those lovely plants round about your table. We had hoped,
as soon as the warm spring should come, to see you all at
Hass Keuy; but this hope we must now relinquish. May
we all at last, through infinite mercy in Christ Jesus our
Lord, be permitted to walk together under those living trees,
by those living fountains of water, which are in the midst of
the paradise of God!

I have the honor to be, My dear Count,
Your very affectionate brother in Christ,
W. GOODELL.

The remarkable outpouring of the Holy Spirit upon the
churches of the United States in 1857 and 1858, and the conversion of a great multitude of souls, was nowhere the occasion of greater joy, and nowhere awakened more fervent
thanksgivings, than in Turkey. Missionaries the world over,
perhaps above all other men and women, are alive to all that
relates to the prosperity of the cause of Christ at home,
knowing that in the divine constitution of things it reacts at
once upon the prospects of the church abroad. They look
to the church at home not as the fountain of divine influence,
but as the channel through which, in a great measure, that
influence is communicated by prayer, and by personal consecration to God's service, to the extremities of the body of
Christ.

While the Spirit was yet poured out from on high, Dr.
Goodell wrote to a friend in this country, who had forwarded
an account of the work: —

"We thank you for sending us that report of the gracious
visit of the Lord of glory to the churches of our native land.
Surely He is walking in the midst of the golden candlesticks

in our beloved country, and holding the stars in His right hand, and from the seven spirits that are before the throne communicating larger measures of divine influence and spiritual blessing than we find recorded in any previous part of the history of the church. Of the 'glorious things *spoken*' of Zion, and promised to her, we had often read before, but by every week's post we now hear of the 'glorious things' actually *done* for her, and our spirits are stirred within us."

These tidings awakened the most earnest expectations of a similar blessing for the young Protestant churches of Turkey, and they excited a corresponding hope that the churches of America would come up with fresh zeal and almost new-born power "to the help of the Lord, to the help of the Lord against the mighty." For one or two years Dr. Goodell, in common with his brethren, continued to await the intelligence of a grand accession to the strength of the church in carrying on its aggressive work among the nations, until, in the beginning of the year 1860, he was moved to address, through the "New York Observer," a series of letters to the Christians of his native land. The first was superscribed, "*To the Hundreds of Thousands of Young Converts in America*," and contained an earnest appeal for an entire consecration of themselves to the service of their divine and chosen Master.

This was followed about a month later by a communication "To the Churches of Christ in the United States of America," in which he urges them to come up to a higher standard of living for God, and with themselves to devote their property to the advancement of the kingdom of Christ in the world. The following is a brief extract:—

"In the great increase that is to be made to the church in the latter days, the Prophet Isaiah sees them coming in crowds, and bringing 'their silver and their gold with them;' that is, devoting their wealth to the name and worship of Jehovah, to be employed in His blessed service. And had any of those left their 'gold and frankincense' behind; or had they left 'the flocks of Kedar,' with 'the multitude of camels' and 'the dromedaries from Midian,' behind them, in the dark regions of idolatry, where they could themselves go back every day to enjoy them, — would they have been received and incorporated among the true Israel? Certainly not. They would have been rejected, as still devoted to idolatry, and possessing substantially the same character as before.

"Now, beloved friends, the present are those latter days of glory foretold by the prophet. And have you looked to see whether the crowds that now come up to join themselves to the Lord are bringing 'their silver and their gold with them?' Have you made any inquiry? Have you gone into any examination of the subject? If you have not, we in Constantinople have; and we have been amazed beyond measure to find that while there has been such a great increase of names to the records of the church, there has been comparatively little addition to the 'whole burnt offerings and sacrifices' made to the Lord."

To the widowed wife of a former missionary to Constantinople, then residing in this country, he sent the following playful invitation to attend the marriage of his daughter, which was to take place a few days later: —

CONSTANTINOPLE, June 26, 1860.

MY DEAR SISTER, — Our daughter Mary expects to change her name on the 6th of July. Will you and Samuel and Frances and Charley grace the occasion by your presence? Do try and come. You will meet many of your old friends, and we will try and arrange every thing pertaining to the ceremony so that you shall get home before dark.

But time changeth all things, and I must not forget that you are no longer in Pera, but have removed to another country. I wonder whether, after our removal to a better country, even an heavenly, we shall be able or be permitted to be present on every grand occasion or great celebration that takes place among the glorified ones above. I know of two bright spirits who had to deny themselves and forego the pleasure of being present on one of the grandest occasions it is possible to conceive. When the Son of God "went up where He was before," and all heaven poured forth to do Him honor, and the high command was given, "Lift up your heads, O ye gates, and be ye lifted up, ye everlasting doors, and the King of glory shall come in," two of the blessed angels could not be present. They could not delay a moment to view the pageant, but must hasten down to a little mountain near Jerusalem, in order to give some directions to eleven poor fishermen. And how many others were sent off in other directions to other worlds we know not. But was it no self-denial in them to be absent from this most blessed occasion?

Let us, then, learn to exercise self-denial here, that it may not seem hard to us there. Let us learn to exercise faith, confidence, and a firm trust in God here, for we shall have to confide in Him for ever.

Always your brother,

W. Goodell.

To another friend in this country, with whom he had long been in correspondence, he wrote: —

"I hope that, in some of the many mansions we may occupy hereafter, we shall be much nearer to each other's habitations than we now are, and that our good Newbury-port friends will be quite in our neighborhood. What blessed introductions await us! And as to our location, and the location of our friends, as to the particular mansions assigned to us or to them, I presume we shall be perfectly satisfied, not having the slightest change to suggest. Well, let us be satisfied with those we now occupy, for they were assigned to us by the same loving Father."

The jubilee of the American Board of Missions was cele- brated in 1860. The occasion was observed with sacred interest at Constantinople. Dr. Goodell was appointed to prepare a historical address, which he did, interweaving his record with numerous personal reminiscences of the deepest interest. He had been associated with many of the earlier missionaries to the different parts of the world; he was present at the ordination of Judson, Nott, Newell, Hall, and Rice, at Salem, Mass., in 1812, two years after the organiza- tion of the Board; he stood on the wharf when the first company of missionaries to the Sandwich Islands sailed from Boston in 1819, one of his own kindred being in that company; down through the whole history of the Board he had watched its work and its progress with an interest exceeded in the case of no other of its missionaries, and in that work he had been honored with bearing no insignificant part. Not among all the friends of this noble institution, so honored of God in sending the tidings of the Gospel through the world, was there one who had been more completely identified with it, or who had prayed with more constancy, or labored more faithfully for its prosperity. And now it was a joyful service to be permitted to celebrate its success by recounting its history, and giving all the praise to God.

On the 6th of November, 1860, Dr. Goodell, who had then resided at the Turkish capital nearly thirty years, made the following expression of his views in regard to the attitude of the government toward foreigners and toward Christianity, and of the results of the issuing of the Hatti Humayoun:—

"When we first came to Turkey, and for many years after, we could not live in Constantinople proper, nor, indeed (after the influence of our labors began to be felt), in any of its suburbs, except Pera. Although other Franks had summer residences in different places, still this privilege was, through the influence of the Armenians, Greeks, and Catholics, denied to us; and it was with great difficulty, and only after long and very strenuous efforts, that we obtained a foothold in Bebek. But the Turks now no longer listen to the representations, or rather misrepresentations, of our enemies, and we live without molestation wherever we choose, even in the very city itself. The change in this respect is certainly very great, and it would be ungrateful to deny it.

"Formerly our schools and our religious assemblies, although they were in our own private apartments, were liable at any time to be interrupted. Being unauthorized, they were irregular, and as such they were without the pale of protection. But now we can open schools and consecrate chapels wherever we please, and we can, in case of necessity, claim the protection of government. Then, all who wished to have religious intercourse with us, or receive any kind of instruction from us, were obliged to come all the way to Pera, however great the distance, and to be received into

our own apartments, however great the inconvenience to
ourselves. Now, 'the kingdom of God is come nigh unto
them,' and we can meet them in their own suburbs and in
their own houses, and we can open both schools and chapels
in their own villages.

" It is said that the grand charter of religious toleration
in Turkey exists only in name, and is virtually a dead letter.
To this it is sufficient to reply that before the Hatti Humayoun there were more cases of persecution reported to us
every week than there are now in a whole year. Then,
much of our time and strength was taken up, and all our
wisdom and influence were employed, in endeavoring to
secure protection for those who were persecuted for righteousness' sake. Now, cases of persecution are only occasional,
and our time and strength are employed in our appropriate
missionary work.

" Again, it is said that the Turks are insincere in their
professions of toleration, and that it is only under foreign
pressure they are ever brought to act in favor of it. But it
would be much more in accordance with truth to say that,
so far as Protestantism is concerned, it is only under such
pressure that they have ever been brought to act against it.
There is, and there always has been, ten times (perhaps I
should say a hundred times) as much influence exerted upon
the Turkish government against liberty of conscience as has
ever been exerted in favor of it. These Armenian and
Greek and Catholic communities are themselves mighty,
and they exert a mighty influence; and they are always
exerting it against each other, each endeavoring to enlist the
Turk on his side. Now, all these mighty communities united
all their mighty energies to oppose Protestantism. To secure the sword of Mohammed in their cause, they spared
neither bribes nor falsehoods; and, furthermore, they were
backed up by the influence of the Greek and Russian and
nearly or quite all the papal governments, through their
representatives, their ministers, consuls, dragomans, and
numerous *attachés* at the Sublime Porte.

" The influence, then, which was, and which still is exerted
upon the Turkish government against religious liberty is
more powerful than can well be expressed. But, blessed be
God! there is now another influence, the pressure of which
they begin to feel, and we most devoutly pray that they may
feel it more and more. Whatever influence the representa-

tives of England and of other Protestant governments have exerted upon the Turkish government in favor of Protestantism, has been mainly in opposition to other mighty influences of a most adverse character. Whoever has read the 'Missionary Herald' for the last forty years must have seen that in perhaps ninety-nine cases out of a hundred our persecutions have come not from the Turks, but from these corrupt churches, — the Turks never of themselves showing a disposition to molest us, and being drawn in to side with our persecutors only when under this terrible outside pressure to which we have alluded.

"But it will be asked, Did not the other European powers unite with England in procuring the Hatti Humayoun? We answer, yes; at any rate, they assented to it; some of them perhaps not really expecting it would ever go into effect, or, at any rate, be of universal application; for, in point of fact, it is more or less opposed to the very principles and practices of their governments at home. And by the persecuting churches here, that part of its provisions which relates to liberty of conscience is regarded as any thing rather than a blessing, for it is really an infringement of their liberty to 'bite and devour one another.' Liberty of worship in their own churches, and according to their own forms, they already had to perfection, and 'they needed no more,' as an intelligent Greek gentleman once said to me. 'What,' said he, in speaking of this document, in reference to liberty of conscience, 'what is the use of this Hatti Humayoun? We had before just as much liberty as we wanted.' And so they had; but, blessed be God! this Hatti Sherif prevents them from abridging the liberty of others. Thus the carrying out of the principle involved in this feature of it strikes terror into all these wicked churches; and it is this which has awakened the wrath of a near neighbor of ours (Russia) almost to frenzy, she calling it '*persecution.*'

"But to the Protestant communities here, and to all who will live godly in Christ Jesus, this Hatti Humayoun is a boon of priceless value. Heretofore its principal use was to secure us from the molestation of these corrupt churches, but we have now begun to test its importance with reference to the Mohammedans themselves. Only a few years since the headless bodies of apostates from the Mohammedan faith might be seen 'lying in the streets of the great city; and for three days and a half their bodies were not suffered to be put into graves;' and, unless flight from the country was possible, nothing better than this was ever expected. But now such apostates may be seen at all hours of the day, walking these same streets without any apparent danger, urging the claims of Christianity even in the very courts of the royal mosques, and teaching and preaching in the chapel, and in the private circle, and sometimes even in the palaces of the great, that Jesus Christ is Lord, to the glory of God the Father. And all this wonderful security is, under God, owing entirely to the Hatti Humayoun."

Mention was made in a previous chapter of a young Greek who welcomed Dr. Goodell on his first arrival at Constantinople, and who was soon after taken into the service of the mission, in which he remained a faithful and devoted laborer, until he was removed by death, March 11, 1861. The following tribute to his precious memory, written by Dr. Goodell at the time of his death, deserves a place in his own memoirs, as well for its historical as for its personal interest : —

"Mr. Panayotes Constantinides was called to the knowledge of divine truth, and to trust in Christ, about thirty years ago ; and through all his subsequent life his path was that of the just, shining more and more unto perfect day. During this time he was variously employed, sometimes for months together, as dragoman to the American legation, but more generally as a teacher, a translator, or a preacher of the Gospel of Christ, under the direction of the missionaries of the American Board. Some of the best of the Armeno-Turkish hymns were composed by him. All the early petitions which the Protestants presented to the Porte, in the terrible persecutions they suffered, setting forth their grievances and asking for redress, were drawn up by him. When the Sublime Porte created a board of instruction, composed of one person from each of the different communities, Mussulman, Jewish, and Christian, Mr. Panayotes was selected to represent the Protestants in that council. When a censorship of the press was established, and one from each community was to be chosen to meet monthly and examine all books proposed for publication, Mr. Panayotes was the one selected on the part of the Protestants for this service.

"But his most important, and what may be called the crowning work of his life, was the help he afforded in translating the Scriptures of the Old and New Testaments into Armeno-Turkish. In translating and revising and carrying through the press several editions of these Scriptures he was a very efficient helper. He was engaged in the work of revision when his Master came and called him home. He had reached the first chapter of Joel when he laid down his pen, and said to me, with a smile, 'I am going home.' And, indeed, he was already almost there. His health had been failing for many months, but he worked on until he could do no more.

"Though he was naturally very timid, yet in his last days he feared no evil. His mind was filled with peace, and his heart overflowed with thankfulness. He had forsaken the religion of his fathers for the sake of Christ; his first wife had no sympathy with him in the change, his older children had left him; but he said to me the very last week of his life, 'I have received a hundred-fold in this life, yea, I have received more than a thousand-fold. From my own blessed experience I can testify that this word of His is true.' When I spoke to him of the blessed labors in which he had been engaged, he replied, 'Yes, but they are not my Saviour; all my works I call only bad; I throw them all away; away with them, I cannot look at them; on every page I have written I see only sin; for salvation I look to Christ alone, and He is all-sufficient.' I fell on my knees by his couch and prayed that the sins with which every page of our translations had been stained might be forgiven, and I commended our brother affectionately to that Saviour who had come to take him to His own glorious kingdom.

"And he has, I doubt not, gone to be with Joseph and David and Daniel, with James and John and Paul, with patriarchs and prophets and apostles, and with his and their Saviour, Jesus Christ. For with all these he seemed much better acquainted than with his nearest neighbors. With the latter he had not associated the hundredth part so much as he had with the former. His conversation had long been with those in heaven, and he seemed to us all to be going there, not as a stranger, but as a fellow-citizen with the saints, and as one of the same blessed household.

"He had formerly expressed a great deal of anxiety about his family and his nation, but he lived to see one of his sons a missionary to the Greeks, in the service of the National

Scotch Church, and one beloved daughter employed as a teacher in the same holy service. He fell asleep in the sixty-fifth year of his age, on the morning of March the 11th, 1861, and the following day devout men carried him to his burial."

In a letter to a friend in this country he speaks of the annual meeting of the mission at Constantinople in June, 1861 : —

" Our annual meeting closed on the 17th inst., and the representation from the different stations in the interior, east and west, was unusually large. There were seventy-nine of us in all, thirty of whom were children. There were sixteen little ones under three years of age. Such a fine assortment of missionary babies I never saw before. Oh that they could all have been photographed in a group! One day I had a prayer-meeting with the mothers and their infant babes. One day Mr. Morgan from Antioch had a meeting with the children, when twenty-five of them took hold of hands and sang, 'There is a happy land,' and 'I want to be an angel.' One day I preached a sermon to the mothers. One day, in concert with the annual meeting at Kharpoot, in far Eastern Turkey, arranged by telegraph, we had in the morning a prayer-meeting for our country, and in the afternoon the annual sermon, the communion, and two baptisms. They at Kharpoot had three baptisms, — one of them William Goodell, the son of our Mary.

" One day was held the anniversary of our auxiliary Bible Society, when Sir Henry Bulwer, British ambassador, presided, and Dr. Schauffler made one of his best speeches. Mr. Morgan, from the Southern mission, gave us many interesting particulars of the work in that field. There are sixteen hundred pupils in the Sabbath school at Aintab, the blessed Bible the only text-book. The Christian song-book we have prepared for them they sing with mighty voice, and this not only in the church, but at home, where many of their ungodly neighbors, even the Turks, can hear and learn. All the filth and offal of the city are carried out of the city into the fields by poor Turkish boys, in bags on miserable donkeys. In returning for fresh loads they jump on and ride without saddle or bridle, and sometimes a dozen of them may be seen riding as fast as they can make the poor creatures go, their faces and hands for days unwashed, their hair streaming in the wind, their clothes all tattered and torn, and they all singing at the top of their voices through the streets of Aintab, 'I want to be an angel,' &c., in the hearing of the Cadi, the Mufti, the Governor, and all others, great and small. These poor boys are never troubled with the bronchitis, and their clear voices are heard at a great distance. And who can tell how many, by hearing those wonderful words, may wake up to a new life, and enter upon new trains of thought and feeling and action."

On reaching the age of seventy he wrote to one of his sisters : —

CONSTANTINOPLE, Feb. 14, 1862.

MY DEAR SISTER MARY, — I am this day threescore and ten years old, — a long time to live in this world, and to find every day food to eat, raiment to put on, and air to breathe. I seem now to be standing on the banks of the Jordan, where I see others passing over, and where I can see the shining throng beyond; and for no worldly consideration would I retrace my steps and turn back into the wilderness. To turn back for any thing earthly is like "taking a leap into the dark," to press forward is like coming to "the general assembly and church of the first-born, whose names are written in heaven." Blessed be God, sin dies and grace reigns. I feel more and more that I have made a most blessed exchange with Christ, giving Him all my nothingness and sinfulness, and taking all His fulness and goodness; and thus, though I find nothing *in* myself worthy of divine acceptance, I find every thing worthy *on* me, viz., His righteousness, " which is to all and upon all them that believe." And thus,

> "I'm a poor sinner, just nothing at all,
> But Jesus Christ is my all in all."

He who has taken care of me these many days and months and years is abundantly able to provide for me and make me happy, when days and months and years are no more. How happy to feel that we shall never be separated from His love, His people, His kingdom ! How happy to be even now walking and living and conversing with the world's Saviour, — *our* Saviour, whom having not seen we love, and of whom we have brighter, clearer, more precious views, than we have of " the shining throng beyond."

Your brother,

WILLIAM.

CHAPTER XXII.

IN the spring of 1862, Dr. Goodell was appointed a delegate to the annual meeting of the Central Turkey Mission, to be held at Aleppo. Although very feeble, he was encouraged by his brethren to undertake the journey, which he did the more readily because it afforded him the only opportunity he would probably ever enjoy of revisiting the scenes of his earliest labors in the East. He was accompanied as far as Alexandretta by several members of his family, who went on to Beyrout, to meet him on his return from Aleppo. At Alexandretta he was joined by his friend and former associate, Rev. S. H. Calhoun. Together they set out on the overland journey to Aleppo, tarrying for a day at Antioch, where they were to be joined by other missionaries. As they were about to engage in their morning worship, before resuming their journey, on Wednesday, the 26th of March, a messenger came in with the tidings that the Rev. Mr. Coffing, of Adana, whom they were expecting to meet, had been shot by robbers or assassins near Alexandretta, and mortally wounded. Mr. Calhoun immediately returned to the place and found him dead. Within about an hour of Alexandretta, Mr. Coffing and his two attendants had been fired on, and all of them wounded. One of the attendants, a pious Armenian, died soon after, but the other, a Moslem, though severely wounded, recovered. The assassins were apprehended after long delay, and one of them executed; the other made his escape.

This occurrence not only excited some degree of apprehension in regard to the safety of travel on horseback through the country, it cast also a shadow over the meeting at Aleppo. But no further violence was offered to any of the travellers.

On this journey an incident occurred showing the impression made upon the minds even of Mohammedans by the consistent lives of those who had embraced true Christianity through the teachings of the missionaries. The impression is quite the opposite to that made by the adherents of the corrupt Oriental churches in their accustomed worship and by their daily walk. Dr. Goodell and his party were obliged to spend a night on the way, at a Turkish *café*. In the morning, finding themselves surrounded by a noisy crowd of Turks, as there was no place for retirement, the question arose whether it was best to have their usual worship in the midst of such a crowd. Dr. Goodell said, " A Mussulman never hesitates to say his prayers at the proper time, wherever he may be, and why should we ? " A portion of Scripture was then repeated aloud, and Dr. Goodell knelt to pray. He had scarcely commenced before the Turks ceased talking. He soon ceased praying in English, and continued his prayer in the Turkish language. He asked the protection and blessing of God upon themselves, and implored temporal and spiritual blessings in behalf of the people of the country, and in particular for those who were then present, entreating the forgiveness of sin, in the name and for the sake of Jesus Christ. As he closed, the " Amen " was heartily echoed by the Mussulmans from all sides of the *café*. When the party had risen from their knees, the Turks clustered around them, inquiring who and what they were. " Are you Protestants ? " said they. " What are Protestants ? " inquired Dr. Goodell. " They are those who do not tell lies," replied one ; " Those who do not cheat," said another; " Those who believe only in the Bible, and try to live as it tells them," added a third. " Yes," said Dr. Goodell, " we are Protestants ! "

His observations, made in the course of his journey and while at Beyrout, show the great changes that had taken

18

place since he first entered Turkey. The following interesting account he wrote at the time : —

"In this Southern field I found myself at once among the
people for whose benefit I had spent the strength of my life;
and no one will be surprised to hear that I felt constrained
to offer special thanks to God for helping me to translate
those glorious words which had there been preached with
the Holy Ghost sent down from heaven, making the desert
blossom as the rose. The place I visited seemed to be a
part of my own great parish, and I was more desirous than
ever before of making a pastoral visitation through the
whole.

"The mission families appeared to be very happy. Although
some of them were alone in the wilderness, and three days'
journey from any others, yet they and their little ones seemed
the picture of contentment and happiness. Instead of saying with a repining spirit, 'How can we sing the Lord's
song all alone in this strange land,' the voice of joy and
praise, of thanksgiving and making melody, was heard in
their habitations. And I would ride far, even through
storm and tempest, to hear again their sweet songs of Zion.
Indeed, all these little missionary spots, with which the
whole country is now dotted, were each one like an oasis in
the desert.

"At some of the missionary stations the Gospel has taken
such root that it seems to be growing up as in its own native
soil, and it is already bringing forth its appropriate fruit.
The work of the missionary, if it be not already completed,
yet seems on the very point of being so; and there is evidently more danger that he will in some instances stay too
long than that he will go too soon. At Aintab, for example,
the church supports its own pastor, its own common schools,
of which, with those in the neighborhood, there are nine, and
takes upon itself the supply of all the out-stations except one.
The missionaries of that place ask for no appropriation except for the theological class, the Female Boarding-school,
and for one out-station. For all the rest the church at Aintab
provides; and for all these various objects, including provision for their poor, and their taxes to government, the sum
total raised the last year was $2,556, averaging $1.25 for
every man, woman, and child in the community. The congregation is already much too large for one pastor, and the

church has recently and very wisely made arrangements to settle another, and thus have two churches instead of one.

"In the good providence of God I was permitted on my way back to join my family at Beyrout. That was my first field of labor, and this was my first visit to it, after an absence of thirty-four years. Nearly half of the original members of the little church gathered there thirty-seven years ago still survive, and are bringing forth fruit in old age; 'but some are fallen asleep.' In their history I was deeply interested. A son of two members of that little church is now a missionary of the Church Missionary Society at Aleppo, and he has the respect and confidence of all the wise and good. A sister of his is the wife of a German missionary in Egypt. His own wife is the daughter of two other original members of that little church, and her sister is an assistant to the deaconesses in their important establishment at Beyrout. All these are hopefully Christians.

"One of the original members of that little church is now living at Sidon, and sustains the reputation of being a worthy, exemplary Christian man, with a Christian family. Another of the original members, when we first knew her thirty-nine years ago, was a worshipper of the Virgin. She is now the excellent wife of one of our own beloved missionaries, one of her daughters is the wife of another, and all her other five or six children, excepting the youngest, are members of the church of Christ. Thirty-seven years ago she became united to Christ, and her own prospects, with those of her children, and of her children's children, were changed for ever. We were happy to sit once more with this aged sister in heavenly places in Christ Jesus, repeating many beautiful hymns and verses of Scripture, and speaking of the way His kind hand had led us. Precious intercourse! A foretaste of what we hope to enjoy more fully hereafter. When we fled from Beyrout thirty-four years ago, this little church of Christ (was it not a little one?) was scattered to the four winds, but 'He hath remembered His holy covenant,' and He is still a God to His people and to their seed after them.

"At Beyrout, one of our first visits was to the Protestant cemetery, a retired and pleasant spot, which I myself 'purchased of the sons of Heth for a possession of a buryingplace,' thirty-six or thirty-seven years ago. Here we stood by the graves of the well-known and well-beloved brethren Fisk (who died at my house in Beyrout), Smith, and Whiting, whose memories are as fragrant as ever, and whose works still follow them. Here, also, is the last earthly resting-place of Peter Abbott, Esq., for many years British consul at Beyrout, who did so much for our protection and for the salvation of an infant mission from the rage of persecution, that his reputation, like that of the elector of Saxony, suffered in consequence. No history of these times would be complete without a distinct recognition of the untiring efforts he made to shield from harm the infant cause of Protestantism in Turkey.

"The changes that have taken place in Beyrout are great, and those that have taken place on Mount Lebanon are still greater. The pride of Lebanon is broken, those high looks are brought low, and that terrible power which trampled upon all that thirsted for God or desired a knowledge of His ways is itself cast down. When we first went to Beyrout, all was dark as darkness itself, and not a ray of light was to be seen on the mountain. All was dead and dry, like the bones in Ezekiel's vision, and there was not even a sign of life. Indeed, the crime of drawing a single spiritual breath had really the death penalty annexed to it, unless foreign protection could in some way be secured. But now how changed! 'By terrible things in righteousness' has God answered the prayers of His people, and avenged the blood of His servants. Now there is life and light and liberty. One can breathe freely without borrowing special leave to do so. Now the waking up of men's minds to eternal things no longer awakens painful apprehension of sufferings beyond endurance. Then every thing seemed to belong to the kingdom of Satan, and he had every thing his own way. Now it is given into the hands of Christ, and He has begun to take quiet possession of the whole.

"I was amazed at the amount of influence and confidence possessed by the missionaries. I well remember the time when they had less influence with the principalities and powers of Mount Lebanon than the very humblest of the down-trodden poor. But in the wonderful overturnings of God's providence 'they ascended up to heaven in a cloud, and their enemies beheld them,' and the influence they are now permitted to exert over Lebanon is extraordinary. Their character is now known and respected; and their names, which were once odious to a proverb, are now held in honor. Indeed, in their case, that promise seems to be fulfilled which was spoken of Zion, 'Whereas thou hast been forsaken and hated, so that no man went through thee, I will make thee an eternal excellency, a joy of many generations.'"

After his return to Constantinople, he received from one of the girls connected with the Female Boarding-school at Aleppo, where the annual meeting was held, a letter, together with a black velvet cap, wrought by their hands and encircled with a double inscription embroidered in Arabic. This cap he continued to wear, as a precious memorial, until the day of his death. It was on his head when he sat in the meeting of the American Board at Chicago, and in all the public meetings that he attended in this country after his final return : —

ALEPPO, Sept. 6, 1862.

DR. GOODELL, SIR, — I have the pleasure of sending you the cap which the girls of our little school in Aleppo promised to make you when you were here. They often ask about you, and all send many salaams, with their best wishes that your life may be spared many years to use many more caps, and still to do much service in the Lord's vineyard. The texts on the cap are (in Arabic) : —
"The hoary head is a crown of glory, if it be found in the way of righteousness" (Prov. xvi. 31).
"The glory of young men is their strength, and the beauty of old men is the gray head" (Prov. xx. 29).
All our little circle are well, and send many regards, including the new little Miss Wortabet.
Yours respectfully,

SAADA GREGORY.

In November, 1862, Dr. Goodell received an urgent invitation from the "Turkish Missions Aid Society" in London to visit England. This society, which was organized in 1854, "to aid the existing evangelical missions in the Turkish empire, especially American," within those eight years had appropriated to the American missions in different parts of Turkey about $70,000. It was an outgrowth of the warm interest felt in England in the work of the faithful men who were seeking to evangelize the races of Turkey. It was two years before, in 1860, that the Earl of Shaftesbury, on taking the chair as president of the society, bore such honorable testimony to the worth and wisdom of these men, in saying, " I do not believe that in the whole history of missions, I do not believe in the history of diplomacy, or in the history of any negotiations carried on between man and man, we can find any thing equal to the wisdom, the soundness, and the pure evangelical truth of the body of men who constitute this mission." The following is the letter of invitation:—

7 Adam Street, London, Oct. 17, 1862.

The Rev. Dr. Goodell:

My esteemed Brother,—I am instructed by our committee to convey to you their affectionate desire for a visit from yourself this year, as a deputation from the missions aided by their operations.

I ventured privately, by the mediation of our beloved brother, Rev. Dr. Perkins, to sound you on the possibility of our obtaining this privilege. He was to have told you from personal experience precisely what you would have to endure in the way of work, and he encouraged me to hope he might succeed in securing your consent.

Our committee will be delighted to welcome you, and although our associations hold their meetings during the wintry months of the first quarter of the new year, the facilities of railroads and hospitable houses everywhere mitigate the inconveniences. All expenses for your coming and going by the first-class comforts by sea and land, from and to Turkey, we gladly meet, that your health may be cherished, and only as much work shall be devolved upon you as your strength will permit. Our winters in England are generally very short and mild, with little snow or frost to last a week. If you could be here in the first week of January, that would be early enough.

Hoping you will give this cordial invitation of our committee your serious consideration, and, *if possible*, give us all the pleasure of welcoming you to Old England,

I remain, Rev. and dear Brother,
With cordial esteem,
Very fraternally yours,
G. R. Birch, *Secy. T. M. A. S.*

Dr. Goodell would gladly have complied with the invitation, in order to make some acknowledgment of the important assistance that the American missionaries had received from their Christian brethren of all denominations in England; but he was not equal, physically, to the service, and he sent to the secretary the following letter, giving his reasons for declining : —

CONSTANTINOPLE, Nov. 19, 1862.

To the Rev. G. R. BIRCH, *Secretary of the T. M. A. Society,* London :

REV. AND DEAR SIR, — Yours of October 17 was duly received, and with great gladness of heart would I accept the kind invitation of your committee to visit England and spend part of the coming winter in the service of your society, did I dare undertake it. It is more than fifty years since I began to listen with admiration to your Christian orators; and the names of Wilberforce and Grant, of Teignmouth and Bexley, of Pinkerton, Paterson, and a host of others, — the venerable presidents, vice-presidents, secretaries, and earnest advocates of your benevolent institutions, — were as household words. And as I read their glowing statements and fervent appeals, my only fear was that they would usher in the millennium before I should be ready to do any thing in the world, and that I should be left with nothing to do, — a fear, however, which I have long since laid aside. I always feel proud to confess that I have pure English blood flowing in my veins; and though "The Times" might insinuate that it must by this time be vitiated, yet, whether somewhat vitiated or somewhat improved, there it is, and I feel it every day, to the very ends of my fingers.

I should so love to visit that wonderful island, and see some of the good friends of whom I have read and thought so much, or whom I have known in the East. I should love to look once more upon the noble countenance of that distinguished statesman of yours, whose name will be remembered with honor to the latest generations for his advocacy in Turkey of the principles of civil and religious liberty, a principle to be recognized not only in Turkey, but in all the surrounding countries. But I am not fit for the service to which you invite me. I have neither the strength, wisdom, nor grace. My work, too, has been to such a degree in my own study, that I know comparatively little of those details of which you would wish me to inform you. My powers of body and mind are failing, and my bodily presence among you would be weak and my speech contemptible. Even my voice has lost all its former edge, and I no longer recognize it as my own.

I therefore wrote to my son-in-law, the Rev. Mr. Barnum, of Kharpoot, whose name was mentioned in connection with mine by our mutual friend, the Rev. Dr. Perkins, when he first informed me of your request. I hoped he would be able to go, but he cannot leave his work. I have therefore written to the Rev. H. Morgan, of Antioch, urging him to go. He will be able to tell you, straight through, from beginning to end, of the whole Zeitoon affair, and will give your society much interesting information from his very interesting field of labor. I hope he will go. And may the good Lord go with him, and give him all the grace and help he may need.

Christian salutations to your committee and to your society. In due season they shall reap if they faint not. And if I never have a personal introduction to them on earth, I hope we may meet on the other side of Jordan, in the green fields of Eden, where the tree of life doth grow, and where no "New York Herald" or "London Times" will ever disturb our harmony or interrupt the flow of our affectionate regards for each other.

Your unworthy, but very affectionate, brother in Christ,

W. GOODELL.

In February, 1863, his labors in the work of translating and revising the Holy Scriptures came to a close. He then completed his last revision of the entire Bible in the Armeno-Turkish language, which he had prosecuted with as much painstaking and prayerfulness as the original translation, which he finished in 1841. This work will now remain a monument to his accurate scholarship, his sound critical judgment, his life-long perseverance, and his scriptural piety, and will hold forth the lamp of divine truth in the Turkish Empire, until the language shall cease to be spoken. As soon as this work was completed, he penned the following letter to his children, copies of which he sent to them in their several and widely separated places of residence:—

CONSTANTINOPLE, Feb. 3, 1863.

To my dear children and grandchildren in Constantinople, Kharpoot, and America:—

You will, I am sure, rejoice, and will unite with me in thanksgiving and praise, that I have been spared so long, and have been permitted to finish the great work given me to do. Though I am now old and feeble, yet my eyesight has been wonderfully preserved, enabling me to read the last proof in the printing of the Armeno-Turkish Scriptures, and to make my last corrections. I now turn my back upon the beautiful country through which I have travelled, and again set my face toward the wilderness, hoping the good Master will see fit to employ me in some way to promote His glory, though hardly expecting it to be so pleasant a service as that in which I have been so long engaged. For the privilege I enjoyed in having that pleasant service assigned me, in such pleasant fields, amidst such living fountains, I ought to be unfeignedly thankful. Every truth in the whole Bible, from Genesis to Revelation, has now come once and again directly before my mind and received my earnest attention. Oh, had I been sanctified through every truth I have translated, as might have been expected, what a good and benevolent man I might have become! But, alas! I know only in part, and only in part do I believe and love. That which is perfect is not yet come. And will it never come? Yes, I hope; not by my work of translation, nor by any other work of mine, but through wonderful mercy in Christ Jesus our Lord, I have hope that "that which is perfect" will surely come.

On completing my work, I invited to dinner my principal helper in the work of translation, Baron Harûtun, and his principal helper in the work of printing, Baron Sarkis; and I reminded them that we must now make the same use of the truth we had translated and printed that other poor sinners do, otherwise we should die in ignorance of the Gospel; that we, like all other poor, dark sinners, needed the Holy Spirit to enlighten us, and to take of the things of Christ and to show them to us; otherwise, notwithstanding all our knowledge of the Bible, we should for ever remain ignorant of God's great salvation. I hope you will pray that all who have had any thing to do in preparing this

18* AA

book, all who hear it, or read it, or preach from it, may be sanctified through the truth it contains. And will you pray especially that your aged father, after having translated those glorious truths for others, and after having preached them to others, may not "himself be a castaway."

I now turn from my work of translation to that of preaching, and I desire your prayers that I may so preach as to save both myself and those that hear me. The poor remnants of my strength and of my days I consecrate to Him whom I have tried to serve these many years, and in whose blessed service I hope to be employed for ever. How long I shall be permitted to preach or to do any other service on earth seems very uncertain, for my health is all broken and gone. Formerly my sleep was sweet and refreshing, and however fatigued I became by night, I was fully restored in the morning. But now I often spend much of the night in utter sleeplessness, and during the long and silent hours I repeat to myself verses of the many beautiful hymns that we have sung together, and this one often among others : —

> "Just as I am, without one plea,
> Save that thy blood was shed for me,
> And that thou bid'st me come to thee,
> O Lamb of God, I come!"

Yes, I come! I come! Where else can I look, where else can I go?

My dear children, — you are all, without one exception, very dear to me, — it seems but a few days since you sat on my knee, tying up my hair in hard knots, and in all sorts of odd ways, to the back of my chair, for your amusement, but to the great annoyance of your good mamma. I am now scarcely fit for any thing else than to sit on the floor with some of my grandchildren around me, to tangle and tie up my hair in the same old-fashioned way. I think both mamma and I should live longer if we had some of our good grandchildren about us to amuse themselves and us. She loves you and prays for you. And so does

Your very affectionate father,

W. GOODELL.

At the same time, he wrote to the Secretary of the American Bible Society, under whose auspices the translation was printed. He commenced his letter in his characteristic style, referring to his personal and lamented friend, the Rev. Dr. Brigham, with whom his correspondence had been previously carried on : —

" MY DEAR BROTHER, — Did our postal arrangements admit of it, I should be tempted to direct this letter to my good brother, the late Secretary, now in heaven. But I hope it will come safely to your own hands, for that great and good society in which our brother took so lively an interest, and for the prosperity of which he labored for so many years," &c.

On the announcement of the completion of this life-work of Dr. Goodell, the compiler of these Memoirs received from a lady, who had been sojourning in one of the islands of the sea, the following letter : —

WILLOWBROOK, March 14, 1863.

DEAR SIR, — I have read with peculiar interest (in this week's " New York Observer ") the account of the completion of the Armeno-Turkish Old and New Testaments by Dr. Goodell. The history of the labors of this veteran Christian soldier takes my thoughts back to the impression made upon my mind several years since by the casual perusal of a tract entitled " The Missionary's Father." There is a link between the prayers of the devoted Christian father and the achievements of his no less devoted son, which should not be lost sight of, now that, through his instrumentality, millions are to rejoice in the possession of the word of God in their own tongue. In the narrative to which I allude, I remember this sentence : " Every foot of his farm, if not ploughed over, was prayed over." Is not this a fulfilment of the promise, " He that goeth forth and weepeth, bearing precious seed, shall doubtless come again with rejoicing, bringing his sheaves with him."

I can never forget what joy the words of the venerated missionary brought to the closing hours of a young man, dying a stranger in a strange land, as I read to him an extract from a sermon preached by Dr. Goodell at Constantinople, on the death of Mrs. Dwight. The trembling believer was venturing timidly down into the valley of the shadow of death, with no tender mother to smooth his pillow, no sister's hand to minister to his relief. At that moment his eager ear caught the words spoken years before in a time of great trouble in a distant land : —

"'And if I go and prepare a place for you, I will come again and receive you unto myself, that where I am there ye may be also.' Our Saviour does not leave us to grope our way into heaven alone. He comes himself to receive those who trust in Him."

This thought entered the soul of the dying man. He started from his pillow, and, with a countenance irradiated with joy, exclaimed, "How beautiful! How beautiful!" Jesus was revealed to him as the "rod out of the stem of Jesse," to comfort him in the valley of the shadow of death.

Blessings on the memory of the missionary's father! Truly his effectual fervent prayers have availed much. What numbers will have reason to bless God for the labors of his eminent son!

Yours very sincerely.

In November, 1863, our national Thanksgiving was celebrated in Constantinople, according to recent custom. The occasion was always one of great interest, the families of the mission, and the Americans who might happen to be in Constantinople, uniting most heartily in its observance, and usually having some social exercises after those of a more strictly religious character. At this time the day was observed in true American style and spirit. Among the sentiments offered was one deriving its significance from the civil war that was then going on at home: "The Union as it was intended to be, and as it shall be," which was responded to by Mr. Goddard, American consul. "The Army and Navy" called up the Rev. Mr. Pettibone. The Rev. Dr. Hamlin proposed, "Our missionary boys and the Federal army," and called upon Rev. Dr. Schauffler, who had a son in the army ; and he responded in an eloquent and patriotic address. On the reading of the toast, "The Constantinople Colony," Dr. Goodell was called on, and gave the following historical reminiscences : —

"My family removed to this place in June, 1831. We had then three children, and we constituted the whole

American colony of Constantinople. In a few weeks oui number was increased by the arrival of Constantine Washington, whose baggage and the most of whose outfit were, a few days before, consumed in that dreadful conflagration which reduced all Pera to ashes. We received him as best we could, and he lived with us nine years.

"A few days before this arrival several distinguished American citizens came from the United States, among whom was the Hon. Mr. Rhind, who had been previously sent by the United States government to make a treaty with the Sublime Porte, and he was now come to exchange ratifications. The treaty itself was made in the village of Bebek, in a little kiosk on the Bosphorus, which kiosk has since been removed. The American and Turkish commissioners met here night after night in the time of Ramazan, and completed their work before those European powers who might have been disposed to exert unfavorable influences had any knowledge of what was transpiring. The Rev. Messrs. Smith and Dwight, arriving at that time on their way to Persia, travelled as American citizens, by special authorization of the Porte, they being the first of our countrymen, it is believed, who enjoyed that distinction. This was in the year 1828 or 1829.

"In this his second visit to Constantinople, Mr. Rhind was accompanied by Mr. Eckford, a celebrated ship-builder of New York. Dr. De Kay, Mr. Eckford's son-in-law, came as physician, and Mr. Rhodes as his foreman. Commodore De Kay was in their company, being in command of the frigate which Mr. Eckford had built in New York, and which he now sold to the Ottoman government. Mr. Eckford was soon employed in the arsenal to build a Turkish fleet, the Porte having lost the whole of its navy at the fatal battle of Navarino. He undertook the work with his characteristic energy, and after his death, which occurred the following year, it was carried on by Mr. Rhodes, until the death of Sultan Mahmoud.

"As not a hotel or boarding-house had escaped the conflagration, these friends came to us, and begged us to take them in; and though we had lost all our furniture, still, as the life of our cook had been almost miraculously preserved (he had been covered by the ruins of the burning house), we opened our doors to them, and the first night made tea for them in a *tenjéré* (a sauce-pan). The same week that

Mr. Rhind and his party arrived came also Commodore Porter, in a United States vessel, being accredited to the Sublime Porte as minister resident from the government of the United States. He was uncle to our present secretary of legation, and father of our two brave naval officers, William and David Porter, who have performed such deeds of valor during the present war. Commodore Porter was our first minister, and continued in office here until his death, a period of eleven or twelve years, a much longer time than has been allowed any of his successors.

" One of the first duties of the new minister was to convey to the Porte the presents which were always given on such occasions. One fan, I recollect, cost $15,000, and other knick-knacks were in proportion. It was early in the morning of the 5th of October that Commodore Porter, having these presents in charge, started from Buyuk-Dèrè, in a caique, to go to the *yali*, or summer residence of one of the Turkish ministers. A heavy black cloud hung in the southwest, and a strange rumbling noise was heard, like distant thunder. My house was on the water. I stepped to the window, and was struck by the very singular appearance of the Bosphorus. It seemed as if some persons were throwing brick-bats or paving-stones into it. Observing the same appearance at a distance from the shore, I concluded for a moment it must be large fish jumping out of the water, but the next instant I was undeceived, as a terrific storm of hail burst over us with a fury not to be described. 'Jehovah thundered from heaven, and the Most High uttered His voice, hailstones and coals of fire.' Every pane of every window exposed to the storm was smashed; every tile of every house was broken to pieces, and the rain poured down in torrents into all our rooms. Several persons received severe contusions, many animals were killed, and, doubtless, many men would have shared the same fate, had it not been so early in the morning.

" And where was Commodore Porter all this while? He and his suite had just passed Therapia when the storm burst upon them. The boatmen, paralyzed, dropped their oars, and the Commodore himself, who had been accustomed all his life to battle and blood, trembled like an aspen leaf. He described the scene afterwards as the most terrific he had ever witnessed.

" Such was the commencement of this little colony, and

such was the commencement of our diplomatic relations to the Sublime Porte. Our diplomatic corps has always had the esteem and confidence of the Ottoman government and of the several foreign legations, having always maintained amicable relations with them; and the various gentlemen composing it, some of them distinguished for their scholarly attainments, have commanded the respect of this little colony for their personal worth, and for the energy with which they have sustained American interests.

" This colony has been increased from time to time both by ordinary generation and by fresh importations from home, of native born and also of naturalized citizens. It has also had much to do in receiving and forwarding fresh importations to form colonies in the regions beyond us. A large number of those whom we loved, whose memories are fragrant, and whose very names are precious to us, have gone to that better land where it is one eternal day of thanksgiving. Many of the children have from time to time been sent back to the land of our fathers, and have been an honor to the institutions where they have been educated. Some of them have been deemed worthy of promotion in the Federal army. Several are at present fighting for the restoration of the Union. May we have occasion next year for a day of thanksgiving over a restored Union, universal freedom, and a solid peace."

These allusions to the civil war in this country were expressive of the sentiments that animated the heart of every missionary of the American Board at Constantinople. Although the representative of our national government at the Sublime Porte was constrained by his sympathy with the Southern cause to resign his position, there was not a man among all those who had gone forth to represent the churches in the service of the Board who wavered for a moment in his attachment to the Union, or who did not heartily sympathize with the national cause and pray for its success. Several of the sons of the missionaries who were then in this country enlisted in the Union army, and were among the bravest defenders of the flag. Among them was a son of Dr. Goodell, alluded to in the following note, which the father pinned to a pair of socks that he placed in a box prepared for the soldiers of the Union army by the mission families at Constantinople : —

"Peace to thy feet, thou wearer of these socks! They were knit by an old lady at Constantinople, the city of the Sultan, who herself had a brave soldier boy in the Union army. And he was one of the thousand men who for their bravery had the honor accorded to them by General Banks of marching into Port Hudson and receiving the submission of the city.

"So let us all be brave to fight the battles of the cross, and we shall come off conquerors, and 'more than conquerors, through Him that loved us, and gave Himself for us.' Thus prays the husband of the lady referred to above. The socks were originally intended for him, but on the forty-second anniversary of their marriage, November 19, 1864, they were taken up anew, to be finished for some soldier boy. So here they are."

CHAPTER XXIII.

AS early as 1856, the year in which the celebrated Hatti Humayoun was promulgated, direct efforts toward the evangelization of the Mussulman population of Turkey were undertaken. These efforts were, of necessity, more quietly made than in the case of the other nationalities. The Turkish government was still jealous over its Mohammedan subjects, and any thing like the noise of a revolution, even of a religious revolution, was peculiarly distasteful to the ruling powers. The Turks are not only strongly conservative, but they particularly dislike any movement that is demonstrative. As Dr. Goodell wrote at one time, " they would rather thousands of Turks should be converted than that any noise should be made about it." The circulation of the Bible among the Mussulmans went steadily on, and Mohammedans dropped in occasionally to hear the Gospel preached. In October, 1859, Dr. Goodell wrote : —

" Within the last five or six years, several hundred copies of the Holy Scriptures every year have been sold to the Turks. The history of these we never knew; but we now begin to find among the Turks those who really seem to be Bible Christians, spiritually minded, who, with no teacher but the Bible, have become wise unto salvation. How many minds are thus awakened, and how many hearts are thus affected, it is impossible at present to say. We are told of thousands ; but if they be counted only by hundreds, or even scores, it is still a great work. Facts are coming to our knowledge every day that fill us with astonishment. It really seems as though the heavens were about to drop down upon us abundantly. A nephew of one of the pashas here, who lives with his uncle, and who was educated by him to be one of the four great Mollas of the empire, is a candidate for Christian baptism."

More than twenty Mussulmans had been baptized at Constantinople, and one of these, Selim Effendi, who had taken as his Christian name Edward Williams, was licensed to preach the Gospel. This work was going quietly on, the American missionaries all pursuing the line of policy which Dr. Goodell had strenuously advised from the very beginning of his work at the Turkish capital, that of avoiding collision with and opposition from the authorities, civil or religious. But all the laborers at Constantinople did not exercise the same prudence. Two missionaries or agents of the Church Missionary Society of England, in the warmth of their zeal, and presuming perhaps on the influence of their government, favored a bold assault upon Mohammedanism. Great excitement among the fanatical Turks ensued, and it soon became evident that whatever were the terms of the Hatti Humayoun, and however it was understood by others, the Turkish government was not disposed to regard it as an unqualified permission to Mohammedans to change their religion.

After this state of things had continued for some time, the Turkish officials, in the month of July, 1864, acting under orders from the Porte, seized eight or ten Mohammedan converts, and thrust them into prison. The prisoners were kept in close confinement, and were not allowed to have any intercourse with their friends. The whole community, native and foreign, was roused. The foreign residents, including the missionaries, met and protested against the action of the government. Unhappily, the English ambassador was a very different man from Lord Stratford de Redcliffe, the champion of religious freedom and the friend of the oppressed. There was every reason to believe that Sir Henry Bulwer had been cognizant for some time of the intended action of the Turkish government, and that he had given either his approbation or his tacit consent to the measures that were adopted.

The storm continued to rage at the capital; but in the mean time the Mussulman converts in prison, and when summoned before the courts, witnessed a good confession, in humility and yet with firmness avowing their belief in the Lord Jesus Christ as the true prophet of God, sent to be the Saviour of the world. As they were not even charged with any other crime than that of being Christians, and as they exhibited the meekness of Christ, together with great boldness in confessing Him, their conduct evidently made an impression upon the Turkish officers and people. In this state of things Dr. Goodell wrote to his friend, the former English ambassador, who was then in England. He was induced to address him for several reasons. The first and chief was, the hope that Lord Stratford might in some way exert an influence with the government at home in behalf of the persecuted, and for the cause of religious liberty in Turkey; another, to remove any false impressions that might have been made upon his mind by the extraordinary course of his successor, who had so grossly misrepresented the policy and proceedings of the American missionaries. Dr. Goodell was unwilling that one whose confidence they had enjoyed so fully in past years should imagine that they had all at once lost their discretion.

CONSTANTINOPLE, Sept. 27, 1864.

To the Right Honorable VISCOUNT LORD STRATFORD DE REDCLIFFE:

On account of my age and infirmities, I should not now venture upon any thing so public as writing to your Lordship, were not the case exceedingly urgent. I know not what your Lordship can do for us, nor, indeed, whether you can do any thing, in the circumstances, which must appear so delicate. But we shall, at any rate, secure your sympathy and your prayers. England has now, for a full score of years, stood up in the view of all the mingled populations of this country as having more sympathy with the Bible than with the Koran, with Protestantism than with Islamism, with truth and justice than with falsehood and oppression, and far distant be the day when she shall cease to occupy that high position. Our former persecutors, the Armenians, express great astonishment at the present posture of affairs. "Is Sir Stratford Canning no longer living?" an ecclesiastic recently asked; "Is his life-work all thrown away?"

The "Levant Herald" accuses us of now doing to the Mussulmans the very things which we complained of them for doing to the native converts, before the establishment of religious liberty. Does the London "Morning Post" understand what it says? Does it know any thing of what we then complained, and for which, through the very energetic, humane, and untiring efforts of your Lordship, we obtained redress? It was not that our religion was reviled, and our names cast out as evil. All this we bore for many years, and could still bear, without rendering evil for evil, or asking for the interference of the civil power. But it was that the converts were thrown into the filthiest dungeons, or banished to the most distant parts of the empire. It was that they were everywhere cut off from bread and water, and from all employment, their houses and land and shops and their protective papers taken from them, and they left without any permission to live or to die. Their condition was truly deplorable.

Now, have any of the missionaries, or any of the helpers, been guilty of doing any thing of this kind to the Mussulman population? If so, in the name of justice, where and when? If not, then is the whole reasoning of the "Morning Post" singularly out of place. In fact, it is altogether irrelevant, and has no pertinence whatever. And is there no friend in England to point out the great error into which the "Morning Post" has fallen, and the great injustice it has done us?

It should be known in England that of all the persecuted Mussulman converts, some of whom have suffered imprisonment, and some been sent into exile, not a single one, so far as I can learn, has been brought to trial, or had a single charge proved, or attempted to be proved, against him. If any individual has spoken unadvisedly against the Koran, or railed against the prophet, as is alleged, let it be proved, that the guilty individual may be suitably punished. But let not a whole community be punished for the sake of one or two, when it has not been proved that any crime has been committed by any one. In the name of the Hatti Humayoun of Turkey and of the Magna Charta of England, every right-minded person should protest against such an outrage.

In all the communications of His Excellency Sir Henry Bulwer, and in various articles I have seen, taken from the " London Times " and the " Morning Post," it is everywhere roundly asserted, or taken for granted, that the American missionaries have entirely changed their policy. Now this is entirely false. We have not changed our policy in any respect, nor have we seen it done by others, who within a few years have come to labor for the Mussulmans, without earnest entreaty and solemn protest on our part.

We therefore deem it unfair to be condemned in this wholesale manner. It is like the treatment of the hunted Mussulman converts, altogether unjust. So far as we, personally, are concerned, it is a small matter. But so far as these persecuted ones are concerned, it calls for prompt action on the part of representatives of foreign powers, and especially of Protestant England.

So H. E. Sir Henry Bulwer, in one of his most important communications to us, which was intended for effect in England, and was published there, places us in altogether a false position, and shows us in a most unfavorable light. Had we entertained the views which he ascribes to us, or rather assumes that we entertain, his reasonings and his advice would have been most excellent; but as such views and such conduct are as abhorrent to our own minds as they are to his, the communication does us great injustice, for the English government and all right-minded Englishmen must feel that we, as thus represented, are most unreasonable, and need to be held in with bit and bridle.

But I fear I am taxing your Lordship's time and patience; I fear, too, I may not have touched upon those points you could have desired me to speak. I hope, however, the few scattered things I have said may serve as hints to enable you the better to understand our present position.

But let me not close without assuring your Lordship that we every day see reason to bless God that He sent you to this country, and used you as an important instrument of great and permanent good to all the nationalities of Turkey. May your declining years be years of great peace and happiness! May your own heart repose confidence and find comfort in those everlasting truths which now, through your instrumentality, the mingled people of these countries are permitted to read and believe and enjoy.

Mrs. Goodell unites in very kind regards for Lady Redcliffe. And may I ask your Lordship to inform Miss Canning that I retain very grateful recollections of her having once piloted me with perfect safety through all the straits and narrows and shoals of the Prayer-book.

I have the honor to be, yours most truly and faithfully,

W. GOODELL.

The reply of Lord Stratford, though carefully and properly guarded with reference to the relations of the governments, and especially in regard to the British representative at Constantinople, expressed the deep interest he had always felt in the cause in which the American missionaries were engaged, and renewed the assurances of his personal friendship : —

UPLEATHAM, Oct. 12, 1864.

MY DEAR AND REVEREND SIR, — The advantage of hearing from you was very acceptable to me, notwithstanding the painful topics to which your letter and its interesting enclosure necessarily referred. You have always held a high place in my esteem, and latterly in my affection also. It is, therefore, natural that I should derive pleasure from any renewal, even at this distance, of our former more frequent communications. I could only wish that it were in my power to afford you, under present circumstances, that support which you received from me in other times, and which you and your fellow-laborers deserve so well at my hands. A feeling of delicacy prevented my going up to Earl Russell with the first representations on the subject of the late vexatious treatment of the missionaries and their converts by the Turkish government. But I wrote to his Lordship in proof of my general concurrence with the deputation, which could not have been introduced to him by an abler or more suitable advocate than the Earl of Shaftesbury. I have since had occasion to confirm my previous opinion in a letter of reply to Lord Chichester, who had written to me in his character of President of our Evangelical Alliance. Whatever may remain to be done is open to consideration.

My absence from London has prevented me from seeing the missionaries who applied for an interview; but Mr. Schmettau had sent me some printed documents connected with the object of their application, and I have directed my eldest daughter, who is in the neighborhood of London, to see them, if she can, and report what they have to communicate. Judging from my past acquaintance with the missionaries, your countrymen, I cannot readily believe that they have suffered their zeal to carry them to any objectionable lengths, and I presume that the converts from Islamism have imbibed the discretion of their teachers, and would not, if it were only for personal considerations, do any thing to provoke the Turkish authorities, or to merit the forfeiture of that liberty of conscience which was distinctly secured to them by the Imperial Charter.

I know not under what suggestions our Foreign Department may have to take its course with respect to the late transactions in Turkey, but I shall be painfully disappointed if any official lukewarmness at Constantinople receives any countenance inconsistent with our anterior policy and the inalienable provisions of the Hatti Humayoun.

Should any thing occur, either before or after my return to London, to require a fresh communication with you, I would not scruple to trouble you with another letter.

Meanwhile, I beg you will accept from my wife and daughters, as well as from myself, the joint expression of our kindest regards and best wishes for your health and happiness.

Believe me, ever truly and cordially yours,

STRATFORD DE R.

In regard to the actual responsibility for the disturbance which arose, and especially with respect to the charge of publicly reviling the prophet, Dr. Goodell wrote at the time to one of his brethren in Turkey:—

"The American missionaries have not changed their policy, but it ought to be known that other missionaries have come in, who from the first have pursued a very different policy. The Rev. Dr. Pfander, of the Church Missionary Society, a very worthy and excellent man, came and opened his batteries against Islamism. We earnestly advised him not to publish those books; we entreated him not to do it; we solemnly protested against his doing it. But this good brother having what the great Dr. Edwards attempted to prove nobody can have, viz., *a self-determining power of the will,* went on and did it; and the effect has been to bring all our missionary and Bible operations into great danger, — the very thing of which we had repeatedly warned him.

"Then there is a Mr. O'Flaherty, an Irishman, who, from being a sergeant in the Crimean war, felt called upon at the close of it to convert all the Mussulmans for whom he had fought so bravely. Some good people in England furnished the funds, and requested us to direct his labors. This we soon found to be impracticable, and we wrote, saying we could no longer assume any responsibility in regard to him. He was then shifted over to some English or Scotch society, and has continued his responsible or irresponsible labors to the present time, holding lectures or meetings up and down the Bosphorus, at all suitable or unsuitable places, talking long and loud, on steamboats or elsewhere, with any one who would ask or answer a question or give him a hearing, and, it may be (though I know not if there be any proof), saying hard things against the Koran and the prophet. Perhaps it will appear at last that he and Dr. Pfander have done more good than any of us; but even this will be no evidence that they acted with Christian prudence and discretion; for the Lord in His wisdom and great mercy sometimes makes use of our imprudences and our indiscretions. But we greatly need here at the present time for British ambassador a man like Lord Redcliffe, whose moral worth and weight of character would be felt, whose sympathies would be with the Bible and not with the Koran, with Christianity and not with Islamism, and who would represent the English and not the Turkish government."

This verdict upon the principles and course of Sir Henry Bulwer was fully confirmed in his speedy recall. He was plainly unfitted to represent the Christian government of England at such a court as that of the Sublime Porte. Wholly without sympathy for the great object and the great work of the Christian missionaries, he was also so ignorant of the facts in the case, and of religious matters in general, as to assert, and insist upon it, that Dr. Pfander was an American, sent out by the American Board; and when the English representative of the British and Foreign Bible Society assured him he must have been misinformed, for Dr. Pfander was from England, and was in the service of the English Church Missionary Society, Sir Henry replied that he himself was an Englishman, and knew what there was in England, and he had never heard of such a thing as the Church Missionary Society.

This storm of persecution and excitement, though violent for a time, was not long in passing over and its occurrence was the means of defining more clearly the true character of the religious charter which the Sultan had granted to his subjects, and of making them more secure in the enjoyment of the privileges which had been guaranteed. It is simply wonderful that this Mohammedan power, which by the creed of Islam is pledged to intolerance, if not to persecution, has given so many and such strong pledges, binding itself to carry out the principles of toleration and protection toward those of other religions.

Dr. Goodell's native politeness and true dignity of heart were never more apparent than when he had occasion to ask pecuniary aid in the work in which he was engaged. This was always done with perfect delicacy, and with the utmost regard for the rights of others; and yet when he made such an application, he did it as though he were presenting a draft which he had received personally from the Lord Jesus, whose is " the earth and the fulness thereof." One scarcely can tell which most to admire in the following correspondence, the Christian propriety and freedom of the application, the heartiness with which the generous response was made, or the scriptural simplicity and beauty of the acknowledgment when the response was received: —

CONSTANTINOPLE, Oct. 4, 1864.

To the Rev. W. ADAMS, D.D., Madison Square, New York:

REV. AND DEAR BROTHER, — Mr. Sarkis Minasian, a native Armenian of Constantinople, but a naturalized American citizen and a good Christian brother, offers to lend us five hundred pounds for two years without interest, on condition that we use it in completing the church which we commenced building several years ago, but had to stop for want of funds.   Five hundred pounds is the estimate of the architect, and he has this day commenced the work under the direction of Mr. Minasian and ourselves.

Now, my dear brother, there are three things we shall want of your good people : —

First, *A Bell*, " to call a solemn assembly " three times every Sabbath day ; not a large one, but such as is used in your factories and public schools ; not too sharp or shrill, but a good one, and rather deep-toned.

Second, *A Melodeon*, to help " lift up a sound on high " when the people have been called together by the bell.   This should be about the size of those in your lecture-rooms.   Our church is about forty-four by twenty-seven feet.   Let it be strongly rather than elegantly made, and let the bell be without the possibility of a crack, for we have no good President Dwight here to recommend " a carrot poultice."

And then, if you give us these two, we want,

Third, *Your Prayers.*   Without the two former your prayers will be too weak to have any perceptible influence at Constantinople; but, with those two, " this service not only will supply the want of the saints," but be " abundant also by many thanksgivings unto God."

Consider what I say, and the Lord give thee understanding in all things.

Your very affectionate brother in Christ,
W. GOODELL.

The Rev. Dr. Adams, on receiving this letter, read it to his congregation, and a collection, which was in keeping with the proverbial liberality of the people, was taken on the spot. It proved more than sufficient for the purchase of the bell and the melodeon, which were immediately shipped, with all expenses paid, to Constantinople.   The following letter of acknowledgment was subsequently received and read by Dr. Adams to his people : —

CONSTANTINOPLE, March 13, 1865.

REV. WILLIAM ADAMS, D.D., — I know not in what Dictionary to find suitable words to express our sense of the obligation we feel to you and your good people for your and their prompt attention to our wants.

The bell is exactly of the size and ring which I described in my letter. It utters its voice sufficiently loud and clear to arrest the attention of most of those who live within the limits of our parish, and summon them to the worship of the great God in the house of prayer, while the six-stop cabinet organ of Mason & Hamlin enables us to discourse sweet music to those assembled there.

Had your church been organized three thousand years ago, and had they been as thoughtful of King David's wants as they were of ours, it would have been celebrated in the 150th Psalm. And when he called upon us to praise God "upon the loud cymbals" and upon "the high-sounding cymbals," he would have added, with an emphasis, "and also upon the six-stop cabinet organ of Mason & Hamlin, furnished by the munificence of Dr. Adams's church in New York."

The church is now finished, the bell hung, and the organ in position, and yesterday the whole was dedicated with appropriate services to God the Father, God the Son, and God the Holy Ghost. In the morning the Rev. Dr. Hamlin preached in Armenian. He was assisted in the services by Pastor Simon, of Pera, who you will rejoice to hear is again with us, and like one of us, as in former happy times. We hope the Lord "will again turn our captivity as the streams of the south." Indeed, it really seems as if He had already begun to do so, and all this, we are quite willing to believe, is owing to the increase in your prayers for us; for as a general thing, as I wrote you before, the more a church increases in her contributions the more does she increase in the frequency, fervency, and efficaciousness of her prayers. And this improved state of things first began to appear just about the time your collection was made to furnish us with the organ and the bell.

In the afternoon of yesterday I preached in Turkish, and observed several Jews and also Turks in the congregation. The house was densely crowded both parts of the day, and as one, in describing the aspect of the assembly, remarked, every face seemed radiant with joy. One native sister said that when she heard the sweet music and still sweeter words she could hardly contain herself, but she felt that she must absolutely break out into an exceedingly loud and not bitter, but joyful cry. Another aged member of the church said she felt like saying, with the aged Simeon, " Lord, now lettest thou thy servant depart in peace." It only remains that we pray earnestly that the place may be filled with the glory of God, and that the Lord may " count, when He writeth up the people, that this and that man were born there."

We do not forget your former contribution to this mission of a communion service, and for the former and the latter rain, the upper and the nether springs, we thank you. In the name of our whole mission, I thank you. In the name of this poor and very feeble church, I thank you. In the name, the precious name, of Christ, we thank you. May all that pass by your beautiful heritage be constrained to lift up their hands and say, " The blessing of the Lord be upon you. We bless you in the name of the Lord."

" The churches of Asia salute you."

Your very affectionate brother in Christ,

W. Goodell.

To an invitation to attend in this country the twenty-fifth anniversary of the marriage of a daughter of one of his former instructors at Andover Theological Seminary, he sent the following reply : —

CONSTANTINOPLE, May 17, 1864.

MY DEAR AND HAPPY DAUGHTER, — Your kind invitation to be present at your " silver wedding," I received last week. And now only three days remain for us to attend to our passports, secure our passage, arrange all our affairs, and complete all our arrangements for a six months' absence from our work. How you could expect that I especially, with all the infirmities of age, could do all this in three days, I cannot possibly conceive. In the other world, where, I suppose, as quick as thought we can find ourselves where we wish to be, such a thing might be possible ; although even there you will recollect that one of the angels, and one made to fly swiftly, was a full half day in getting to Daniel, and that another, sent to him with most important despatches and answers to prayers, owing to difficulties on the way, was full three weeks in getting to him, and this though another very mighty angel came to his help. Sure you must have supposed that all the angels in heaven would be at our service, and would take turns in carrying us on their wings, to enable us to reach in good time your silver wedding.

I forwarded without delay your invitation to Dr. Schauffler. And did we suppose you would have such a time as John Gilpin had, I am sure he would almost start right off, even though he had to walk on the sea some of the way, and all the way on foot; for he has recently celebrated his own silver wedding, and his heart is full of the brightest and happiest thoughts on the subject.

Oh if he could be there, what a time you would have! But you can, and I hope will, have the presence of One whose thoughts towards you are precious beyond expression, who can turn your water into wine, and every curse into a blessing, and make every bitter thing sweet.

Your father's, your husband's, and your own friend,

WILLIAM GOODELL.

Conscious that his work of preaching the Gospel with his lips was drawing near its close, and desiring still to speak in his own familiar terms to those for whose salvation he had spent nearly all his life, Dr. Goodell, during his last year at Constantinople, prepared for the press forty-eight of the sermons in Turkish which he had preached to the people; in order, as he said, " that they may the more readily 'remember the words that I spake unto them while I was yet with them.'" These sermons were published in a volume, accompanied by a farewell letter to the Protestant churches in the Turkish empire. The sermons were soon scattered abroad, and being written not only in the language but in the idiom of the people, they were read and heard with great eagerness. A portion of them were translated into the Bulgarian language, and were read over and over again by the Bulgarians in the northern part of the empire. They were afterward translated into Armenian by the wife of the native pastor at Kharpoot, in Eastern Turkey, and by the liberality of a few Christian friends in this country the volume was stereotyped, published by the American Tract Society, and one edition after another speedily exhausted. They are still preaching the Gospel of Christ in different languages, in various parts of Turkey.

The following is the letter to the evangelical churches in Turkey. Even in its English dress it will be read with an interest akin to that excited by the last words of Paul the aged to the elders of the church of Ephesus, as he met them at Miletus, on his last journey to Jerusalem: —

TO THE EVANGELICAL CHURCHES IN TURKEY.

DEAR BRETHREN AND SISTERS IN THE LORD, — It is more than forty years since I left my native country and came to Turkey, and about one-third of a century since I made Constantinople my home. I am now old, and I know not the day of my death. I am also feeble, and cannot reasonably expect to continue long. All my powers of body and mind are failing, and I am going to the house appointed for all living. For all your kindness to me and mine since the first day I came among you, you have my sincere thanks. And you have also my fervent prayers for your temporal and eternal well-being.

In your hands I leave the Scriptures of the Old and New Testaments, which, with the important help of some of you, I translated into Armeno-Turkish for the benefit of those of you who use only or chiefly that language. With these Scriptures you have also a Commentary on the Gospel of Matthew, which also with your aid I prepared for you in the same language. And I am now putting into the hands of the printer more than forty of the sermons which some of you may recollect to have heard me preach to you, in order that you may better "remember the words I spake unto you while I was yet with you." And whether these words be " the words of truth and soberness"; whether they be in strict conformity to God's holy word, — you must search and see for yourselves. Blessed be God! you now have the whole Bible in your native language, and you need not, and must not, remain ignorant of its holy doctrines and sublime teachings.

When we first came among you, you were not a distinct people, nor did we expect you ever would be ; for we had no sectarian object in view, it being no part of our plan to meddle with ecclesiastical affairs. Our sole desire was to preach

Christ and Him crucified.   Our object was precisely the
same as that of the missionaries to that ancient church in
Persia.   The labors of those missionaries have produced no
separation in that church ; but they have been permitted to
labor side by side with the bishops and priests, to preach in
their houses of worship, to assist in supporting and superin-
tending their schools, and to do much in every way to enlighten and elevate that whole community.

But if instead of giving the missionaries a cordial welcome
among them, they had anathematized and persecuted to the
death all those who loved the truth and wished to live a
godly, conscientious life, the consequence would have been,
that those persecuted suffering ones would have been forced
to appeal to the civil powers for protection, as you had to do
here.   And the civil power there might have found it necessary, in order to afford this protection in conformity with
ancient usage, to separate those persons from their former
connection, and acknowledge them as a distinct community,
entitled to all the protection and privileges of any other
community in the empire.   This you know was the case here.
The Sublime Porte, to save you from perishing, was compelled to separate you from the old Armenian community.
This is your present condition ; and this condition you should
" accept with all thankfulness," and use it for your own and
your children's good.

And, my brethren, if you do not now remain, or speedily
become, a holy, happy, united people, securing the confidence
and commanding the respect of all around you, you have
none to blame but yourselves ; for in being good and doing
good, no people on earth ever enjoyed a higher freedom than
has been bestowed upon you.

Among my last words of adieu to you, let me exhort you
to bear with one another's infirmities, " forgiving one another,
even as God, for Christ's sake, hath forgiven you."   Be honest in your dealings both with the world and with one another,
always keeping your accounts written in a fair hand ; and
this even in all business transactions with your own relatives
and Christian brethren ; for memory is imperfect, and impressions are not always to be trusted.   In this imperfect
world, the only safe way is to keep a book-account of all
pecuniary transactions.

Train up your children in the way they should go.   Remember that they have souls as well as bodies, and if it be

your duty to provide food and raiment for their bodies, so is it your duty to provide instruction for their immortal minds. See that they have suitable teachers and suitable books. Teach them also yourselves, especially on the Lord's day, and bring them with you to the sanctuary, that they may assist in singing the high praises of our God, and that they may receive the blessing of the God of Jacob.

Labor to support, as soon as possible, your own civil, educational, and religious institutions; and be always ready to assist those more needy than yourselves.

Be kind to the poor and to the sick, and visit the families of affliction, of want, and of sorrow. In all these respects, be Jesus Christ's men and women; that is, do as you think He would do if He were among you. Hasten to the relief of those who are in distress. Have little prayer-meetings in the neighborhood of those who are unable to attend public worship. Have little meetings also for the young, and for those who are beginning to seek after God, and to desire a knowledge of His ways.

If the Lord bless you with a pastor, honor him, love him, and pray for him. Do all you can to assist him, and to strengthen his hands and encourage his heart in his labors for your good. The relation of a missionary to you is not intended to be permanent, and it should not be continued longer than is absolutely necessary. While it continues it calls for mutual candor, forbearance, and kindness; but it should, as soon as circumstances will permit, be superseded by the pastoral office. This should be a permanent relation; labor to make it so. And besides providing what is suitable for the support of your pastor, if you now and then make him a small present, as a token of your love and of your appreciation of his services, though by reason of your poverty it be no more than a choice apple or orange, it will awaken anew his interest in you and his prayers for you.

When a stranger enters your place of worship, direct him at once to a suitable seat, or give up your own to him. It might be well to make it the duty of the door-keeper to be on the alert to seat all strangers. This is comparatively a small matter, but Christian courtesy, and even common politeness, requires attention to it. Should such a stranger come a second or third time, take it for granted that he desires to find the way of life, and lose no time in seeking an acquaintance with him; not for the sake of holding up to ridicule his former belief, or the ceremonies and errors of his church, but for the sake of leading him to the Scriptures of truth, the fountain of living waters. Twenty-five or thirty years ago, such a stranger could hardly appear in sight without being at once hailed and introduced to the whole brotherhood, receiving from you all exhortations without stint, and being followed also with your fervent prayers. Let not your former zeal degenerate into cold indifference.

But I must conclude. And now, "my brethren, dearly beloved and longed for. my joy and crown, so stand fast in the Lord, my dearly beloved" (Phil. iv. 1). "If there be therefore any consolation in Christ, if any comfort of love. if any fellowship of the Spirit, if any bowels and mercies, fulfil ye my joy, that ye be like-minded, having the same love, being of one accord, of one mind. Let nothing be done through strife or vainglory, but in lowliness of mind let each esteem other better than themselves" (Phil. ii. 1–3). And now, how can I better take my leave of you, and express to you my very last words, and the very best wishes of my heart, than in the language of Paul in 2 Cor. xiii. 11: "Finally, brethren, farewell. Be perfect, be of good comfort, be of one mind, live in peace; and the God of love and peace shall be with you." Amen.

Your very affectionate brother in Christ,

W. GOODELL.

19*

CHAPTER XXIV.

THE time at length came when, in consequence of advancing years and increasing infirmity, it was necessary that Dr. and Mrs. Goodell should make some change. They were no longer able to bear the responsibilities of housekeeping in that distant land, and it was evident that their earthly labors were drawing near an end.   It was suggested that their son and daughter, the Rev. Herman N. Barnum and his wife, should remove to Constantinople, from their field of labor at Kharpoot, in Eastern Turkey, to be with them in their declining years.   But this was deemed undesirable, on account of the great importance of the Eastern field, in which Mr. Barnum had been eminently successful; and the venerable couple decided to return to America, and spend their last days with their children, who were anxious to welcome them to their homes.   This decision Dr. Goodell communicated to the Board in a letter, dated Constantinople, March 2, 1865, in which he said : —

"It would be our desire to live and die, and be buried, among the people for whose good we have spent the strength of our life and the vigor of our days ; but this cannot be.   It is a sad conclusion to which we have come, but, after much thought and consultation, we are unable to come to any other. When we left America the first time, in 1822, I do not recollect that either of us shed a tear.   We sailed from New York, having already taken leave of our friends in New England.   When we sailed the second time, in 1853, and left five children standing on the wharf in Boston, not one of whom had yet found a home, we sat down and wept.   But at the very thought of leaving our work in Constantinople, together with our beloved associates, and all the dear objects of our prayers and labors in the East, our head seems ready at once to become waters, and our eyes a fountain of tears. Of all our separations, this seems the hardest to bear. Forty-three years ago we had youth and courage, being strong and hopeful. Now, youth and strength and energy are gone. Then we had much confidence in ourselves; but we would still confidently put our hand in His, and go confidently and cheerfully wherever He may lead us, whether it be from the eastern to the western continent, or from this world to the other.

"When we left America the first time, it was to go to Jerusalem. That was our destination; but we have never been there. Now we set our faces toward the New Jerusalem, and I hope we shall not fail of arriving there. It is not so much America as it is heaven to which we would now direct our eyes and thoughts. For though life itself may yet be spared for several years, our life-work must be nearly or quite done, and we feel that 'we are going home, to die no more.' We have the prospect of finding among our beloved children a suitable room, where we can breathe our last prayers, and we hope to find a corner in some cemetery, where we can rest in quietness till the bright morning of the resurrection.

"The work of missions appears to me more and more excellent and glorious, as I begin to feel that my connection with it is drawing to a close. I bless God for the great privilege of being connected with it for so long a time. My unworthiness appears exceedingly great, and I wonder at the divine patience and forbearance towards me. To the Prudential Committee, and to all the members of the Board, to the secretaries and treasurers, and especially to you, my dear brother, do I feel under great obligations for all your and their kindness. 'I die, but God will surely visit you;' and you shall not labor in vain. He will raise up other and better instruments, and will surely perform the oath He sware to His Son. All the land promised shall assuredly be His for an everlasting possession. And blessed be all those who are in sympathy with Him. I regret no sacrifice I may at any time have made for Him. Sacrifice for His dear sake is no sacrifice. No: it is honor, it is happiness, it is privilege, high and sacred."

If the parting was sad to them, it was not less so to the large circle of American and English friends at Constantinople, to whom they were bound by the strongest ties of Christian love and personal friendship. With some of the families they had been associated on terms of great intimacy and mutual confidence and love, for more than a quarter of a century. To them all Dr. Goodell was like a father, tenderly beloved, and held in the highest respect.

In anticipation of their departure, a large number of the foreign residents at the Turkish capital made arrangements for an expression of their regrets, and of their respect and attachment. They assembled for this purpose on Thursday, June 8, 1865, at the Hotel d'Angleterre, where they had invited Dr. and Mrs. Goodell to meet them. The "Levant Herald" had the following account of the proceedings: —

"It had been known for several weeks that the Rev. William Goodell, D.D., of the American Mission to the Armenians, was about to retire from the scene of his labors, and return with his family to America. Dr. Goodell is in his seventy-fourth year, and has spent forty-three years in active missionary labor in the East, during thirty-four of which he has resided in this city. In these circumstances it need be no wonder that his long residence among us, his public position, his professional labors, and his inestimable personal virtues, should have endeared him to all who have resided here any considerable time, and made them contemplate his withdrawal almost as a personal bereavement. It needed but a simple suggestion to secure the expression of these feelings in an address to their venerable friend, accompanied by the gift of a timepiece as a memorial of esteem from the older British residents here. The presentation took place in the presence of a numerous assemblage of British and American residents. Charles S. Hanson was called to the chair, and, observing that the meeting was held for the purpose of taking leave of their venerable friend, requested the Rev. Dr. Schauffler to open the proceedings with prayer. He then called upon the Rev. Dr. Thomson, of the British and Foreign Bible Society, to read the address which had been prepared, and of which the following is a transcript: —

" ' CONSTANTINOPLE, June 8, 1865.

" ' DEAR DR. GOODELL, — We have asked you to meet us on this occasion, that we may express to you publicly those sentiments of esteem and regard which we all entertain for you personally, and that respect and admiration with which we look back upon your long and unblemished career of Christian usefulness in this city, — sentiments which we feel all the more deeply in the near prospect of your withdrawal from among us.

" ' Several of our number can remember that when you first arrived here in 1831, there was no chaplain to minister to the British residents, and consequently none to address to them in their own language the word of life, to dispense to them the sacraments, or to pour the consolations of the Gospel into the sorrowing heart. Your disinterested and laborious services at that period are still gratefully remembered by many of your friends, and they doubt not that a more enduring record of them is preserved on high. As members of other churches and of a different nationality, though one intimately connected with your own, we have long highly appreciated that catholic Christian love with which you have ever welcomed good men of every denomination, winning their confidence by your cheerful cordiality of manner, while your whole character and deportment, chastened by wisdom, and pervaded by Christian principle, never failed to instruct and encourage all who had the privilege of your acquaintance. Nor can we omit to refer to the edification and enjoyment with which we have often listened to your lucid, faithful, and impressive expositions of divine truth, while we pray that we may more than ever be guided by that faith and hope in our Lord Jesus Christ, which it has always been your happiness to proclaim.

" ' But though it has been chiefly as a minister of Christ, preaching among us in the English language as opportunity occurred, that we have come in contact with you, we are well aware that, after all, such services formed but a very small portion of your public labors. We well know that your most vigorous years and your most devoted efforts were consecrated to the high enterprise of presenting to the Armenian people a translation of the whole word of God in a language known to almost all of them, and to very many of them the best if not the only means of access to their intellect and feelings. The divine Head of the church has permitted you not only to finish this great work, but to republish in a revised edition the whole Armeno-Turkish Bible once, and the New Testament in the same form several times ; and, more cheering still to the Christian missionary, He has given you to see not a few instances in which your labors have been blessed by the Spirit to the conversion and edification of your fellow-men. By these labors, as well as by your Commentary and your published Sermons, you have left an inestimable legacy of divine truth to the Armenian nation, in whose grateful remembrance we doubt not your name will long be honored as pre-eminent among the noble band of American missionaries in this country.

" ' It would be out of place to advert to every thing that occurs to us on this occasion ; but permit us to assure you and all the members of your family that, while we humbly submit to the arrangements of infinite wisdom and goodness, we part from you with deep and unfeigned regret, accompanying you and yours with our best wishes, and praying that your declining years — and may they still be many — may be cheered and supported by the comforts of the Spirit, and the love and reverence of your friends in your native land, until at last you be called from your labors of love on earth, to the rest that remaineth for the people of God.

" ' We have now to request your acceptance of this timepiece, as a memorial, however inadequate, of the sentiments which we all entertain towards you, and as something to remind you in after years of many in Constantinople who love and revere you. May we not even hope that it may be long regarded by your children and your children's children as a simple but emphatic testimony to the worth of an honored parent, and an incentive to all of them to imitate his example.

" ' T. Hardy, C. S. Hanson, Mrs. C. S. Hanson, Charles La Fontaine, Mrs. Rumball, Rev. Zabanski. Rev. H. T. Knapp, Mr. and Mrs. E. La Fontaine, T. Millingen, H. T. Hanson, E. F. Ede, G. B. Marshall, Thomas Baker, R. T. Buck, Rev. C. B. Gribble, Rev. A. Thomson, D.D., T. H. Charnaud, James Binns, John Rowell, Robert Hayden, E. Grace, T. R. Thomson, George Bill, W. Sellar, W. B. Hopper, R. T. Allan, John Seager, G. H. Clifton, T. R. Parry, W. Dann, Mr. Wright, Rev. C. S. Newman, Henry Lamb, Thomas Turner, R. Sarrell, M. D., Mrs. Sarrell, Miss E. Whittet, Miss A. Ewan, Thomas Swan, F. Guarracino, Misses Walsh, Rev. A. Tomery, T. Herdman, Mr. W. Kerr.' "

Mr. Hanson, in a few appropriate words, presented to Dr. Goodell the testimonial, with the address engrossed on vellum. Dr. Goodell, with deep emotion, in replying, referred to the peculiarly pleasant intercourse he had always enjoyed with the British families, with one of which — Mr. Hanson's — he had been most happily associated from the time of his first arrival, in 1831. Nothing had ever occurred to break the harmony of his intercourse with them all. His official services had been cheerfully rendered for their benefit, in public and in private; and they had as cheerfully responded to his calls for aid in his work, and most liberally when the native Christians were enduring persecution and in want. He concluded with an assurance of his unfailing remembrance and affection for all his friends at Constantinople.

The following is the inscription on the timepiece, a valuable clock: —

"In grateful recollection of his eminent ministerial services in the cause of his divine Master, not only amongst the Armenians in Turkey, to whom, as a missionary of the American Board, he was especially deputed. but also among the British and other communities; and with admiration of his talents and labors in translating the word of God into Armeno-Turkish, with affectionate regard also for his noble catholicity of spirit, for his gentleness and discretion, and with best wishes and prayers for his happy return and peaceful sojourn in his native land, this timepiece is presented by members of the British community

"TO THE REV. W. GOODELL, D.D.,

on his departure from Constantinople, after a ministry of forty-three years in the East."

The Rev. Dr. Hamlin, President of Robert College, followed with a few remarks, in the course of which he characterized the occasion as one of many which evidenced the deep sympathy and mutual esteem which subsisted between the British people and their brethren in America, and expressed the confident hope that the Christians of both countries would continue to co-operate in the diffusion of Scripture truth. He assured all present that there was not an American missionary in Turkey who did not feel as grateful to their British friends for this testimonial to their venerable father, as if it had been bestowed upon himself. The Rev. Dr. Riggs, of the American Mission, then offered prayer.

Other testimonials of affection from different families and persons were added. Among the most grateful was one presented by twenty-six of the missionary children, one of whom was blind, to whom Dr. Goodell returned the following note of acknowledgment: —

To Blind Charlie, Chairman of the Children's Committee, together with all the other members.

VERY DEAR CHILDREN, BABIES AND ALL, — On being waited upon yesterday by your honorable deputation, we re membered the proverb, that " in some places it never rains but it pours, and that sometimes .the most abundant and refreshing showers come last." Certain it is, that no kindness shown us, and no honors rendered us, have so moved our feelings as yours have done.

We read over with great interest all your names, and remembered all the dear faces that belong to them, not only all the older faces, but even the baby faces also; and we pray that you may all hereafter, in the kingdom of our Father, shine as the sun in the firmament.

And we beseech you to pray for us that we may not be puffed up and exalted above measure by these abundant revelations of honor made to us these last days. We love to be loved; and it is very pleasant to be remembered by our friends, and especially by the children; and we shall not cease to have you in most loving and prayerful remembrance.

Please, God, let Charlie live, and Willie, and Clara, and Nellie, and Henry; yea, all the dear ones at Bebek, Pera, and Galata, and Haas Keuy, and Constantinople, with those that have gone to sea!

We cannot reward you, dear children, for your kindness to us, so unworthy; but if you will honor Christ, who is infinitely worthy of all you can bestow on Him, He will reward you a thousand-fold. He will crown you with eternal joy.

We do not expect to look again upon your sweet faces here below, but we hope we shall meet you all —

> " On the other side of Jordan,
> In the sweet fields of Eden,
> Where the tree of life doth bloom."

Pray for us, that we may not fail of crossing safely over to the other side; and we also will pray for you. And may the Lord Jesus Himself take us all up and carry us in His own blessed arms, and then we shall be safe.

Your very loving friends,

W. GOODELL, and
A. P. GOODELL.

The Hon. E. Joy Morris, United States ambassador to the Sublime Porte, on the eve of the departure of Dr. Goodell, accompanied the presentation of a valuable token of his regard with the following note : —

UNITED STATES LEGATION,
BUYUK-DÈRÈ, June 28, 1865.

Rev. W. GOODELL, D.D. :

MY DEAR SIR, — I beg you to accept the accompanying silver service as a memorial of the baptism of our daughter Roumelie, and also of the great esteem entertained for you by Mrs. Morris and myself. Most deeply do we regret your departure from Turkey, where your Christian life and virtues are so widely known and appreciated. In my intercourse with men I have never met with one who, in his actions, speech, and manner of life, more truly represented the excellencies of the Christian character. The daily walk of such men as yourself shows what moral beauty and sublime virtue there is in the true Christian character.

With Mrs. Morris's and my own most affectionate regards to Mrs. Goodell and daughters, and the hope that you may all safely arrive in America, and there pass the rest of your life in peace and happiness among your kindred, I remain,

Most affectionately and truly yours,
E. JOY MORRIS.

Before leaving Constantinople, Dr. Goodell went into the city proper and spent several days, visiting from house to house, conversing, singing, and praying with the families over whom he had had a pastoral care, — many of whose members he had been instrumental in leading into the fold of the great Shepherd. When he had taken leave of one of these families, and was passing out of the door, a little boy about eight years of age seized his hand, and, looking up into his face, said, out of the promptings of his own heart, " When you are gone away I will be a preacher here in your place." He laid his hands on the head of the boy and blessed him. In speaking of the incident in a public address after his return to this country, he said: " I now commend this little boy to your prayers. I do not remember his name, but no matter, the

Lord will know what little boy you mean, especially if you tell Him it was the little fellow who has engaged to be a preacher in my stead."

He devoted several days to farewell calls upon the families in the suburbs of Constantinople, native as well as foreign, for whom he had lived, and labored, and prayed; and they thronged his house to give him their salaams and to receive his farewell blessing. The evening before he was to sail, about a hundred of the people came to sing a farewell hymn which they had prepared, expressive of their obligations to him. He received them as a father would his children who came to take their leave, but he told them their hymn should be in praise of Christ instead of himself. The day that he was to leave, many of the old Armenians, as well as the Protestants, came to his house; and among the crowd that followed him, weeping, to the wharf, were some who had stoned him and spat upon him in the days of the persecution.

" Amid many tears and benedictions," he left Constantinople on the 27th of June, 1865. His heart clung to it as the scene of his labors, where he had witnessed so many wonderful displays of the grace of God, and he still yearned after the work that he was laying down for ever. Here, as the pioneer of a noble band of soldiers of Christ, he had planted the standard of the cross, thirty-four years before. From the steamer on which he sailed he wrote to his daughter, then in the far East: " As we swept round Seraglio Point, and I caught the last glimpse of Constantinople and its magnificent surroundings, I kept saying in my heart, ' Farewell, thou beautiful city, may thy moral beauties soon equal all thy natural! I should love to preach the Gospel to thy people once more.' "

On board the steamer he met the Algerian chieftain, Abd-el-Kadr, who had signalized himself as the protector of the Christians during the massacre at Damascus in 1860. This kind and liberal-hearted Mussulman conversed very freely with the missionary in regard to his own checkered career, and made many inquiries respecting the Turks of Constantinople who had become Christians. Dr. Goodell tarried a short time at Athens, and then sailed for Marseilles, reaching Paris on the 7th of July. At London he rested quietly for a few days, and on the 20th sailed from Liverpool, and ar-arrived at Boston on the 3d of August.

At the monthly concert in Park Street church he made an interesting address on the condition and prospects of Turkey, and again spoke on the same subject at Roxbury. After visiting several friends in Boston and the neighboring towns, he went to Hartford, to the home of the Rev. Isaac Bird and Mrs. Bird, with whom he left this country in 1822, and with whom he had been intimately associated in missionary labor for many years at Malta and Beyrout. He preached at Hartford, and delivered addresses at various places in the vicinity. Wherever he went he was called upon to give some account of his work in the East, and he was always ready for the service.

CHAPTER XXV.

IN October, 1865, the American Board held its fifty-sixth annual meeting at Chicago. Although feeble in body and in voice, he desired to share once more in the hallowed interest of the yearly gatherings of the society, in whose service he had worn out the energies of his life. From the time when a mere youth he left his father's house, and went out alone and unaided to acquire an education, he had known no other purpose in living but to promote the great object of this institution, — the publication of the gospel of salvation among the nations of the earth. Now that he had come to the borders of the river, and was about to pass over to the other side, to the land of rest, he had a strong desire to mingle once more with those who were to guide and carry on the work.

Probably nothing connected with the meeting at Chicago excited greater interest at the time, or will be remembered with more pleasure, than his venerable presence, which was a benediction in itself. With his aged form bent with years and toil, his beaming countenance, his snow-white beard, his head wearing the Oriental cap, on which was inscribed in Arabic characters the motto, "The hoary head is a crown of glory, if it be found in the way of righteousness," wrought by the hands of Eastern converts to the cross, and still more by his cheerful bearing, his spiritual conversation, none the less spiritual because flavored with his sparkling humor, he made an impression which will ever be associated with this anniversary of the Board.

An incident that occurred during the meeting illustrates his love of practical humor. One day, while the great congregation was gathering, he took his seat on the floor of the hall, when two ladies came in and sat next him. One of them turned and asked him if he was acquainted with Dr. Goodell. He said he was. She then asked if he saw him on the stage. He looked up and down the platform, and at length said he did not see him there, and he thought he was not among the gentlemen on the stage. She then asked him if he would not be so good as to look over the hall, as she was very anxious to get a sight of him, which he did, looking in all directions. At length, turning rather abruptly toward her, he said, " Why, madam, he is sitting just next to you." She looked first at her friend who was with her, then at him, and it was some time before she could comprehend what he meant. When she awoke to his meaning she was covered with confusion, and said to him, " Why, sir, I am so ashamed." He replied, " And I am so ashamed too."

His voice was too feeble for him to address the great assembly, but he spoke frequently at the smaller gatherings, and it was suggested to him by one of the officers of the Board to prepare a letter that should be read by some one in his stead, before the Board should adjourn. Accordingly near the close of the meeting he rose on the platform and said : —

" When I went from my native country, in 1822, it was to go to Jerusalem ; that was my destination, there I expected to live, to labor, and to die and be buried, arising again at the resurrection of the just. I have never been there. I have now set my face toward the New Jerusalem, taking Chicago on my way." (This allusion awakened loud and long applause.)

" As my voice and my strength will not allow me to address this large assembly, I have, since my arrival here, prepared my thoughts, and addressed them to the respected President of this Board, and will now request Mr. Dodge to read the paper to the Board."

To the Rev. MARK HOPKINS, D.D., LL.D., *President of the A. B. C. F. M.:*

VERY HONORED AND DEAR SIR, — Including two years which I spent as an agent of the Board, it is now more than forty-five years since I entered the service, and came under the direction of the American Board of Commissioners for Foreign Missions, and about forty-three years since I received a commission from your Prudential Committee to labor as a missionary under their direction, among the mingled peoples of Asia Minor.

On account of my age and infirmities it should be known that I am no longer able to perform the active duties of a missionary, and having no voice or strength left to address this great congregation on the subject, I choose to come in this way by letter, and place in your hands, honored sir, the commission which I received about forty-three years ago. Not that I wish my connection with you to be really ever sundered, unless you yourselves should consider it desirable for the sake of the good cause; for when I entered this holy service it was for life, nor do I wish it to terminate but with my life. I wish it to be understood that it is not through any feeling of discouragement that I now retire from the field, for the work never appeared to me more hopeful than it does now. Nor is it through any dissatisfaction with the Board, with the Prudential Committee, or with any of my brethren and sisters of the mission. More kind, more considerate, and more affectionate brethren and sisters, than those with whom it has been my happiness to be associated, earth never saw, nor can I easily be made to feel that even the millennium itself will ever produce any thing better. That the Prudential Committee and the Secretaries may have committed some mistakes is not strange; the only strange thing is that they have not committed more, and greater. One thing is certain, were I to live my life over again, and were it left to my choice, I would again enter the service of the American Board of Commissioners for Foreign Missions, and I would again put myself under the direction of the same Prudential Committee, and I would again choose to carry on my correspondence with the churches through the same beloved and respected Secretaries.

I remember when the whole American Board could at their annual gatherings be easily accommodated in an ordinary parlor: now they can hardly be accommodated in any of our largest churches. I remember when it was thought impossible for the American churches to undertake the support of three missionaries in foreign lands, and a deputation was sent to England to see if the London Missionary Society would not come to their help and pledge themselves to support one and a half, or at least *one* of the three. " A little one has become a thousand," or rather *thousands, many thousands,* and " a *small* one a *great nation.*"

I consider it a mark of special favor, and worthy of special notice and of devout gratitude to God, that I am permitted to bring to you the same dear companion of my life. whom, amidst your prayers and benedictions, I led forth forty-three years ago ; and although she has less of youth. and it may be, in the estimation of the world, less of beauty than she had at that time, yet in my estimation she is not less worthy of all the confidence and all the affection she began to claim and received from me forty-eight years ago.

Contrary to the repeated and expressed wish of many of our friends, that we might have no family, God has given us nine children. One of these, the daughter of a missionary, the wife of a missionary, and a missionary herself, we left in the land of the Moslem, at Kharpoot, near the banks of the Euphrates, where, with her husband, the Rev. H. N. Barnum, and their beloved associates, they are telling the good news of salvation to the perishing around them. Seven of my children are in different parts of this country, no two of them being found in the same place ; and one has, we trust, gone to a better country, even a heavenly.

The Rev. Mr. and Mrs. Bird, who sailed with us from America, and were our associates at Beyrout, still survive. Two of their children are engaged in the missionary work, — a son, Mr. William Bird, on Mount Lebanon, and a daughter, Mrs. Van Lennep, at Smyrna, and all their other children are occupying posts of usefulness.

Of all the missionaries of this Board I think of but three who are older than myself, — the Rev. Mr. Thurston, of the Sandwich Islands, whom I knew at the Theological Seminary, Andover ; the Rev. Levi Spaulding, in India, whom I knew both at Dartmouth College and at Andover; and the Rev. Dr. King, of Athens, whom I knew at Andover, and who, with his fellow-laborer, Pliny Fisk, welcomed us to Beyrout.

And may I ask your special prayers for us poor old men?

for though we are almost through the wilderness, and are even now in sight of the promised land, yet we remember that the children of Israel, after they had been wandering in the wilderness forty years, and were already on the very borders of the land long desired, and could actually look over and see the green fields and vine-clad hills, yet even there many of them perished.   Pray for us, beloved friends, that we may not fall after the same example of unbelief.

We die, but God will surely visit you.   Fisk and Parsons of former times, and the beloved Dodd and Morgan of the present, were not suffered to continue, by reason of death. But Jesus lives ; His cause is marching on and His kingdom is near, and still nearer coming ; and of that kingdom, yea, and of the increase of that kingdom, there shall be no end.

With this faith, and in the midst of all these bright hopes, I now retire from active service, but still desiring to be useful, and begging your committee to point out to me, from time to time, any way in which they may think I can render some small service.

May you, honored sir, long be spared to preside over this great body on these joyful occasions.   And may you, and all this congregation, see the eternal good of God's chosen, and rejoice with His inheritance.

Your aged, very affectionate, but very unworthy fellow-laborer in Christ Jesus, our Lord,

W. GOODELL.

CHICAGO, Oct. 3, 1865.

From Chicago he went to visit a brother in Wisconsin, stopping often by the way, going and returning, to address numerous assemblies.   His visit at Auburn Theological Seminary, in returning, will long be remembered by those who were students at the time, as if it had been a call from one of the patriarchs.   He addressed them in their public gathering, and conversed personally with several who had a missionary life in view.   He went thence to Mount Holyoke Female Seminary, in which he had ever taken a deep interest ; and in New York City was once more at home with the beloved friend of his youth, and the son of his honored preceptor, Rev. William Adams, D.D.

He spent a day at the residence of Rev. S. Irenæus Prime, D.D., on the Hudson, who made the following mention of the visit in the "New York Observer," of Nov. 30, 1865 : —

"It is only in idea that I write by the fireside. In these warm Indian summer days, the fire has gone out, and if there were any leaves on the trees I would go out too. One of these delightful genial days has been spent with a venerable and lovely old man from a far country, long known to the religious world as one of our missionaries at Constantinople. Twelve years ago I sat with him in his house on the Bosphorus, and was now glad to welcome him to mine on the Hudson.

"Seventy-three years ago William Goodell was born in Templeton, Mass. He grew up to boyhood there, and at Phillips Academy in Andover was prepared for college. While here his uncle, Solomon Goodell. sent to the principal, Mr. Adams, to ask if the boy was 'worth raising,' and learning that he was, the good uncle sent him a yoke of fat oxen 'to draw him over the hills of learning.' From Andover he went to Dartmouth College, graduating in 1817, and then to Andover Theological Seminary, where he completed his course in 1820. During these years of study, a young man by the name of Temple was his room-mate, and afterwards his fellow-missionary to the East: the distinguished Daniel Temple, of the Smyrna mission, who returned to this country a few years ago in feeble health, and died. It so occurred in providence that Dr. Goodell arrived here on a visit just in time to preach the funeral sermon of his old chum and life-long friend.

"These men were beautiful types of two contrasted kinds of piety. Temple was inclined to take more serious, perhaps darker and more desponding, views than Goodell, whose buoyant spirits were always rejoicing in the sunlight. I have often told a story which I repeated to the good man at dinner, and asked him if it were true: One day at Andover, while they were sitting in their room together, Temple said to Goodell, with a heavy sigh (*ab imo pectore*), 'Ah, me! I don't see how I shall ever get through the world !' 'Why,' replied Goodell, 'did you ever hear of anybody who stuck fast by the way?' The doctor laughed heartily at the story and said it did not originate with himself.

20

" Then I ventured to tell him another, which he said was true, and true of himself and his early friend : Just before they went abroad as missionaries, they were visiting together at the house of a hospitable lady in Salem, Mass., who said, after welcoming them, ' Mr. Temple, take the rocking-chair.' ' No, madam, if you please,' said Mr. Temple, ' I will take another, missionaries must learn to do without the luxuries of life.' ' Well,' said the lady, turning to Mr. Goodell, ' You will take it.' ' Oh, certainly,' he replied, ' missionaries must learn to sit anywhere ! '

" These two men had diversities of gifts, but the same spirit. They were constant correspondents (exchanging a let-ter a week, I believe) as long as both were alive.   While they were at different stations in the East, Mr. Temple once wrote to Mr. Goodell, referring to the long fraternal cor-respondence that had been carried on between them since they first met at Phillips Academy in Andover, and expressing anew the great regard that he had for his beloved brother ; but there was one thing he had long wished to say to him, and he knew it would be received in the kind spirit in which it was written.   It was that he sometimes thought his good brother Goodell laughed a little too much for one in his position.   Brother Goodell replied, with his usual frankness, that he had no doubt he deserved the reproof, but he added, ' You know, brother Temple, I have always to do the laugh-ing for both of us.'   And so the account was made per-fectly square between them again.   In later life Mr. Temple overcame his early tendency to despondency, and became more cheerful in his work ; but through life they doubtless proved the truth of the saying, ' the boy is father of the man.'

" Forty-three years ago Dr. Goodell sailed with his wife, who is now here with him, from New York for the Oriental world, to carry the word of life to the perishing on the shores of the Mediterranean.   At Malta he mastered the languages of the East, and at Beyrout for some years he pursued his labors.   In 1831 he was removed to Constantinople, where he has spent the balance of his useful life.   He has preached there in several different languages, — English, Arabic, Ar-menian, Greek, Turkish, and Italian.   But the great work of his life was translating the Holy Scriptures into the Ar-meno-Turkish language, which he did alone, — a work that fairly places his name alongside of Wicklif and Tyndale.

He has lived to see it published and widely read among the people of that benighted land.

"Worn out with years and toil, and unable to bear the labors of the pulpit or the study, he has come home to pass the evening of his days among his children and friends. With his snow-white beard, and his form bent with age and bodily weakness, he is venerable and singularly interesting in appearance. Feeble as he is, his vivacious and playful intellect is as clear and lively as ever, while his conversation, always seasoned with the salt of grace, is also seasoned with another salt, the Attic, which imparts a peculiar flavor to his words in the social circle.

"Paul himself could scarcely write a more diversified chapter of 'remarkable experiences' than Father Goodell, if he should condense into a few chapters the story of his life. The trials of childhood and youth, his struggles into the work to which he was called, perils by land and sea, plundered by Arabs, his life attempted by poison among the Turks, living in the midst of the plague that killed a thousand and more daily, and fires that swept off every house but eight where he dwelt: such is an outline of the life he has led, yet he is the same genial, pleasant, cheerful man that he was when he took the rocking-chair in Salem, nearly a half-century since.

"It was a joy to have the blessed old man here; to have him sit in the old, oak chair under the leafless branches of the trees, and so become part of the associations that make up the charm of rural life. We owe such men a debt of gratitude beyond all means to pay. He has been our representative all these long years in the Eastern world. He has borne our burden of life's duties there. And what an example to our youth is he! Not one of them but has a better prospect of usefulness than he had, yet what a work he has done! I would love to have the crown that will one day take the place of his Turkish fez! For well do I know, when a few more suns shall have set, and his goes down, that he will shine as a star in the firmament, and ages hence, when the names of great men have been forgotten, many whom he has turned to righteousness will bless the name of William Goodell.

"IRENÆUS."

On the 23d of December, Dr. and Mrs. Goodell reached the home of their son William Goodell, M.D., at Philadel-

phia, which was to be their own until they should be called
to the mansions prepared for them in the skies.   Together
with Mrs. Goodell he became connected by letter with the
Central Congregational Church in Philadelphia, then under
the pastoral care of the Rev. Edward Hawes.   He identified
himself at once with this church, and according to his bodily
strength became an active worker in seeking to promote its
edification and the usefulness of its members.   He took the
charge of a large Bible class, composed chiefly of professional
and business men, who regarded it as a great privilege to sit
at his feet, to imbibe his spirit, and to receive the truth at
his lips.   He regularly attended the social as well as public
services of the church, now and then in a few words, and
occasionally by more extended addresses, suggesting to others
the precious truths of the Gospel which had been a cordial
to his own spirit, cheering them with its consolations and
encouraging them with its hopes.   His presence and bearing
were always like the traditional memories of the Apostle
John in his old age, who, when unable to say more, would
say to the people of God as he met them, "Little children,
love one another."   Frequently he would rise in the social
meeting, and with great impressiveness repeat some hymn
that breathed his own feelings.

In February, 1866, as he was returning on the Sabbath
from his Bible class, he fell on the ice and broke his arm.
Owing to his advanced age and great feebleness, it was feared
the accident would be attended with serious consequences to
his general health and vigor, but he recovered from it with
remarkable celerity.   While he was confined to his room by
this accident, a friend called on him, and in the course of
conversation spoke of a meeting that was to be held at the
church in the evening of the same day.   Dr. Goodell immediately expressed his earnest desire to attend, and said he
thought he should be able to do so.   Mrs. Goodell remon-
strated, assuring him it would be at great risk, and that he
ought not to think of such a thing.   He turned to his wife

with his peculiar quizzical look, and said, "A man's foes shall be they of his own household."

As soon as he was able to use a pen, he wrote to the Rev. Dr. Schauffler, of Constantinople:—

PHILADELPHIA, March 2, 1866.

MY DEAR BROTHER,—It is now almost five weeks since I have used my pen. I take it to-day for the first time since I fell and broke my arm, and my first letter is to you, one of the oldest and best friends I have remaining on earth. This right hand has written many things, and I have resolved that whatever it may write hereafter shall be in a greater degree to the honor and glory of Christ than many of its former scribblings.

With my left hand I can do nothing in the way of writing, and very little in any other way. I am amazed that it should have lived with me now more than seventy-four years, and yet should have learned so little. It must have seen my right hand do hundreds and thousands of things, and yet it seems ignorant of every thing. It must be, I think, that my right hand did not let my left hand know what it did, and this shows the importance of not interpreting the Bible too literally.

. . . If you have never given special thanks to God for the discovery of ether and chloroform, I pray you do it without delay, for what a wonderful blessing it must have been in the army hospitals! I myself could not endure to have any one touch my arm without fainting at once. But when I was put under the influence of ether and chloroform combined, though I sat bolt upright and knew all that was going on, and saw the whole, yet I felt no faintness and no pain whatever. Indeed, I was perfectly comfortable. The arm was broken completely, a little below the shoulder. But it must have been set remarkably well, for I have already thrown off my splints and bandages, and find this arm as straight as the other. I can now feed and dress and undress myself, and I now lift up both hands and exclaim, Praise be to God, I have two good arms still. And with this same right hand I am now writing you, my brother. Praise be to God, too, that I had the best of surgeons in my son, and the best of nurses in my own wife.

Your faithful friend and brother,

W. GOODELL.

When it was thought safe for him to venture out, he went to meet his Bible class, but in returning homeward he was caught by a sudden gale of wind and was literally thrown upon his head. His hat protected him, and prevented his sustaining any injury beyond a few scratches on his face. His broken arm was not injured. After this occurrence he wrote to a friend, " I never go out now without offering up the prayer, ' Hold thou me up and I shall be safe.' And, indeed, I have heard of worse falls than those Dr. Todd and Dr. Poor and myself had.* But the good Lord is able to preserve us from every evil, moral as well as physical."

With returning spring he was much invigorated, and during the summer he made an extended tour, which was as truly a missionary tour as any that he had ever undertaken in his Oriental field. Wherever he went, his presence and his voice were constantly pleading the cause of missions, and commending the Saviour, in whom he trusted, to the love and confidence of all. He first accepted an invitation to Vassar College, at Poughkeepsie, where he had a charming sojourn. Thence he went to Utica, to visit the family of one of his missionary associates; then to Canandaigua, to visit his eldest sister, where, on arriving, he learned that two days before, while walking in her garden, she suddenly fell and never spoke again. In his own record of the event he said, " *She* had been making great preparations to welcome me, while *the Lord* was preparing to receive her."

While at Canandaigua he wrote in his journal : —

" *Sunday morning, June* 10. Preached for Dr. Daggett. In the afternoon addressed the Sabbath school, and in the evening made a missionary address.

" *Monday morning, June* 11. Conducted the opening exercises of the Young Men's Seminary. Talked with some sixty or seventy young men. Made two calls on sick people, with whom I talked and prayed. One little boy very ill with typhoid fever. Visited him several times, and taught him this little verse : —

* Drs. Todd and Poor had both fallen on the ice about the same time, and each had an arm broken.

> "'Almighty God, I'm very ill,
> But cure me, if it be thy will;
> For thou canst take away my pain,
> And make me strong and well again.

> "'Let me be patient every day,
> And mind what those who nurse me say;
> And grant that all I have to take
> May do me good, for Jesus' sake.'"

On one occasion during this journey, after he had made a public address, as he was about to leave the church he saw a lady with a child standing in the aisle as if waiting to speak with him. He learned that the little girl had begged her mother to stay with her, as she wished to speak to Dr. Goodell, and ask him a question. As he was passing down the aisle the little girl stepped up to him and said, " Have you ever seen the Lord Jesus?" He replied "No," and added that he expected one day to see Him in all His glory. The child seemed disappointed, and said, "You spoke about Him just as if you knew Him well," and added, that as he had been where the Saviour once lived, she thought he must have seen Him. This impression a child would naturally receive from his conversation and address, which were those of one who lived and walked with Jesus.

An incident somewhat in contrast with the above occurred about the same time, as he was addressing a Sabbath school in one of the churches of New York City. With his venerable form and snow-white beard, and with his kindly beaming face, he seemed the very impersonation of good-will to the children to whom he was speaking words of loving instruction. A little girl in the school was so much struck with his appearance that she turned and whispered eagerly to her teacher, "Is that Santa Claus?" the resemblance perhaps being heightened in her estimation by the black velvet cap, with the Arabic inscription, which he always wore in public.

At various places in Western New York he preached and addressed congregations on the Sabbath and during the week.

He spent several days most delightfully at Palmyra, with the Rev. Dr. Eaton and family, whose church was a school and a home for missionaries, several of its members having been trained up for service in the East. At this place he spent an afternoon with the family of Mr. Beckwith, with whom he had sojourned forty-six years before, when he visited Canandaigua as an agent for the Board, just after leaving the Theological Seminary.

From New York he went into New England, to comply with numerous invitations he had received. He was several days with missionary friends at Sturbridge, Mass., where he preached on Sabbath morning, and made an address on missions in the evening. Early on Monday morning he left Sturbridge to attend the Commencement exercises at Andover Theological Seminary.

He enjoyed a festival in meeting with beloved friends at Andover, a place made sacred by the scenes of his early life and of his consecration to the service of Christ. Of this, and many similar occasions in his summer's journeyings and sojournings, he remarked that he met with so many good people, and had with them so much sweet communion, it seemed to him like a foretaste of the society of heaven. He made one more pilgrimage to his native town, and sought out once more " the old place where my father prayed and gave us all to God;" and after visiting Amherst, where he addressed the students of the college, he was privileged to attend another meeting of the American Board at Pittsfield, the last that was held while he was an inhabitant of earth.

He reached his home at Philadelphia on the 15th of October, having been absent about five months, during which he had preached every Sabbath but one, and had made public addresses nearly every day in the week.

He soon commenced, in compliance with the oft-repeated request of his children, to write out for them the reminiscences of his life. He had always declined doing so on account of his unwillingness to speak or write of himself, but as soon as he entered upon the work, he became deeply interested in the review of his life, and in making the record. As he walked the floor of his room dictating to his youngest daughter, who for years had been his amanuensis, the events of his early life came back to him with such freshness that he seemed literally to be living his life over again; and as one scene after another rose up vividly before him, he indulged freely by turns in laughter and in tears. These reminiscences, as far as he was spared to complete them, form the earlier pages of this volume.

On Saturday evening, Feb. 16, 1867, he finished the letter giving an account of "How he found a wife," which he closed by commending the beloved companion of his youth and of his old age to his children, as worthy of all the love and trust he had reposed in her. The next day he was apparently in perfect health. He attended the morning service in the church, and in the afternoon was at the Sabbath school. He remained longer than usual with his Bible class, to arrange with them for the support of one of two young men at Robert College, Constantinople, for whom he had engaged to provide. On returning home, though much wearied, he said to Mrs. Goodell, "I am so happy; I think I shall get one of these boys started in his education, and if one is provided for, I am sure God will raise up means for the other." Then folding his hands upon his breast, as was his wont, and seated in his chair, he fell asleep.

In the evening he joined the family in their worship, asking them to sing his favorite hymn, "Come to Jesus, just now," which he had been delighted to hear and to sing every day for years. In his prayer he mentioned every one of his children by name, asking God to bless each one with the blessing most needed. He prayed for his "Eastern and Western" friends, that God would "remember them all, and reward them for all their love and kindness." He listened then to the reading of a sermon on the prophecies, in which he was greatly interested; and, after some social conversa-

20*

tion, retired, apparently as well as usual, bidding each one of the family a cheerful " Good-night."

About midnight he had a violent attack, apparently cf a bilious character, attended with difficulty in breathing. He suffered much during the night, but the next morning he rose, dressed himself as usual, though he did not leave his room. All day he was in much bodily distress. He repeatedly said, " I never was so ill in all my life before." In the afternoon a birth-day letter came from his daughter Isabella, which, at his request, was read to him a second time. An expression in the letter of thankfulness that his life had been spared so long to his children, and the wish that he might yet have many happy years to come, called forth a smile of pleasure in the midst of his distress. In the course of the day he received a note with a gift from a beloved friend in Newburyport, Mass. The note was dated on his birth-day, February 14 (St. Valentine's day). He dictated a few words of reply, in his own playful style, saying, he had scarcely expected to receive a valentine, but as it was sent on the seventy-fifth anniversary of his entrance into the world, he should receive it as a birth-day gift; and added, that the day had been so peaceful and happy, it was with him " one continued psalm of thanksgiving."

About five o'clock in the afternoon he was undressed, and lay upon a couch, quite free from pain. He sent word to one of the members of the church that he should not be able to attend the meeting of the teachers of the Sunday school in the evening, and asked them to remember him in their prayers. He then fell asleep; but presently awoke in a restless state, and exclaimed, " I am so tired." In a few minutes it was evident that his hour for entering into eternal rest had come; and, before the family could all be gathered around his couch, he had gone up to continue the thanksgiving song, with the multitude around the throne, " redeemed out of every kindred, and tongue, and people, and nation."

The funeral services were attended at the Central Congregational Church, with which Dr. Goodell was connected. They were conducted by the pastor, Rev. Edward Hawes, assisted by the Rev. E. R. Beadle, D.D., pastor of the Second Presbyterian Church, Philadelphia, and formerly a missionary of the American Board to Syria; and by Rev. George W. Wood, D.D., one of the secretaries of the Board, who had been associated with Dr. Goodell as a missionary at Constantinople.

His dust now sleeps in the Woodlands Cemetery, West Philadelphia.

Mrs. Goodell, the loving and faithful companion of his entire ministerial and missionary life, who had shared in all his toils and trials, who had been with him in all his perils, who had accompanied him in his journeys by land and by sea, and who had lived to return with him to their native land, and now to see him depart to "a better country, even an heavenly," was to tarry a little longer before being permitted to join him in the mansions above.

She continued to reside with her son, Dr. William Goodell, in Philadelphia, until the summer of 1871, when, in the seventy-second year of her age, the summons came for which she had been hopefully waiting. During her last illness, which, though short, was severe, she spoke freely of her departure; and even before it was thought by others that her end was near, she said, that, while she was in possession of all her faculties, and was able to express her thoughts, she wished to say that she was very happy in the thought of dying. Her trust in the Redeemer and her peace of mind were unbroken to the last.

The day before she became unconscious she was permitted to embrace once more her son and daughter, the Rev. Herman N. Barnum, D.D., and wife, with their children, who had returned to this country for a brief season from their mission work on the banks of the Euphrates. Her last prayer was now granted, her last desire fulfilled, her work on earth was all done; and early on the morning of the

11th of July, from the same chamber from which the spirit of her beloved husband had ascended to heaven, from which, on the 7th of March, 1870, her daughter Isabella had gone up to meet him, she, too, went up to join her beloved, and to meet, in the home of their Father, the many from the lands of the East whom they had been instrumental in turning to righteousness.

CHAPTER XXVI.

THE concluding chapter of these Memoirs of Dr. Goodell is devoted to tributes to his memory from some of his early and life-long associates in the missionary work. The first is from the pen of Rev. Isaac Bird, with whom he sailed, in 1822, for their common field of labor in the East. Mr. Bird still survives, enjoying a green old age, at Great Barrington, Mass., in the home of his son, Mr. James Bird, who married the eldest daughter of Dr. Goodell.

The writer of the following brief sketch had the privilege of being a classmate and intimate companion of William Goodell during the three years of his theological studies, and also of being his associate missionary for seven years in Malta and Syria, as well as his familiar correspondent to the time of his decease. Precious is the memory of the many seasons in which we took sweet counsel together and walked to the house of God in company. Precious the seasons in which our united households knelt at the domestic altar, and the years during which our hearts shared the same joys or sorrows, according to our successes or disappointments in our mission work.

The life of our brother was remarkably uniform and consistent. As teady as the needle to the pole, so steadily his eye seemed fixed on what, in childhood, his catechism had taught him to consider "the chief end of man." A model of industry, he was always busy about something, but having about as much anxiety for the morrow, concerning what he should eat or what he should drink, or wherewithal he should be clothed, as have the fowls of the air or the lilies of the field After entering on his course of education, his whole time was scrupulously occupied either in intense application to study, or in unbending his mind by a walk, or in conversation, or in familiar correspondence with his friends. He had by nature a slender constitution, unable to endure long-continued muscular or mental exertion, or long-continued confinement in one place, but, by a wise apportionment of work and respite, his health and usefulness went on together.   He had no general prostrations to complain of, never longed for the relief of a vacation, never petitioned for a furlough from duty.   While others were enjoying rides over the country, or resorting to hunting or fishing excursions, he was teaching school, or aiding some church by holding religious meetings and making religious visits from house to house.

His desire, as much as in him lay to *live peaceably* with all men, led him, without a word, to yield his position to any one who he thought had a higher claim, and where this was not the case he would yield, rather than maintain any dispute.   If he had grieved any one in regard to a difference of opinion, or some plan of proceeding, and afterwards discovered that he had been wrong, he would confess the error though long after the other party had forgotten it.   Letting alone contention "before it be meddled with" was one of his golden rules, and not only did he most studiously avoid any breach of it himself, but it stung him to the heart to see it broken by any of his Christian brethren.   In the dining-hall at the Theological Seminary one day, a student sitting near him was engaged in the discussion of some exciting topic, and, excited by the remarks of his antagonist, broke out in a passion, using violent language.   Goodell was electrified.   With an earnest look, and a countenance full of astonishment, he said: "Brother D., that's wicked.   You mustn't let the sun go down."

He cherished *bright hopes and large expectations.*   Those who have been familiar with the style of his mission journals and letters will remember how sanguine and inspiring were his anticipations.   He was watching for the morning, and when the first dawn appeared he hasted to arouse his brethren, that they might be partakers of his joy.   The day may have lingered somewhat beyond his first expectations, but he lived to see it shine brightly over the whole field of his labors.

He was a man of *courage* as well as a man of peace.   He was surrounded by bigoted and fanatical Moslems and papists, exposed to the decisions of unjust judges and the slanders of the highest ecclesiastics.   Petty persecutions and threats of the most violent kind were used to intimidate him, so that, in reviewing some of the scenes through which he passed in Syria, he said he had often wished for some Obadiah to take and hide him in a cave till the impending indignation should be overpast.   Yet when the calamity was actually upon him he proved himself fully equal to the occasion.   Once when debarred from his family for a time, he continued to visit them in spite of the prohibition.   When Greek pirates came and attacked Beyrout by land and by sea, he went forth with his pockets full of tracts and distributed them among them.   When his house was assailed by a band of wild Arabs, some of whom were battering down his door, and others pointing their muskets at his head, he stood in his window expostulating with them, and warning them not to offend the great God and the Sultan. And when they rushed up to his chambers he withstood them, and as they were bearing off his goods snatched them out of their hands.

In his living he was *frugal*, in all his expenses strictly *economical*, and in his accounts very *exact*. The money he lived on was the Lord's; he had no right to any of it but what was necessary to do the Lord's work. On leaving home he was expecting to be stationed at Jerusalem; he arrived in Syria, and was there stopped on his way; he was disappointed: his soul would have felt as pure and thrilling a delight in visiting the Holy City as other men who go thousands of miles to visit it. A very few dollars would have enabled him to go there, and yet he lived five years in Syria and never went. He did not *dare*, he said, for his own pleasure, *to spend so much of the Lord's money*. The Treasurer's books will probably show that, at least during his residence in Syria, he never received for his own use the whole amount of his small nominal salary.

Dr. Goodell was celebrated for his *promptness and punctuality.* His domestic cares had their appointed hours, and, unless from some special preventive, were attended to in their time. He retired and rose early. His seasons of devotion had their appropriate place, and any material delay in his meals not only annoyed him as a violation of order, but sometimes unfitted him physically for his duties. At no business appointment had his friends to wait for him. He interrupted no worshipping assembly by a tardy entrance. His debts were paid; his reports to the Board, &c., were uniformly ready, when due.

In his public performances, as well as in his general style of writing, he was a pattern of *simplicity.* His language was chaste, his words common and well chosen, his sentences short, his aim evidently being first of all to be understood. In *speaking*, his utterance was very uniform, but prevented from being tediously monotonous by the frequent emphatic force with which he brought out many of his short phrases. He had in his delivery no excessive emotion, no transports of enthusiasm, but an appearance of sober, undoubted conviction of the truth of what he uttered, and the presumption that the truth would force its own way to the heart, without power of voice, or vehemence of gesture. Yet in his younger days, when an important thought was to be uttered, he would straighten up, set his eye steadfastly upon the audience, and with quivering lip throw forth the sentiment with marked effect. In *prayer* he spoke in much the same voice and manner as in his preaching. He was never pathetic, but conversed with the Deity in calm, deliberate, familiar, though solemn language, using frequent Scriptural quotations and allusions, and not uncommonly introducing the names of persons and places prayed for.

He had a large share of one of Paul's peculiar qualifications for a bishop, — he was *apt to teach*. Giving instruction was an employment which to him brought its own reward. He was "apt" in it because he loved it. It was doubtless his pleasure in this employment that made him so popular and influential in his early schools. On reaching his mission station in the East, he could not wait for the slow process of acquiring the language of the natives, but made use of the few first words he could learn, and then went on to speak and learn, until in a short time he was able to bear an intelligent part in familiar conversation. He learned portions of Scripture, and when visitors called, from curiosity or otherwise, he took occasion to read to them the Ten Commandments or the Lord's Prayer. Next he made little addresses to the children in the mission school, and from this began to preach short expository sermons to a group of beggars, to whom, in imitation of his Master, he dispensed both the living and the perishable bread. If what he said to them was understood, it was well; if there were parts that were not understood, it was well, so far as he was concerned. At his evening family devotions he instituted the custom of reading a chapter of the New Testament in Arabic, assisted by his two Armenian teachers and others, he himself giving a prepared commentary on the whole. It is probable that by this exercise, rather than by any other human instrumentality, both these eminent teachers were brought to a saving knowledge of the truth. To how many other persons at home and abroad he was made the spiritual father, must be left for another world to reveal; but we may be very sure that no man can go through this world preaching as he preached and living as he lived, without being instrumental in turning a no small number from the error of their ways unto God.

His life was as *happy* as it was useful. He set out early in his Christian course by a whole surrender of himself to his Divine Master; and the Master in His good providence appointed for him a service quite congenial to his taste. Of Paul, the persecutor and murderer, it was not unfitly announced, "I will show him how great things he must *suffer* for my sake." But of this man we may say, as David sang, "Thou hast given him his heart's desire, and hast not withholden the request of his lips." He desired to be a missionary, and his request was granted; he reached his foreign destination, and it fell to his lot there to do the very kind of work he would have chosen. Instead of constant travel by sea and land, having no certain dwelling-place, and having the Spirit's witness, in every city, saying that bonds and afflictions awaited him, his was the blessedness of the man whose delight was in the law of the Lord, and whose very work and business it was to meditate in that law day and night. As we hold up this man of God for an example to be imitated, it will be very natural to affirm that all Christians, and all men, indeed, ought to be as holy and heavenly-minded as he. This may be true. But it is evident that few comparatively ever attain that eminence, and certainly it must be confessed that if it is by divine truth that we are sanctified, a man whose mind has been a channel through which a flood of that truth from the fountain of God's word has been running for forty years, must have a great advantage over others.

When Dr. Goodell had finished his great work in the East, — the translation and final revision of his Turkish Bible, and had prepared a volume of sermons for the Armenian nation, — the infirmities of age, which were seriously increasing upon him, led to his removal from the field, that he might close his life among his children and among his American friends. He could not, however, endure the thought of retiring to rest in idleness, but desired to the end to be, in some humble sphere, busy and useful. So we find him attending meetings of the Board, preaching in the churches, making addresses, assisting in prayer-meetings, in Bible classes, and Sabbath schools, to the delight and edification of the Christian people among whom he moved, and all this down to the last week of his life.

Like Enoch, he walked with God, and was not, for God took him. The manner of his departure was not like dying, but simply a being taken away. We may imagine that, when he closed his eyes, he thought himself subsiding into one of his daily refreshing slumbers, and when the music of the heavenly choir first struck on his ear, and when with all his new powers he joined in and shouted spontaneously the hallelujah chorus, he thought himself simply enjoying an ecstatic dream. But till the heavens be no more, he shall not awake, nor be raised out of his sleep. He rests from his labors, and his works do follow him. The influences which he has set in operation are following him here below, working to complete the holy purpose he had in view. The truth he preached, and his hallowed example, are stamped indelibly on the hearts of many who are now following him as he followed Christ. The volumes of his writings, especially the book of God which he has given to an enterprising nation, are now preaching to hundreds where he preached to one.

The following recollections of Dr. Goodell are furnished by the Rev. Cyrus Hamlin, D.D., long his associate in the mission, and now the President of Robert College at Constantinople : —

On the morning of Feb. 3, 1839, I entered, with my youthful wife, the hospitable dwelling of Mr. and Mrs. Goodell, on the heights of Pera, and looked out with enraptured eye upon the Golden Horn, the Turkish fleet, containing still some of the huge hulks which got away from Navarino, but above all upon the glorious city crowned with its domed and minareted mosques. We were to hold with that beloved and honored missionary family twenty-five years of uninterrupted Christian intercourse and sympathy of the closest nature. While it was a family of that harmonious structure that constitutes a unit, I am to speak only of its always beloved and lamented head.

One of my first impressions of Dr. Goodell was that he was a thorough New Englander, a true-born Yankee. The impression was doubtless true, or had a truth in it, yet it were easier to argue in the negative than affirmative. Instead of any apparent shrewdness, he had great apparent openness and simplicity. Instead of reserve and scrutiny, he had mirthfulness, wit, humor, and a contagious laugh. Instead of mechanical craft and skill, so common to New England, he " could never make a cider-top that would hold! "

But he had substantially Puritan theology, Puritan saintliness, and Puritan patriotism. He had them, however, in his own way. His saintliness was adorned by the most sparkling cheerfulness. Divine truth was taught, not after the manner of Hopkins or Emmons, but just as the great Master himself taught it, with clear and simple illustrations for edification. He had a steady, fervent, and pure patriotism. He always prayed for his native land, for its material, civil, and religious interests. He rejoiced to have sons to take part in the great contest for freedom. Still, he was a cosmopolitan. He never forgot to pray for England. Turkey, China, Japan. Queen Victoria has few subjects who have prayed for her more constantly, devoutly, sincerely. He prayed for the Sultan with unwavering faith, that God could control all his counsels and purposes for His own glory and the accomplishment of His eternal designs. The year 1839 was a dark and trying one at Constantinople. Some of the missionaries were in other portions of the field, at a great distance. Those native brethren who had openly given their testimony for Christ and His Gospel were in prison or exile. The Sultan demanded of our minister resident the expulsion of all the missionaries. No one could salute us in the streets without exposing himself to the then terrible anathema which was the judgment of God upon the soul, — conflagrations, the Egyptian rebellion, the treason of the Capudan Pasha with the whole fleet, repeated reports of the plague breaking out here and there, the apparent cessation of the missionary work, all made the year a memorably sombre one. But Goodell's cheerfulness held its position against all these assaults. He believed it would all work together for good, as it manifestly did. There was no darkness nor weakness nor confusion in the government and plans of God, and therefore he held on the even tenor of his way, praying always with all prayer and supplication in the spirit, and watching thereunto.

In all these difficult times Dr. Goodell was wise in counsel. He had a certain quick intuitive sagacity of judgment, with the least possible formality about it. After others had expressed their views, he would often make a suggestion, in form a mere suggestion, and yet it would hit the nail so fairly on the head as to drive it home at a single blow. The circumstances of his life called forth this quality. Himself the ardent lover of peace, with a smile and a blessing for all, he lived in turbulent times, amid pestilences, persecutions, and revolutions. In Beyrout, his house was attacked and plundered by the Arabs. In Constantinople, violent persecutions frequently scattered to exile or imprisonment those who had begun to feel after the light and liberty of the Gospel. The machinations of a crafty, numerous, and powerful enemy must be met, and his plans thwarted. Often an innocent man would be accused of some abominable or shameful crime, and abandonment of the Gospel offered as the only condition of deliverance. To unmask the hypocrisy, to thwart the crafty and unscrupulous iniquity, to meet the enemy with weapons of the right temper, often called for all the wisdom, firmness, sagacity, and judgment of the missionaries. In these exigencies and perplexities Dr. Goodell's judgment was often like that of James', to which all the apostles and the whole church gave immediate assent. But it would be expressed in the fewest possible words, without any argument to support it. It would often come in a way and manner that required none. It was an *intuition*, an insight, a flash of light, that revealed the whole object towards which we were earnestly gazing in the dimness.

Dr. Goodell's wit and humor and mirthfulness may have sometimes appeared in excess to a casual observer, not to those who knew him best. It was natural to him. He saw with a quick eye and a ready sensibility all the humorous things of life and of human character. Nothing escaped his notice, and no sooner did a fit object present itself than his shaft struck it.

He taught his brethren and all around him how to pray. This came in the way of his work, duty, life. position. But, what was in some respects far more difficult, he taught them how to laugh. Who that remembers him will ever forget his laugh? Who that knew him ever refused to join it? He laughed heartily, honestly, truthfully, merrily, just as he felt at the moment. But he never pursued it. He never pushed it. His mirth left not a trace in his spirit. It was like a flitting summer cloud, whose shadow adorns, not obscures, the landscape over which it flits. The sunshine seems all the purer and nature all the lovelier for these passing shadows. So were Goodell's wit and mirth. They left the soul in the sunshine of God's love, and in perfect sympathy with holy themes, quite ready to enter with uncovered head the holy of holies. One is often reminded of father Temple's reproof, " Brother Goodell, do you expect to enter heaven *laughing?* " " I don't expect to go there *crying*," was the quick reply.

Another beautiful trait of Dr. Goodell's character was his power as a bond of peace and harmony. His cheerful piety, his supreme devotion to his Master's cause, his quick sympathy with all who were visited by any trial whatever, his unselfishness, his love of all social enjoyments, his entering with all his soul into every one's amusements, playing marbles or blindman's buff with all the zest of boyhood, — these, in symmetrical combination, made him the natural centre of social life. He penetrated it with his own spirit. He held it together, and made all the missionary families like one family.

When I first knew him, in 1839, he seemed to me to have a feeble constitution, and to have done already his missionary work. And yet he continued to labor for more than twenty years with unfailing diligence. This was due in part to his perfect *regularity of life.* He had a time for every thing, and every thing in its time. This is the way to make the most of life. But, more than this, he had a rare wisdom to know and grace to do just what he was able to do, *and then stop.* He had not a particle of that indolence that would make him stop short of that point, and conscience and judgment would not let him go beyond. How many missionaries have cut short their days for the want of this wisdom and grace!

The best comment upon his character was the universal respect, affection, regret, grief, expressed by so many of different races and religions at his departure. His memory is embalmed in all our hearts. We shall not look upon his like again, nor will the millennium bring together a more charming circle of Christian friends than that over which he presided before his eye was dimmed or his natural force abated.

When the tidings of the death of Dr. Goodell reached Constantinople, the Rev. William G. Schauffler, D.D. (who had joined the mission the year following the arrival of the subject of these Memoirs), preached to the American and English residents a commemorative discourse, of which the following is an extract: —

By far the greater part of the missionary life of our friend was spent at Constantinople. After his flight from Syria to Malta he began at that island the great work of his life, — the translation of the Bible into Armeno-Turkish; and there he translated into the same dialect " The Dairyman's Daughter," the first tract, so far as I know, ever printed in that language. This tract and a New Testament in Armeno-Turkish, given away by him at Nicomedia in 1832, began, by the blessing of God, the good work at that place, and thus inaugurated that better day which was soon to dawn upon the spreading realms of Asia

Minor, where just now a fresh outpouring of the Spirit of God is enjoyed by our brethren. This, his great Bible work, he continued here, revising and improving it, publishing and re-publishing it under a constantly growing demand, to nearly the end of his missionary life. He left it behind him, complete with references, in the hands of about one and a half million of Armenian people, who either read that dialect only, or who are as familiar with it as they are with the Modern Armenian. This Bible is the Bible of all the revivals and hopeful conversions among the Armenians who are confined to that language in Tur-key, and even in the Russian and Persian provinces. Together with the version of the Bible into the Modern Armenian, it is the Bible of the first native Protestant churches in all the East-ern countries short of India. It is the Bible under the influence of which the first Osmanlee family was converted to God, the first-fruits of Achaia. And from this blessed book, in the very element of which he spent every day of his missionary life, not to say of his Christian life, there proceeded all his plain, home-spoken, practical sermons, in English and in Turkish. A volume of the latter, and a farewell letter to the people he so much loved, were his last bequest to them.

His influence among his missionary brethren was great and good. He laid the foundation of the missions of the American Board in Turkey. A short-lived attempt made at Smyrna under the auspices of a private circle of Christian people in America being excepted, he was the first American missionary who settled in Turkey, and this place was the first station. And upon this station, and more or less upon the mission, he imprinted his peculiar character, — I mean that of entire freedom from self-seeking ambition, spiritual arrogance, and ecclesiastical aristoc-racy and dogmatism. He was the servant of all, and he taught the rest of us so by precept and example. I was impressed and delighted, when, a year after him, I arrived here, to see how ready he was to let others do the most encouraging and creditable work, or to report the most cheering intelligence to the Board. He was always ready to be the last. Free also from all sectari-anism and proselytism, properly speaking ; all the proselyting he ever was guilty of was that from the world to Christ, from unbelief to faith, from death to life, and that simply by the word of truth, which liveth and abideth for ever. So Christ and the apostles proselyted. Even the existing native Protestant churches were formed, not by his nor by our seeking, but providentially and necessarily when Bible readers were excommunicated, per-secuted, imprisoned, bastinadoed, hunted down by their own patriarch, his bishops and his priests, and after they had been repeatedly refused re-admission into the church in which they were born, and which they solemnly declared they still loved as their mother, unjust and cruel as she was.

In the cultivation of this unselfish, unsectarian, and mutually confiding spirit, not this station only, but the entire mission, was for many years so perfectly united that every vote was unanimous, and on every subject there existed but one opinion. It appeared to me oftentimes that our relation as missionaries and as Christians was as perfect as could be expected on earth, and that if any worldly or sceptical man wanted to see Christian love and harmony, we could invite him to look into our inmost feelings toward each other, and to judge for himself. If human nature has since then occasionally shown its infirmities amongst us, it was not the senior missionary who set the example.

As he was everybody's friend, so his Christian cheerfulness and his innocent, artless humor made everybody his friend, and his rare familiarity with the Bible, the book of his heart, and his happy and often novel and striking quotations from it, while they raised a smile or drew a tear, testified to his thorough intimacy with the divine word. These quotations are, in fact, proverbial among his friends, and will long continue to live among them in the form of pleasing and profitable anecdotes. Thus when the family were burnt out in the great Pera fire of 1831, they fled as they were, and though they had lost every thing they had, he asked for no special appropriation from the Society, but when the small number of their friends near by, and some in America, sent them help, he said, as in the case of Job, all his brethren and sisters also came to him and bemoaned and comforted him, and " every man also gave him a piece of money and every one an ear-ring of gold," and 'the Lord blessed his latter end more than his beginning." When, some years ago, I took leave of the mission to engage in the service of the two great Bible societies, and expressed to the assembled mission my thanks for their kindness and the confidence they had so long bestowed upon me, assuring them of my abiding interest in their work, and asking the continuance of their Christian affection and fellowship, this was most affectionately reciprocated by them; and when that exchange of kind feelings was over, my old friend, passing around behind the assembly to my side of the house, said to me, in a subdued tone of voice, " The Lord do so to me and more also if aught but death part thee and me." This was his spirit toward his friends.

The Bible was his light, prayer his rod and staff, and faith and love his element. During thirty-three years of closest intimacy with him I have seen him in various vicissitudes of a missionary life, — but always the same. We passed together through six annual campaigns of plague, from 1832 to 1838. I saw him within his habitation one Saturday night, in 1833, when the fire from a neighboring conflagration was pouring so thick upon his roof that I thought the house could not stand another hour. The house was saved, and the next morning we had our English service in it. I saw him in the dark days of reckless persecution against the Gospel, and its followers driven from their houses, beaten, crushed; I heard him wrestle for their souls and for their deliverance from the death-grasps of their relentless persecutors. Not enough for him to kneel down in our seasons of prayer, but, with his face on the floor, he poured out his soul and prayed for those poor sheep with a simplicity and urgency enough to melt a stone. And are not such prayers heard in heaven?

Sympathizing with others in their straits, he was always cheerful in his own. Once, when the American Board was in pecuniary distress, he reduced the comforts of his table, which were never great, because he wanted to sympathize with them in their troubles. But at another time, when family trials had rendered his salary insufficient, unwilling to ask for help from the Board, which he could have had for the asking, he quietly cut off from his table the coffee in the morning and the tea in the evening, till an unasked-for, unexpected, providential help from friends in America enabled him to restore the accustomed comfort to his family board.

In all the vicissitudes of a missionary life, all his social relations, in his intercourse with his family at home and his friends around, he was always the same confiding, contented, humble, happy Christian man. In society, native or foreign, high or low, he moved with the same ease, not from any finish of artificial training in his youth, but from the native soundness, simplicity, modesty, and benevolence of his heart and mind, pervaded by the spirituality of his inner life, and guided by a peculiar soundness of judgment as to what was fitting at the place and in the society he was in.

This remark reminds me of very numerous instances in our missionary deliberations, often on difficult, responsible, and complicated subjects, when he would put the question and suggest the right measure, often with such clearness as to secure at once the concurrence of the whole station or mission; and he did so, not as the result of any profound or acute reasoning on the subject, but simply as the verdict of a judgment thoroughly clear and sound. I could mention cases when in later days, in my judgment, the mission had reason to deplore their dissent from him in the measures to be adopted. But in these cases (they were not frequent) he invariably submitted to the majority, and did it unhesitatingly and honestly.

At last, the end of a well-spent missionary life drew near, and, as his health and strength were manifestly failing fast, he turned his face toward the land of his fathers, but still more toward "the land of pure delight, where saints immortal reign." Not Boston, not New York, not Philadelphia, but the New Jerusalem, was the city he sought, and now has found.

APPENDIX.

The compiler of these Memoirs, while engaged in their preparation, furnished for the "Princeton Review" (October, 1875) a historical sketch of the action of the Turkish government on the subject of "Civil and Religious Liberty" during the present century. The official documents, which were gathered from various sources, are transferred to these pages, as having special interest in connection with the subject of this volume. It is believed that they are not elsewhere accessible in this complete and continuous form. They were all issued during the residence of Dr. Goodell at Constantinople. The first document, the history of which is given at page 240 of the Memoirs, is the Hatti Sherif of Gûl Hané, issued by the Sultan, Abdul Medjid, Nov. 3, 1839.

HATTI SHERIF OF GÛL HANÉ.

It is well known that, during the early ages of the Ottoman Monarchy, the glorious precepts of the Koran and the laws of the Empire were ever held in honor. In consequence of this the Empire increased in strength and greatness, and all the population, without exception, acquired a high degree of welfare and prosperity.

For one hundred and fifty years a succession of incidents and various causes has checked this obedience to the sacred code of the law, and to the regulations which emanate from it, and the previous internal strength and prosperity have been converted into weakness and poverty; for, in truth, an empire loses all its stability when it ceases to observe its laws.

These considerations have been ever present to our mind, and since the day of our accession to the throne the thought of the public good, of the amelioration of the condition of the provinces, and the alleviation of the national burdens, have not ceased to claim our entire attention. If we take into consideration the geographical position of the Ottoman Provinces, the fertility of the soil, and the aptness and intelligence of the inhabitants, we shall attain the conviction that, by applying ourselves to discover efficacious methods, the result which, with the aid of God, we hope to obtain, will be realized within a few years.

Thus, then, full of confidence in the help of the Most High, supported by the intercession of our Prophet, we consider it advisable to attempt by new institutions to attain for the provinces composing the Ottoman Empire the benefits of a good administration.

These institutions will principally refer to these topics: —

1. The guarantees which will insure our subjects perfect security for their lives, their honor, and their property.

2. A regular method of establishing and collecting the taxes.

3. An equally regular method of recruiting, levying the army. and fixing duration of the service.

In truth, are not life and honor the most precious blessings in existence? What man, whatever may be his detestation of violence, would refrain from having recourse to it, and thereby injuring the government and his country, if his life and honor are exposed to danger? If, on the contrary, he enjoys perfect security in this respect, he will not forget his loyalty, and all his acts will conduce to the welfare of the government and his fellow-subjects.

If there is no security for their fortune, all listen coldly to the voice of their Prince and country; none attend to the progress of the common weal, absorbed as they are in their own troubles. If, on the other hand, the citizen possesses in confidence his property, of whatever kind it may be, then full of ardor for his own affairs, the sphere of which he strives to extend in order to increase that of his own enjoyments, he daily feels his love for his Prince and his country growing more fervent in his heart. These sentiments become within him the source of the most laudable actions.

It is of the highest importance to regulate the imposition of the taxes, as the State, which in the defence of its territory is forced into various expenses, cannot procure the money necessary for the army and other branches of the service, save by contributions levied on its subjects.

Although, thanks to God, our subjects have been for some time delivered from the scourge of monopolies, falsely regarded hitherto as a source of revenue, a fatal practice still exists, although it can only have the most disastrous consequences: it is that of the venal concessions known by the name of *Iltizim.*

Under this system the civil and financial administration of a province is intrusted to the arbitrary will of an individual, that is, at times, to the iron hand of the most violent and covetous passions; for, if the administrator is not good, he cares for nothing but his own advantage.

It is therefore necessary that, in future, each member of the Ottoman Society should be taxed in a ratio to his fortune and his ability, and that nothing further should be demanded from him.

It is also necessary that special laws should fix and limit the expenses of our forces on land and sea.

Although, as we have said, the defence of the country is of paramount consideration, and it is the duty of all the inhabitants to furnish soldiers for this end, it is necessary to establish laws to regulate the contingent which each district should furnish, according to the requirements of the moment, and to reduce the time of active military service to four or five years, for it is both committing an injustice and inflicting a deadly blow on the agriculture and industry of the country, to take, without regard to the respective populations of the districts, more from one and less from another than they are able to furnish, at the same time it is reducing the soldiers to despair and contributing to the depopulation of the country to retain them during their whole life in the service.

In fine, without the various laws, the necessity of which has been recognized, the Empire can neither possess strength, nor wealth, nor prosperity, nor tranquillity. On the contrary, it may hope for them all from the existence of these new laws.

For this reason, in future, the cause of every accused party will be tried publicly, in conformity with our divine law; and until a regular sentence has been pronounced, no one can put another to death, secretly or publicly, by poison, or any other form of punishment.

No one will be permitted to assail the honor of any one, whosoever he may be.

Every person will enjoy the possession of his property of every nature,

21   E E

and dispose of it with the most perfect liberty, without any one being able to impede him. Thus, for example, the innocent heirs of a criminal will not be deprived of their legal rights, and the property of the criminal will not be confiscated.

These Imperial concessions extend to all our subjects, whatever religion or sect they may belong to, and they will enjoy them without any exception.

Perfect security is, therefore, granted by us to the inhabitants of the Empire, with regard to their life, their honor, and their fortune, as the sacred text of our law demands.

With reference to the other points, as they must be regulated by the concurrence of enlightened opinions, our Council of Justice, augmented by as many new members as may be deemed necessary, to whom will be adjoined, on certain days which we shall appoint, our minister and the notables of the Empire, will meet for the purpose of establishing the fundamental laws on these points relating to the security of life and property and the imposition of the taxes. Every one in these assemblies will state his ideas freely and give his opinion.

The laws relating to the regulations of the military service will be discussed by the Military Council, holding its meeting at the palace of the Seraskier. As soon as the law is decided upon, it will be presented to us, and in order that it may be eternally valid and applicable, we will confirm it by our sanction, written above it with our Imperial hand.

As these present institutions are solely intended for the regeneration of religion, government, the nation, and the Empire, we engage to do nothing which may be opposed to them.

As a pledge for our promise, we intend, after having deposited this in the hall which contains the glorious relics of the Prophet, in the presence of all the Ulema and Grandees of the Empire, to take an oath in the name of the Almighty, and cause the Ulema and Grandees also to swear to that effect.

After that, any one of the Ulema or Grandees, or any other person whatsoever, who violates these institutions, will undergo, without regard to rank, consideration, or credit, the punishment appointed for his guilt when proven. A penal code will be drawn up to this effect.

As all the functionaries of the Empire will receive from this day a suitable salary, and those whose functions are not at present sufficiently rewarded will be advanced, a rigorous law will be passed against the traffic in favors and appointments, which the divine laws reprove, and which is one of the principal causes of the decay of the Empire.

The enactments thus made being a complete renovation and alteration in ancient usages, this Imperial Rescript will be published at Constantinople and in all the towns of our Empire, and will be officially communicated to all the Ambassadors of friendly Powers residing in Constantinople, in order that they may be witnesses of the concession of these institutions, which, with the favor of the Almighty, will endure for ever.

May the all-powerful God have us all in His holy keeping!

May those who commit any act contrary to the present institutions be the objects of the divine malediction, and eternally deprived of every kind of happiness!

The following are the Pledges given by the Porte and the Sultan, in consequence of the beheading of the Armenian in 1843, mentioned on page 291 :—

"The Sublime Porte engages to take effectual measures to prevent, henceforward, the execution and putting to death of the Christian who is an apostate.

"March 22, 1844."

"Declaration of His Highness, the Sultan, to Sir Stratford Canning, at his audience on the 23d of March, 1844 : —
"Henceforth neither shall Christianity be insulted in my dominions, nor shall Christians be in any way persecuted for their religion."

The First Protestant Charter, Ministerial in its character and authority, as stated on page 330, was issued in 1847. It is as follows : —

PROTESTANT CHARTER OF 1847.

To His Excellency The Pashah Comptroller of the City Revenue :
Whereas, The Christian subjects of the Ottoman Government professing Protestantism have experienced difficulty and embarrassments from not being hitherto under a special and separate jurisdiction, and naturally the Patriarch and the Heads of the sects from which they have separated not being able to superintend their affairs ; and
Whereas, It is in contravention to the supreme will of his Imperial Majesty, our Gracious Lord and Benefactor (may God increase him in years and power), animated, as he is, with feelings of deep interest and clemency towards all classes of his subjects, that any of them should be subjected to grievance ; and
Whereas, The aforesaid Protestants, in conformity with the creed professed by them, do form a separate community :
It is his Imperial Majesty's supreme will and command, that, for the sole purpose of facilitating their affairs and of securing the welfare of said Protestants, the administration thereof should be henceforward confided to Your Excellency, together with the allotment of the taxes to which they are subjected by law ; that you do keep a separate register of their births and deaths in the bureau of your department, according to the system observed with regard to the Latin subjects ; that you do issue passports and permits of marriage, and that any person of established character and good conduct chosen by them to appear as their Agent at the Porte for the transaction and settlement of their current affairs, be duly appointed for that purpose.
Such are the Imperial Commands, which you are to obey to the letter.
But although passports and the allotment of taxes are placed under special regulations which cannot be infringed upon, you will be careful that, in pursuance of his Majesty's desire, no taxes be exacted from the Protestants for permits of marriage and registration ; that any necessary assistance and facility be afforded to them in their current affairs ; that no interference whatever be permitted in their temporal or spiritual concerns on the part of the Patriarch, monks, or priests of other sects ; but that they be enabled to exercise the profession of their creed in security, and that they be not molested one iota, either in that respect, or in any other way whatever.
RESHID, *Grand Vizier.*
Nov. 15, 1847.

This Charter, not having the authority of the Sultan, was liable to repeal. Accordingly a new Charter was granted to the Protestants by the Sultan, Abdul Medjid, in 1850, as stated on page 352 : —

IMPERIAL PROTESTANT CHARTER OF 1850.

To my Vizier, Mohammed Pashah, Minister of Police at my Capital, the honorable Minister and glorious Counsellor, the Model of the World, and

Regulator of the Affairs of the Community, who, directing the public interests with sublime prudence, consolidating the structure of the Empire with wisdom, and strengthening the columns of its prosperity and renown, is the recipient of every grace from the Most High. May God prolong his glory.

When this Sublime and August Mandate reaches you, let it be known that,

Whereas, Hitherto those of my Christian subjects who have embraced the Protestant faith have suffered inconvenience and difficulties, in consequence of their not being placed under a separate and special jurisdiction, and in consequence of the Patriarchs and Primates of their old creeds, which they have abandoned, naturally not being able to administer their affairs; and

Whereas, In necessary accordance with my Imperial compassion, which extends to all classes of my subjects, it is contrary to my Imperial pleasure that any one class of them should be exposed to trouble ; and

Whereas, By reason of their faith, the above-mentioned already form a separate community, it is, therefore, my Royal compassionate will, that, by all means, measures be adopted for facilitating the administration of their affairs, so that they may live in peace, quiet, and security.

Let, then, a respectable and trustworthy person, acceptable to and chosen by themselves, from among their own number, be appointed, with the title of "Agent of the Protestants," who shall be attached to the department of the Minister of Police.

It shall be the duty of the Agent to have under his charge the register of the members of the community, which shall be kept at the police. The Agent shall cause to be registered therein all births and deaths in the community. All applications for passports and marriage licenses, and special transactions of the community, that are to be presented to the Sublime Porte, or to any other department, must be given under the official seal of this Agent.

For the execution of my will, this, my Royal Mandate and August Command, has been specially issued and granted from my Imperial chancery.

Hence, thou, the minister above named, in accordance with the explanations given, will execute to the letter the preceding ordinance; except that, as the collection of capitation tax, and the delivery of passports are subjected to specific regulations, you will not do any thing contrary to them. You will not permit any thing to be required of them, on pretence of fees or expenses, for marriage licenses or registration.

You will see to it that, like the other communities of the Empire, in all their affairs, and in all matters appertaining to their cemeteries and places of worship, they should have every facility and needed assistance. You will not permit that any of the other communities should in any way interfere with their rites, or with their religious concerns ; and, in short, in no wise with any of their affairs, secular or religious ; that thus they may be enabled to exercise the usages of their faith in security.

And it is enjoined upon you not to allow them to be molested an iota in these particulars, or in any others, and that all attention and perseverance be put in requisition to maintain them in quiet and security. And in case of necessity, they are permitted to make representations regarding their affairs through their Agent to the Sublime Porte.

When this, my Imperial will, shall be brought to your knowledge and appreciation, you will have this August Edict registered in the proper department, and cause it to be perpetuated in the hands of the above-mentioned subjects, and you will see to it that its requirements be always executed in their full import.

Thus be it known to thee, and respect my sacred signet.

Written in the holy month of Moharrem, A. H. 1267 (November, 1850).

Given in the protected city of Constantinople

Even this did not fully protect the Protestants. Its provisions were disregarded by the governors of some of the provinces, and persecution of the Protestants continued. In 1853, another Firman was issued, and sent to all the governors, as well as the head-men of the Protestants, requiring that the previous Charters should be strictly enforced.

IMPERIAL FIRMAN OF 1853.

Let attention be given to the unchangeable, constant, and perpetual execution of the provisions contained in this, my High Firman; and let care be taken not to contravene it.

To Sdepan, the chosen and honorable Vakeel of the Protestant Christian community! May your honor be increased! When my High Firman reaches you, know that the all-just and sovereign God, the gracious giver of good, according to His divine, excellent, and boundless goodness, having caused my Imperial and August person to reign in regal glory; and having elevated me to the lofty and Imperial rank of Caliph, I give thanks and glory that so many cities and diverse classes and subjects, nations and servants, are committed to the hand of my most just Caliphate, as a special divine trust. Wherefore, in accordance with the benevolence due from my civil and spiritual power, and also in conformity with the excellent custom of my Sultanship and my sovereignty, being favored by the divine goodness and aided from above, since my succeeding to the happy Imperial throne, I have used all my care to secure perfect protection to each class of all the subjects of my government, and especially, as in all former times, that they may enjoy perfect quiet in the performance of religious rites and services, without distinction, in accordance with my true and honest Imperial purpose and my benevolent will; and my Imperial government, continually and without ceasing, watches for the same.

And since the good and useful effects of these measures are at all times plainly manifest, it is my Imperial desire that no improper or disorderly thing, of whatever kind, be thoughtlessly occasioned to the faithful subjects of my kingdom of the Protestant faith, and that the special privileges granted by my Imperial government, concerning religion and matters pertaining to it, be in all respects perpetually preserved from all detriment. And as it is my Imperial will that no injury, of whatever kind, or in whatever manner, come upon them, therefore, this most righteous Imperial edict has been written, that those who act against it may know that, exposing themselves to my Royal indignation, they shall be punished. Notice has been given to the proper authorities, so that there may not be the least ground of excuse, if there should happen in any way a neglect of this ordinance.

And this, my firm decree, has been issued from my Royal divan, to make known and establish it as my Imperial purpose, that this thing shall be carried into full and complete execution. Wherefore, you, who are the above-mentioned Vakeel, on learning this, will always move and act in accordance with the demands of this, my High Firman, and carefully abstain from any thing at variance with these things; and if any thing shall occur contrary to this, my decisive order, you will forthwith make it known to the Sublime Porte. Know this to be so, and give credence to my Imperial cypher.

Written in the last of the month Shaban, 1269.

The following is the celebrated Hatti Humayoun of 1856, issued by the Sultan, Abdul Medjid, in compliance with a demand from the European Powers that the death-penalty for a change of religion should be abolished. See page 385.

HATTI HUMAYOUN OF 1856.

Let it be done as herein set forth.

To you, my Grand Vizier, Mehemed Emin Aali Pasha, decorated with my Imperial Order of the Medjidyé of the first class, and with the Order of Personal Merit; may God grant to you greatness and increase your power!

It has always been my most earnest desire to insure the happiness of all classes of the subjects whom Divine Providence has placed under my Imperial sceptre; and since my accession to the throne I have not ceased to direct all my efforts to the attainment of that end.

Thanks to the Almighty, these unceasing efforts have already been productive of numerous useful results. From day to day the happiness of the nation and the wealth of my dominions go on augmenting.

It being now my desire to renew and enlarge still more the new institutions, ordained with the view of establishing a state of things conformable with the dignity of my Empire and the position which it occupies among civilized nations; and the rights of my Empire having, by the fidelity and praiseworthy efforts of all my subjects, and by the kind and friendly assistance of the Great Powers, my noble Allies, received from abroad a confirmation which will be the commencement of a new era, it is my desire to augment its well-being and prosperity, to effect the happiness of all my subjects, who in my sight are all equal and equally dear to me, and who are united to each other by the cordial ties of patriotism, and to insure the means of daily increasing the prosperity of my Empire. I have, therefore, resolved upon, and I order the execution of, the following measures: —

The guarantees promised on our part by the Hatti Humayoun of Gûl Hané, and in conformity with the Tanzimat, to all the subjects of my Empire, without distinction of classes or of religion, for the security of their persons and property and the preservation of their honor, are to-day confirmed and consolidated; and efficacious measures shall be taken in order that they may have their full and entire effect.

All the privileges and spiritual immunities granted by my ancestors, *ab antiquo*, and at subsequent dates, to all Christian communities or other non-Mussulman persuasions, established in my Empire under my protection, shall be confirmed and maintained.

Every Christian or other non-Mussulman community shall be bound, within a fixed period, and with the concurrence of a commission composed, *ad hoc*, of members of its own body, to proceed, with my high approbation and under the inspection of my Sublime Porte, to examine into its actual immunities and privileges, and to discuss and submit to my Sublime Porte the reforms required by the progress of civilization and of the age. The powers conceded to the Christian Patriarchs and Bishops by the Sultan Mahomet II. and his successors shall be made to harmonize with the new position which my generous and beneficent intentions insure to these communities.

The principle of nominating the Patriarchs for life, after the revision of the rules of election now in force, shall be exactly carried out, conformably to the tenor of their firmans of investiture.

The Patriarchs, Metropolitans, Archbishops, Bishops, and Rabbins shall take an oath on their entrance into office, according to a form agreed upon in common by my Sublime Porte and the spiritual heads of the different religious communities. The ecclesiastical dues, of whatever sort or nature they be, shall be abolished, and replaced by fixed revenues for the Patriarchs and heads of communities, and by the allocation of allowances and salaries equitably proportioned to the importance of the rank and the dignity of the different members of the clergy.

The property, real or personal, of the different Christian ecclesiastics shall remain intact; the temporal administration of the Christian or other non-Mussulman communities shall, however, be placed under the safeguard of an assembly to be chosen from among the members, both ecclesiastics and laymen, of the said communities.

In the towns, small boroughs, and villages, where the whole population is of the same religion, no obstacle shall be offered to the repair, according to their original plan, of buildings set apart for religious worship, for schools, for hospitals, and for cemeteries.

The plans of these different buildings, in case of their new erection, must, after having been approved by the Patriarchs or Heads of communities, be submitted to my Sublime Porte, which will approve of them by my Imperial order, or make known its observation upon them within a certain time.

Each sect, in localities where there are no other religious denominations, shall be free from every species of restraint as regards the public exercise of its religion.

In the towns, small boroughs, and villages, where different sects are mingled together, each community inhabiting a distinct quarter shall, by conforming to the above-mentioned ordinances, have equal power to repair and improve its churches, its hospitals, its schools, and its cemeteries. When there is question of the erection of new buildings, the necessary authority must be asked for, through the medium of the Patriarchs and heads of communities, from my Sublime Porte, which will pronounce a sovereign decision according to that authority, except in the case of administrative obstacles. The intervention of the administrative authority in all measures of this nature will be entirely gratuitous. My Sublime Porte will take energetic measures to insure to each sect, whatever be the number of its adherents, entire freedom in the exercise of its religion.

Every distinction or designation tending to make any class whatever of the subjects of my Empire inferior to another class, on account of their religion, language, or race, shall be for ever effaced from the administrative protocol. The laws shall be put in force against the use of any injurious or offensive term, either among private individuals or on the part of the authorities.

As all forms of religion are and shall be freely professed in my dominions, no subject of my Empire shall be hindered in the exercise of the religion that he professes, nor shall be in any way annoyed on this account. No one shall be compelled to change his religion.

The nomination and choice of all functionaries and other *employés* of my Empire being wholly dependent upon my sovereign will, all the subjects of my Empire, without distinction of nationality, shall be admissible to public employments, and qualified to fill them according to their capacity and merit, and conformably with rules to be generally applied.

All the subjects of my Empire, without distinction, shall be received into the civil and military schools of the government, if they otherwise satisfy the conditions as to age and examination, which are specified in the organic regulations of the said schools. Moreover, every community is authorized to establish public schools of science, art, and industry. Only the method of instruction and the choice of professors in schools of this class shall be under the control of a mixed Council of Public Instruction, the members of which shall be named by my sovereign command.

All commercial, correctional, and criminal suits between Mussulman and Christian, or other non-Mussulman subjects, or between Christians or other non-Mussulmans of different sects, shall be referred to mixed tribunals.

The proceedings of these tribunals shall be public; the parties shall be confronted, and shall produce their witnesses, whose testimony shall be received, without distinction, upon an oath taken according to the religious law of each sect.

Suits relating to civil affairs shall continue to be publicly tried, according to the laws and regulations, before the mixed provincial councils, in the presence of the governor and judge of the place. Special civil proceedings, such as those relating to successions, or others of that kind, between subjects of the same Christian or other non-Mussulman faith, may, at the request of the parties, be sent before the councils of the patriarchs or of the communities.

Penal, correctional, and commercial laws, and rules of procedure for the mixed tribunals, shall be drawn up as soon as possible, and formed into a code. Translations of them shall be published in all the languages current in the Empire.

Proceedings shall be taken, with as little delay as possible, for the reform of the penitentiary system, as applied to houses of detention, punishment, or correction, and other establishments of like nature, so as to reconcile the rights of humanity with those of justice. Corporal punishment shall not be administered, even in the prisons, except in conformity with the disciplinary regulations established by my Sublime Porte; and every thing that resembles torture shall be entirely abolished.

Infractions of the law in this particular shall be severely repressed, and shall besides entail, as of right, the punishment, in conformity with the civil code, of the authorities who may order and of the agents who may commit them.

The organization of the police in the capital, in the provincial towns, and in the rural districts, shall be revised in such a manner as to give to all the peaceable subjects of my Empire the strongest guarantees for the safety both of their persons and property.

The equality of taxes entailing equality of burdens, as equality of duties entails that of rights, Christian subjects, and those of other non-Mussulman sects, as it has been already decided, shall, as well as Mussulmans, be subject to the obligations of the Law of Recruitment. The principle of obtaining substitutes, or of purchasing exemption, shall be admitted. A complete law shall be published, with as little delay as possible, respecting the admission into and service in the army of Christian and other non-Mussulman subjects.

Proceedings shall be taken for a reform in the constitution of the provincial and communal councils, in order to insure fairness in the choice of the deputies of the Mussulman, Christian, and other communities, and freedom of voting in the councils. My Sublime Porte will take into consideration the adoption of the most effectual means for ascertaining exactly and for controlling the result of the deliberations of the decisions arrived at.

As the laws regulating the purchase, sale, and disposal of real property are common to all the subjects of my Empire, it shall be lawful for foreigners to possess landed property in my dominions, conforming themselves to the laws and police regulations, and bearing the same charges as the native inhabitants, and after arrangements have been come to with foreign powers.

The taxes are to be levied under the same denomination from all the subjects of my Empire, without distinction of class or of religion. The most prompt and energetic means for remedying the abuses in collecting the taxes, and especially the tithes, shall be considered. The system of direct collection shall gradually, and as soon as possible, be substituted for the plan of farming, in all the branches of the revenues of the State. As long as the present system remains in force, all agents of the government and all members of the Medjlis shall be forbidden, under the severest penalties, to become lessees of any farming contracts which are announced for public competition, or to have any beneficial interest in carrying them out. The local taxes shall, as far as possible, be so imposed as not to affect the sources of production, or to hinder the progress of internal commerce.

Works of public utility shall receive a suitable endowment, part of which shall be raised from private and special taxes, levied in the provinces which shall have the benefit of the advantages arising from the establishment of ways of communication by land and sea.

A special law having been already passed, which declares that the budget of the revenue and expenditure of the State shall be drawn up and made known every year, the said law shall be most scrupulously observed. Proceedings shall be taken for revising the emoluments attached to each office.

The heads of each community and a delegate, designated by my Sublime Porte, shall be summoned to take part in the deliberations of the Supreme Council of Justice on all occasions which might interest the generality of the subjects of my Empire. They shall be summoned specially for this purpose by my Grand Vizier. The delegates shall hold office for one year; they shall be sworn on entering upon their duties. All the members of the Council, at the ordinary and extraordinary meetings, shall freely give their opinions and their votes, and no one shall ever annoy them on this account.

The laws against corruption, extortion, or malversation shall apply, according to the legal forms, to all the subjects of my Empire, whatever may be their class and the nature of their duties.

Steps shall be taken for the formation of banks and other similar institutions, so as to effect a reform in the monetary and financial system, as well as to create funds to be employed in augmenting the sources of the material wealth of my Empire.

Steps shall also be taken for the formation of roads and canals to increase the facilities of communication and increase the sources of the wealth of the country. Every thing that can impede commerce or agriculture shall be abolished. To accomplish these objects, means shall be sought to profit by the science, the art, and the funds of Europe, and thus gradually to execute them.

Such being my wishes and my commands, you, who are my Grand Vizier, will, according to custom, cause this Imperial Firman to be published in my Capital, and in all parts of my Empire; and you will watch attentively and take all the necessary measures that all the orders which it contains be henceforth carried out with the most rigorous punctuality.

The Hatti Humayoun was communicated by the Sultan to the representatives of Great Britain, France, Austria, Russia, Sardinia, and Turkey, who met, in February, 1856, to form the Treaty of Paris. The following is an extract from the Treaty : —

"NINTH ARTICLE. — His Imperial Majesty the Sultan having, in his constant solicitude for the welfare of his subjects, issued a Firman, which, while ameliorating their condition, without distinction of religion or race, records his generous intentions towards the Christian population of his Empire; and wishing to give a further proof of his sentiments in that respect, has resolved to communicate to the Contracting Parties the said Firman emanating spontaneously from his sovereign will.

"The Contracting Powers recognize the high value of this communication. It is clearly understood that it cannot in any case give to said Powers the right to interfere, either collectively or separately, in the relations of His Majesty the Sultan with his subjects, nor in the internal administration of his Empire."

Cambridge: Press of John Wilson & Son.

530 BROADWAY, NEW YORK,
November, 1875.

ROBERT CARTER & BROTHERS'

NEW BOOKS.

Forty Years in the Turkish Empire.

Memoirs of Rev. William Goodell, DD., late Missionary at Constantinople. By E. D. G. Prime, D.D..................................... 2.50

Dr. Goodell was the first American Missionary at Constantinople, his wife the first American lady that ever visited the Turkish Capital, and they both remained at this post in labors of usefulness, until in their old age they returned to this country to die among their kindred. This volume is largely autobiographical, being compiled from Dr. Goodell's Letters and Journal, containing also his personal Reminiscences written during the last year of his life. He was inimitable as a letter writer, and everything that came from his pen was marked by spirituality, a peculiarly apt use of Scripture language, and a spice of wit that enlivened his conversation and his writings to the day of his death.

Autobiography and Memoir of Dr. Guthrie.

2 vols., 12mo... 4.00

"His stories which give sparkle and zest to the narrative, and greet us on almost every page, are woven together in a picture of Scottish life that is wonderfully graphic." —*Harper's Magazine.*

The Works of Thomas Guthrie, D.D.

9 vols. In a box. (The works are sold separately)...................13.50

D'Aubigne's History of the Reformation

In the TIME OF CALVIN. Vol. 6... 2.00

D'Aubigne's History of the Reformation

In the TIME OF CALVIN. 6 vols...12.00

D'Aubigne's History of the Reformation.

5 vols. in 1. 8vo., 3.00; in 5 vols., 12mo................................ 6.00

Without doing violence to historical truth, he seems to invest history with all the charms of romance, and with the enthusiasm and skill of a poet he sketches on the historic page his fascinating and life-like pictures.

Hugh Miller's Works.

New edition, very neat.   10 vols., 12mo..................................15.00

FOOTPRINTS OF THE CREATOR... 1.50

OLD RED SANDSTONE.. 1.50

SCHOOLS AND SCHOOLMASTERS....................................... 1.50

TESTIMONY OF THE ROCKS... 1.50

CRUISE OF THE BETSEY... 1.50

FIRST IMPRESSIONS OF ENGLAND...................................... 1.50

POPULAR GEOLOGY... 1.50

TALES AND SKETCHES... 1.50

ESSAYS.   HISTORICAL AND BIOGRAPHICAL......................... 1.50

HEADSHIP OF CHRIST.. 1.50

From the late Professor Agassiz :

"There is in HUGH MILLER's geological works a freshness of conception, a depth of thought, and a purity of feeling rarely met with in works of that character."

Hugh Miller's Life and Letters.

By PETER BAYNE.   2 vols.. 3.00

Mr. BAYNE carries the absorbed reader with him through the whole period, unfolding leaf after leaf of the history of a life, certainly one of the most interesting and striking as well as useful of this century.

By the Author of "The Wide, Wide World."

THE LITTLE CAMP ON EAGLE HILL.................................... 1.25

WILLOW BROOK.. 1.25

SCEPTRES AND CROWNS.. 1.25

THE FLAG OF TRUCE.. 1.25

BREAD AND ORANGES.. 1.25

THE RAPIDS OF NIAGARA... 1.25

The Say and Do Series.

Comprising the above 6 vols. on the Lord's Prayer.   In a neat box 7.50

"Every new work of fiction by this gifted author we receive with a cordial welcome, for we know that it will be an addition to that pure, elevating, and delightful class of books which we may love as the fireside literature of our country. She writes for the home circle."—*N. Y. Observer.*

By the same author :

The Story of Small Beginnings.	House of Israel..................... 1.50
4 vols. In a box............... 5.00	The Old Helmet.................... 2.25
Walks from Eden.................. 1.50	Melbourne House................. 2.00

Elsie's Santa Claus.
By Miss JOANNA H. MATHEWS, author of the "Bessie Books."…. 1.25

Miss Ashton's Girls.
By Miss JOANNA H. MATHEWS. Comprising "Fanny's Birthday Gift," "The New Scholars," "Rosalie's Pet," "Eleanor's Visit," "Mabel Walton's Experiment," and "Elsie's Santa Claus." 6 vols. In a box……………………………………………………………. 7.50

By the same author:

The Bessie Books. 6 vols…… 7.50   Little Sunbeams. 6 vols…….. 6.00
The Flowerets. 6 vols………. 3.60   Kitty and Lulu Books. 6 vols 6.00

"The children in Miss MATHEWS' stories are perfectly natural. They get into trouble and get out of it. They say sweet things, and sharp things, and funny things, yet all the time childish things. They illustrate the right and the wrong, but in either case in a manner to attract to the former."—*Albany Express.*

Dare to Do Right Series.
By Miss JULIA A. MATHEWS. 5 vols……………………………… 5.50

"Miss JULIA A. MATHEWS' boys are as live and wide-awake as any one could wish, into mischief, now and then, like the majority of boys, yet frank and manly withal, and not ashamed to 'own up' when they find themselves in fault."—*Hearth and Home.*

Coulyng Castle; or, a Knight of the Olden Days.
By AGNES GIBERNE. 16mo……………………………………… 1.50

By the same author:

Aimee; a Tale of James II…. 1.50   The Curate's Home…………. 1.25
Day Star; or, Gospel Stories… 1.25   Floss Silverthorn…………. 1.25

The Odd One.
BY Mrs. A. M. MITCHELL PAYNE. 16mo……………………… 1.25

By the same author:

Cash Boy's Trust…………. 1.00   Rhoda's Corner…………. 1.25

Fred and Jeanie: How they learned about God.
By JENNIE M. DRINKWATER. 16mo…………………………… 1.25

By the same author:

Only Ned………………… 1.25   Not Bread Alone…………. 1.25

Brentford Parsonage.

By the author of "Win and Wear." 16mo.............................. 1.25

By the same author:

WHO WON?... 1.25
MABEL HAZARD'S THOROUGHFARE.................................. 1.25
DOORS OUTWARD.. 1.25

Win and Wear Series. 6 vols. 7.50 Ledgeside Series. 6 vols....... 7.50
Green Mountain Stories. 5 vols 6.00 Butterfly's Flights. 3 vols..... 2.25

Imogen; a Tale.

By EMILY SARAH HOLT..,.. 1.50

By the same author:

Isoult Barry. 16mo.............. 1.50   Ashcliffe Hall. 16mo............ 1.25
Robin Tremayne. 12mo........ 1.50   Verena. 12mo...................... 1.50
The Well in the Desert. 16mo 1.25   White Rose of Langley. 12mo 1.50

Mind and Words of Jesus, Faithful Promiser, and Morning and Night Watches.

By J. R. MACDUFF, D.D. All in one vol. RED LINE EDITION.
Handsomely bound in cloth, gilt... 1.50

By the same author:

Footsteps of St. Paul............. 1.50   Hart and Water Brooks......... 1.00
Family Prayers...................... 1.25   Memories of Olivet............... 2.00
Memories of Gennesaret........ 1.50   Noontide at Sychar............... 1.50
Memories of Bethany............ 1.00   Memories of Patmos............. 2.00
Bow in the Cloud.................. 0.50   St. Paul in Rome................... 1.25
Grapes of Eschol................... 1.00   Tales of Warrior Judges......... 1.00
Sunsets on Hebrew Mountains 1.50   Comfort Ye, Comfort Ye......... 1.50
Thoughts of God................... 0.50   The Healing Waters of Israel.. 1.25
Prophet of Fire..................... 1.50   The Gates of Prayer.............. 1.00
Altar Incense........................ 1.00   A Golden Sunset................... 0.35
Shepherd and his Flock......... 1.50   Clefts of the Rock................. 1.50

The Pilgrim's Progress.

Twenty full-page pictures. Handsomely bound in cloth. Gilt
and black, 4to... 2.00

"The CARTERS have done a good service to the cause of juvenile literature in publishing the 'Pilgrim's Progress' in a style more attractive for boys and girls than any other edition before the public."—*Christian Observer.*

Nurses for the Needy.

By L. N. R.. 1.25

The Golden Chain.

By Miss MARSH.. 0.90

Four Years in Ashantee.

By RAMSEYER and KUHNE.. 1.75

Twelve Months in Madagascar.

By Dr. MULLENS... 1.75

Little Brothers and Sisters.

By MARSHALL. 16mo... 1.25

New A. L. O. E. Books.

AN EDEN IN ENGLAND. 16mo., 1.25; 18mo......................... 0.75
FAIRY FRISKET... 0.75
THE LITTLE MAID.. 0.75
THE SPANISH CAVALIER.. 0.75

Alice Neville and Riversdale.

By C. E. BOWEN. 4 illustrations... 1.25

All about Jesus.

By Rev. ALEXANDER DICKSON. 12mo... 2.00

"I have read it with the delight which every reader of the 'Pilgrim's Progress' recalls. Compared with the current literature of the time it produces a feeling akin to that of one who passes from barren sand into the verdure and fragrance of a spring garden, when each lily and rose is still touched with the morning dew, and rejoicing in the early sunshine."—*From Judge John K. Porter.*

This book has been re-printed in England at the earnest request of Mr. MOODY, *who gave away nearly 100 copies to friends in Great Britain before parting, each containing his autograph.*

Nature and the Bible.

By J. W. DAWSON, L.L.D., Principal of McGill University, Montreal, Canada. With ten full-page illustrations......................... 1.75

"It contains the well-considered opinions of one who is a student of nature, and of the sacred record as well. The questions considered are of interest to a great many, both in the religious and scientific world."—*Presbyterian.*

The Shadowed Home, and the Light Beyond.

By Rev. E. H. BICKERSTETH, author of "Yesterday, To-day, and Forever." 1.50

By the same author:

Yesterday, To-Day, and Forever.

12mo. edition, mor., 5.00; full gilt, 3.00; cloth........................ 2.00
Cheap edition, 16mo... 1.25

The Reef, and other Parables.

By Rev, E. H. BICKERSTETH. 16 illustrations............................ 1.25

Dr. Williams on the Lord's Prayer.

12mo... 1.25

Dr. Williams on Religious Progress.

12mo... 1.25

The Suffering Saviour.

By F. W. KRUMMACHER... 1.50

The Works of James Hamilton, D.D.

Comprising "Royal Preacher," "Mount of Olives," "Pearl of Parables," "Lamp and Lantern," "Great Biography," "Harp on the Willows," "Lake of Galilee," "Emblems from Eden," and "Life in Earnest." In 4 handsome uniform 16mo. vols....... 5.00

Earth's Morning; or, Thoughts on Genesis.

By Rev. HORATIUS BONAR, D.D......... .... 2.00

The Rent Veil.

By Dr. BONAR... 1.25

Follow the Lamb; or, Counsels to Converts.

By Dr. BONAR... 0.40

*Carters' Cheap S. S. Library.   No. 1.

Fifty vols. in neat cloth. In a wooden case. Net....................20.00

*Carters' 50-volume S. S. Library.   No. 2.

Net...20.00

These fifty choice volumes for the Sabbath School Library, or the home circle, are printed on good paper, and very neatly bound in fine light-brown cloth. They contain an aggregate of 12,350 pages, and are put up in a wooden case.

The Wonder Case.
By Rev. R. NEWTON, D.D. 6 vols. In a box............................. 7.50

The Jewel Case.
By the same. 6 vols. In a box.. 7.50

Golden Apples ; or, Fair Words for the Young.
By Rev. EDGAR WOODS. 16mo.. 1.00

The Scottish Philosophy. Biographical, Expository, Critical.
By JAMES McCOSH, LL.D., President of Princeton College. 8vo... 4.00

By the same author :

Method of Divine Government 2.50	Logic....................................	1.50
Typical Forms...................... 2.50	Christianity and Positivism....	1.75
The Intuitions of the Mind.... 3 00	Royal Law of Love. Paper...	0.25
Defence of Fundamental Truth 3.00	Reply to Tyndall...................	0.50

Christian Theology for the People.
By WILLIS LORD, D.D., LLD. 8vo... 4.00

Christianity and Science.
A Series of Lectures, by A. P. PEABODY, D.D., of Harvard College 1.75

A Lawyer Abroad.
By HENRY DAY, Esq. Twelve full-page illustrations................... 2.00

The Period of the Reformation——1517 to 1648.
By Prof. LUDWIG HAUSSER. Crown 8vo.................................... 2.50

*Songs of the Soul.
Gathered out of many Lands and Ages. By S. I. PRIME, D.D.
Elegantly printed on fine paper, and sumptuously bound in Tur-
key Morocco, 9.00 ; cloth, gilt.. 5 00

Thought Hives.
By Rev. T. L. CUYLER... 1.75

The Empty Crib.
By Rev. T. L. CUYLER... 1.00

Cheap Editions of Important Theological Works.

CHARNOCK ON THE ATTRIBUTES...................................... 3.00

McCHEYNE'S WORKS. 2 vols. in 1.. 3.00

DR. CHALMERS'S SERMONS. 1105 pages............................ 3.00

LEIGHTON'S COMPLETE WORKS.. 3.00

DICK'S THEOLOGY. 2 vols. in 1.. 3.00

JOHN NEWTON'S WORKS.. 3.00

*JOHN HOWE'S WORKS. 2 vols., 8vo.................................. 5.00

THEOLOGICAL SKETCH BOOK. 2 vols. in 1.......................... 3.50

DR. JOHN BROWN ON THE DISCOURSES AND SAYINGS OF
   OUR LORD. 2 vols. in 1.. 3.50

*MURDOCK'S MOSHEIM'S CHURCH HISTORY. 3 vols......... 5.00

*THE WORKS OF JONATHAN EDWARDS. 4 vols., 8vo.........12.00

DAVIES' SERMONS. 3 vols... 3.75

SETS IN BOXES.

A. L. O. E. Library. 37 vols..28.00
*Cheap S. S. Library.   No. 1..20.00
*Cheap S. S. Library.   No. 2..20.00
The Jewel Case. 6 vols.......... 7.50
The Wonder Case. 6 vols...... 7.50
Win and Wear Series. 6 vols. 7.50
Green Mountain Stories. 5 vols 6.00
Ledgeside Series. 6 vols....... 7.50
Butterfly's Flights. 3 vols.... 2.25
The Bessie Books. 6 vols...... 7.50
The Flowerets. 6 vols........... 3.60
Little Sunbeams. 6 vols....... 6.00
Kitty and Lulu Books. 6 vols 6.00
Miss Ashton's Girls. 6 vols... 7.50
Drayton Hall Series. 6 vols... 4.50

Golden Ladder Series. 6 vols 3.00
Dare to Do Right Series. 5 vols 5.50
Tales of Christian Life. 5 vols 5.00
Tales of Many Lands. 5 vols. 5.00
Ellen Montgomery. 5 vols... 5.00
Stories of Vinegar Hill. 6 vols 3.00
The Say and Do Series. 6 v. 7.50
Story of Small Beginnings. 4 v 5.00
Young Ladies' Biog. Lib'y. 5 v 5.00
Ministering Children Library.. 3.00
Little Kitty's Library. 6 vols. 3.00
Harry and Dolly Library. 6 v. 3.00
Rainbow Series. 5 vols......... 3.00
Primrose Series. 6 vols........ 3.00
The Lily Series. 6 vols........ 2.00

HELPS TO BIBLE STUDY,

PUBLISHED BY

ROBERT CARTER & BROTHERS.

---

*MATTHEW HENRY'S COMMENTARY ON THE BIBLE.

In 9 volumes, 8vo., cloth,   -   -   -   -   **$27.00**

In 5 volumes, quarto, sheep,   -   -   -   **25.00**

It would be easy to name commentators more critical, more philosophical, or more severely erudite; but none so successful in making the Bible understood. In the words of the late JAMES HAMILTON, D.D., who has done as much as any man to promote the circulation of HENRY'S Commentary, "It has now lasted more than one hundred and forty years, and is at this moment more popular than ever, gathering strength as it rolls down the stream of time; and it bids fair to be the Comment for all coming time. True to GOD, true to nature, true to common sense, how can it ever be superseded? Waiting pilgrims will be reading it when the last trumpet sounds, Come to judgment!" Or, in the words of Dr. ALEXANDER, "Taking it as a whole, and as adapted to every class of readers, this Commentary may be said to combine more excellence than any work of the kind which was ever written in any language."

*POOL'S ANNOTATIONS ON THE BIBLE.

3 volumes, royal 8vo.,   -   -   -   -   -   **15.00**

RICHARD CECIL says "POOL is incomparable."

EDWARD BICKERSTETH says "Judicious and full."

T. H. HORNE says "He who wishes to understand the Scriptures will rarely consult them without advantage."

*HORNE'S INTRODUCTION TO THE STUDY OF THE BIBLE.

One volume, royal 8vo., sheep,   -   -   -   5.00

"An indispensable work for a theological library.   *   *   *   It is a work of gigantic labor. The results of the research and erudition of scholars of all countries and in all time are here faithfully garnered."—*Evangelist.*

KITTO'S BIBLE ILLUSTRATIONS.

4 volumes, 12mo.,   -   -   -   -   -   -   7.00

"I cannot lose this opportunity of recommending, in the strongest language and most emphatic manner I can command, this invaluable series of books. I believe for the elucidation of the historic parts of Scripture, there is nothing comparable with them in the English or any other language."—*John Angel James.*

DR. HANNA'S LIFE OF CHRIST.

3 volumes,   -   -   -   -   -   -   -   4.50

"We can most heartily commend the 'Life of our Lord' by Dr. HANNA."—*Congregational Quarterly.*

"Sabbath-school teachers will find Dr. HANNA's work very helpful."—*S. S. Times.*

"From a perusal of these volumes we believe that the sympathetic reader will carry away a more distinct image of the character and life of Christ, and his relation to his contemporaries, than he can gain from the more brilliant page of PRESSENSE, or the more elaborate discussions of NEANDER.'"—*North British Review.*

DR. JACOBUS' COMMENTARIES.

Genesis, 2 volumes in one, - - - -	1.50
Exodus. Part I, - - - - - -	1.00
Matthew and Mark, - - - - - -	1.50
Luke and John, - - - - - -	1.50
Acts, - - - - - - - -	1.50

The value of Dr. JACOBUS' Notes is evinced by the fact that over ONE HUNDRED THOUSAND VOLUMES of them have been sold in this country alone, without counting the circulation in Great Britain.

Drs. HODGE, GREEN, and others of Princeton, say : "The excellent Commentaries of Dr. JACOBUS have deservedly attained a high reputation. They present, in a brief compass, the results of extensive erudition, abound in judicious exposition and pertinent illustration, and are, moreover, distinguished by doctrinal soundness, evangelical character, and an eminently devout spirit."

RYLE ON THE GOSPELS.

7 volumes, 12mo, - - - - - - 10.50

OR SEPARATELY:

Matthew, - - - - - - - - 1.50
Mark, - - - - - - - - 1.50
Luke, 2 volumes, - - - - - - 3.00
John, 3 volumes, - - - - - - 4.50

"We know of no comment that, as a whole, gives as much satisfaction in the study of the Divine Word as this."—*Christian Instructor.*

"Those who are engaged in teaching others will find in them a treasury, full of edifying and instructive suggestions."—*Episcopal Register.*

BONAR'S BIBLE THOUGHTS AND THEMES.

Genesis—Earth's Morning, - - - - 2.00
Old Testament, - - - - - 2.00
Gospels, - - - - - - - - 2.00
Acts and the Larger Epistles, - - - 2.00
Lesser Epistles, - - - - - - 2.00
Revelation, - - - - - - - 2.00

"The condensed riches of Bible truth."

DR. HODGE'S COMMENTARIES.

Corinthians, 2 volumes, - - - - - 3.50
Ephesians, - - - - - - - 1.75

"Dr. HODGE'S Commentaries ought to be in the hands of all readers of the Bible, in families, in Sabbath-schools and Seminaries."—*Observer.*

DR. CROSBY ON JOSHUA, - - - - 1.00

DR. GREEN ON THE BOOK OF JOB, - - 1.75

"The thanks of the christian public are due to the scholarly and devout Prof. W. H. GREEN, of Princeton, for a modest, but as we think, exceptionably valuable little treatise on the Book of Job."—*Congregationalist.*

HORNE ON THE PSALMS, - - - - 2.50

BRIDGES ON THE PROVERBS, - - - 2.50

HAMILTON ON ECCLESIASTES. (Royal Preacher). 1.25

MISS NEWTON ON THE SONG OF SOLOMON,   1.25

BROWN ON THE DISCOURSES OF OUR LORD,   3.50

ARNOT ON ACTS. (Church in the House).   -   2.50

HALDANE ON ROMANS, -   -   -   -   -   3.00

CHALMERS ON ROMANS,   -   -   -   -   2.50

*BROWN ON ROMANS,   -   -   -   -   -   2.00

McGHEE ON EPHESIANS,   -   -   -   -   3.00

LILLIE ON THESSALONIANS,   -   -   -   2.00

*SAMPSON ON HEBREWS,   -   -   -   -   3.00

MISS NEWTON ON HEBREWS, -   -   -   -   1.50

DR. BROWN ON FIRST PETER,   -   -   -   3.50

BUTLER ON THE APOCALYPSE, -   -   -   1.50

THE BOOK AND ITS STORY, -   -   -   -   1.50

FRESH LEAVES FROM THE BOOK AND ITS STORY, 2.00

BOWES, THE SCRIPTURE ITS OWN ILLUSTRATOR, 1.50

DRUMMOND ON THE PARABLES, -   -   -   1.75

DYKES ON THE SERMON ON THE MOUNT. 3 vols.,   3.75

THE WORD SERIES. By Miss WARNER. 3 vols.,   4.50

THE FOOTSTEPS OF ST. PAUL. By Macduff,   1.50

FRASER'S LECTURES ON THE BOOKS OF THE
        BIBLE. 2 volumes,   -   -   -   -   -   4.00

THE CHRIST OF HISTORY. By JOHN YOUNG,   1.25

NATURE AND THE BIBLE. By DAWSON,   -   1.75

BLUNT'S COINCIDENCES AND PALEY'S HORÆ
        PAULINÆ,   -   -   -   -   -   -   -   1.50

PALEY'S EVIDENCES, Edited by Prof. NAIRNE,   1.50

978219

Printed in Great Britain by
Amazon.co.uk, Ltd.,
Marston Gate.